FIFTEEN COLONIAL THEFTS

'An eloquent and powerful book! The editors, Sela K. Adjei and Yann LeGall, have brought together an invaluable collection of forgotten histories around fifteen colonial thefts. The authors show with rigour and depth that colonial conquest was not only about erasing, expropriating, dispossessing, extracting, exploiting, but also looting and trafficking. They make the case for unconditional restitutions and returns.'

—Françoise Vergès, author of *A Programme of Absolute Disorder: Decolonizing the Museum*

'This book brings much needed diversity to a debate that has for too long focused on a very few cases often mainly seen from a European perspective. It is a great introduction to the history behind the restitution process and the confrontation of different perspectives that it engenders.'

—Felicity Bodenstein, lecturer in Contemporary Art History and Heritage, Sorbonne Université

'By focusing on colonial violence in such a straightforward way, this volume not only reminds us of the nature of colonialism itself, but also of the unabated necessity to continue scrutinising museum collections and work towards restitution.'

—Larissa Förster, Department of European Ethnology, Humboldt-Universität zu Berlin

FIFTEEN COLONIAL THEFTS

A GUIDE TO LOOTED AFRICAN HERITAGE IN MUSEUMS

Edited by Sela K. Adjei and Yann LeGall
Foreword by Peju Layiwola

First published 2024 by Pluto Press
New Wing, Somerset House, Strand, London WC2R 1LA
and Pluto Press, Inc.
1930 Village Center Circle, 3-834, Las Vegas, NV 89134

www.plutobooks.com

Copyright © Sela K. Adjei and Yann LeGall 2024

The right of the individual contributors to be identified as the authors of this work has been asserted in accordance with the Copyright, Designs and Patents Act 1988.

British Library Cataloguing in Publication Data
A catalogue record for this book is available from the British Library

ISBN 978 0 7453 4952 7   Hardback
ISBN 978 0 7453 4954 1   PDF
ISBN 978 0 7453 4953 4   EPUB

This book is printed on paper suitable for recycling and made from fully managed and sustained forest sources. Logging, pulping and manufacturing processes are expected to conform to the environmental standards of the country of origin.

Typeset by Geraldine Hendler
Simultaneously printed in the United Kingdom and United States of America

CONTENTS

Acknowledgements IX

List of Artworks X

List of Illustrations XI

FOREWORD by Peju Layiwola XIII

INTRODUCTION: Fifteen in a Thousand: How to Tell the History of Colonial Conquest, Anti-Colonial Resistance and Looted African Heritage
Sela K. Adjei and Yann LeGall 1

◆ **PART I: THE BATTLEFIELD** 19

1. The Treasure of Samori Touré
Felwine Sarr and Bénédicte Savoy 21

2. The Manifesto of the Sudanese Mahdī: Banners as Artefacts of Empire
Fergus Nicoll and Osman Nusairi 35

3. [Conversation] *IsiHlangu* from the Anglo-Zulu War of 1879
'We need to infuse African-ness in museums'
Mwelela Cele and Yann LeGall 47

4. The Plunder of '*Adibo Dali*' and Why Looted Cultural Goods Need to Return to Dagbon
Alhaji Sulemana Alhassan Iddi, Elias Aguigah, Marlena Barnstorf-Brandes, Michael A. Gyimah, Jan König and Ricarda Rivoir 59

5. A War Coat of the Anufo / Tchokossi From Northern Togo to the Field Museum in Chicago
Julia Kennedy, Foreman Bandama, Christopher J. Philipp and Kokou Azamede 71

PART II: THE ROYAL PALACE 85

6. Hiding and Returning Asante Regalia
The Journey of an Ancestral Messenger (1970–2024)
Nii Kwate Owoo 87

7. A Plaque from an Ngolo *Etana*
The Looting of Architectural Heritage as a Token of Colonial Violence
Richard Tsogang Fossi and Jeanne-Ange Wagne 99

8. [Conversation] Subverting Firepower
A German Cartridge Upcycled as Snuffbox, Symbol of Chagga Resistance
Konradin Kunze, Sarita Lydia Mamseri, Gabriel Mzei Orio
and Mnyaka Sururu Mboro 111

9. In Defence of Theft?
On the Theft and Restitution of Ngonnso' and Punitive Exhibitions
Godfrey B. Tangwa and Fogha MC Cornilius Refem, alias Wan wo Layir 125

10. The Long Journey of the *Bocio* of Three Danxomè Kings
Didier Houénoudé and Gaëlle Beaujean 137

PART III: THE SACRED 149

11. Degodding Maqdala
Emanuel Admassu and Eyob Derillo 151

12. *Nkisi nkonde* of Chief Ne Kuko of Boma
The Tragic Spoliation of a Sacred Sculpture
Placide Mumbembele Sanger 163

13. [Conversation] The *Ngadji* of the Pokomo
On Revolutionary Responses, Release and Relationships
Njoki Ngumi and Adéọlá Naomi Adérẹ̀mí 177

14. Where are Nehanda's Remains?
A Zimbabwean Search in the Context of Shifting Museum Politics
Njabulo Chipangura, Farai Chabata and Lennon Mhishi 189

15. *Byéri*
Ancestor Guardian Figures of the Kwasio People in Southern Cameroon
Yrine Matchinda and Sebastian-Manès Sprute 201

Abbreviations 214

Notes on Editors, Contributors and Artists 215

Endnotes 229

Appendix: List of Museums and Collections discussed 269

Index 277

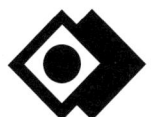

ACKNOWLEDGEMENTS

The editors are grateful to all the contributors and artists who have participated in this adventure. We are aware that it was tough for everyone to meet the tight deadlines and keep up with the flow of emails. Thanks for making the time and putting so much effort into the volume.

Our warmest thanks to Bénédicte Savoy and Dan Hicks for their precious feedback on the structure of the volume, as well as to David Castle, Jonila Krasniqi, Thérèse Wassily Saba and Robert Webb for believing in the project, helping in making it into a book, and dealing so professionally with the many chapters and illustrations.

We are blessed to feature Jack A. Batchelor's typeface Bobby Grotesque in this book and thank him for lending it for this project. First used to memorialise the death of Sheku Bayoh (1983–2015), this typeface reminds us that design is not exempt from political meaning. We also take this opportunity to honour the memory of all people of African descent who were murdered by police or died as a result of state violence, including that of Lamin Touray, shot down by German police in late March 2024 as we were correcting the last version of this book. Black Lives Matter.

We are incredibly grateful to the students of Sela K. Adjei at the Multimedia Production Department of the University of Media, Arts and Communication, Institute of Film and Television. These talented students – Kweitsu Nene Addo Francis, Amelia Cherbu, Emmanuel Amon, Grace Yeboah, Samuel Arhin and Nana Kwame Appiah – have contributed the newly designed symbols interspersed with some original Adinkra symbols that mark the end of each chapter in this volume. Their new designs, created as part of Sela K. Adjei's design pedagogy projects, are deeply rooted in indigenous West African symbolism. They reflect artistic skill and a profound connection to Africa's cultural heritage. These symbolic endpieces add a unique layer of meaning to the content in each chapter. We extend our sincere thanks to the students for their creativity, dedication, and for sharing a part of their cultural heritage with our readers. We are honoured to showcase their designs and believe it adds a unique and meaningful layer to the reading experience.

This project is an output of the DFG-AHRC project 'The Restitution of Knowledge' and would not have been possible without the financial support of the Open Society Foundation and the German Research Foundation. We are also forever grateful to Elsa Goulko and Eyke Vonderau for sharing with us the burden of bureaucracy and handling it so masterfully.

Finally, the editors would like to thank their own friends and family members, who accompanied this venture by providing them with invaluable support in the ups of downs that such a journey entails.

FOREWORD

Peju Layiwola

I

Permit me to begin in an unusually rave way by stating my sincere opinion about this book. Any reader who goes through each chapter carefully and patiently as I did would be rewarded with an uncommon insight. The multiple fields that *Fifteen Colonial Thefts* brings together – history, activism, intergenerational memory, cinema and the arts – paradoxically make the core objective of the book clearer and all the more achievable. The chapters are remarkable in their rigour and approach, particularly in terms of how they extend the claims for recovery and restitution of appropriated cultural assets to forgotten backwaters of the relationship between Africa and Europe, be they past instances of oppression and inequality, or current post-colonial connections. Having scoured the innermost recesses of museum storage rooms in far flung places to ferret out useful evidence, contributors then proceed to present their cases and urging with strong points on the project of restitution. They have verified such evidence against the Klieg light of observations offered by African knowledge bearers, be they oral or scribal historians. The result is therefore an invaluable compilation of proof that can be a buttress for various cases for unconditional restitution of cultural heritage. The data, as would be seen, are not only fresh but have also been presented in readable language and style. As a result, what Fergus Nicoll and Osman Nusairi call the 'uneven encounter' between Africa and Europe (see Chapter 2), or what the editors of the volume, Sela K. Adjei and Yann LeGall, have chosen to characterise more straightforwardly as an 'encroachment', is relived on the pages of this book, with authentic and accessible research aided by beautiful illustrations in pen and ink. The contributors, energised by a commitment to humanity and to increasing knowledge on the history of colonial dispossession, past and present, have emerged from their geographical, racial, disciplinary and intellectual islands to collaborate and restore erased or elided moments in African history for the readers, and indeed for Africans. As any reader would eventually notice, the results are newer and wider implications for current and future relations between Africa and Europe or the so-called Global North.

FOREWORD

II

Looted cultural assets taken away to the West by the 'victorious' colonial powers are perhaps the most useful evidence that imperialism resorted to what is now considered to be disproportionate use of force against hapless people in civil unrests and resistance skirmishes. As many chapters in this book suggest, the items taken away as 'war booties' and intended to show off the valour of Europeans have today been transformed into assets of immensely high value because of what they now represent, unintentionally, about the disparaged African mind and creative capacity. In their very instructive entry on the Flags of the Sudanese Mahdi, Fergus Nicoll and Osman Nusairi argue that, '[c]ontrary to the derogatory and supercilious labels ascribed by the British invaders – that the Mahdists were "savages", "dervishes" and "fuzzy-wuzzies" – banners are evidence of a society that prized literacy' (Chapter 2). If colonial officers and anthropologists aimed to erase evidence and sanitise atrocities when extracting, removing and storing cultural heritage off-stage and off-view in the backrooms of Western museums, those items are emerging today and making important statements about how 'enlightened' Europe managed their relations with Africa. They are a witness to Europeans of today who knew little or nothing, or who pretend to know little or nothing, about their ancestors being involved in some of the atrocious wars in human history in which they plundered the human and cultural resources of Africa. Requests for the restitution of artefacts and other treasures continue the long entanglement of Africa with Europe. Documented delays in keeping to the agreements reached in some of the transactions or the implicit and explicit refusals to do so in others are now generating a restitution narrative as part of the complex engagement of the two continents. So, in simple terms, the presence of Africa's cultural heritage in Western museums and attempts that are made to recover parts of this material heritage would memorialise the plunder and pain of the contact. The details of imperial brigandage are etched in specific cultural assets. Many of them have been excavated from their supposedly 'safe' repositories in European museums for readers of this volume. At the moment, these belongings, effigies, entities, drums and architectural elements are, in my opinion, threatened with erasure and obliteration, namely, rendered silent and useless, by two overlooked factors. The first is large-scale ignorance of their existence, which a volume of this nature attempts to resolve. The sheer multiplicities of the plunder producing similar results would have made the 'war booty' so common as to degrade their specific value. The second is the loud narratives of restitution which have built up around specific looted cultural assets in specific domains or geographies, such as the Benin Bronzes.[1] While such narratives may have been doing a great job in the general call for restitution, they are also, no doubt, drowning the nuances of the discourses that 'small' and specific unheard cases can bring to the effort for recovery and restitution. The need for practical efforts to unstrap all items from the snares of guaranteed erasure and obliteration, if they remained in Europe, is real and urgent. Coordinating the work of scholars, artists and activists, who have gathered data and evidence from multiple sources, can do wonders. It cannot be overstated that this volume is an intellectual effort in that direction.

III

On 1 November 2023, an event of immense significance in memory and heritage studies took place in the Southern Tanzanian region of Songea. The event, which has unfortunately not been given the attention it deserved apart from reportorial in a few news media outlets, was the visit of the German President, Frank-Walter Steinmeier, to the Majimaji Memorial Museum during which he publicly asked 'forgiveness' of Tanzanians for atrocities that Germany committed during the colonial era. The Majimaji Museum commemorates the eponymous anti-colonial uprising of the 1900s in which about 300,000 people were killed in what was then German East Africa, a territory that comprised today's Tanzania, Burundi, Rwanda and parts of Mozambique. Facing a crowd of Tanzanians that included the descendants of Chief Songea Mbano, one of the leaders of the resistance who was executed by the Germans, President Steinmeier declared: 'I would like to ask for forgiveness for what Germans did to your ancestors here… What happened here is our shared history, the history of your ancestors and the history of our ancestors in Germany'.[2] The scenario evoked here shows clearly how the progenies of victims and victimisers are facing each other courageously at the Songea site of colonial horror to reflect on the mis/deeds of their ancestors. President Steinmeier, on whom a greater burden falls, is clearly seeking to open another page for the history of Africa–Europe 'encounters' and relation to unfold.

The Songea event is epochal for two reasons. First, we need to understand that the German president's apology is uttered in the wake of several others made earlier by rulers of erstwhile colonial nations such as Emmanuel Macron of France and King Charles of Britain. It is therefore not entirely new. But it dredges up for further contemporary scrutiny the confuted logic of Darwinism on which colonisation was arguably based. Without a doubt, war has been a significant part and definer of human social experience and history up until the current moment, as illustrated in the events that are still unfolding in the Middle East and Europe. However, it is incontestable that we now live in a political modernity where physical strength must be used cautiously against the backdrop of various hamstrings in international relations. The intellectual support that competing imperial nations received to activate their colonisation of 'weaker' territories has now been replaced by a superior knowledge, one that demonstrates that an economy of cooperation would produce better results. Much as this is my personal opinion, it is underlined by the evolution and growth of supra-national war-dissolving political entities such as the European Union and its ilk across the continents. In that context, actual and symbolic spoils of war or the treasured trophies of violence, such as those discussed in this book, now carry with them ambivalent meanings. How can societies that hold on to ideas and values such as human rights, social justice and the sanctity of life (no matter how contested these epithets might be) also hold on to the cultural patrimony of others, justified or otherwise? In my opinion, this question is crucial to any efforts at normalising relations between Africa and Europe, especially where it concerns the issue of looted cultural assets taken away in the era of colonisation.

The second epochal importance of Steinmeier's appeal is how it can be seen literally as seeking a closure to a certain type of tendentious discourse about colonisation. In that case, the German president has an unusual ally in the Nigerian scholar Olufemi Taiwo, whose controversial book *Against Decolonisation: Taking African Agency Seriously* questions the pervasiveness and rationale of an unending discourse of coloniality.[3] Steinmeier and Taiwo seem to envisage a 'new' moral order in a 'peaceful' world for the descendants of colonial victims and victimisers. For Steinmeier, who is the offspring of a perpetrator of colonial carnage, there can be no better site to appeal for a new beginning than the archive and site of the crime. His plea for cooperation in 'communal processing' is precisely the kind of appeal that the descendants of oppressors can make upon finding themselves in an awkward position in a world transformed by liberal values. For Taiwo, who presents himself as speaking for the descendants of victims, his assumption (perhaps, presumption maybe more appropriate) is the kind of confident posture that the descendants of the oppressed can take in invoking truce, to enable progress in human social evolution. In both cases, we see attempts at putting a handle to the direction of a more benign Africa–Europe engagements and relations. And for us, who are onlookers, the issue is how to create a 'new' language and narrative that recognises that humanity is now more linked than ever before, which requires new words and approaches to describe current realities. We are all united in conceding that humanity must look at itself critically, reassess histories and do the needful in terms of what Steinmeier calls 'communal processing' that would lead to practical results on the 'repatriation of cultural property', both in Tanzania and other places in Africa.

Steinmeier's Songea visit and gestures are hallmarked by a missionary symbolism that recalls Africa's initial encounters with Europeans. It therefore needs to be considered and engaged as a performance. In other words, it needs to be approached with a healthy dosage of scepticism. So, crucial questions remain. Does his engagement with the descendants of victims of colonial crimes at the crime scene suggest indeed, that a benign phase in Africa–Europe or North–South relations is about to begin or should now begin? Would the new encounter erase or overlook the past and its pain? Can the past be so easily transcended? When would action go beyond speech in that crucial effort at 'communal processing'? How would such action translate in terms of soothing and palliating the pains of the past? I presume that these must be the unvoiced questions and thinking of the descendants of the Maji Maji resistance heroes as they listened to Mr. Steinmeier. The answers to these questions are as difficult to develop, as finding a logical basis for the engagement of Africans with the children of their tormentors. However, we cannot deny that while the visit of Mr. Steinmeier dredges up and projects a painful memory, it at least offers a way of dealing with it. It is in this regard that I see this volume as work in progress on heritage and restitution, aligning with other contested fields, such as geopolitics, memory, economic inequality, extractivism and questions of reparations.

IV

In conclusion, I am intrigued by the reconstruction of underprivileged and overlooked histories of forgotten territories and encounters presented here. The authors of the various chapters show that uncomfortable histories and narratives seeking retrieval and narration have been hibernating in plundered cultural assets stowed away in various parts of the world. The scale and complexity of 'unequal encounters' between Africa and Europe is only just beginning to be revealed and understood as historians, artists and activists unearth more and more stories of dispossession and oppression. It is emerging in defiance of whitewashing contemporary transcontinental migrations, cooperation and bridge-building among descendants of victims and victimisers. Memory, pain, hope and other stories abound in the literal and symbolic tapestries of Mahdist flags and fabrics, in the patterns of shields of the AmaZulu, in the guardian role of the *byéri* of the Mabi, as well in the absence of a headgear from Dagbon. They are also present in how the 'upcycled' tobacco cartridge snuffbox of Tanzanian Mangi Meli tells the heroic story of victory as well as the defeat of the Chagga people's resistance (Chapter 8). All of these have come to us, the readers of this volume, on the basis of collaborations forged between the children of colonial victims and victimisers. It is safe for us to assume that such a gesture of collaboration shows an eagerness to put a closure to painful memories of ancestral deeds and misdeeds without necessarily erasing the memorials. The authors of the chapters and, indeed, the children of victims and victimisers have chosen to see, assess, interpret and track these cultural assets, these material witnesses of the past, based on their common humanity. But as the book shows, they have etched their view of things in the 'correct' language, one that addresses and is consistent with the violence of the era.

INTRODUCTION

Fifteen in a Thousand
How to Tell the History of Colonial Conquest, Anti-colonial Resistance, and Looted African Heritage

Sela K. Adjei and Yann LeGall

August 2023: the chapters of this book start trickling in, one draft after another, in our mailboxes. The artists working on the illustrations are putting pen and ink on paper to produce their representations of the looted African cultural assets addressed in this volume. Meanwhile, the British Museum stands in the eye of the storm. One of their former senior curators is being accused of having stolen an estimated 1,500 to 2,000 items from the museum collection and of selling them on the market over the course of a decade – not on the darknet, but simply through the popular auction platform eBay. After two years of internal investigation, the then director of the most famous 'ethno-colonial' museum in the world, Hartwig Fischer, was compelled to fire the alleged thief and, subsequently, to resign from his position. What an irony for an institution that had been dubbed 'the world's largest receivers of stolen property'.[4] In other words, the thief had been outsmarted by another one. While the art market and the museum sector debated on the scheme and the worth of the items that disappeared right under the museum's nose, the scandal also provided a platform for renewed calls for the restitution of looted cultural heritage housed at the British Museum. Not only did this public embarrassment undermine the commonly expressed argument that the collections were safer in London than anywhere else,[5] it also rekindled demands to return artefacts to their country of origin, where they had originally been stolen from. As the former British Museum director told the press after the scandal leaked, they were 'determined to put things right, … working alongside outside experts to complete a definitive account of what is missing, damaged and stolen' and 'throw[ing] efforts into the recovery of objects'.[6] In the context of transnational debates on restitution, this statement rubbed up advocates for the return of the Parthenon Marbles to Greece or the Benin Bronzes to Nigeria the wrong way. As anthropologist Dan Hicks wrote in the thick of the affair: 'The British Museum's longstanding claim to be the safest possible repository for world culture was falling apart in slow motion, and with it went the last remaining credible argument against cultural restitution.'[7]

This scandal felt like the cherry on the cake in a decade marked by ever-growing critique against museums, especially so-called 'ethnographic' or lofty 'world' museums holding looted cultural heritage. Since 2010, a plethora of publications have criticised museum politics from different viewpoints, addressing colonial loot, restitution claims, issues related to decolonising institutional structures, staff politics, funding ethics, curatorial agendas and unequal structures of cooperation with artists, civil society and other communities.[8] If many museums today pretend to have embarked on a decolonial turn in their practice and in the ways they consider their collections, it is essential to remember that ethnographic museums per se are colonial institutions, and that the history of their collections is inextricably connected with the theft of irreplaceable effigies, statues, symbols of power and with the confiscation of personal belongings and private property. This appropriation and plunder took place alongside the destruction of entire societies, with military expeditions being the preferred modus operandi of British, French, German and Belgian colonial troops during the imperial era for conquest, subjugation and loot. Prominent anthropologists and art dealers of the late nineteenth and early twentieth centuries unabashedly admitted that they considered plunder as the most efficient way to get hold of unique pieces of non-European material culture.[9] The famous German art dealership J.F.G. Umlauff – to which more than 300 entries in the collection of the British Museum and more than 1,000 at the Ethnological Museum in Berlin can be linked[10] – and its director Heinrich Umlauff conceded in a catalogue showcasing their Cameroonian collection sent in 1914 to museums across the world:

> If you consider the rich material of idols, masks, carvings, drums, weapons, household utensils, etc., you might be led to believe that such things are easy to obtain. In reality, the situation is quite different. [Africans] are very attached to their things and especially to old, inherited family pieces. In normal circumstances, they can hardly be persuaded to give away … old masks and sacred objects. … Only in times of war or in the case of great expeditions are conditions more favourable, when power exerts a certain pressure.[11]

INTRODUCTION

A Thousand Asymmetrical Wars, Hundreds of Thousands of Spoils

So far, books dedicated to colonial loot have mostly dealt with exemplary cases, like the Benin Bronzes, a boat from the island of Luf in Papua displayed at the Humboldt Forum in Berlin, or El Penacho, the crown of Aztec king Motecuhzoma, at the Weltmuseum in Vienna.[12] Henrietta Lidchi and Stuart Allan published a comprehensive volume on spoils of war in 2020, but restricted the scope of their study to the British Empire and military collections.[13] Many studies on colonial provenance have also failed to convey the perspectives of descendants of the dispossessed, especially those that discuss colonial history in Africa. In 2022, a report by the non-governmental initiative Open Restitution Africa pointed out that only one in twenty-four authors on restitution of African cultural heritage is in fact African.[14]

Addressing fifteen contexts of asymmetrical wars and foregrounding the expertise of African and Afro-diasporic historians, curators, artists and activists, the present volume takes debates on colonial looting and restitution of African cultural heritage to another level. Some of the cultural assets under scrutiny are kept under lock and key in cold storage rooms, almost forlorn (see Chapters 2, 4, 5, 7 and 8). Others are, as we write, shown to museum visitors under glass cases in permanent exhibitions (see Chapters 1, 3 and 6). Communities also yearn for the return of these relics and ancestral remains, but some remain to be found (see Chapters 7 and 14), or the claims of their descendants remain unanswered (see Chapter 13). In turn, others have made first steps on their way back to Africa (see Chapters 6, 9 and 12) or were even repatriated and welcomed home (see Chapter 10). Lastly, we also need to remember that magnificent pieces of African cultural heritage with more than dubious provenance are still being auctioned and sold off for millions of euros on the art market, against the will of community members (see Chapter 15). While this book does not pretend to run the gamut of issues linked to looted African heritage, this array of contexts is evidence of the ubiquity of loot, of racial (and intersectional) violence perpetrated by ethno-colonial museums, and of the high stakes linked to their fate, be they spiritual, socio-economic or political. Bringing together manifold voices and positions in the debate on colonial history, museum studies and restitution, this volume is proof that, when those voices come together, they speak in unison regarding transparency and better access to collections. Following Felwine Sarr and Bénédicte Savoy's call for a 'relational ethics', many authors in this book argue for a museum practice that respects not only the descendants of these belongings' former owners, but also the knowledge of African experts on their cultural heritage. As Godfrey Tangwa and Fogha MC Cornilius Refem wittily term it in their chapter on Ngonnso', the violence committed in the past through 'punitive *expeditions*' and the humiliation that ensued should not perdure through 'punitive *exhibition*' of colonial loot (see Chapter 9).

INTRODUCTION

Taking asymmetrical wars as a common denominator, this book gives a sweeping – but far from exhaustive – overview of the participation of museums in the violent mechanisms of 'dispossession' and 'dislocation' (see Chapters 1, 3 and 7). What colonialists called 'punitive' actions, a term also used in far-right and neo-Nazi jargon,[15] were not retaliation measures against 'unruly barbarians', as colonial rhetoric wished us to believe, but more often massacres committed by colonial troops against sovereign communities and nations. Several historians and anthropologists have dissected this 'imperial epistemology predicated on reversing the relationship between invaders and invaded', a colonial militarist rhetoric which sought to put the blame on indigenous communities for their fate.[16] Dan Hicks even talked of a 'World War Zero', a concept from which we would like to distance ourselves, as the compound rather evokes in the mind of readers more or less comparable belligerent parties and fails to encompass two features that were central to these conflicts: first, the conquering impulse behind the dispatch of European-led troops, which implies a defensive motive for entering these conflicts by most indigenous communities, since they felt that their sovereignty was threatened; second, the prevalent asymmetry in terms of forces involved and technology available to these belligerent parties, apart from a few exceptions. These exactions started at the beginning of the nineteenth century, the blockade of Mokha by the East India Company in 1820 and the French attack on Algiers in 1830 being two prime examples of this rhetoric of retribution. They became a military routine at the height of the imperial era, especially after the Berlin Conference of 1884–1885, during which European powers divided the African continent among themselves. Up until the First World War, colonial powers forced African rulers to sign what they called 'treaties of protection', pieces of paper that Tanzanian historian Buluda Itandala more rightfully termed 'treaties of subjugation'.[17]

These expeditions were generally accompanied by the confiscation of means of subsistence, the appropriation or destruction of spiritual and political symbols (effigies, relics, thrones, sceptres, banners, architectural elements…), and by the murder of generations of anti-colonial leaders. The spoils of war were then divided among expedition members along strict rules of command. As Henrietta Lidchi and Stuart Allan describe,

> in the British imperial context, the prize system … allowed for auctions to be undertaken in situ, to raise prize money for distribution through the conquering army or to be sent home for auction with the same purpose, keeping aside certain items reserved for the Crown.[18]

In Imperial Germany, the Berlin Ethnological Museum became *de jure* a central repository for colonial spoils of war. The Federal Council (*Bundesrat*) ruled in 1889 that collections acquired during expeditions financed by the Colonial Department of the Foreign Office should first be offered as gifts to this museum before being sold to other institutions or landing on the art market. Military museums, like the Musée de l'Armée in Paris, the Zeughaus in Berlin, or the handful of regimental museums in the UK were de facto spoiled with loot coming directly from the hands of both high- and low-ranking officers. Directors of ethnographic museums also entertained close correspondence with members of the military, in order to be first in line to acquire or buy African belongings from communities that had been stripped of their sovereignty.

Most African collections in ethnographic museums in Europe in fact stem from contexts of imperial rule (1800s–1960s).[19] It is during this period that many of those institutions were born and witnessed an exponential increase of their holdings. For instance, between 70 and 80 per cent of the Africa collection at the Berlin Ethnological Museum was acquired before the end of the German colonial empire in 1919.[20] More than half of the collections of its direct concurrent at the time, Stuttgart's Linden Museum, also came before 1920. In France, about 65 per cent of African collections at the Musée du Quai Branly – Jacques Chirac (formerly, Musée du Trocadéro) stem from before 1960, the year in which an unmatched number of African countries declared their independence. Across the English Channel, the British Museum's Department of Africa, Oceania and the Americas collection had about 54,000 entries when Botswana gained its independence from British colonial rule in 1966.[21] It is therefore evident that hundreds of thousands of belongings were taken under duress, in the context of despotic regimes and unequal relations of power where resistance to conquest and exploitation was met with military oppression. Most of these instances of extreme violence are still unaccounted for. They provided fruitful terrain for the shameless confiscation of personal belongings, sacred artefacts and ancestral heirlooms, contexts of acquisition that the British Museum has euphemistically called 'contested means' in an addendum to its online collection (see also Chapter 13).[22] These asymmetrical conflicts were often punctuated by summary executions and the snatching of human remains, as happened with Lusinga in 1884 (see Chapter 12), Hassan bin Omari in 1895,[23] Mbuya Nehanda in 1898 (see Chapter 14), or in the Kilimanjaro region in 1900 (see Chapter 8).

In their report commissioned by the French president, Felwine Sarr and Bénédicte Savoy listed well-known instances of blatant pillaging: Algiers in 1830, Magdala in 1868, Kumasi in 1878, Ségou in 1890, Abomey in 1892, Benin City in 1897 and Tibati in 1898. At nearly the same time, Savoy galvanised the German media and the museum scene when she exclaimed in a dramatic manner: 'I would like to know how much blood can be found on a [museum] artwork'.[24] She did not mean blood from sacrifices of animals as witnessed in Akan, Dagomba or Ewe rituals performed on drums; she meant chemical (albeit perhaps not as strikingly red as the ones on this book's cover) and archival traces that would prove that people were murdered before their belongings were taken away. Five years down the stretch, Savoy and her team in Berlin, a team to which one of us belongs, were able to list 181 military expeditions led by German colonial troops in German Cameroon, 60 in German Togoland, that

INTRODUCTION

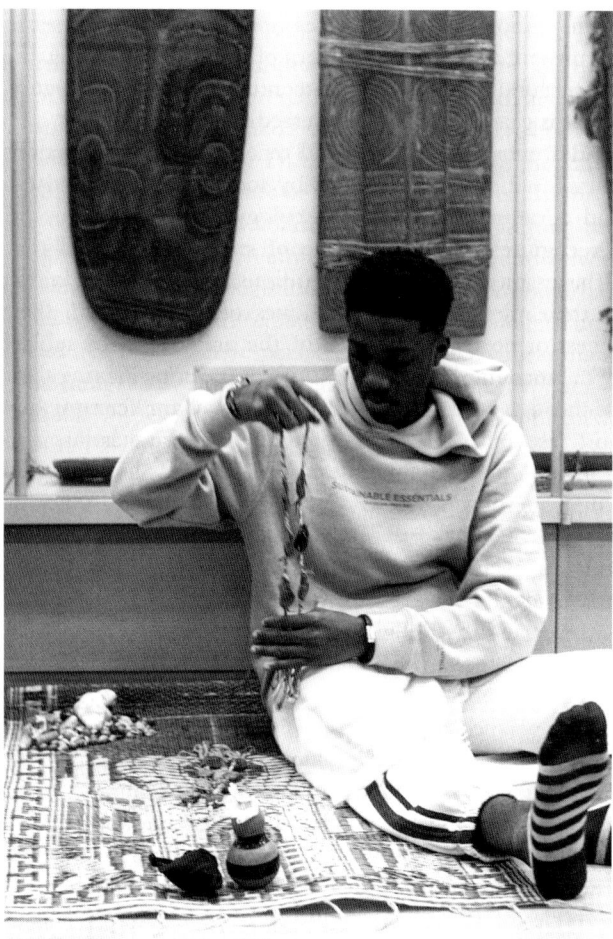

Figure 0.2: *Afa* diviner Celestino Kofi Voncujovi engaged in *afa* reading at the open storage of the Overseas Museum in Bremen, as part of the transnational Legba-Dzoka Project. Photo: Sela K. Adjei.

In a quest to align their core values and institutional policies to the concept of the 'new museology', some museums have acknowledged and reconsidered their social responsibilities in relation to the long-standing debates plaguing Western cultural institutions. Consequently, over the last few decades, other museums have corrected their ways of tackling specific problems which negatively taint the social role of museums as 'universal sites' of knowledge, pedagogy and culture. For instance, the Museum der Kulturen in Basel, Switzerland, superimposed a watermarked caveat across the pages (2993) of a digitised catalogue detailing African inventories in their collection which reads: 'Please note that many designations in this list have been identified as faulty, outdated or as racist abuse since the inventories' original conception.' In 2012, the Smithsonian amended their historical records by publishing a list of 'Cultural Terms Not in Use' in their bid to 'reverse' epistemic violence, traumatic colonial histories and to also align their institutional practices with new museum ethics. Serious consideration was finally given to appropriate naming and cataloguing of collections in culturally sensitive ways that ensured they caused neither confusion nor offence. Given that a substantial portion of these cultural assets were amassed during the colonial and apartheid era, the South African collection particularly poses several challenges to the Smithsonian in this respect, a situation that highlights epistemic violence and the broader implications of changing museum terminologies and classifications in contemporary times. The K-word, a racist term that has been used to refer to Black South Africans, was for instance everywhere in the catalogue and database. Being offensive, this word was therefore included in the Smithsonian's list of 'Culture Terms Not in Use'.[37] Because removing discriminatory terms from catalogue records can risk erasing the racist history of museum collections, the Smithsonian provides digitised versions of original catalogue cards that display historical records with the K-word present but crossed out. This example demonstrates how traces of the colonial past can remain visible, while refraining using racist terms in the searchable online record. The Victoria and Albert Museum, the German Lost Art Foundation and other institutions have also made similar attempts in their online inventories to reflect these inequalities and power imbalances in the mode of acquisition and the description of this cultural heritage.[38]

Yet, the rationale behind the museum's retention of archaic terms might lack a sound basis to a conscious visitor. Derogatory terms and problematic approaches to museum classification and heritage management still persist. Appalling stories and culturally insensitive information built around looted collections were constructed during a time when unequal global structures and a disrespectful attitude towards Africans were prevalent and often went unquestioned. Eurocentrism has never stopped being the norm, especially in the museum sector. This entrenched Eurocentrism not only influenced the narratives and information surrounding looted collections but also manifested harshly in real-world scenarios, evidencing the depth of cultural insensitivity. A poignant example of this can be seen in events that unfolded at the turn of the twentieth century, which starkly illustrate the consequences of such a skewed worldview. Consider the 267 African men, women and children 'imported' from the Congo to Brussels in 1897 as 'exhibits' merely to gratify Leopold's racist whims. In an elaborate display, set up a mere three months after the British expedition against Benin, these Africans were transported by train to Brussels's Gare du Nord and settled in specially created villages in Tervuren, showcasing a sharp contrast between what the metropole considered as 'uncivilised' and 'civilised' lifestyles. The artificial villages featured a 'river village', 'forest village' and a 'civilised' one, inhabited by the 'Pygmies' from the Congo. The inhabitants of the first two 'uncivilised' villages displayed their 'native' practices with tools, drums and canoes they brought from home, while being exhibited in bamboo huts during the day like 'zoo animals'. Adam Hochschild recounts that:

> Leopold himself came to see the Congolese, his dream made flesh, and was introduced to one of their chiefs. Told that some of the Africans were suffering from indigestion because of snacks and candy given them by the public, he ordered up the equivalent of a don't-feed-the-animals sign. The placard said: THE BLACKS ARE FED BY THE ORGANIZING COMMITTEE. They were fed and slept in the royal stables. The local press titillated its readers by speculating about whether the 'uncivilized' Africans were 'dangerous'.[39]

Taking into account these shocking histories and recent developments, scholars and museum staff ought to acknowledge and take up discussing the various tensions still prevalent in revisionist museum practice today. Specifically, there's a need for a thorough examination of how Eurocentric methods of labelling, organising, displaying and documenting cultural assets – often acquired through looting – continue to shape contemporary museums. A stubborn adherence to what Hannah Turner describes as 'dirty data' in Western museum cataloguing, seems an irresponsible way to deal with the violent histories associated with the cultural assets illegally held in museums' so-called 'protective custody'.[40] A generic term like 'object', for instance, is quite inaccurate in representing the vast myriad of cultural assets, ancestral heirlooms, sacred artefacts, royal regalia and human remains – which, in many cases, include trophy heads and ancestors whose remains were dug up from desecrated graves.[41] In this sense, the use of 'object' without contextual pedagogy, objectifies and strips museum collections of their humanity, cultural value, spiritual essence and quite often, obscures the violent histories associated with them. Gordon Gibson, anthropologist and former curator at the Smithsonian National Museum of Natural History, expressed his discontent by stating:

> I continue to be dissatisfied with the very unsystematic, inconsistent and cumbersome manner in which ethnological materials are being described for the catalog. Functions, techniques, basic materials, shapes, vernacular names – all appear, singly or in combination, as 'name of object'.[42]

With the 'discovery' of the so-called 'New World', and the resulting imperial expansion and colonial conquests in Africa, not only did Europeans illegally seized the land and the cultural heritage of colonised populations which became war booty. The discriminatory philosophies (of Hegel, Hume, Kant etc.) which prevailed during the so-called 'age of enlightenment' influenced European perception of African art and culture and fuelled racist thinking. This bleak era saw European ethnographers mislabelling African art. In their Eurocentric minds, 'primitive'[43] 'fetish'[44] 'objects' did not 'meet the aesthetic criteria' of what they judged as 'pure art'[45] or 'civilised art' worthy of appreciation and aesthetic contemplation. Historically, in maintaining their colonial apparatus, Europeans denied Africans the capability of producing art, since they regarded most sacred sculptures, masks and ritual implements as 'fetish-power objects'[46] or strictly utilitarian devices.[47] Gradually, African artworks were categorised interchangeably as 'rarities' or 'curiosities'. Cabinets of curiosity and their descendants, that is, public museums, displayed everything deemed 'exotic', 'extraordinary' and 'rare' from the living and the non-living, and were 'exalted' to mysterious settings. European kings, noblemen and artists also had 'curio' cabinets displaying African art in their private collections. The status of African art remained uncertain for centuries, until Victorian European writers labelled them as 'art objects'. With the so-called 'discovery' of African art by twentieth-century modernists like Picasso and Matisse, the status of these cultural and aesthetic assets was upgraded, leading to their inclusion in museum collections under the label of 'art objects'.

In practical terms, there is still no conclusive solution to record traumatic histories and flag racist bias in museum databases. It will take time. The key to addressing all these problems lies in collective efforts. In other words, it is the responsibility of stakeholders and advisory boards to ensure high-quality research and proper education within cultural institutions, while acknowledging the limits of dealing with 'dirty data' and colonial bias in their holdigs. Envisioning epistemicides in academia and cultural institutions, Ghanaian philosopher Kwasi Wiredu urged African intellectuals to adopt a 'doubly critical stance' towards inherited colonial culture and its insidious educational frameworks. In other words, they should not forget to draw on their own cultures and language when developing new approaches in cultural history. Philosophical decolonisation, in his view, extends beyond critiquing doctrines: it also encompasses developing fundamental concepts, being therefore 'an examination of validity rather than the exposure of invalidity'. It rests upon the critical examination of Western frameworks upon which museal cultures were erected, and 'of those elements of culture that play significant roles in the constitutions of meanings in the various African worldviews'.[48]

In editing this volume, trying to avoid using the term 'object' was tough. This term indeed presupposes that a subject is gazing at, defining and manipulating a thing devoid of agency. But if some of the looted cultural assets are imbued with spiritual power, how could they not have agency? We have tried to convince the authors to refrain from using the word 'object' for this diverse array of paraphernalia, royal insignia, effigies, ancestral guardian figures, human remains and (personal) 'belongings', the latter being a worthy suggestion by archaeologist Goodman Gwasira and author Priya Basil.[49] Here, we have chosen to encompass them under the umbrella term 'cultural assets' from Africa. Whenever possible, the authors provide names in local languages, for example, *isiHlangu, bocio, vigango* and *ngule malang* (see Chapters 3, 10, 13 and 15). We also encountered various alternative terms, such as the alluring 'treasure' of Samori Touré (see Chapter 1), mostly foreign denominations used interchangeably to represent personal affairs here, royal insignia or sacred sculptures there.[50] Godfrey Tangwa and Fogha MC Cornilius Refem, however, defended their use of the term 'object' to describe effigies with agency and sacred sculptures exhibited in Western museums. Their rationale was based on the premise that agency is not inherent to the thing itself, but rather 'relational' (see Chapter 9, also 10). By employing and purposefully highlighting the term 'object', these authors aimed to depict authentically the contextual existence of the effigy of Ngonnso', while also advocating for her redefinition. Evidently, all these concerns related to inconsistent terminology in Western anthropology are connected to contentious issues, many of which remain unresolved among scholars of African art history and Africa-based intellectuals. These debates are historically rooted in the epistemic violence which occurred during the clash of civilisations between Europe and Africa, sometimes euphemistically called 'colonial encounters'. This book wants to make clear that this clash involved violent acts of conquest of land and people.

Artistic Interventions and Orality: Challenging the Ethnographic Gaze and Scientific Authority

Speaking of encounters: the first moment of contact between us and African heritage in museums usually takes place either in an exhibition or by browsing pictures taken by conservationists and museum staff online. These shots of musealised cultural assets feign neutrality: they are placed standing in front of a neutral background or lying on unwrapped foil of acid-free paper, taken out of storage drawers and shelves for a brief moment, just enough time to adjust focal length and for the shutter to open and close. Museumgoers are allowed to take their own snapshots of the cultural assets displayed and can thereby, to a certain extent, produce an image that challenges the way these cultural assets are displayed to the public. More daring, some activists opted for 3D scanning, thereby bypassing museum regulations but also stealing the assets' digital identity.[51] Conservation photography, with its peculiar light, frame and position, is subject to unbending institutional and methodical conventions. Photography is an integral part of museum practice and its normative discourse. By displaying inanimate cultural assets detached from social contact, digital databases try to give the impression of a neutral perspective. But this gaze can never really show how these belongings were used before they were taken away from their owners and turned into museum displays or boxed collections. There are often cultural codes that decide whether a statue can

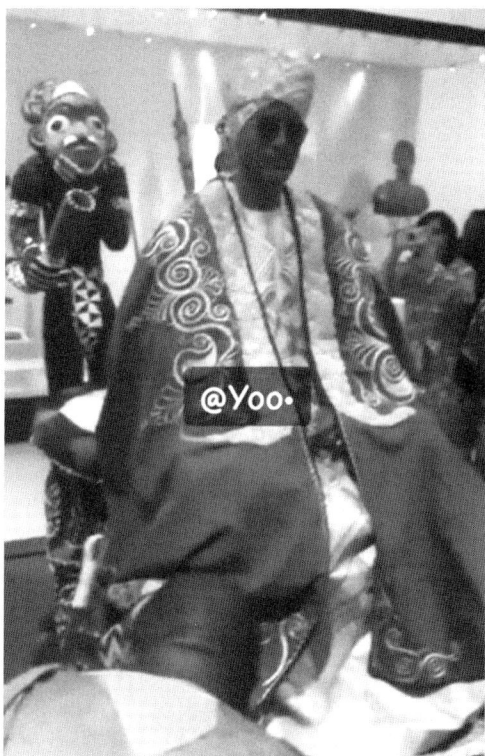

Figure 0.3: Screenshot of a video showing the King of Bamum climbing up and sitting on *Mandu Yenu* at the Humboldt Forum in Berlin. Original video by Yannick Ondua, http://bit.ly/manduyenu11062023 (accessed 12 January 2023).

be shown – and to whom.[52] It might indeed be inappropriate to gaze at sacred effigies, masks used in ceremonies, let alone at intimate items of clothing. Drums would prefer being hit and heard than portrayed as silent remnants. If nobody is allowed to sit on a throne, can it still be called a throne? The King of the Bamum kingdom (in today's Cameroon) shattered these conventions of museum display when on 11 November 2023 at the Humboldt Forum in Berlin, he offhandedly climbed upon his ancestor's throne, *Mandu Yenu* (see Figure 0.3).

To counter the ethnographic and colonial gaze, we decided against featuring photographs of African cultural heritage as stand-alones and chose to foreground this relational aspect in the illustrations. Additionally, we got artists on board who could contextualise the cultural assets under scrutiny. The result is a patchwork of illustrations drawn by nine creative minds from the African continent and curated by Sela K. Adjei. All produced in pen and ink, they subvert this proto-colonial style, a format widely used in the nineteenth and twentieth century to illustrate colonial narratives such as military reports, voyages of discovery or ethno-geographic studies of non-European land and people. We also scouted around to feature illustrators from the region or country where the colonial thieves operated. Through this approach, we encouraged each illustrator to capture the critical visual narratives in this volume to properly represent their country's colonial history.

Finally, contrary to Judeo-Christian understandings of history, where the written word has authority over other forms of historiography, in many African cultures, history is recorded by elders or griots. It is conveyed in diverse forms, including storytelling, public reciting, music, and also in dance and textile patterns. Local historians, like *gonje* Alhaji Alhassan Sulemana, pass on the stories they heard to their descendants and beyond (see Chapter 4). The past is narrated through dialogue and song in the public space, like the *baraza* in East Africa (see Chapter 8). Each section of this book, hence, includes a chapter that was not the product of writing, but of talking. We called them 'conversations' and hope they will offer a dynamic alternative to the Western academic format of edited volumes. In these chapters, the authors digress, wander around and reflect on the (sometimes very personal and emotional) value of these histories for them, their families and their peers. These conversations are, to our minds, much needed alternatives to provenance research reports and scientific articles, and we invite our readers to imagine the context in which those dialogues took place, as well as the sound of these contributors' voices.

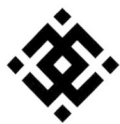

PART I

THE BATTLEFIELD

This first part of the book discusses paraphernalia and personal belongings that were grabbed or looted during or in the immediate aftermath of battle. Museums today are filled with African weapons such as spears, arrows, quivers, swords and axes. Shields and armour also testify to the cost in human lives: some preserved in museum storages are visibly pierced with bullet holes, such as the famous Gweagal shield exhibited at the British Museum, a material remnant of the violence of British encroachment on the continent that we today call Australia.[53] In the contexts of colonial – and mostly asymmetrical – wars in Africa, colonial troops confiscated weapons and equipment, even though many fireweapons that local communities used against them were in fact the result of European import.[54] Finally, other types of trophies were brutally taken from the enemy: war flags, drums, but also human remains of fallen warriors and leaders.

In the British Army, the most valuable pieces were reserved and presented to the Queen while the remainder of the capture was divided as so-called prize, or prize money. During the colonial era, army museums acquired plenty of spoils of war that they put on display as trophies. The Musée de l'Armée in Paris, the Zeughaus in Berlin or the National Army Museum in London are prime examples of this celebration of imperial conquest and military prowess through exhibits. Yet, some of those pieces looted on the battlefield were also interesting for anthropologists and thereby landed in other kinds of museums. Others were auctioned off, or, if the museums had already acquired heritage from a given region or community, considered as a double and therefore sold or transferred to smaller institutions or other museums abroad. Part I will explore the lives and afterlives of some of this war booty which fills ethnographic and military museums in Europe and beyond.

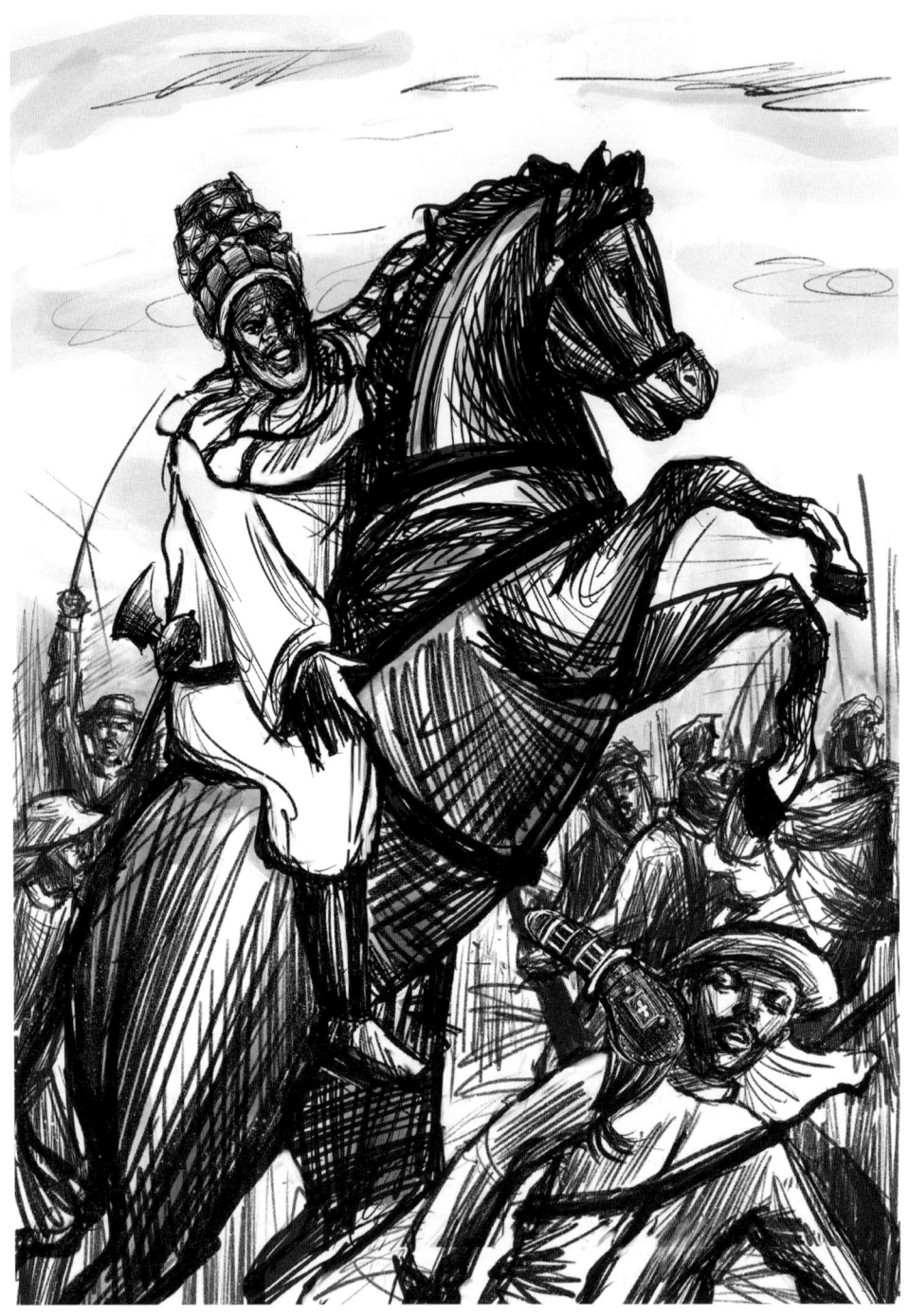

Artist: Chigozie Obi

CHAPTER 1

The treasure of Samori Touré

Felwine Sarr & Bénédicte Savoy

In the post-colonial psyche, Samori Touré is seen as a hero of African resistance to French colonial expansion. In 1984, the Ivorian reggae singer Alpha Blondy dedicated a song to him: 'Bory Samory' (literally 'Run, Samory!'), in which he is remembered – alongside his rival Babemba Traoré, but also Patrice Lumumba, Steve Biko or Martin Luther King – as one in a series of Black anti-colonial figures victim of colonial and racist violence. Founder of the Wassoulou Empire, in a territory currently located between Guinea, Mali, Burkina Faso and Côte d'Ivoire, Samori Touré opposed the French and the British invasion of West Africa for two decades. In autumn 1898, he was the target of a campaign of reprisals led by the French general Henri Gouraud. He was arrested and deported to Gabon, where he died two years later. 'Samori's treasure', seized upon his surrender, were twelve crates valued at over 200,000 francs at the time. In his memoirs, titled *Au Soudan: Souvenirs d'un Africain*, Gouraud notes:

> With the treasure, Samory's souvenirs are leaving, some to the Musée de l'Armée (Army Museum): the saddle, the sabre, the almamy's war bonnet, one of his rifles…, *dialas* [cowrie shells], the necklaces of Saranké Mory and Ahmadou Touré, some strange rings, a match holder and above all Saranké Mory's war boubou, a rich piece. Besides, we are also sending General [Edgar] de Trentinian the battle axe, the fly swatter made from an elephant's tail wrapped in silver and the sabre that Sarankégny Mory handed over to me when he surrendered.[55]

Today, some of these belongings are kept in the Musée de l'Armée in Paris. The late marabout Cheikh Ousmane Badji paid them an official 'visit' in the late 1960s. A red file containing some forty documents bears witness to this visit and the reactions it provoked, particularly among those in charge of the Musée National des Arts d'Afrique et d'Océanie, formerly Musée des Colonies, where part of Samori's 'treasure' was kept at the time.⁵⁶ These documents are evidence of the keen and precocious interest shown by the independent state of Guinea under President Sekou Touré in recovering Samori's paraphernalia. They also testify to the intellectual, emotional and mystical enterprise of an Islamic religious and community leader eager to reconnect with the founder of the Wassoulou Empire.

A pan-African legend, Samori Touré is also one of the figures in pre-colonial historiography about whom we know the most. In addition to oral history and archival documents, photographs and personal belongings have enabled historians to reconstruct many aspects of his political and military biography in the century following his death, especially after the decade of African independences. Today, we know more about Samori Touré, his empire, his family, his beliefs, his understanding of war and trade, diplomacy, law and taxation, and even his clothing, than we do about most of the African sovereigns who had to fight European armies in what anthropologist Dan Hicks has described as 'World War Zero': a world war *avant la lettre* waged for 30 years by Europe across the entire African continent, not a succession of micro-campaigns ('punitive expeditions') as a peculiar historiographical euphemism has customarily led us to think.⁵⁷

Anyone who has ever tried to reconstruct the actions of African emperors, kings and chiefs harassed around 1900 by German, French, British or Belgian armies knows how difficult it is to 'shift' the perspective provided by colonial sources in order to understand the position of the other side, the 'opponent', the 'African chief', the one who left little to no written trace. African leaders had a complex network of vassals, children, wives, troops, arsenals, horses, treasures, libraries, jewels and so on. In the case of Samori, generations of historians both in Africa and in Europe have perused the archives (military, diplomatic, museum, literary). They offer a reconstruction that is, if not truly faithful or complete ('truly' does not exist in these fields), at least a polyphonic and critical reconstruction of the events that led this son of a Malinke merchant, born around 1830 and deprived of his mother at an early age, to become the head of a vast empire, to engage in armed resistance against colonial powers and, finally, to go into exile. The eminent Ghanaian historian Albert Adu Boahen set the tone and the general framework for this historical work in the sixth volume of *Histoire Générale de l'Afrique*. In a detailed article, he described the 'Islamic Revolutions or djihād' of which Samori Touré was a key player in West Africa before 1870.⁵⁸ The same volume also devotes an almost entire chapter to the leader of the Wassoulou Empire, entrusted to the best expert of the time, Yves Person, who in the 1970s had devoted his career of 'the Almami', as Samori is sometimes called.⁵⁹ The investigation continued in the seventh volume of the *Histoire Générale* with a new chapter by Albert Adu Boahen, co-authored by M'Baye Gueye and titled 'African Initiatives and Resistance in West Africa'.⁶⁰ Even today, this work remains a benchmark in the field of Samorean research. In recent years, this work has been accelerated by the brilliant investigations of young academics who, thanks to a triple turn – iconic, acoustic and material, that is, 'object turn' – have chosen to use sources hitherto considered peripheral or neglected by traditional historiography: phonography, photography, film and museum collections. In this respect, Elara Bertho's work on the hundreds of photographs representing Samori Touré in various mainly French archive collections (2018) and on the screenplay of an unrealised film by Ousmane Sembène (2016), Angie Epifano's study of Samori's relics kept at the Musée de l'Armée in Paris (2020) and Olivier Kodjalbaye Banguiam's examination of African collections formed by French officers during the colonial conquest (2016) deserve particular attention.[61] The following pages are not intended to reconstruct the military carnage that led to the collapse of Samori's empire, his arrest and deportation; nor to recall the Almami's involvement in the Islamic conquest through brutal raids, his military tactics, his scorched earth policy or the trade in human beings. They focus on the link between the capture of heritage, military confrontations, the neutralisation of cultural assets in Western museums, and the question of their return to the regions and the societies from which they were taken for a resocialisation.

Capture

There is quite a lot of information on the booty confiscated by the French army after the arrest of Samori Touré in September 1898 in a small town in the west of today's Côte d'Ivoire, not far from the borders with Liberia and Guinea. But this spectacular capture was not the first. French museums acquired items associated with Samori or his close circle as far back as the 1880s. Olivier Kodjalbaye Banguiam revealed that the administrative archives of the Musée d'Ethnographie du Trocadéro in Paris inform on the shipping of human remains as early as 1883. On 10 July 1883, the French officer Louis Archinard, best known for his looting in 1890 of the possessions of El Hadj Omar Tall, aka 'the treasure of Ségou', wrote: 'You asked me for skulls from the Niger valley, I collected two from Samory warriors killed in Bamako'.[62] From the 1880s onwards, European museums in fact incited soldiers, civilians, missionaries and scholars to collect material samples of African cultures that had been or were to be subjugated by arms, and to ship them to the colonial metropoles. Beyond a simple military logic legitimised by decades of law on booty, the taking of cultural entities and their integration into ethnographic collections seemed, from the European point of view at the time, to be key for accessing and generating knowledge, something that observation alone could not guarantee.

Museums sometimes issued precise instructions as to which items should be selected and how they should be packaged. On their return from Africa for home leave or during their summer holidays in France, colonialists got into the habit of depositing their best finds in museums, whether in Paris or elsewhere. Yet, the provenance of these African belongings was not always well documented. This is illustrated by archives related to Archinard, who, in the middle of the summer of 1883, wrote on a sheet of paper: 'I left a number of objects from Niger and from Samory's army with the concierge [caretaker] of the Musée d'Ethnographie at Trocadéro. I'm just passing through Paris on my way to my family...'.[63] In France, the spoils of Captain Louis Archinard are among the most significant and the least studied. In total, there are probably more than a thousand cultural assets in French public collections listed as successive 'gifts' from this French general or his widow. At present, it is difficult to determine with any certainty what can be linked to his confrontations with Samori. At the Musée du Quai Branly – Jacques Chirac, only a few items are associated with his name. Four amulets inventoried in 1889 with other cultural assets were probably taken from the corpses of soldiers.[64] At least one other amulet was probably obtained in the same macabre circumstances. Archinard included it in the same lot and, according to the catalogue, it originated from a town in the Wassoulou region. In addition to these donations by Archinard, the Quai Branly's inventory lists a dozen of items linked to the Almami or his entourage: an arched harp that entered the museum in 1882 and which was reportedly '[t]aken at Kemera in Samory's camp'; 'a hunting headgear from the people of Samory' and a 'special headgear of Samory's *sofas* [soldiers]' entered the collection in 1889 and 1892 respectively; two hats made of basketwork and leather with a 'special shape relative to the soufa [sic] chiefs of Samory' entered in 1892.[65] Besides, three spears, a harpoon (!) and a 'cutter' were donated to the museum in the 1950s and were reportedly 'part of a set of weapons that belonged to Samory's personal guard' but remained in the family of a soldier for several decades. They entered the collection along with a 'parasol' which, according to the inventory, 'belonged to Samory' himself.[66] Like all wars waged by the European powers against African sovereigns at the time, the battles between Samori's troops and the French were, from the 1880s onwards, the occasion for acquiring war trophies, traces of which can be found in all ethnographic museums of Europe.

But it is with the events of 1898 that 'Samori's treasure' is generally associated. The surprise arrest of the warrior chief in the early hours of 29 September 1898 was followed, according to a detailed report by Henri Gouraud, by several hours of searching and amassing material goods. Most particular among them were weapons and gold. Gouraud, who graduated from the military academy in Saint-Cyr as an infantryman in 1888, was only a captain when he obtained the rendition of Samori in 1898, earning him immense renown in France and the rank of Chevalier of the National Order of the Legion of Honour. The words he used to describe his seizure were part of a long military tradition of confiscation. We will not dwell on the legal and military implications of these practices, since they are largely dealt with in this entire volume. Suffice to say here that the law on pillage and its product, war booty, were well established at the end of the nineteenth century. Many of Samori's contemporaries on the African continent and in the rest of the world had by 1898 already first-hand experience of its implications: from the looting of the summer palace in Beijing by

British and French troops (1860) to the plunder of Magdala in today's Ethiopia by the British (1868, see Chapter 11), to the sacking of Abomey by the French army (1892, see Chapter 10) and that of Benin City by the British (1897), amplified by the illustrated press of both countries, world public opinion associated colonial wars with the capture of cultural assests often deemed fabulous in their form or materiality. In this field, fantasies and anticipation of gain, narratives of extraordinary military feats, and abundant iconography were part and parcel of the mechanisms of appropriation.

Gouraud was no exception to the rule. In *Au Soudan: Souvenirs d'un Africain*, two chapters are devoted to the subject: 'The Spoils' and 'The Treasure'.[67] Both describe the accumulation of wealth confiscated from the enemy. As in many similar stories, the question of how to divide the spoils is central, as the French army had not perfected the British way of redistributing prize money. Gouraud recalls one of his subordinates asking him: 'Captain, I have never seen so much gold, do you think we'll be left with a bit of it?' To which he retorted: 'I believe there is a regulation on shares. I'll ask if it can be applied to us.' The general continues, 'I asked. I was told that the regulations did not apply to Sudanese troops.'[68] The topos of the soldier or low-ranking officer being wronged by regulation on prize money is not uncommon. It can also be found in accounts of the capture of Abomey in 1892. Its counterpart was a national pathos that dictated that the wealth wrested from the vanquished would be bequeathed to the French state. Archinard, for example, in the context of the 'treasure of Ségou', forced the officers to sign 'a pledge that they would do everything in their power to ensure that nothing is taken away and that the State obtains the whole treasure'.[69]

What did the 'treasure' consist of, according to sources provided by Westerners? And what can be located today? As Daniel Foliard writes, in the African context at the end of the nineteenth century, the discovery and confiscation of war treasure was not only a military objective but also a form of justification: in the face of anti-colonial criticism stirring up the parliaments of colonial metropoles at the time, governments needed to justify the high cost of taxpayers' money spent in conquering the African continent. Making these treasures attractive, cultivating rumours about them, and publicising their eventual capture eventually helped garner support for military conquest. It was not in the interest of the victorious officers in Africa to play down the scale of their finds – quite the contrary.[70] Hence, a mixture of precision and vagueness in Gouraud's own description of the treasure of Samori. On several occasions, he specified that he was drawing an inventory, a way of signalling a sense of order and responsibility. However, apart from the human remains, weapons, ammunition and livestock that would remain in French West Africa, he only gave a brief description of the 'treasure': a few emblematic possessions with military trophy value, 'the saddle, the sabre, the war bonnet of the almamy, one of his rifles', as well as 'the battle axe, the fly-catcher… and the sabre' given by his son, and 'above all the war boubou of Saranké Mory, a rich piece', which we already mentioned in the introduction. The rest remains rather vague: '*dialas*', 'necklaces', 'strange rings' and a 'match holder'. For the remaining portion, Gouraud provided an exact figure, namely, 'a treasure amounting to 230,000 francs'.[71] According to historian Yves Person, it consisted mainly of 'gold dust'.[72]

Gouraud also mentioned the 'twelve crates' in which this treasure was transported by the French military. But traces of this shipment have been lost in the archival sources known to date. Several clues suggest: 1) either that its integrity was altered even before it was transferred to the metropole; or 2) that some items thought to have been taken from the treasure were circulating in 'French Sudan', although their provenance could not really be verified. During a scientific expedition in 1899, the botanist and biologist Auguste Jean Baptiste Chevalier related, not without racist prejudice vis-à-vis local troops:

> I was just robbed of 500 fr[ancs] consisting mainly of gold objects from Samory's treasure that I was bringing back as curiosities. This theft, which took place in the very interior of the Post Office in Bobo, could only have been committed by a tirailleur or a boy. You could hang them all without being able to obtain half a confession.[73]

If correct, the hypothesis of a treasure scattered as curiosities suggests that the colonial troops sorted out Samori Touré's belongings after his capture and a process of inventory. As it had been the case with the treasure of Ségou, the assets deemed of minor value would have then been sold on the spot. Another possibility is that some officers kept parts of the seizure under wraps so they could generate profit from informal sales. The final option would be to grant commonplace cultural assets a prestigious provenance – that is, 'Samori treasure' – in order to increase their symbolic value and hence their price with unsuspecting buyers, as was the case in France and Great Britain after the looting of the Yuanmingyuan, Beijing's Old Summer Palace. Here, it is impossible to give a final answer. The fact is that the integrity of 'Samori's treasure' – and therefore its ethnographic or scientific value as a coherent whole formed by one of the most powerful emperors in West Africa before colonial territorial and administrative partition – played no part in the discourse and practice of the French military in the aftermath of Samori's surrender.[74] On the contrary, the French followed a military and, so to speak, magical logic that was called *translatio imperii* ('transfer of power') in medieval times. The young officer Gouraud recalled in his memoirs sending three unique attributes of power to the governor of the then 'French Sudan', General Edgard de Trentinian: 'the battle axe, the fly swatter made from an elephant's tail sheathed in silver and the sabre given to me by Sarankégny Mory when he surrendered'. In this military logic, to grab and confiscate the symbols of someone else's power was to take on and appropriate his very power. It would be hard to find a clearer expression of the archaic faith of the military in the 'loaded force' of personal belongings.

Dislocation

The 'treasure of Samori', or what remained of it after its dislocation (not only in the original sense of 'separation, disintegration, scattering of the elements of a whole' but also in the medical sense of a 'break'), resurfaced in Paris in an unexpected place: the Universal Exhibition of 1900. Unexpected because this show was certainly not conducive to the expression of the treasure's initial prestige, its power or its symbolic force. There, Samori's belongings were indeed competing with other energies considered quasi-supernatural at the time. Placed under the auspices of the 'electricity fairy', the exhibition offered a host of technological attractions: a 3-km two-speed moving walkway; an illuminated Ferris wheel like the one at the 1893 exhibition in Chicago; a giant screen by the Lumière brothers, who showed animated images to the public for the first time; a siderostat to capture the stars; the first Paris metro line; and, in the United States pavilion, the now legendary *Exposition des Nègres d'Amérique*, conceived among others by the very young leader of the civil rights movement for Black Americans, the sociologist W.E.B. Du Bois, who used his now-famous photographs and graphs to demonstrate the value of social, cultural and economic contributions of Black US citizens.[75] Looking back at this juxtaposition of avant-garde technologies and socio-political achievements more than a century after the Universal Exhibition, the anachronism of putting on display in Paris a war treasure captured in West Africa is striking.

In a guide of the exhibition, we learn that 'Samori's treasure' – or what was designated as such – was presented to the public at the 'Palais de la Colonisation' at the Musée d'Ethnographie du Trocadéro in a series of subjects related to the colonies:

> Berlitz's method for the propagation of the French language, souvenirs from explorations in the Sudan (including Samory's treasure brought back by Mr d'Anthonay, which includes, along with the crown, so many objects and jewels of worked gold of great value), railways penetrating the colonies…[76]

Apart from the incongruity of this juxtaposition, the mention of a 'crown', absent from military sources related to Samori's arrest, and that of a Monsieur d'Anthonay are intriguing. They corroborate the suspicion that there was not one, but several 'treasures of Samori' on French territory at the time, their authenticity being back then probably less important than the prestigious name of the defeated chief. In 1900, Léon d'Anthonay was at the head of a vast heating and ventilation industry. He was also the author of a book dedicated to 'rubber in the French Sudan', the properties of which he had studied in the field in the very region where Samori had been arrested a year earlier. A section of the Universal Exhibition was devoted to this raw material extracted in Africa. Should we go as far to imagine that he acquired part of the 'treasure' on the spot? In matters of provenance, prudence suggests that we shouldn't take this step. All the more so when considering another report on the Universal Exhibition which mentions Raoul Lartigue, an officer who was actually involved in Samori's arrest: 'Major Lartigue exhibited jewellery from Samory, his Qur'an, chased silver handles, necklaces and bracelets. The weapons of the black conqueror, his rifle and those of several of his *sofas* made up a panoply'.[77] To date, no trace of the Almami's Qur'an in French public museums has been found.

The questionable authenticity of all those descriptions of the treasure, including those that immediately followed Samori's arrest, make it difficult to retrace how this section of his alleged 'treasure' came to be displayed six decades later in the 'gallery of conquests' at the Musée des Arts Africains et Océaniens (MAAO), formerly Musée des Colonies (1931–1935), and Musée de la France d'Outre-Mer (1935). Two black-and-white photographs in the collections of the Musée du Quai Branly – Jacques Chirac show a tall octagonal display case that showcased, according to the handwritten note attached to one of the photos, 'Samory's treasure. Dialla; necklace; arms'.[78] In one of the two photos, some kind of crown sits on top, labelled in the visitors' guide at the time as the 'crown of Samory'.[79] Interestingly, none of the artefacts photographed are today associated with Samori's name in the collections of the Musée du Quai Branly, the heir to the MAAO. However, the 'battle axe' with its wooden handle decorated with iron rings and its head of prominent metal buttons is familiar to the eye: it was not transferred to the Musée du Quai Branly but is kept at the Musée de l'Armée.

In fact, of the items explicitly mentioned by Gouraud in his account of the arrest, only five can be clearly identified today. One was donated to the Musée Municipal de Montauban by Louis Bratière, a sergeant involved in Samori's arrest who was born in the city of Montauban. It is labelled as a 'saddle cloth of the King of Haut-Niger Samory Touré',[80] and appears to correspond to the 'green velvet' one that Gouraud reported to be a gift from one of Samori's wives, a cloth she herself had received from 'the French government and which bears a crescent and a star in gilded metal'.[81] The other four pieces are now displayed together in a showcase at the Musée de l'Armée in Paris, an institution supervised by the Ministry of Defence, and not the Ministry of Culture like most national museums in France. Founded according to an intellectual and institutional logic that differed from those of ethnographic museums, the Musée de l'Armée possesses the most prestigious and most certainly authentic elements of the 'treasure of Samory'. Or, to use the names chosen by the institution, the 'war tunic of Sarankegny Mori, son of Samory Touré' (inventory number 2300); 'Samory Touré's war headgear, wrapped in a diala (turban)' (inventory numbers 2292 & 2301); 'Samory's fly-chaser' (inventory number Cd485-5) and 'the axe used for commanding troops, Samory's mace' (Cd489-3) mentioned earlier. Here are therefore two belongings Gouraud originally intended for the Musée de l'Armée (the bonnet and the 'war boubou') and two others that were initially handed over to the

Governor of French Sudan, General Trintignan. According to information provided by the Musée de l'Armée, the first two were gifts from Colonel Audéoud, Gouraud's superior. An old postcard from 1920 bears witness to how these belongings were shown in the 'Aumale Hall' at the Musée de l'Armée: behind a Tuareg warrior mannequin riding a stuffed dromedary, a display case devoted to Samori is visible (see QR code). The caption reads: 'Samory's saddle and arms, taken by Gouraud in 1898'. The saddle is no longer on display.

At the end of this description of the scattered fragments of 'Samori's treasure', several observations can be made. First, as it is now preserved in France, the treasure does not form a homogeneous, coherent or truly known whole. Second, a multitude of officers contributed to the translocation of its various elements, meaning not only the geographical transfer to France, but equally the transformation of their function. As they became museum collections exhibited to the French public, these belongings lost their initial properties. Their power has been thereby both restrained and frozen. Third, between the arrival of the artefacts in Paris around 1900 and the 1960s, there was a great deal of institutional to-ing and fro-ing between the various Paris museums, notably the MAAO and the Musée de l'Armée. This means that, today, the 'treasure of Samori' cannot be truly associated with a fixed location. Fourth, the symbols of power that the French confiscated in the field because they were endowed with implicit force and associated with leadership in the Wassoulou Empire are today treated in the museums that preserve them as simply material samples, with neither mutual nor privileged relationship with their former owner or his descendants. Finally, the taxonomy of museums takes no account of the knowledge and beliefs associated with these possessions. 'Samory's treasure' is approached neither from the perspective of an ontology or sociology of the cultural asset, nor in terms of power and agency, nor in a dialectic between victors and vanquished, between the living, the dead and the inanimate, between the physical and the metaphysical nature of things.

Reconnection

This tunic, richly decorated with silver plates, was seized from Sarankegny Mori when the French captured Samori and his court at Guélémou (today's Côte d'Ivoire) on September 29, 1898. Gift from Colonel Audéoud, 1899.[82]

The information at the Musée de l'Armée appended to the display of one of the most extraordinary West African talismanic shirts kept in a European museum highlights the apparel's provenance and the circumstances – humiliating for some, rewarding for others – of its change of ownership. It is in keeping with the ancient logic of the trophy, in the original sense of the term: 'the armor of a defeated enemy, which in Antiquity was set up against a tree trunk', is here exposed in a glass case to the gaze of visitors. Its conservation in a public place, however, brings about other questions, such as those recently explored by art historian Angie Epifano. Based on the few elements of the 'treasure of Samori' preserved in France, she sketches out a reconstruction of what she calls 'the cultural system' of the Samorian state, a system that, destroyed with the arrest of its leader, can only be imagined today by bringing together scattered documents, material culture and oral accounts: 'This system', Epifano argues, 'consisted of physical objects – such as clothing, headdresses, fly-chasers and axes – as well as performative experiments, public ceremonies, and political negotiations', whose form and impact the author sets out to retrieve.[83]

Drawing on the 'Samorian regalia', she sees them as valuable sources of economic, artistic, symbolic and even religious history. Without repeating Epifano's whole argumentation here, which someone with intimate knowledge of West African Islamic traditions could certainly have deepened, let us retain her ability to 'make objects speak' without doing violence to them, in other words, without damaging the element of mystery encapsulated in them. Unlike Parisian museums, who are quick in using intrusive scanners, Epifano makes no attempt to unravel the meaning and content of Sarankegny Mory's incomparable tunic and its hundred or so embossed or openwork silver capsules, rectangular or oblong, some lined with bright red fabric, carefully fastened by leather loops along the lines of the indigo-dyed blue and black garment. She assumes that their content is apotropaic (i.e. protects from evil forces), and certainly includes suras from the Qur'an. Above all, she sets out to demonstrate that this 'spiritual armor' – whose silver capsules were supposed to shine in the sun, perhaps giving the wearer the feeling of attracting Allah's protective light – is also the expression of a commercial mastery of the Niger region that gave Samori Touré and his entourage 'access to incalculable material wealth, like silver, indigo, and red fabric'. Epifano concludes: 'The tunic is indicative of the State's innovative reimagining of non-Malinké aesthetic traditions to create a distinct system of regalia that mirrored the State's control of trade routes.'[84]

In the 1970s, when in the aftermath of independence African intellectuals started calling for the restitution (or at least long-term loans) of cultural assets looted by colonial powers, they argued in self-aware and empowering terms. These treasures would help young African nations in their effort to 'pave their own way' through better understanding of pre-colonial history, crafts, beliefs and creativity in Africa. In this context, Nigerian archaeologist Ekpo Eyo, among others, underlined the importance of developing a properly African historiography of material culture extracted from the continent in the nineteenth century and now on display in Western museums. In the introduction to his famous volume *2000 Years of Nigerian Art* (1977), he stressed the need for this heritage in exile to be reintegrated into a history and science conceived from the African continent, one that should not be satisfied with how Western historians made sense of these works, one that would demonstrate how European categories and terminologies often remained unworkable, if not totally useless, for understanding and studying African material cultures:

> If Europe has chosen to divorce art from religious or other social contexts, this does not amount to advancement, in fact some would regard it as a retrograde step. For the African the importance of a sculpture lies outside the realms of aesthetics; it has to do with the reconciliation of his life with his environment – with the problems of birth, survival, well-being, longevity, death and reincarnation: the whole life-cycle. It is only in terms of these social and religious contexts – indigenous African ideas, philosophies, religions, economies and politics – that the meaning of a sculpture may be found, or that it may be of direct benefit to the community.[85]

In the case of Samori, it was cinema that embodied this intellectual and epistemological reappropriation, with the (regrettably) aborted film project of Ousmane Sembène. The red archival folder we found at the Musée du Quai Branly and mentioned in the introduction contains the photographic and filming permits granted to the Senegalese director in 1971, as well as a precise list of cultural assets he would have liked to feature. This took place the year when the first formal restitution claims emanating from Nigeria and Zaire reached Europe. When asked to draw up a list of Samori's belongings and specify their exact provenance in view to a possible restitution, the head curator at the MAAO firmly noted:

> All these objects, whatever their origin, are ... national property. To remove them from the inventories, it is necessary that the Parliament votes a law authorising it. However, a favourable ruling would lead to a revision of the status of all collections (and probably of all museums that hold objects of foreign origin), which would lead to numerous international negotiations. *In any case, it would set a dangerous precedent.*[86]

Nothing was returned and this first attempt to get back looted African heritage was buried in oblivion, like many others.

Today, with almost all of Africa's cultural heritage still housed in European museums, 'Samory's treasure' at the Musée de l'Armée being a telling example, the question of intellectual and spiritual reappropriation of these cultural assets and belongings is becoming increasingly acute. More than ever, dialogue on restitution must make it clear to public opinion in the countries concerned, both in Africa and in Europe, that the aim, however desirable it may be, is not simply to monitor the return of cultural assets from their point of forced exile to their point of origin – or their new destinations for that matter. Further, and above all, it is essential for the institutions who own them and those who will one day repossess them to set off mechanisms for reappropriating their meaning, their geopolitical and their poetic values, and for foregrounding the fact that these important cultural heritage materials acquire meaning through social relations, not when being pinned in display cases like insects in entomological collections. In the case of the 'treasure of Samori', moreover, we need to reflect on the question of borders inherited from colonisation. For these relics, should they return one day, can no more be accommodated in the restricted space of a state than their original owner was willing and able to realise.

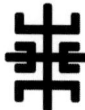

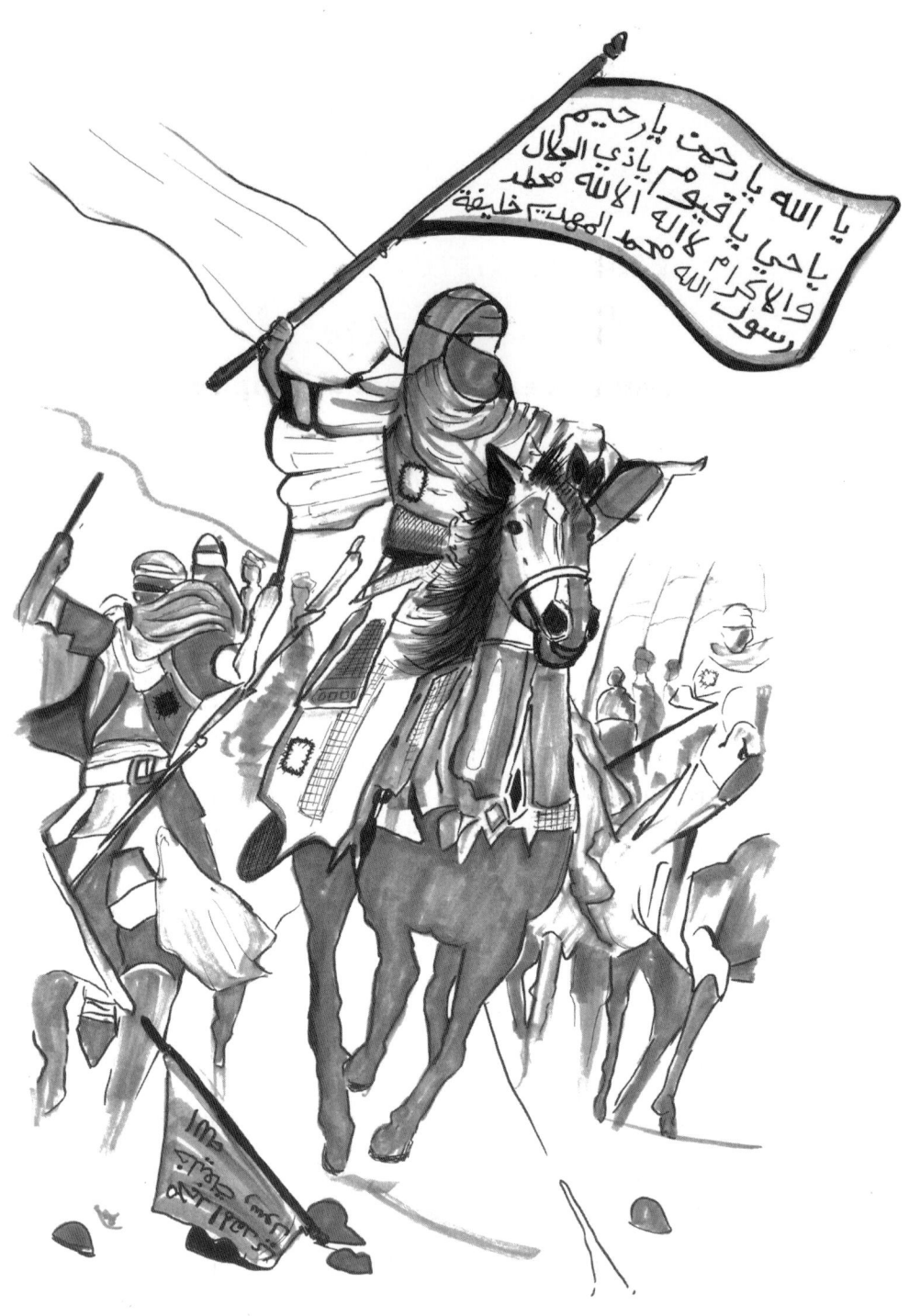

Artist: Assil Diab

CHAPTER 2

The Manifesto of the Sudanese Mahdī
Banners as Artefacts of Empire

Fergus Nicoll and Osman Nusairi

Artefacts from Britain's colonial wars in Sudan in the 1880s and 1890s can be found in at least sixty-five museums, art galleries, royal palaces, stately homes, academic archives and private collections around the world – in England, Scotland, Sudan, but also at the Smithsonian Institution in Washington, DC, and the State Hermitage in St Petersburg. The vast majority, however, are in the possession of the regiments that served, variously, in Lord Wolseley's failed mission to extract Major-General Charles Gordon from the besieged capital at Khartoum, the serial battles and skirmishes in the vicinity of Sawākin on the Red Sea Coast and – most of all – in the slow but relentless punitive invasion under Sir Horatio Herbert Kitchener during the late 1890s.

Tens of thousands of Sudanese were killed during this advance in a series of grotesquely asymmetrical battles: at Firka on 7 June 1896; at Abū-Ḥamad on 7 August 1897; on the River ʿAṭbara on 8 April 1898; and in the final destruction of the Mahdist forces north of Omdurman beneath the Kararī hills on 2 September 1898. During this last encounter, British and Egyptian troops, with their Sudanese auxiliaries, fired 523,119 bullets and 3,697 artillery rounds in under three hours, accounting for an estimated 10,800 Sudanese fatalities and 16,000 wounded. After the battle, 'vast quantities of rifles, swords, spears, banners, drums and other war material were captured on the battlefield.'[87] As the war reporter George Steevens wrote, the so-called Battle of Omdurman was 'not a battle but an execution'.[88] By way of further retribution, Kitchener tacitly sanctioned the widespread killing of wounded Sudanese fighters. This was denounced at the time by another war reporter who noted that 'many officers heartily disliked the slaughter of the wounded, and would have forbidden it if left to their own initiative'.[89] Kitchener denied the charge, calling it a 'disgraceful libel' and claiming in his official account that he had done all that he could 'to relieve suffering amongst the enemy'.[90] Kitchener also denied, again in contradiction of eyewitness accounts on both sides, that his gunboats had targeted Sudanese fighters fleeing from the battlefield and that his troops had been indulged in a three-day looting spree involving the pillaging of Omdurman. Even after the formal surrender, General Archibald Hunter and his men hunted through Omdurman for battlefield survivors: 'most surrendered, but we had to kill some 300 or 400'.[91] Meanwhile, one Sudanese fighter who had survived the battlefield recorded how the invaders had been given 72 hours to take what they could find:

> We suffered many troubles during the three days when the city was thrown open to the soldiers. They entered homes, seizing anything their hands could reach... Remarkably, there were no violations of personal honour: they were satisfied with money, portable items and jewellery. ... On the second day, two English soldiers entered our home and took two Medjidi riyals and two candlesticks; then came three Sudanese soldiers, who barged into the women's quarters and started gathering up all the copper, beads, money and jewellery.[92]

There was some variety in the language used to describe the multitude of artefacts that were taken from the dead and dying on the battlefields of Kitchener's southward advance, stolen from private homes and official buildings during the sack of Omdurman or purchased as souvenirs in the aftermath of the conflict. Lt. the Marquis of Tullibardine was assigned as a 'galloper', ferrying important battlefield updates to and from the commander of Kitchener's Egyptian cavalry. His letter home the day after the uneven encounter on the 'Aṭbara on 8 April 1898 was candid:

> I have got 10 or 12 large spears for you and a few swords, also some fish-hook spears, one small flag, etc., and one good footman's gibbeh.[93] ... I galloped past a beautiful beaten copper war drum, but could not pick it up; also saw some nice suits of chain armour; but the infantry got all the nice loot.[94]

That disappointment in the poor quality of his personal haul was echoed after Omdurman five months later:

> I have got you some loot, but not very good – i.e. valuable. I have got 2 or 3 drums, some good spears (best one lost), a sword or two, gibbas, coats of mail, some good steel caps, one good flag, shields, but as I came in late, 3 days, I got nothing of value ... At present I am in treaty with a native of even less conscience and of considerably more pluck than myself to get two finials off the top of 2 pepper boxes [turrets] on the Mahdi's tomb.[95]

By contrast, official accounts tended to avoid using the L-word – even if, at the most formal level of written orders, there was a systematic, approved looting process, in which troops were given carte blanche to take what they could find, subject to certain rules. When Lt.-General Sir Garnet Wolseley wrote his *Soldier's Pocket-Book* in 1886 – codifying not just general military behaviours across the empire but also his own campaign experiences in Canada (1870), West Africa (1873–1874) and Egypt (1882) – the process was so well established that the *Pocket-Book* had its own detailed section on 'Prize Money'. In principle, Wolseley decreed, 'all booty taken in war legally belongs to the Crown, and should not under ordinary circumstances be appropriated or distributed without the Sovereign's sanction.'[96] Outlining a detailed procedure that began with the selection of officers to act as prize agents, the spoils of the recent conflict were to be collected and auctioned off to raise the prize money that would subsequently be shared according to rank. In the Sudan wars, all such injunctions were largely ignored, apart from a choice selection of artefacts that senior staff, perhaps with an eye to advancement, dutifully handed over to Queen Victoria. Hundreds of artefacts, claimed by individuals or battalions as their rightful seizure, ended up as officers' mess trophies or personal souvenirs. It was an outcome that contrasted markedly with the Benin expedition just one year earlier, after which division of the spoils was 'more disciplined and less triumphalist'.[97]

The scale and voracity of British trophy hunting in Sudan was matched by only a few other imperial expeditions, among them Benin 1897. Sudanese loot was far less valuable in monetary terms: there were no jewels, gold coins or silken garments to be found in the Khalīfa 'Abdullāhi's impoverished fledgling state. But thousands of Sudanese artefacts are still tucked away in storage cabinets and drawers, carefully wrapped in acid-free paper: invisible and often forgotten. A small percentage are on permanent display, in museums, art galleries and private estates across the UK and beyond, but the vast majority form part of a hidden hoard: the colourful patched tunics worn by Mahdist fighters; their swords, spears, rifles, pistols, knives, axes and artillery pieces; their shields, helmets, powder horns and ammunition bandoliers; their drums of beaten copper and carved wood; saddles for both horse and camel; medieval armour, passed down from generation to generation, and the quilted garments worn underneath; their coins, water-bottles, food bowls, necklaces, slippers and satchels; their prayer-beads, prayer-books, copies of the Qur'an and even school work-boards with the day's lessons still visible in dark ink.

Even sections of the Mahdī's own tomb – far more than the finial that Lord Tullibardine's haggling netted him to adorn his ancestral home – were ripped from the ruins of its deliberate destruction by Kitchener's artillery and dispersed into the luggage of his soldiers and the newspapermen who covered the campaign.[98] In the aftermath of battle, surviving Sudanese families exploited this hunger for trophies. 'During our brief stay in Omdurman,' recalled one war correspondent, 'every variety of loot was hawked about the camp for sale.'[99] Indeed, several years after the conflict was over, artefacts from the Mahdīa – the 14-year period of Sudan's first indigenous independence under Muḥammad Aḥmad al-Mahdī himself and his successor – were still available for purchase by visitors from outside Sudan, including the territory's earliest tourists.

But the most desirable souvenir from the battlefield was the flag carried by the Sudanese in battle. Dozens of Mahdist banners can be found in at least twenty-two collections in the UK alone.[100] In November 1898, gloating about 'the bill of costs that the wretched Dervishes had to pay Sir Herbert Kitchener for their little outing at Omdurman', the *Navy and Army Illustrated* featured the Khalīfa 'Abdullāhi's own black banner, captioned 'The Death Flag', as the a centrepiece of photograph showing 'a selection of very characteristic Dervish weapons and war material'.[101] Later that month, the same banner, a 'great black standard, riddled by bullets', was the highlight of an extraordinary post-war exhibition at the Banqueting Hall in London of 'the loot of Ferkeh, Hafir, Atbara, and Omdurman … lent by officers who have taken part in the Sudan expeditions.'[102] The centrality of the flag reflected the recognition by British officers and soldiers alike that the banner represented the men underneath it – not least because the Sudanese fought with such determination to keep the flags flying in the face of relentless firepower. Courage was one thing; however, the significance of the flags went far beyond the simple rallying of troop units.

The use of banners by followers of Muḥammad Aḥmad 'Abdallah and, later, the Khalīfa 'Abdullāhi stemmed from Sudan's Sufi tradition, in which flags were a public expression of individual or collective adherence to a *ṭarīqa* (fraternity), prominently displayed at all ceremonies. While varying in shape, colour and specific message, common features included the testimony (*shahāda*) that 'There is no God but Allah; Muḥammad is the messenger of Allah', the name of the fraternity's founding saint and/or, most simply, 'Allah'.[103] As the leader of an important branch of the Sammānīa fraternity, Muḥammad Aḥmad must have had his own banner, even before his declaration on 29 June 1881 that he was *al-mahdī al-muntaẓar* (the expected rightly-guided one) and *khalīfat rasūl allah* (successor to the Prophet Muḥammad). This assertion, reproduced on banners, became a portable manifesto:

لا اله الا الله محمد رسول الله

محمد المهدي خليفة رسول الله

> There is no god but Allah; Muḥammad is the messenger of Allah
> Muḥammad al-Mahdī is the successor to Allah's Messenger

This manifesto was replicated on hundreds, possibly thousands of banners during the *Mahdīa*. Only one surviving flag has been claimed to have been that of the Mahdī himself. Today, it is in Scotland: one of five preserved at the Highlanders'

Museum at Fort George outside Inverness. A brass inscription on the flagstaff claims it to be the 'Original flag of Mahomet Ahmed the Mahdi Captured on the Final Defeat of the Khalifa at Um Dibericat [Umm Dibīkarāt] on Nov 24 1899.'[104] It was not: as we shall see, its true function was dramatically different.

Muḥammad Aḥmad's claim to be the Mahdī provoked consternation among the orthodox religious establishment. The 'ulamā', al-Azhar-trained legal and religious scholars in Khartoum and Cairo, responded with outrage and legal arguments, challenging the credentials of an individual they insisted was an impostor, and rehearsing instead the legitimacy of the Ottoman Sultan as the bona fide leader of the faithful. But it was when ideological outrage turned to military action on Jazīra Abā, the self-declared Mahdī's White Nile island base, that the Sufi banner first became part of the paraphernalia of conflict. On 24 October 1881, a small force was despatched to the island to detain the dissident sheikh and bring him to Khartoum for questioning. An oral history of the period, compiled by 'Alī, one of the Mahdī's two surviving sons, from the sworn testimony of those who had taken part, provides vivid evidence of the use of banners in this, the first of many military encounters with the colonial state. As the soldiers disembarked from the steamer moored on the riverbank, Muḥammad Aḥmad made his dispositions for the imminent fight. These preparations included the rapid creation of five new banners, four of which acknowledged specific Sufi saints.

> On all five banners was written the statement of *tawḥīd* [Allah's singular nature]. On four of the banners were inscribed the names of Allah's followers: Sheikh ['Abd-al-Qādir] al-Jīlānī *walī allah*;[105] Sheikh Aḥmad al-Rifā'ī; Sheikh Ibrāhīm al-Dasūqī; and Sheikh Aḥmad al-Badawī.[106] The fifth flag, however, had no writing on it. … After appointing his lieutenants (*muqaddamīn*), the Mahdī asked for an inkwell and wrote on the fifth flag: 'Muḥammad al-Mahdī is the Successor of Allah's Messenger.'[107] Above this, he wrote: 'O Allah! O Ever-living, O Everlasting, O Lord of Majesty and Generosity'.[108] All this took place during the time before daybreak.[109]

In this way, the Sufi banner, hitherto a relatively static item involved in rituals or positioned in cemeteries, was reinvented and customised as battle paraphernalia. Examples of this invocation of Sufi saints survive in several UK collections, including that of the Highlanders' Museum:

يا الله يا رحمن يا رحيم يا حي يا قيوم يا ذا الجلال والاكرام

لا اله الا الله محمد رسول الله الدسوقي ولي الله

محمد المهدي خليفة رسول الله

> O Allah, the Compassionate and Merciful | O ever-living, everlasting, Lord of Majesty and Generosity
> There is no god but Allah [and] Muḥammad is his Prophet | al-Dasūqī is a friend of Allah
> Muḥammad the Mahdī is the Successor of the Prophet of Allah[110]

After this initial skirmish at Jazīra Abā, the Mahdī's forces – now dubbed *anṣār*, after the earliest followers of the Prophet Muḥammad – achieved considerable successes against a succession of expeditionary forces despatched by the occupation government. Flags were observed in every major encounter during the Mahdī's steady advance on al-'Ubeiḍ, then Khartoum. What kind of manufacturing process had evolved at this highly mobile stage of the *jihad* is unknown: the *baraka* (blessing) of the Mahdī's own writing on a banner was immense but the numbers involved suggest that the work must have been delegated. Describing a significant skirmish at al-Marābī on the White Nile on 29 April 1883, a senior British officer observed the enemy forces with their flags 'inscribed with the Mahdi's own rendering of the Koran'.[111] Preparing for an attack on administration forces in the Nuba Mountains a year earlier, the Mahdī had gathered his banners. The editor of one hagiographical account noted:

> After the sunset prayer on Monday eve ... the Mahdi came out of his house, unsheathing his sword and uttering the *takbīr* [i.e. saying '*Allahu akbar*']. He said that he had been informed by the Prophet to advance against the Turks. ... During the night, the divisions came in succession to the Mahdi, and he ordered them to advance towards the enemy. ... The author explains the virtue of using flags (*rāyāt*) in battle, stating that this had also been the practice of the Prophet.[112]

The word *rāya* is crucial. It signified both the physical fabric, with its stitched manifesto, and the men formed up beneath it, divided from that earliest battle at Jazīra Abā into contingents of varying size. And just as the flag was more than just a military rallying point, the unit was more than just a bunch of men. It was a unit of social cohesion, often of clansmen or simply individuals from the same town or region, in which collective and individual welfare was maintained. If a member found himself short of anything, the *rāya* took care of it – and the Mahdī himself ordered that if a new recruit 'does not have a brother to take care of him financially and has not yet been integrated in the banners', he could count on support from the collective treasury, the *beit al-māl*.[113] That is not to say that the Mahdī did not use flags in metaphorical form as well. On 22 May 1882, he wrote to a senior government officer to deliver a long, point-by-point rebuttal of the government's arguments against his own *daʿwa* (call), warning that the Prophet Muḥammad himself would lead the *anṣār*, 'along with 'Azrā'īl, King of Death, carrying a black flag in my army's vanguard'.[114]

As the Mahdī's campaign progressed, two factors prompted important changes in the presentation and content of *anṣār* banners. The first was a basic colour coding. This followed the Mahdī's appointment, in direct imitation of the Prophet Muḥammad, of three designated successors who also served as administrative and military deputies. These *khulafā'* commanded substantial divisions named for the flag under which they paraded, marched and fought. The Black Banner (*al-rāyat al-zarqā'* [literally 'blue']) was assigned to 'Abdullāhi al-Ta'īshī, who had primacy among the three and who was heard to express his pride that on his earliest encounter with the Mahdī, the latter had appointed him one of his flag-bearers. 'Alī wad Ḥilū was given the Green Banner (*al-rāyat al-khaḍrā'*), while the Red Banner (*al-rāyat al-ḥamrā'*) went to one the Mahdī's close relatives, Muḥammad al-Sharīf. According to Ibrāhīm Fawzī, these new dispositions immediately followed the Mahdī's victory in the Nuba Mountains on 30 May 1882.[115]

A number of letters written personally by the Mahdī during subsequent campaigns dealt, variously, with permissions to raise new banners on behalf of specific communities, the wider organisation of forces under their respective banners, the assignment of named individuals and their followers to the *rāya* of the Khalīfa 'Abdullāhi – and one decree was addressed by the Mahdī to the entire population as 'his beloved people of the banners'.[116] In 1881, even before Muḥammad Aḥmad began calling himself the Mahdī, he illustrated the value of the flag in the community in a letter to a follower:

> It has come to our knowledge that your banners were burned among the property you lost when your home caught fire. May Allah reward you and mend what has been lost and damaged! We are sending you more material: take it and may it be blessed. This piece of cloth can be divided into a number of bands, so make three or four banners as you see fit. The backs should be plain white or black, as should the writing, as you see fit.[117]

The second factor was the decision, taken by the Khalīfa 'Abdullāhi in October 1886 – eighteen months after the premature death of the Mahdī – to link the approved colour scheme with the Sufi saints proclaimed on the Mahdī's very first banners. This ruling appeared to contradict the Mahdī's own prior decision to abolish all the Sufi brotherhoods as potentially divisive. Given his own pre-eminence, he regarded them as redundant: all sects, legal schools and religious texts were proscribed, with the exception of the Qur'an, a digest of daily prayers and invocations (*al-rātib*) and his own proclamations (*manshūrāt*).[118] In reversing his master's exclusivist doctrine, it has been suggested that the Khalīfa 'Abdullāhi was reshaping his propaganda for an imminent invasion of Egypt, where the Rifā'ia, Dasūqīa and Badawīa sects had considerably larger followings than in Sudan. In any case, the Khalīfa's edict of October 1886 prescribed a standard text followed by five possible formulae tailored for the respective fraternities: the Black Flag for Aḥmad al-Rifā'ī, the White Flag for al-Dasūqī, the Red Flag for al-Badawī, the Green one for al-Jīlānī, and the Yellow Flag, each terminating with the manifesto of the Mahdī.[119]

With *anṣār* recruitment intensifying and new fronts emerging, the Mahdī and his successor needed manufacturing facilities to create more banners. Flag production, therefore, like other written propaganda, became the responsibility of the *beit al-māl*, a department that handled financial affairs, quartermastery and logistics. In an ironic precursor to the looting of Sudanese artefacts, the *beit al-māl* controlled all the loot (*ghanīma*) that had been taken by the *anṣār* in their successive victories over Ottoman-Egyptian occupation forces. These spoils included tent material, printed fabrics with sophisticated European designs and the military uniforms worn by their defeated enemy, all of which were cannibalised: ripped up, stitched and dyed to make new flags and new patches for their stylised uniforms.[120] A Green Flag in the collection of the Royal Engineers' Museum at Gillingham – reputedly used by General Gordon as a tablecloth – has recycled some beautifully printed material of unknown but certainly non-indigenous provenance, simply superimposing the manifesto in matching appliqué.

Contrary to the derogatory and supercilious labels ascribed by the British invaders – that the Mahdists were 'savages', 'dervishes' and 'fuzzy-wuzzies' – banners are evidence of a society that prized literacy. Before the Ottoman-Egyptian invasion and occupation of 1821, Sudanese Sufi communities had boasted as many as 270 highly literate holy men, many of them trained at al-Azhar in Cairo. Founding several schools apiece, each might train several hundred youngsters – only boys – during their lifetimes.[121] The primacy of the written word remained after the Mahdī's victory: colonial artworks, imported culture, even architecture were all eradicated with the destruction of Khartoum – but the government printing press was preserved. Dubbed the Stone Press (*matbʻat al-ḥajar*) it was moved, along with its surviving Egyptian employees, to the new capital at Omdurman. Its output over the fourteen years of the Mahdīa was remarkable, if inevitably partisan. When Kitchener's forces reached Omdurman in September 1898, they dutifully logged both the names of surviving personnel and the books they had produced: multiple volumes of the Mahdī's writings, bound and unbound; copies of the *Rātib*, a bespoke collection of Qur'anic quotations and Sufi prayers; and biographies of the great man.

As importantly, the large table at the Stone Press became a banner factory. Production accelerated and the flags, most with their manifesto stitched onto the background cloth in appliquéd letters in a variety of colours, were then handed over to the *beit al-māl*. Local women, as well as Europeans and other captives, were involved in the manufacturing process: selecting swatches of looted materials, dying indigenous cottons, and stitching on the various manifesto formulae. At their best, *anṣār* banners were beautifully made, featuring elegant script, straight lines, coherent word spacing and skilful appliqué work. Not all flags were produced in approved workshops, however, especially before the centralisation of production, so a consistent standard of workmanship, calligraphy or even spelling was never guaranteed. Enthusiasm occasionally eclipsed competence, with some banners so poorly executed that it is hard to believe that they were drawn or sewn by anyone literate. One of the first Mahdist banners to be seen by the British public, illustrating a book about the Battle of Tūfrīk on 22 March 1885 on the Red Sea Coast, features a standard, if minimal, manifesto but in almost indecipherable script.[122] Similarly, the red banner of a leading general named ʿAbd-al-Raḥman al-Nujūmī – now in Omdurman in the proud possession of the Mahdī's most senior living descendant – is also crude in the extreme.

To the dying days of Mahdist rule in Sudan, possession of a banner meant unquestioned status – and the manifesto it bore was an expression of a collective identity for which fighters were willing to risk their lives. Their importance as paraphernalia of war was made clear by their storage in a small round structure about 20 feet high alongside the *beit al-amāna*, where artillery pieces, rifles, powder and bullets were all kept.[123] One of the Khalīfa's European prisoners recalled how, collected together, the flags:

> present the appearance of a small forest of staves. The great black flag of the Khalifa Abdullah towers high above them all. … Immediately after morning prayers the leaders proceed to the flag yard, each takes his flag, and they all stand in line in the open space in front of the *beit el amana*.[124]

At Kararī, that same great black flag, which would later dominate the spread of loot featured in the *Navy and Army Illustrated* and in London's Banqueting Hall, was subjected to sustained and deliberate British gunfire, making its protection a deadly duty. The tale of its capture differed strikingly according to the teller. 'It was a huge black flag stuck in the ground with a pile of dead around it, killed at long ranges,' the Marquis of Tullibardine wrote the following week, adding that the British company assigned to pick the flag had to 'pour volleys' of gunfire into the heap of wounded *anṣār*.[125] The Sudanese military historian ʿIsmat Ḥassan Zulfū, by contrast, recorded the testimony of Sudanese survivors:

> The custodians of the black banner raced on foot behind its bearer, who was on horseback. They halted and planted the banner … Despite bullets raining from three brigades in the direction of the unmissable target, the custodians began to gather rocks and stones to support the huge banner, the mast of which was more than 20 feet high. Because of the gunfire, a great number of the party fell under the flag, to be replaced by others who kept shooting at the advancing troops. The standard was now exposed to fire raining down from north and east. Holes appeared in the fabric. As one man fell, another would rally to it but soon machine-gun fire devoured all around it to the last man. The enemy arrived at the flag. One hundred dead bodies and twice as many wounded were found around the standard.[126]

Of the hundreds of *anṣār* banners that must have flown over the Khalīfa 'Abdullāhi's army that day at Kararī – as at Tūshka on 3 August 1889, on the River 'Aṭbara and in other Sudanese defeats at British hands over the previous decade – a relatively tiny number, perhaps no more than fifty, can still be found in publicly accessible collections. It is certain that a few are preserved with respect, even reverence, in private homes in Sudan, 125 years after the brutal ending of Sudan's first experiment in independent nationhood – and that replica banners in black, green, red and yellow have been created for historical pageants and community events since. In the public domain, however, it remains a lasting irony that it is British museum collections – usually military collections showcasing the war loot of the 1880s and 1890s – that give us the best chance of tracing the characteristics and chronology of this fascinating aspect of the *Mahdīa*.

In fact, the massacre north of Omdurman on 2 September 1898 was not the absolute end: that came more than a year later, after Sudan's new ruler, the ennobled Lord Kitchener of Khartoum, despatched a force to track down and eliminate the Khalīfa 'Abdullāhi and his remaining followers.[127] The last stand came at Umm Dibeikarāt, in the arid central region of Kordofan, on 24 November 1899 – and the last flag flown by the Khalīfa was one of surrender. Even as the British were advancing up the Nile over the previous three years, 'Abdullāhi had been considering ways of stopping them without enormous loss of life. In May 1897, he had sent an emissary to Constantinople with an extraordinary proposal: If you will stop the British, we will renounce the *Mahdīa*, I will stop calling myself by the title Khalīfa and we in Sudan will agree to become a self-governing Ottoman principality – just like Egypt.[128] It had not worked: the Ottomans were suspicious of the letter's provenance and Kitchener's advance proceeded relentlessly. After the serial bloodletting up to and including Kararī, the Khalīfa was seemingly ready at last to surrender. The flag he was carrying at the final encounter at Umm Dibeikarāt – the banner mistakenly attributed to the Mahdī himself – was a white flag of surrender. The calligraphy is exquisite and stitched in silk with great skill, attention to grammatical detail: this is no shoddy appliqué mass production item. It bears an extremely rare, if not unique, formula, in which the two parts of the *shahāda* are separated over two lines, with the addition of an appeal for safe passage in the first line and an appeal to the Ottoman ruler, Abdülhamid II, in the second:

لا اله الا الله الأمان الأمان

محمد رسول الله السلطان السلطان

There is no god but Allah | Mercy! Mercy!
Muḥammad is the Prophet of Allah | The Sultan! The Sultan![129]

The appeal did not succeed. After an hour of fighting, in which the Sudanese again sustained heavy casualties, the bulk of the force surrendered while their commanders knelt to pray. They were killed on their unrolled sheepskin prayer mats: the Khalīfa ʿAbdullāhi, alongside his most loyal lieutenants, Aḥmad Faḍīl Muḥammad and ʿAlī wad Ḥilū, his two surviving sons and one of the Mahdī's few surviving sons, Ṣiddīq.[130] The British were not interested in the nuances of an Arabic flag.

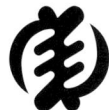

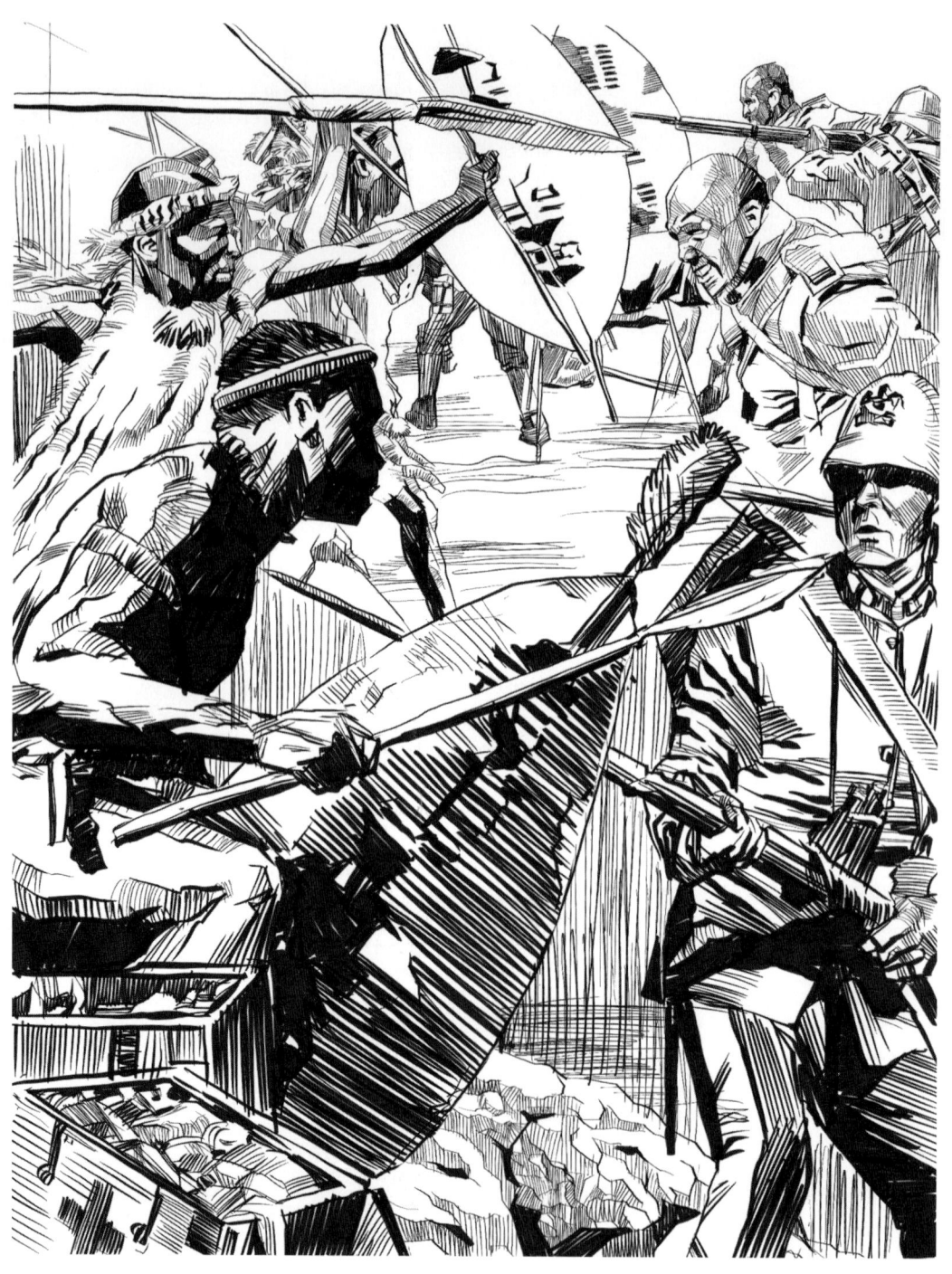

Artist: Sindiso Nyoni

CHAPTER 3

Conversation

IsiHlangu from the Anglo-Zulu War
'We need to infuse African-ness in museums'

Mwelela Cele and Yann LeGall[131]

Yann LeGall: Dear Mwelela, thanks for accepting our invitation to share your expertise on the history of the Zulu kingdom. Let us start with something lighter before we get to the core of the onion.

Two weeks ago, South Africa won the 2023 Rugby World Cup, beating England in the semi-finals. Rugby is cultural heritage from the British Isles, a sport that was exported through colonial occupation to former colonies. In international confrontations, we often see the empire strike back, showing that they have learnt to master the art, something also witnessed in the case of cricket. In view of the history of British colonialism in South Africa, how do you interpret the Springboks' victories over England like the most recent one?

Mwelela Cele: History often connects with sports. A match against England is not like any other match. First, England is a great team, and the stakes are at their apex when the Boks meet them in a World Cup. It happens mostly in the last stages, so the team who wins might go on to become world champion. In fact, there were two World Cup finals where we played against England, in 2007 and 2019, and we beat them twice. I remember in 2007, I was watching it in a very interesting place: the Zulu Jazz Club, a club in Durban. On the screen, they showed the face of Prince Charles – now King Charles – with Prince William and Prince Harry sitting in the crowd. Jokes were flying in the club. Because if you think of English colonial occupation and settler colonialism, the different wars (Frontier Wars, Anglo-Zulu War, the South African War, the Bambatha Rebellion/Zulu rebellion, etc.), there is a symbolic value to this kind of arena, especially for South Africa. Considering the salt in the wounds, victory is all the sweeter.

Yann: From the battle on a pitch to the historical battlefield, now. Here is a photo of spears exhibited at the Pitt Rivers Museum in Oxford. One of the African spears in this display is labelled as a 'stabbing assegai with head bound on, found after the battle of Isandlwana in 1879 when the Zulus attacked a British column and defeated it. Collected by Major A.H.T.H. Somerset.' In the permanent exhibition, nothing more is explained on this context. Could you recall for our readers what this battle was and in which context did it take place?

Mwelela: Let me start by contextualising the war of 1879. At the time, the British Empire did not want to accept the Zulu kingdom as an independent nation. To them, it represented, on the one hand, a problem that should be solved and, on the other, a threat to the colony of Natal. First, a problem because, to support the extraction of natural resources, the British needed workers for the mines in the colony of Natal. Right across the border, in Zululand, the inhabitants did not work for extractive purposes, but for their self-sufficiency, mostly in cultivating their farms, watching over their cattle and defending their kingdom. This was tantamount to what the British saw as a functioning society, one that was based on forced labour and exploitation. So that system had to be dismantled. Second, the British feared that Zulu warriors could just cross over to Natal and take the colonial stations unawares. This is why the Crown appointed people – like Lord Chelmsford – who had gained experience in frontier wars in the Eastern Cape, conflicts that I would label as wars of dispossession, where the British use military force to depose local rulers one after the other, dispossessing the communities from their cattle and their land. The frontier wars were the first step towards British annexation of the whole of South Africa, the Anglo-Zulu War a second step, leading to full colonial annexation in 1897.

Now, what led to the Battle of Isandlwana? On 11 December 1878, the British High Commissioner Sir Bartle Frere[132] sent an ultimatum to Cetshwayo kaMpande, king of the amaZulu, claiming that Cetshwayo had not honoured the promises he had made to Sir Theophilus Shepstone – known in Zulu history as Somtsewu – at the time of his coronation in 1873.[133] The ultimatum stipulated that the age regiment system of the Zulu nation should be abolished, that young men should be allowed to marry without the king's blessing, that the king should control killings within Zululand, that all missionaries who had been chased away from Zululand should be allowed to return, and finally that the sons of Chief Sihayo kaXongo Ngobese, namely, Mehlokazulu, Bhekuzulu and Mkhumbikazulu, as well as the Swazi Prince Mbilini waMswati, were to be surrendered and fines must be paid for their raids into Natal and the Transvaal.[134]

The ultimatum was part of a manipulative strategy of provocation. As Jabulani S. Maphalala put it: 'No self-respecting Zulu king could have accepted those conditions. If Cetshwayo had accepted them he could have been overthrown either by some powerful generals or some members of the royal family.'[135] The age regiment system was indeed one of the central knots of the social and military fabric of the Zulu nation.

The age grade tradition divided tasks among *amabutho* (regiments) that ranged from preparing rituals, ceremonies and collecting taxes, up to settling political disputes and managing administration. In this system, the men matured with people of their age, taking rites of passage together. To force the king to relinquish such social structure for educating young men and his right to give consent to marriage was a way to attack the very core of Zulu society. As far as the return of missionaries is concerned, this would mean that the king would allow colonialists with books to convert his people. Finally, Chief Sihayo was very important to King Cetshwayo, a trusted ally. Based at Rorke's Drift, he functioned as a buffer on the border between Natal and Zululand. His son Mehlokazulu was in fact Cetshwayo's aid. To be an aid meant to be someone very close to the king, someone who accompanies him, someone who has the privilege to see him in private settings, when the king is eating for instance. Therefore, demanding that the king surrender his aid was like forcing him to deliver his groom or protégé.

As expected, King Cetshwayo rejected the ultimatum, letting it expire on 11 January 1879. The British used it as an excuse to invade. On the very same day, the British army under Lieutenant-General Lord Chelmsford encroached in Zulu territory. The strategic plan of the British commander was to advance in three main columns. This colossal army was eventually to join forces at oNdini, King Cetshwayo's Great Place or headquarters. In his book *The Last Zulu King: The Life and Death of Cetshwayo*, C.T. Binns described the various positions the British columns:

> The right column, under the command of Colonel Pearson, was posted at Fort Pearson, on the Lower Tugela Drift, near the Ultimatum Tree …, a total of about 300 mounted men, 1,500 European infantry and 2,000 [African soldiers]. The centre column under Colonel Glyn [and Chelmsford], a total of about 300 mounted men, 1,300 European infantry and 2,500 [African soldiers] was to cross into Zululand at Rorke's Drift … The left column, under Colonel Evelyn Wood, was based on Newcastle and Utrecht and was made up of [about sixteen companies] and a small contingent of 300 [Africans].
>
> In addition to the three main columns there were two subsidiary forces, the first, under Colonel Durnford … based at Fort Cherry, near Kranskop, was formed primarily for the protection of the Border … The second subsidiary force, under the command of Colonel Rowland, was stationed at Luneberg, north of the River Pongola [and] was to defend the Transvaal border.[136]

Having learned from his *izinhloli* (reconnoitres) that the British had invaded, Cetshwayo assembled the Zulu army at kwaNodwengu, King Mpande's great place on the afternoon of Friday 17 January. The Zulu army was commanded by Ntshingwayo kaMahole Khoza.[137] His co-commander was Mavumengwana kaNdlela Ntuli.[138] Having been ritually prepared for war, the troops left kwaNodwengu in the late afternoon of the same day. According to Ian Knight, it was one of the largest armies ever assembled by the Zulu kingdom, and the most important *amabutho* were present in force. Inkosi Ntshingwayo commanded the left column, and Mavumengwana commanded the right column. King Cetshwayo advised the army that they should avoid attacking entrenched positions. He directed: 'you will march slowly so as not to tire yourselves.'[139] As the Zulu army marched through emaKhosini valley, 'the women, children and old men watching them with pride, it seemed that nothing on earth could ever stop them.'

The Zulu army comprised the following regiments: on the extreme right were the uNokhenke, uMcijo, uDududu, iSangqu and iMbube, in the centre the iNgobamakhosi and uMbonambi, while the uDloko, uThulwana, iNdluyengwe and iNdlondlo were on the left. According to historian John Laband, the king held back a large body of reinforcements at oNdini, because he suspected that a British mounted force might rush past his armies into the very heart of the kingdom, or that a further, sea borne, column might try to land in the region of St Lucia Bay. He also suspected that the British would draw the amaSwati into the war to help them invade his kingdom.[140] Cetshwayo gave clear instructions to the commanders of his armies: they were to drive the enemy back into Natal but should not lead their regiments into British territory. His strategy was to crush the aggressors quickly and then use that advantage to open negotiations for peace. Thus commenced the Anglo-Zulu War, which comprised the following main battles: on 22 January 1879, the Battle of Nyezane and Isandlwana; the Battle of Hlobane on 28 March; the Battle of Khambula on 29 March; and the Battle of Ulundi on 4 July 1879.

The sequence of the Zulu army's march was as follows: on 17 and 18 January, they travelled 25 km and reached isiPhezi ikhanda near the Mpembeni River. 'Five months later its track was still evident, the long grass all trodden down in one direction as if a huge roller had passed over it.'[141] The army spent the night there and *izinhloli* were sent out to monitor British troop movement. On 19 January, the *amabutho* marched another 15 km. They split the two columns, and marched parallel and within sight of each other. They slept on the tableland east of Babanango Mountain before travelling 20 more km to reach the northern slopes of Siphezi Mountain. On 21 January, the army marched for another 15 km, moving in small, detached groups to the steep and rocky Ngwebeni valley, wide enough to shelter a huge army, well-hidden because they were concealed by the Nyoni heights from Isandlwana. The *izinhloli* reported that the British centre column was positioned at the base of Isandlwana, amounting to nearly 1,800 British soldiers and their African affiliates. By late evening on 22 January 1879, over 1,200 had been killed by the Zulu army. Only about 55 British soldiers and possibly nearly 200 African affiliates were still alive. The British Empire had experienced the most humiliating defeat of its history.

The Zulu army won the battles fought at Isandlwana and Hlobane, but the British won those fought at Nyezane, Khambula and Ulundi, defeating Cetshwayo less than 10 km away from his headquarters in oNdini. According to Bhekiziwe Peterson, the defeat of Cetshwayo and the Zulu nation heralded the defeat of the last sovereign African polity in the then two Republics and two Colonies of South Africa. The industrial revolution, following the discoveries of minerals, was, for its part, to also exercise a cataclysmic impact on the relations between the imperial centre and the colonial regime, capitalists, white citizens and, on the other side, African kingdoms and the increasing numbers of poor and landless peasants and city dwellers. Battles over the control of land, labour, space, movement and instruments of discipline and coercion were to become the signal factors around which the development of South Africa was to be brokered during the twentieth century.[142]

Remembering the military prowess of the Zulu kingdom, historian Jeff Guy added a qualifier to this statement, contending that the Anglo-Zulu War proved to be an 'embarrassing example of imperial ineptitude' to the British Conservative Government.[143]

Yann: I sent you links to collection entries showing *isiHlangu* (iconic Zulu shields), as well as another shield and personal belongings attributed to the amaZulu kept at the Museum of Archaeology and Anthropology in Cambridge,[144] the Pitt Rivers Museum in Oxford,[145] and the British Museum in London.[146] These are part of a much larger number of spoils from the Anglo-Zulu War of 1879. To what extent is the presence of these looted belongings in English museums known to South Africans?

Mwelela: Many South Africans might not know exactly what was taken and what can be found in museums or archives, but we know that a lot was taken during the colonial era. Still, the system of apartheid made it difficult for generations of South Africans to access museums and archives, and therefore understand that cultural aspect of preservation and historical research, despite having access to education. Because of segregation, most people did not actually grow up with access to museums and libraries, let alone having knowledge of the role of these institutions.

I remember in 2006, when I was working at the Luthuli Museum, I paid a visit to Mama Mrs Maponya, whose husband, a struggle veteran named Selbon Maponya, had been personal secretary to Chief Albert Luthuli, former President General of the ANC between 1952 and 1967. Maponya had been incarcerated on Robben Island for about six years for his activities in the anti-apartheid struggle. As a bookworm, he used to collect books, and his widow and I found a lot of interesting stuff in his house. Then, she said to me 'you know, we burnt a lot of the stuff. We didn't know that this is important, or that someone will be interested in it, like historians or museum staff. We were running out of space, so some of my late husband's writings, we just put it on fire.' In the 1940s, there was only one library for Black people here in Natal, at the Bantu Social Centre in Beatrice Street (now Charlotte Maxeke Street). In the collective psyche, libraries, archives and museums were rather linked to academic institutions, colleges, technical universities, not family or local history.

So even if people have always known that belongings, archives, and other kinds of material were taken – just like during apartheid when letters, etc. were seized by the government – there is a disconnection between those institutions and the people whose stuff is in there. Even before the release of political prisoners in the 1990s, the apartheid regime had set up a huge bonfire to reduce to ashes a lot of the archival documents that were evidence of racial violence, such as police records, books, letters, papers, speeches.[147] We know that, in different times of oppression, there has been a deliberate appropriation and destruction of the material taken from us. But as far as the preservation of this material is concerned, most South Africans wouldn't know where it can be found today.

Yann: How do you assess the way the *isiHlangu* are framed and of the information available online?

Mwelela: The model and methods used for showing cultural heritage and museum collections is a Western model. We need to find a way of infusing African-ness in museums to challenge that Western model of preservation and display. We need to bring the element of sacredness, especially in case of weapons, because someone might have been stabbed by that weapon. In Africa, we have cleansing ceremonies. What if those weapons were never cleansed after the war? What if the blood that was on that shield was just washed?

Besides, as the famous writer Herbert Isaac Ernest Dhlomo demonstrated as early as in the 1940s, some of this material should not be displayed in such a manner. Let me quote from his time-old and very enlightening article about *isiHlangu*:

> The Zulu attached great importance to the shield. Obviously, it had more meaning and use than that of being a mere defensive weapon. First it was a kind of flag or coat of arms of the tribe. We know that Shaka punished severely those warriors who did not return with their flags, the shields, after a battle. It was not a question of cowardice or even of having sustained defeat. Even if you fought valiantly and skillfully and even conquered the enemy, your duty was to bring back your shield and not to lose it. It was a matter of honour, of patriotism, of ideals, of the significance of the shield in tribal life. Flags must not remain in enemy hands or on foreign soil. … When a great commander fell in battle, the shield or shields were used to cover up his body, [with] the warriors 'lowering' their shields in respect and silent tribute.
>
> The shield was known to have medical efficacy. Before the armies went out to battle, herbal and other preparations were sprinkled over them, and, naturally, parts of these potents fell on the shields. In this sense, the shield was a doctored

instrument. Now, in Zulu eyes, it is fatal to let any of your doctored (as bodily) articles fall into the hand of your enemy, especially if the said articles were doctored primarily to give you power over him, for he can use them to return the evil to you – using your strength against you (*ukuzidlisa ngobakho ububende* – to hoist yourself with your own petard).

In addition, shields were central in distinguishing *amabutho* from each other. For every battle, regiments would assign singular patterns and distinctive colours to their *isiHlangu*, which thereby served 'both as a military uniform and as insignia of age'.

In different cultures in Africa, especially southern Africa, weapons have their own sacredness. They belonged to a certain person and there is family attachment to those heirlooms. If a head of a family or an elder die, their weapons will be kept in a special place (see also Chapter 4). When looking at this material and reading some of the labels – like the one that says 'taken from a dead chief at Ulundi' – you know that you are looking at belongings that were not gifts but grabbed after someone was killed, in total disregard to local cultures of remembrance.

Some of these shields and weapons are from 1879. If they are displayed, there should be proper context and respect given to this material. Those vague descriptions are not enough. It requires some kind of history from below, to inform the public on what exactly was happening, who was the aggressor, the invader, and who was responding to this attack and why they responded in this way. If someone sees a spear online and the only information available is that it was taken in 1883, the time of the Zulu civil war, it should be explained that this war took place within a system of divide and rule that the British designed and used to topple the Zulu kingdom. If it's 1879, well there were about four or five battles that took place with various regiments and different outcomes. There are still families today who come from far away to the sites where those battles took place to pay respect to the dead, some even participating in re-enactment performances. So, if people pay their respects to the dead, why shouldn't their belongings be also respected?

In August 2023, I was on the site where the Maphulumo uprising took place in 1906, led among others by Ndhlovu kaThimuni and Mbombo kaSimbindumalo. There, descendants of some of the thousand people who were killed by colonial forces told us, heritage experts: 'our ancestor comes to us in dreams, saying that their spirit is still not at rest.' The direct descendants of the victims asked if we could help erecting a memorial to commemorate the dead of this anti-colonial movement. When we met with the community members, one of the elders there told us he has kept a sword that had belonged to an English soldier. Others told us they have cartridges from British rifles (see also Chapter 8). The memory is still very real: people mentioned the names of relatives who were killed, since precise genealogies are passed on from generation to generation. For instance, I know the name and the deeds of my great-grandfather who was born in 1868 and died in 1944. Our family histories often outlive more than five generations. People go as far as knowing which one of their ancestors died at Isandlwana. The acclaimed author, poet and professor Otty Nxumalo told us that his father did not go to school because his grandfather fought at Isandlwana and proclaimed that his son would not get education from the people he had fought against. This is why I'm saying these weapons should be displayed with respect, because if you have a relative that died during one of those battles, and then you happen to see these belongings online, you cannot stop yourself from thinking: 'is this my great-great-grandfather's shield?'

Besides, the information should not only be available in English. Nelson Mandela once wrote: 'when you speak … English, well many people understand you, … but when you speak [their language], you know you go straight to their hearts.'[148] Museums should make efforts to speak the languages of the weapons. If it's taken from KwaZulu, its language is isiZulu, if it's from Qonce in the Eastern Cape – formerly known as King William's Town – it should be isiXhosa. Some South Africans have children and grandchildren who study or are working overseas. When their family members pay them a visit in London, New York or Oxford, their chances of going to a museum together are quite high, aren't they? If someone from that area happens to stumble on these online collections, or visits those museums, and read isiZulu or isiXhosa, they will feel a degree of respect and inclusion.

Yann: The British Museum also holds two staffs that allegedly belonged to the King Cetshwayo kaMpande.[149] What does the presence of Cetshwayo's confiscated belongings there evoke to you?

Mwelela: In late June 1879, right before the Battle of Ulundi, a very sad thing happened. The British burnt down the *inkhata* of the Zulu nation – not today's political party but the original meaning of it, namely, the 'sacred grass coil' which unified the nation, made with medicine and particles, kept within the homestead of the king.[150] Rulers obtain their strength from symbols of power. Can you imagine if we had burnt down material that belonged to Queen Victoria or Elizabeth, or if we had preserved it here in South Africa, keeping it in a museum? Do you think King Charles would declare 'guys, keep it and display this for educational purposes?' [laughs] I think the royal family and many English people would feel insulted. The preservation of spoils of war, especially personal belongings of rulers in Africa, is just another public announcement that says: 'We defeated you. See, we dispossessed your king.' This is a very powerful symbol. It conveys the side of the conqueror and, without proper contextualisation, risks sending the wrong message to onlookers.

Now let's recall the fate of King Cetshwayo. After the war, he was taken prisoner, exiled and incarcerated in the Castle of Good Hope near Cape Town.[151] Meanwhile, the British divided the kingdom into thirteen regions led by chiefs who had shown some form of loyalty to the colonial government. From 12 July 1882 to 24 September 1882,

Cetshwayo was sent to Britain to meet Queen Victoria and English notables, and to argue his case. Political protest by his supporters in Zululand, Natal and Britain, led to his return in 1883. Four of the thirteen appointed chiefs in Zululand were opposed to his return, namely, Zibhebhu kaMaphitha of the Mandlakazi, Hamu kaMpande of the Genetsheni faction of the Zulu royal lineage, Mfanawendlela, the Zungu chief, and John Dunn, colonial hunter and so-called 'adventurer'. Still, on 10 January 1883, King Cetshwayo arrived at Port Durnford. His rivals refused to accept his intronisation and, in July 1883, attacked the King's Royal Palace in oNdini. From the battle of Msebe to oNdini, Zibhebhu's Mandlakazi and Hamu's Ngenetsheni decimated Zulu leadership, killing many notables as well as thousands of their supporters. Subsequently, King Cetshwayo made his way to the White Mfolozi and moved to the Nkandla Forest, the territory of an old friend and supporter, Chief Sigananda kaSokufa of the amaCube people. There, the king lived in a small homestead known as eNhlweni. He was also sheltered in Sigananda's personal stronghold, an inaccessible cave behind a waterfall. After pressure from the British Resident at Eshowe, the administrative centre of the Zulu Native Reserve, the king surrendered himself on 15 October 1883. He moved with his followers to the Gqikazi homestead, next to the Eshowe Police Station. Within four months, on 8 February 1884, King Cetshwayo died unexpectedly at about the age of fifty. He was buried in the Nkandla Forest. Until today, the circumstances of his death are unclear and there is speculation on foul play.

The interesting thing about these sticks at the British Museum is that they are very similar to the sticks that are at the KwaZulu Cultural Museum in Ulundi, but there is a real difference in the way they are described in the metadata. The label in Ulundi informs that they were presented to Chief Mangosuthu Buthelezi in 1976, and that they had originally belonged to King Shaka and were subsequently bequeathed to his successors, King Dingane, King Mpande and King Cetshwayo. Taking into account this evidence that belongings were passed on from one king to the other, the information on the previous owners of the sticks kept at the British Museum – 'CL Norris Newman; Cetshwayo kaMpande' – is probably incomplete, if not completely incorrect. What if they were family heirlooms from former Zulu rulers like Shaka, and not Cetshwayo's own?

Yann: In the preface to Ron Lock's history of the Anglo-Zulu War, Prince Mangosuthu Buthelezi wrote:

> Although the war and its aftermath was a tragic disaster for the Zulu kingdom and its people, I have learned in life never to be filled with bitterness. What is important is that the truth of what happened on that fateful day … be told to future generations.

Yet, in his book, Lock speaks of an enduring 'resentment for 150 years of subjugation'.[152]

When addressing the presence of ancestral remains of Black South Africans in museum collections at home and abroad, historian Ciraj Rassool also speaks of 'unfinished business' between Europe and South Africa, and between White and Black South Africans. Is there 'unfinished business' between the Zulu nation and the British Crown?

Mwelela: No, despite all the bloodshed, I think it is a story of reconciliation. Even long before 1994 and the abolition of apartheid, in 1947, the British royal family were on tour in South Africa: King George VI, his wife and their children, including she who would later become Queen Elizabeth II. They travelled to several places and met with traditional rulers in King William's Town, in the Transkei and in Natal. They travelled to Eshowe, the former centre of British colonial administration, where they met with the then upcoming king, Cyprian Bhekuzulu kaSolomon. The question before their arrival in Eshowe was: who will write the welcoming speech and read it? The kings will shake hands, of course, but someone is going to stand there and greet the British delegation. Greetings are social rituals of paramount importance in southern African cultures. This task of utter significance fell on the responsibility of a very respected scholar of the time, Charles Mpanza, a great orator who was a prominent figure at Radio Zulu. He read the original speech in isiZulu. For the translation, Chief Albert Luthuli was chosen to read the English version. Luthuli had been educated in an American missionary station, spoke with an American accent. Less than five years after this visit, he became the president-general of the ANC and would go on to win the Nobel Peace Prize. So, the people entrusted to lead a path to reconciliation were high-ranking notables of the Zulu kingdom. This is evidence that this history of wars and conflicts is a history where no bitterness or resentment perdures among political representatives. Still, it is being told and retold from different perspectives, with TV shows inspired from this history, like *Shaka iLembe*, breaking records of audience in the whole of Southern Africa.[153] We might soon see a series on the Anglo-Zulu War in which the *isiHlangu* would probably occupy a prominent role.

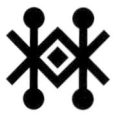

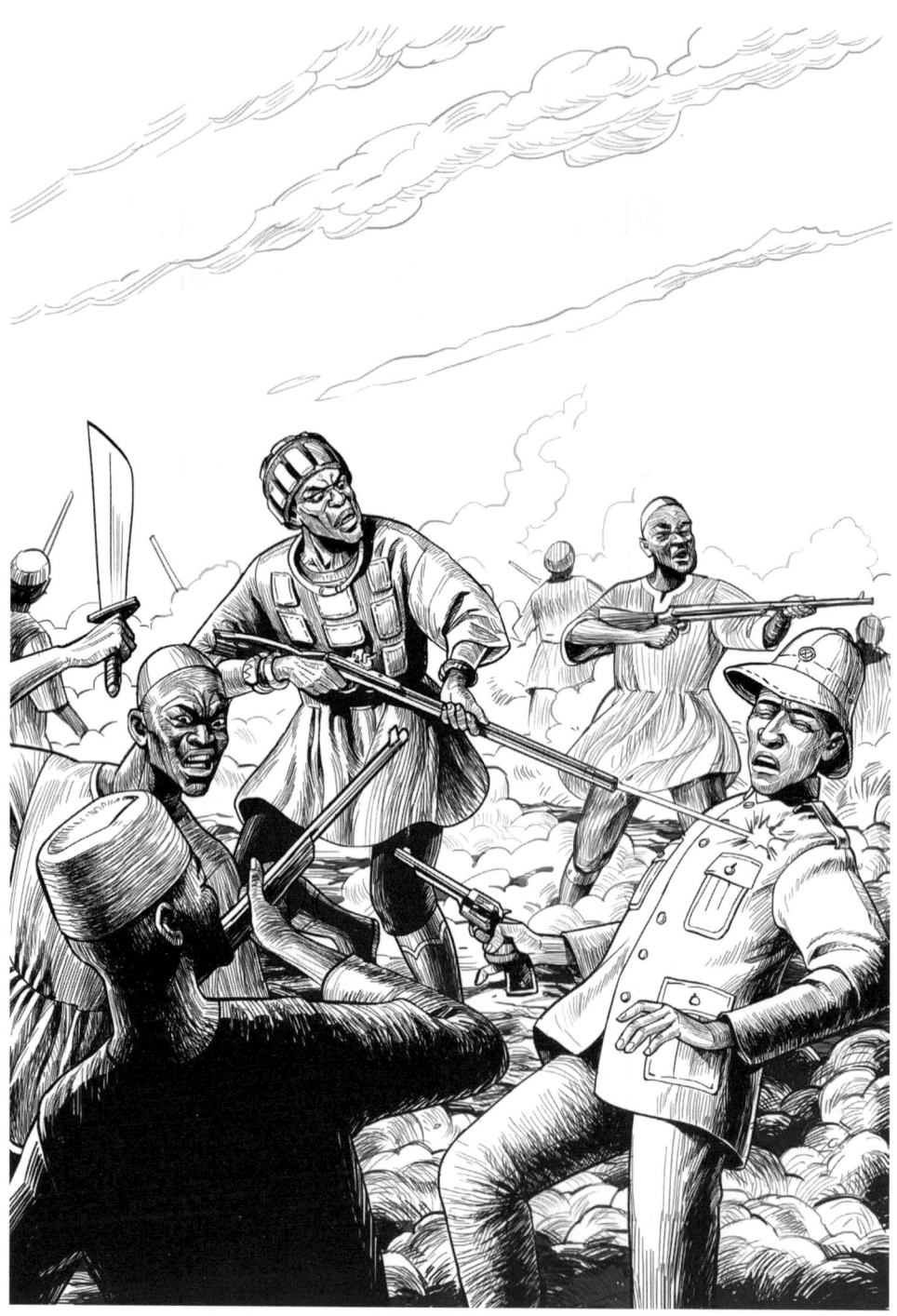

Artist: El Carna Mpesum

CHAPTER 4

The Plunder of 'Adibo Dali'
and Why Looted Cultural Goods Need to Return to Dagbon

Alhaji Sulemana Alhassan Iddi, Elias Aguigah,
Marlena Barnstorf-Brandes, Michael Gyimah,
Jan König and Ricarda Rivoir[154]

Even if your father's legacy bequeathed to you is a tattered headgear,
you must strive to death to acquire and protect it.
– A popular Dagbani maxim

At the Grassi Museum für Völkerkunde in Leipzig, Germany, one of the storages is located in the main building's basement. To access it in 2023, we first crossed a large pathway where all kinds of building material, exhibition furniture and vitrines are stored. We then stepped through an airlock and put on surgical gowns and masks. After that, the manager of the African collections, Julia Pfau, led us through long, clinical corridors with pipes running along the ceiling. The corridors were lined with shelves: some were rolling hand crank storage racks, others glazed cabinets from which figures, masks, drums and other carvings from different parts of the world gazed at us. In a separate room, Julia Pfau took six items out of their cabinets and set them up on tables. They were still lying in their cardboard boxes and wrapped in paper that she delicately unfolded to make them visible to us. Among them was a cotton headgear with leather pouches attached to it. Its index card indicated that it had been taken from Dagbon, in today's Ghana, and that it was sold to the museum by a certain 'v. Massow'.

This visit at the museum marked the first time when all the authors of this article met each other: one Ghanaian and three German researchers who worked with the collections from the former German colony of Togoland at the Grassi Museum, a researcher from Berlin, and Alhaji Sulemana Alhassan Iddi, the official *gonje* (historian)

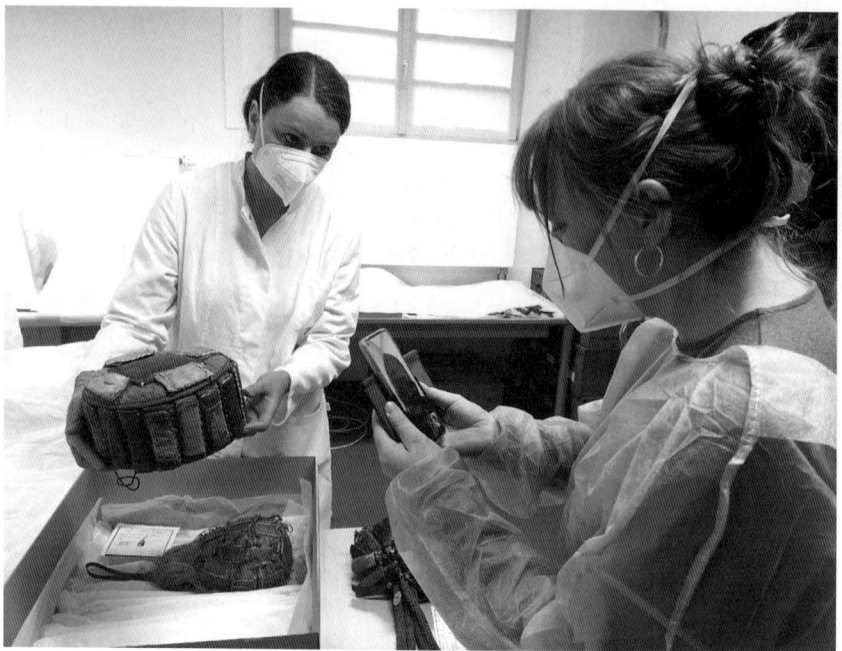

Figure 4.1: Provenance researcher Ricarda Rivoir and collections manager Julia Pfau showing the *gboguno zipligu* to Alhaji Sulemana Alhassan Iddi via video call. Photo: Elias Aguigah.

of the current Ya Na (king) of Dagbon. Still, not all of us could be there physically, walking through the basement storage. Alhaji Sulemana could not travel to Germany and, to remedy this, we took out a phone and called him. We turned on the camera and showed him the items, one after another (Figure 4.1). An intense conversation ensued. Each of us had specific expertise on these cultural assets from north-eastern Ghana and on their histories. Still, it was a discomforting feeling that the person who knew the most about them was only able to participate remotely in this visit.

Alhaji Sulemana holds a major role as far as Dagbon history is concerned. Moreover, he had been searching for these looted items for many years before being able to see them.[155] In 2022, his efforts connected with the Germany-based researchers working on the headgear attributed to 'v. Massow'. Eventually, in November 2022, Michael Gyimah, Ricarda Rivoir and Jan König travelled to Ghana, where they met the *gonje*. More than 120 years after these heirlooms were taken away from Dagbon, they showed photographs of eight items held by the Grassi Museum in Leipzig to various members of the Dagomba society in Yendi. This encounter emerged from two years of previous provenance research,[156] that led to the identification of at least 31 items in Leipzig as war booty, looted during a German military expedition launched against the West African kingdom in December 1896. In Dagbon, this colonial war is remembered as the Battle of Adibo, or *Adibo Dali* (literally 'the day of Adibo'). At the heart of this chapter are not only the plunder of war regalia from the battlefield and their subsequent absence, but also the long-lasting and devastating impact of this brutal colonial campaign.

Dagbon and Germany: Tensions, Conquest and *Adibo Dali*

When Yendi became the capital of the Dagbon kingdom in the fifteenth century, it came to assume a central role in the political, social, economic and historical status of West Africa. The city developed into a thriving multicultural trading centre that linked the region's most important caravan routes from the Maghreb, Timbuktu and Hausa countries to the north, as well as trade routes from Ashanti and other destinations in today's southern Ghana. In 1819, almost eight decades before the German invasion of eastern Dagbon, the English traveller and author Thomas Edward Bowdich recorded accounts of Yendi he had heard from Ashanti merchants:

> Yahndi is described to be beyond comparison larger than Coomasie, the houses much better built and ornamented. The Ashantees who visited it, told me, they frequently lost themselves in the streets […]. The markets of Yahndi are described as animated scenes of commerce, constantly crowded with merchants from almost all the countries of the interior. Horses and cattle abound and immense flocks are possessed even by the poor class.[157]

It was this political and economic power that lured the Germans to take control of the area, their people and their resources.

During the so-called Berlin Congo Conference of 1884–1885, Britain and Germany split Dagbon among themselves without consulting African representatives. The territory straddled between the Gold Coast and German Togoland. For the Germans, who had annexed a ten miles coastal stripe between today's Lomé and Aného, the control that Dagbon enjoyed over this flourishing trade undermined their colonial aspirations to rule over the hinterland, leading them to accuse the Dagomba of unsettling the trade routes. In 1896, after the Germans had burnt down the city of

Salaga, located south of Yendi, the ruler of Dagbon, Ya Na Andani, retorted that 'it is the white man who makes the roads unsafe'.[158] Andani's defiance upset the Germans who were worried of losing their grip on inland territories to the British in the west and the French in the east. Driven by this anxiety, they launched a rash military campaign to subjugate eastern Dagbon and secure Sansanné-Mango 'at all costs before the French', who had embarked on a similar mission dispatched from the Dahomey coast.[159]

On 23 November 1896, 4 Germans, 91 soldiers of the so-called police troops and 277 porters departed from Kete Krachi.[160] The expedition was led by lieutenant Valentin von Massow and colonial administrator Hans Gruner. For the people living between Kete Krachi and Sansanné-Mango, the German attack turned out to be a catastrophe. Massow and his troops left a trail of destruction, starting in Nanumba land, south of Dagbon. They advanced towards Yendi, burning down one village after the other. Seeing the danger, Ya Na Andani tried to rally as many warriors from his vassal cities as he could. Despite the short notice, 5,000 to 10,000 *kambonsi* (warriors) gathered on a hill near Adibo, about ten miles south of Yendi, to intercept the troops. On Friday 4 December 1896, a market day in Yendi, the expedition arrived in Adibo and both sides prepared for a battle.

As historian Emmanuel Tamakloe reported in 1931, the Dagomba war leader Kambon-Nakpem Ziblim Wag-biegu held a speech to motivate his troops in which he exclaimed: '*Silminga yi-la kuom-na, O-nye la zaham*,' that is, 'the white man is come from the water, he is a fish'.[161] In *A Drummer's Testament*, a website that documents Dagomba oral history sources recorded by John Chernoff and Alhaji Ibrahim Abdulai, the griots tell that Ya Na Andani called the *silminga* (whites) 'red monkeys'.[162] However, Alhaji Sulemana points out differences between oral history accounts from western and eastern Dagbon, the latter stemming from first-hand survivors of the German occupation. Eastern Dagomba narratives in fact tally with Tamakloe's record and have called the invaders *nisala zahim* (human fish). Red monkeys, *nisala zahim*, or *silminga*, no matter how they were called, their troops fired with breech-loading rifles the Dagomba called *sarimana*. These were much faster, stronger and more accurate than the muzzleloaders of the *kambonsi*.[163] At least 430 Dagomba fell, including 40 of the *sapashinnima* (war leaders) and their commander, Kambon-Nakpem Ziblim Wag-biegu. On the German side, three porters died and twenty-two people were wounded, including one German sub-officer, who would later succumb to his injuries. The remaining Dagomba dispersed and Ya Na Andani's advisors took him safely to a village, away from Yendi. Meanwhile, Massow's troops burned down Adibo and two more villages on the way before entering the capital. They found the city deserted, so they proceeded to plunder and set it on fire, quarter after quarter, including the royal Gbewaa Palace. Due to a poor appreciation of the Dagomba forces and insufficient ammunition, the Germans feared a possible retaliation by Andani's troops and left Yendi the same day.

On their way to Sansanné-Mango, Massow had at least nine other Dagomba and Bikpakpaam (Konkomba) villages burnt down. The expedition arrived in Sansanné-

Mango shortly before the French, so the Germans were able to strengthen their claims on northern Togoland. Yet, even though large parts of Dagbon were destroyed, Ya Na Andani was still alive and not willing to accept the conditions imposed by the colonialists. He even proclaimed that, as long as he lived, no white man should set foot in Dagbon. The proclamation actually came true: the Ya Na died in August 1899 and, until then, the Germans had not attempted to bring Dagbon completely under their control. Andani's death was followed by succession quarrels, which the German colonial administrator Friedrich Rigler used to his advantage: in early 1900, he launched a second military campaign against Yendi that eventually subjugated what was left of eastern Dagbon to German rule.[164] With two campaigns of destruction, plunder and a subsequent restructuring of the political and economic spheres in line with German colonial interests, the two wars of occupation brought a flourishing, centuries-old African civilisation to an abrupt end.

Loot from Dagbon Shipped to Germany

Even though the Germans admitted plundering Yendi and other parts of Dagbon, it is still difficult to determine the exact number of items that were taken. Colonial archives are deficient, even faulty at times and full of propaganda. In contrast, oral history passed on from people who experienced German occupation up to current generations indicates that war regalia such as bulletproof smocks, headgears, weapons, whiskers, animal skins, *saba* (imbued amulets), drums, horse saddles, royal chairs and stools, and war flags could not be retrieved on the battleground in Adibo. The Dagomba have always known that many of their belongings were looted. After the two campaigns and for the next fourteen years, Dagbon oral history reports that other valuables, such as elephant tusks, lion and leopard hides, special beads called *kpatana*, *lima* and *gmanamsi*, golden and silver items, were forcefully or cunningly taken away. For example, on festive occasions, when wealthy women, merchants and chiefs appeared in their beautiful attires and gold and silver jewellery, the Germans coveted them. They invited the local chiefs for dinner in their bungalows and, while sharing a meal with the Dagomba elite, told them of their interest for those items and requested them to offer those valuables voluntarily, as gifts for the German Kaiser. While some people surrendered their belongings, others could not easily relinquish the ornaments, even under duress, as they were a centuries-long inheritance that had been bequeathed to their grandparents and parents. Those ornaments were collective property and had to be preserved for future generations at all costs. In many cases, the Germans managed to get hold of them, either as tax payments or simply by confiscating them.

Despite the unreliability of colonial archives, it is possible to retrace some of the scattered loot in different German ethnographic collections. For example, in his diary on 16 December 1896, Valentin von Massow lists the most precious items among his spoils of war:

> I have got a couple of very interesting things. Among them, those I value the most are the flag or standard of Yendi, the seat cushions of the King of Yendi, the King of Adibo's suitcase, and a hat that reportedly belonged to Serkin Bindiga duká kasan Dagomba [the Hausa denomination for the Dagomba war leader].[165]

Was it the same hat we found at the Grassi Museum in Leipzig? Possibly. Alhaji Sulemana and other Dagomba representatives were indeed able to identify the leather-patched headgear at the Grassi Museum as a *gboguno zipligu* (bulletproof headgear) worn by a *sapashinnima* at *Adibo Dali*. Massow's diary entry indicates that it could have belonged to Kambon Nakpem Ziblim Wag-biegu, who was killed on the battlefield.

In addition, we established a direct link between *Adibo Dali* and thirty-one items in the collection of the Grassi Museum. For instance, the art dealer Adolf Diehl acquired a large bundle of West African belongings at the auction of Massow's estate in the colony and sold them with more than 700 other items to the museum in Leipzig in 1900 for the overall price of 10,000 Marks (€77,000 or £66,000 today). Among them are two items that Dagomba stakeholders identified as *kabre* and *dangbe*, both used in battle and endowed with representative functions, as explained in the following section.[166] Furthermore, Massow's mother sold a *gboguno* (bulletproof smock) to the museum, while colonial administrator Hans Gruner, second-in-command at *Adibo Dali*, gifted another one to the museum in 1901 which must have been taken from a fallen Dagomba warrior.

Gruner shipped many items from the region to other German museums as well. Among them, he sent fourteen items he labelled as 'Dagomba' to the Museum für Völkerkunde in Berlin in 1898. For one of them – a seat cushion – he precisely indicated that it came from Yendi. Even though Massow explicitly mentioned taking away seat cushions of the Ya Na from the Gbewaa Palace in his diary, evidence that Gruner also participated in the looting of the palace is lacking. He could have taken it away from a regular Yendi household as well. Today, this cushion does not appear in the database of the Berlin Ethnological Museum. In 1901, however, five years after *Adibo Dali* and one year after Friedrich Rigler's second military expedition, the assistant director of the Berlin Museum für Völkerkunde, Felix von Luschan, sent 123 items from Rigler's collection to Karlsruhe, among them a 'leather cushion of King Mohamma Andani'. After a trade in 1935, this shipment, which included the seat cushion, was transferred to the Reiss-Engelhorn Museum in Mannheim.[167] Still, it remains unclear whether Rigler grabbed it himself in 1900 or acquired it from one of the Germans who fought at *Adibo Dali*. Accordingly, it is unsure whether the seat cushion from Massow's diary, the one Gruner sent to Berlin, and the one in Mannheim are the same. Even the claim that it belonged to Ya Na Andani is questionable.

Similar inconsistencies in colonial archives appear when examining the trajectory of the alleged 'flag or standard of Yendi' that Massow mentioned in his diary. According to the archival records of the Ethnological Museum Berlin, Felix von Luschan coveted it and succeeded in acquiring it for the museum in Berlin. But the inventory number originally assigned to the flag is absent from the current database.[168] Just like with the seat cushions, another item partly matches Luschan's description of Massow's trophy: a flag or standard sent to the museum by the colonial administrator Friedrich Rigler. And just like the seat cushion, Rigler claimed that this war flag had belonged to Ya Na Andani.[169] However, Alhaji Sulemana's expertise proved Rigler's claims to be wrong: he identified the item inventoried under the number III C 13167 at the Berlin Ethnological Museum as a religious war-related item called *kabre* or *loow* rather than a war standard. Accordingly, the current location of the original war flag, called *farankang* in Dagbani, is still unknown.

Massow, Gruner and Rigler were not the only ones who took away Dagomba cultural heritage. Gaston Thierry, a German officer who fought at *Adibo Dali* and whom Massow entrusted to burn down Yendi, also shipped his spoils of war to Germany. His collection at the Linden Museum in Stuttgart includes four items from Dagbon: an iron stick with a hook, two scintillating armlets, and a fan. The Field Museum in Chicago, which bought the lieutenant's estate after his death (see Chapter 5), also holds five additional Dagomba armlets. These are only a handful of many traces of *Adibo Dali* and the German conquest of Dagbon found in ethno-colonial museums. It is important to remember here that the colonisers often mislabelled items due to their poor knowledge of local cultures, languages and political situations.[170] There are probably many more looted Dagomba belongings in museum storages and private collections. Only further investigations by experts from Dagbon in museum depots can shed light on the opacity of colonial archives.

Significance of Dagomba Belongings

The items looted from the battlefield are of high significance and value to Dagomba families. This brings us back to the maxim at the beginning of this chapter: 'Even if your father's legacy bequeathed to you is a tattered headgear, you must strive to death to acquire and protect it.' This rule of conduct underlines the importance of caring for your ancestors' legacy, as it is a fundamental step in maintaining your own family identity. All items that were forcefully or cunningly taken away from Dagbon are Dagomba property; they should be regarded as Dagbon's legacy. They have spiritual, cultural and social significance to their rightful owners and communities. As Alhaji Sulemana points out, the flag (*farankang*) for instance stood as a symbol of cultural identity imbued with the hopes and aspirations of Dagomba people. This item that Massow and Luschan described as a war standard landed at the Berlin Ethnological Museum in 1901, but its whereabouts is currently unknown. The continuous absence of closure in this affair harms the dignity of Dagbon. German cultural institutions must strive to find the *farankang* and facilitate its restitution.

To appreciate the significance of the war regalia seized after *Adibo Dali*, one has to learn about the importance of self-defence in Dagomba culture and the value they attach to the bodies of fallen warriors, as well as their paraphernalia, chairs, leather pillows, walking sticks imbued with *damle* (talismans), horses, caparisons of horses including the saddles, reigns, footrests and many more. The social class of the *worizohinema* or warrior class, together with the *Kambon-sapashinnima* (descendants of Ashanti warriors) form the backbone of the Dagbon fighting force. If a warrior dies in war, their regalia used in their last battle serve as symbols of their sacrifice and are henceforth imbued with their soul or spirit. They will be preserved for following generations to cherish with pride and dignity. When a warrior dies with his horse on the battlefield, the survivors must retrieve the saddle and ensure that it returns to their family. It is therefore common to see centuries-old saddles hung on ropes or poles in the homes of descendants. During the annual *bugum* (fire) and Yam festivals, these heirlooms are taken out for sacrifices of water and blood of fowls, goats and rams to remember their deceased owners. In Dagbon, the death of a warrior in war is an honour. If their remains or regalia are taken away by the enemy as trophies of war, this is a humiliating experience.

Furthermore, Dagombas believe in reincarnation and in the spiritual and protective power of heirlooms for their clan or communities. The souls or spirits of those who died in war may reappear as a new-born baby in the family. If the baby is deemed a reincarnation of a family member who died at war, the regalia are used for sacrifices before the baby is given a name. In addition, it is widely believed that if the child gets sick, rituals with family heritage might help bring the child on the path to recovery. With the loss of those artefacts, many war survivors and relatives felt their protective shield had been lost.

Therefore, the forceful takeover of the items from eastern Dagbon has led to the loss of identities connected to the items. The brutal appropriation of material culture disrupted the transmission of this identificatory and historical significance. With the loss of a generation of warriors and their belongings, many families were forced to flee from eastern to western Dagbon and other parts of the country. Along with the reckless burning down of houses and other property and the strategic alignment of local economies with German interests, this loss contributed to a massive displacement of people from the area to other regions outside Dagbon.[171] War regalia and the remembrance of the fallen warriors continue to play a central role in Dagomba society, no matter how much time has passed since Dagbon's last wars. Their absence causes continuous pain and humiliation.

Shaping the Future: Access, Remembrance, Restitution and Justice

The encounter between Alhaji Sulemana and the Leipzig museum's research team – Michael Gyimah, Ricarda Rivoir and Jan König – in November 2022 allowed our group to combine knowledge and begin tracking down the looted items.[172] The aim was to address the presence of Dagomba cultural heritage held by the Grassi Museum and engage with different stakeholders in Yendi. Out of 70 items, Michael Gyimah selected eight belongings based on his knowledge of customs in Dagomba culture. During the trip to Yendi and its surrounding area, the researchers met over 150 people to whom they showed photographs, talked about the colonial past and discussed the looting at *Adibo Dali*. The pictures showed not only the items, but also the storage, the researchers' work in the depot and parts of the museum's exhibitions.

At the sight of the photographs, numerous members of the Dagomba society such as traditional leaders, historians, youth and children, women's groups, artists, etc. recognised the items, located them in the context of *Adibo Dali*, and clearly expressed demands for restitution. In most cases, these demands were accompanied by the prospect of displaying the items and making them accessible for both the local population and tourists. The stakeholders asked for specific items that their forefathers had reported missing from the battleground at Adibo: among them, the stool and sandals of Kambon Nakpem Ziblim Wag-biegu. Other interlocutors were surprised not to see the guns of their slain warriors, knives, trousers and necklaces in the photographs. This prompted the research team to extend the scope of their project and look for those belongings in other German museums and depots. Alhaji Sulemana made clear that inquiries about the whereabouts of these items in Dagbon were frequent and that the search for them had already begun: in 2019, the NGO Yendi Heritage and Resource Center (YHRC) launched the North-Eastern Ghana–German Heritage Programme. Up until our meeting in Yendi, the biggest hurdle of the programme had been a lack of an overview of the cultural-political or bureaucratic structure of German collections and institutions, as well as the difficulty in accessing information on those collections.

Almost everyone in Yendi, young and old, knows about the violent downfall of the Dagbon Kingdom, marked by the defeat at the Battle of Adibo and the losses, destruction and looting that accompanied it. The fierce resistance of Dagomba warriors is an essential part of remembrance culture in Dagbon. In addition to their spiritual and identificatory significance, the *gboguno zipligu* and the other looted items represent historical witnesses to this story of violence and resistance. Had the people had an opportunity to claim these heirlooms earlier, they would have done so long ago in fulfilment of the popular maxim. In Germany, on the contrary, only very few people know about this history. Up until now, German colonialism has been barely addressed in school curricula. Thanks to the relentless work of largely diasporan activists and scholars, awareness of colonial continuities and current neocolonial dynamics is growing. But the German colonisation of today's Togo and eastern Ghana, let alone the atrocious wars of conquest like the 1896 expedition against Dagbon, remains very much at the outer margins of German collective memory.

Dagbon's vibrant remembrance of the past, conveyed through songs and stories, is also marginalised in Ghanaian national memory. Michael Gyimah, who is not Dagomba but has spent years studying cultural spaces in Ghana, was able to identify what he saw in the storeroom of the Grassi Museum at first glance, but the story of how these items ended up in the collection was unknown to him. The same can be said about many other Ghanaians who are not Dagomba. In this transnational process, what is at stake is the recognition of Dagbon's history and memory. Negotiations on restitution – or apologies and reparations for that matter – cannot be done without the Dagomba.

The fact that the looted items have been lying in their cardboard boxes in museum depots for over a hundred years and, in most cases, have received little or no attention since their violent appropriation, is a clear sign of the gap between Germany's lack of interest in the historical significance of *Adibo Dali* and its position as a milestone in Dagbon's history. German institutions that hold cultural heritage from the regions affected by this war of conquest should facilitate access to their holdings and archival records, work towards restitution, and make these processes transparent so that the general public becomes part of this historical and political acknowledgement of the past. Dialogue and exchange of information in restitution processes can offer a fertile ground for building future-oriented relations between the people of Dagbon and the German public.

Collectively, we have taken the first steps towards the return of Dagomba items by informing civil stakeholders in Yendi on the whereabouts of the items that we could localise so far. Subsequently, the YHRC sent requests for restitution to German museums. To keep the flame alive, we need long-term partnerships that enable people from Dagbon to visit museum storerooms in Germany to search, identify and catalogue all respective items. As a direct representative of civil society of Yendi, the YHRC stands ready to partner with museums, but also with other state and non-state agents.[173] But because German law still regulates the process of de-accessioning and returning cultural heritage, unfortunately, restitution is incumbent upon negotiations at the national level. On the Ghanaian side, the Ghana Focal Team on Reparation and Restitution of Illegally Trafficked and Stolen Cultural Heritage and Artifacts was established by the Ministry for Tourism, Arts & Culture in 2020. This board of experts could serve as an important mediator between governmental and non-governmental stakeholders and emphasise the special cultural and historical value of the items to ensure that they are ultimately returned to Dagbon.

In Yendi, ideas for the future of the items are already being discussed. Public presentation can admittedly enhance the touristic attractiveness of the region. More importantly, it will empower the local population by providing access to the knowledge, skills, history and spiritual values that the items embody. Reconnecting them with their rightful owners can help people reclaim and restore their dignity, pride and sense of belonging. The humiliation and shame that has blotted Dagbon's self-image will be a thing of the past. Finally, restitution will present an opportunity to honour the slain heroes and heroines of the wars of resistance against German colonialism. Through its return, the *gboguno zipligu* will represent so much more than what its index card in Leipzig tells us: not only is it exemplary of a violent history of conquest forgotten by the colonisers but remembered by those who resisted; its future can also steer a long journey towards restorative justice.

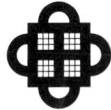

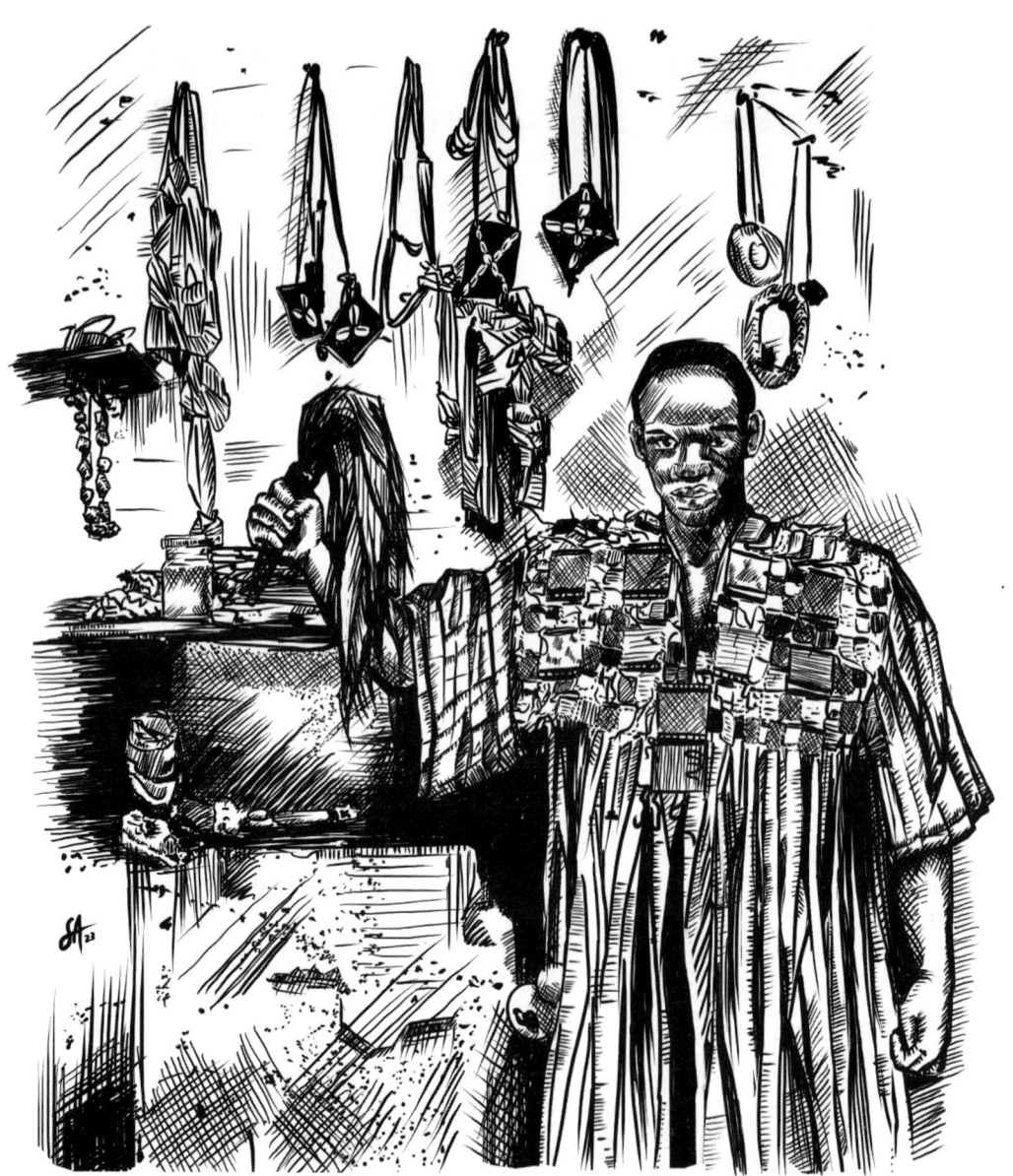

Artist: Sena Dede Ahadji

CHAPTER 5

A War Coat of the Anufo/Tchokossi
From Northern Togo to the Field Museum in Chicago

Editors' note:
This chapter is composed of two sections, one by staff members at the Field Museum focusing on the history and status of this war coat in their collections, and a response by Togolese professor Kokou Azamede, which addresses the meaning of the presence of this war cloak in relation to Togo's collective memory of colonialism and the blueprint of transnational partnerships in the cultural sector.

The Telling Biography of the Field Museum's Togolese War Cloak

Julia Kennedy, Foreman Bandama and Christopher J. Philipp

The Field Museum in Chicago houses nearly 6,000 items of African cultural heritage that were acquired in the years between the museum's inception in 1893 and the outbreak of the First World War in 1914. As is well documented, this period was punctuated by horrendous acts of colonial European subjugation of Africa and its resources included cultural heritage. Therefore, it should not come as a surprise that European colonialism, directly and indirectly, bequeathed most African pieces to contemporary museums throughout the Global North. The processes that brought these collections here no doubt involved the stripping of the cultural assets' original contexts as they passed through the hands of dealers, collectors and museum ethnographers, but the collections continue to evolve and acquire new meaning and roles. Even by calling them 'collections', one risks cementing the items' imposed identity as 'collectibles' rather than the belongings with unique values and meanings they were in their original contexts. The term should invite scrutiny, dialogue and post-colonial redressing. This chapter attempts this critique by exposing the telling journey of a so-called 'war cloak' from Mango, Togo, collected by colonial German army officer Gaston Thierry.[174]

Reconstructing an item's story is often riddled with questions and dead ends, but modern museum researchers have an ethical and moral obligation to confront their ugly pasts by reopening the accession files and asking uncomfortable questions to address the colonial practices that built many of today's museums and their holdings. All the same, the views expressed in this paper are those of the researchers and not the institution. Additionally, by working 'top-down', that is, relying on accession files generated on the bases of information volunteered by the collectors, we are fully aware of our handicap because colonial actors seldom recorded and often misrecorded the values of the items they collected. Nevertheless, we can reasonably assume that many of these cultural assets must have been precious belongings or attractive heirlooms that caught the attention of the covetous eyes of colonial officials.

One such item is the 'war cloak' now housed in the Field Museum's Collections Resource Center. The coat – made of heavy woven cotton in its natural colour and partially lined in the same material dyed blue – is constructed of narrow strips to confer volume and ease of movement. It is adorned front and back with dozens of protective amulets. The amulets, wrapped variously in leather, reptile skin, yarn, velvet and animal fur, contain talismans, symbols and verses from the Qur'an on folded paper and pieces of wood. The Islamic practice of making and wearing amulets is centuries old and fairly well represented in the Field Museum's collections from across the continent, which include examples from Cameroon, Nigeria, Senegal and Somalia; but we know that indigenous African religions also have similar practices.[175] The presence of protective amulets on this particular garment is poignant in light of the well-documented violence and fear inflicted upon the people of Sansanné-Mango by the German collector and army officer Gaston Thierry.[176] The garment highlights the brutality of Thierry's reign: a powerful protective garment, believed to safeguard the wearer, turned into a curio as it was taken from its owner and country of origin.

One can imagine the circumstances under which Thierry could collect the belongings of a warrior. Perhaps it was taken following an armed conflict or stolen from a house during a raid by Thierry. Maybe its wearer, noting changes in their lifestyle as a result of German and French incursion, sold it or traded it for items more useful to a new farming livelihood.[177] The former seems the most likely given what we know about Thierry's behaviour during his tenure in Sansanné-Mango, where he conducted 'one punitive expedition after another … resulting in abundant spoils of war'.[178] But the local people were far from passive bystanders to European action. Local politics, conflicts and community life continued independently while the community actively resisted colonial rule, and it is critical that we do not dismiss their agency in this story. Thierry's notes do not illuminate the specifics of the acquisition, but his peers and archives of the colonial government give hints on the size of the spoils that he amassed through military campaigns. We can, however, trace the garment's journey after its removal from Togoland to Germany, and eventually to the United States. In other words, the chain of provenance can be reconstituted only after the time the war cloak was taken off the shoulders of its African wearer.

That story begins at the Ethnological Museum in Berlin, where his collections were being held when Thierry was killed conducting another violent expedition in the north of the colony of Kamerun, in today's Nigeria. His brother, obliged to handle Thierry's estate, sought a buyer for Thierry's 'duplicate' collections, which Berlin had declined to purchase, but it offered to hold on to them until a buyer was found. While negotiating prices with contacts in Berlin and Cologne, Thierry's brother received an American offer, via an unnamed middleman, of 1,000 marks (the equivalent of over $US8,000 in 2023) for the remaining items in the collection.[179]

Correspondence in the Field Museum archives reveals the actors behind that anonymous transaction: Otto Finsch, naturalist, collector and director of the Municipal Museum in Braunschweig, and the Field Columbian Museum. Finsch had decided to act as an unofficial intermediary between the US and German museums, not in his official capacity at the Municipal Museum, but as a collector and ethnographer. In a letter dated 14 April 1905, Finsch offers curator George A. Dorsey 'a most interesting collection from the Togo-Hinterland […] every specimen has the very location, having been collected at the various places by a former Yeoman officer'.[180] The inclusion of this limited provenance information was evidently deemed sufficient, as Dorsey soon recommended the purchase of the collection to his director, Frederick Skiff, citing the same reason. Skiff approved the purchase of 217 items for $250.00 (roughly $US8,700 today) in late April 1905.

Finsch was already known to Dorsey and Skiff, having done business with them as a collector in previous years, and leveraged that relationship to facilitate the sale of the Thierry collection. Finsch himself was no stranger to colonial plunder. He considered himself a scientist, but the effect of his work was the same as colonialists like Thierry: the (oftentimes violent) removal of Africans' belongings into the hands of Western museums. Finsch's expertise was in Oceania, particularly German New Guinea, and many items he acquired reside in the Field Museum today. Interestingly, Finsch's name had supplanted Thierry's in reference to the collection as early as October 1905, when the museum's annual report announced that it was 'secured through the kindness of Dr. Otto Finsch'.[181] In the eyes of the public, Thierry's name, and all that it implied, were already disassociated from the belongings he took. While likely unintentional, this type of omission or mistake can resound through time. Records that lack blatant evidence of violence, such as the name of a feared colonial enforcer, have served to obscure museums' complicity in colonial brutality. In the case of the 'war cloak', fortunately, the Field Museum documentation retained Thierry's name as the original source for the extraction of these West African cultural assets. Still, the museum's inconsistent application of the designations 'source', 'collector' and 'donor' in the early decades of its operation is one way provenance information can become lost with time.

Thierry's brother quickly accepted the American offer, instructing Berlin to ship the materials to Hamburg. Thereafter, the responsibility and expense for the two crates could be taken on by the Chemnitz branch of Marshall Field & Co., who would send the collection to New York with one of their outgoing shipments. Marshall Field, entrepreneur and founder of the eponymous department store chain, donated the funds necessary to form the Field Columbian Museum in 1893. In 1905, the Field family remained closely associated with the institution as trustees. This unexpected advantage in shipping costs may well have enabled the Field to outbid Thierry's other contacts.

The crates arrived safely in Chicago, and a count of 226 items was officially recorded on 10 August 1905. When pieces like arrows are counted individually, as they are in the museum's database today, that number grows to over 900. About three-quarters of the collection is made up of arrows and a handful of other weapons. Garments and personal adornments are the next most represented category, followed by pieces of cloth. The remainder includes baskets, horse tack, fans, bells and wooden figures. Of these, eight are currently exhibited in the public galleries to show Hausa textile, leather and basketry practices. It is likely that many more were displayed in the years before the existence of reliable exhibition records. The authors have not found any definitive evidence that the war cloak was ever on display, although a similar example from Cameroon was featured in a previous iteration of the Africa galleries.

Today, the collection of Gaston Thierry makes up virtually all of the Togolese collection cared for by the Field Museum. Because Thierry's reputation for cruelty and plunder was recorded even by his contemporaries – 'Mr. Gaston Thierry ... is said to have shot down natives like wild animals', noted a German MP in a 1905 court record – one can assume that most of the items were taken under coercion.[182] At the very least, all were obtained from people living under the threat of violence from their colonial administrator. Over a century later, as museums are just beginning to reflect on their role in nineteenth- and twentieth-century imperialism, colonialism and racism, we are forced to confront the fact that Thierry (and countless others) effectively acted on behalf of European and American institutions. The plunder of Africa's cultural patrimony for financial gain was only possible, and even sanctioned, because of museums' rapacious appetite for the 'unfamiliar', the exotic and the so-called 'primitive'.

Acknowledging North American museums' complicity in European colonial enterprise necessitates revisiting early collections and their documentation. Unsurprisingly, the Thierry documentation available to us focuses on the interactions and transactions among major drivers of the political economy of looting in late nineteenth- and early twentieth-century Africa. There is no shortage of European perspectives on collecting in archives of the time. The missing piece of the puzzle, of course, is the voice of the African makers and owners of these items. Study of belongings' journeys to the Field Museum may help us to reconstruct the connections between cultural assets and their former owners, modern source communities and meanings. The war cloak is only one example of thousands awaiting rediscovery and reactivation by communities: among the 1.5 to 2 million items in the anthropology collections of the museum are approximately 24,000 cultural assets from the continent of Africa and roughly 124,000 archaeological remains from African sites.

This work has already begun in several areas of the world: the Field Museum actively engages various descendant communities in the Americas, the Pacific islands and Southeast Asia to govern access to their ancestral collections. Staff prioritise heritage visits to collections and offer culturally appropriate care for belongings (as instructed in consultation with communities) whenever possible. The museum strives to continually improve the conditions in which it stores items and has constructed facilities that enable access to the collections. Its Collections Resource Center not only mitigates preservation risks to the collections but accommodates large heritage groups and features flexible space for study and ceremony. The museum employs a staff of repatriation specialists who field repatriation requests and return ancestors and belongings to their places of origin. Conservators have begun to consult and invite artists and craftspeople from their respective source communities to preserve and repair the items of their expertise. While these efforts cannot repair the damage inflicted by collectors and anthropologists on behalf of the museum, staff today can find ways to reduce harm and promote the interests of descendant communities.

It is not yet possible to expand all of these practices to every language or culture group represented in the collections. The scope of the work depends not only on staffing and monetary needs, but also on the willingness of community members to work with a colonial institution. Reciprocation of some kind is critical in shifting the relationship between the museum and source communities from the old, extractive model. Increasingly, this means digital and physical access to collections. Expanding digital access (a useful tool, albeit not a replacement for physical access) to collections is a practical step the museum can take in this process – a process that need not look the same for all peoples and collections and can result in outcomes unique to the communities involved. Public interest in museum content and projects waxes and wanes over time, and partnerships forged with staff members may be lost as staff changes. Relationships with external collaborators end; such is the reality of working with members of the public and it does not necessarily constitute a failure. Still, lack of institutional support undercuts individual efforts towards partnership. If engagement is deprioritised, the museum and descendant communities will continue to lose vital connections with descendant communities. This has been the case for the Field's association with African and African diaspora groups thus far, but the museum still wishes to connect with groups on the African continent, African expatriates in Chicago and African-Americans. Crucially, we must remember that communities are stakeholders of the museum's collections and exhibitions need not be an element of that relationship at all.

The need for restitution, repatriation and healing is only increasing in the face of growing world inequality, environmental challenges heavily impacting post-colonial regions, and continuing racism. The role of museums will likely, and necessarily, see radical changes in the coming decades. The Field's continuing relevance will depend on its relationships with the dynamic, living communities from which the collections it cares for derive. The way forward lies in making the museum itself a more dynamic and living entity, one that can respond to a thousand different cultural and individual preferences with receptivity and flexibility, prepared to build stakeholders directly into its processes.

What does all this mean for the 'war cloak' and the rest of Thierry's acquisitions? This article opened with an acknowledgement of the evolving role of collections that have ugly acquisition biographies. Although the belongings in question came into European hands as stolen loot, descendent communities may now decide to give some of those pieces an educational role. Consider the ongoing Field Museum and Cameroonian Bamum Kingdom relationship: during a 2023 Black History Month presentation by representatives of the Bamum people in the Chicago area, presenters mentioned that there exist nearly 70,000 Cameroonian people who now reside in the USA and Canada, many of whom will not be able to visit Cameroon in their lifetime. However, the Field Museum offers those individuals a way to connect with their history through the collections that have been on view in the Field Museum's Africa exhibit for over 30 years. The exhibit was made in collaboration with and led by the late Bamum prince, historian and anthropologist Dr Aboubakar Nijasse Njoya. Thanks to his input and the use of the collections in Chicago, the Bamum Kingdom has a platform to celebrate their heritage, and share with all other visitors to the museum. This is an example of a descendant community re-activating both colonial and contemporary collections through collaborative use.

The museum should tap into this power to acknowledge the difficult past and highlight the ingenuity of the African communities from which these cultural assets were taken. This does not happen by keeping collections inaccessible, but will happen through collaborative care, research and exhibitions. The Field Museum has identified Africa as part of its strategic vision and the decades-old Africa Hall is slated for reimagination. Such a platform is the ideal place for educating current generations, not only about the painful past but also about the great African achievements in technology and craftsmanship. Nonetheless, museums should not assume that communities who have seen their material heritage stolen necessarily desire this type of collaboration. Dialogue and listening are the integral first steps to ensuring mutual, long-term benefit.

Togolese Cultural Heritage from Colonial Contexts in Collective Memory and Transnational Partnership

Kokou Azamede

The colonial history that we, the Togolese people, have learned from teaching materials inherited from a neo-colonial francophone system largely omit mentioning colonial plunder. When it comes to the violence of colonial domination, whether under the yoke of the German Empire or that of France, the Togolese imaginary is rather nourished by oral tradition through stories passed on by our ancestors. Togo's collective memory is opaque, and the looting of cultural heritage has not been a subject usually discussed in public. The collective psyche mostly remembers the brutality and the suffering under colonisation, especially the military expeditions that facilitated the appropriation of cultural heritage. These campaigns took place in conditions of violent conquest and were carried out in deliberate secrecy vis-à-vis the local population. Besides, the memory of those who accompanied the German colonialists and helped them in their plundering enterprise was clearly biased. Before examining the meaning of looted cultural assets such as this war cloak from Mango, let me briefly address this truncated memory of colonialism in Togo.

Collective Memory and Colonial Violence in Northern Togo

When it comes to collective memory of the German colonial period, Togo is a very interesting case. The persistence of Togolese nostalgia for German domination is a question that has been examined many times.[183] Still, post-colonial memory is not as uniform as many believe. For several decades, an instrumentalisation of German colonial history in Togo for political and commercial ends has led foreign observers to suggest that the entire Togolese nation has retained a positive memory of the German colonial era. But it is important to recall how this manipulation of the past ensued.

In 1960, at the dawn of Togo's independence, President Sylvanus Olympio sought to curtail French interference in Togolese public affairs. To achieve this, his government fast-tracked the Federal Republic of Germany to becoming one of their closest politico-economic partners. Already then, this aroused national sympathy for the

Federal Republic bordered on amalgamation with Germany's colonial past. Olympio's distancing from France would prove fatal: allies to neocolonial French power assassinated him in 1963.[184] In the 1980s, President Eyadéma Gnassingbé forged a close bi-national partnership in which the colonial past was incorporated, becoming ultimately a historical friendship between Togo and Germany.[185] This instrumentalisation of the past for geopolitical and commercial purposes had a profound influence on national opinion, which has since given the impression of sympathy for the German colonial era.

However, investigations of the past and enquiries carried out among different communities throughout the country have demonstrated that national memory is in fact split in two. On the one hand, there is indeed a nostalgic impression of German colonisation in southern Togo. This was the area where the colonial administrative structures were established, infrastructure that is still used today, especially in the administrative sector, and are therefore part of the daily lives of Togolese people. This contrasts with the absence of French traces of meaningful infrastructure,[186] hence the lack of a feeling of admiration vis-à-vis the French colonial era. In addition, the evangelisation of the people of southern Togo by German missions through conversion to Christianity left a rather positive impression on the people. Missionary schools indeed produced the first Togolese intellectual elites, products of a Western system of values. In a nutshell, the everyday lives of southerners in Togo are connected to positive impressions of the German colonial past in the region through tangible (buildings, roads…) and intangible (faith, religion…) traces. On the other hand, the north of Togo was the recruitment base, the pool of 'human resources' that the colonists displaced to the south through exploitation and forced labour for the construction of the infrastructures I just mentioned. So, the north has no nostalgic memory of this past – quite the contrary. All the testimonies we have gathered speak of brutality, murder and war. These effects of colonisation left deep scars and have been recounted from generation to generation, right up to the present day. Post-colonial memory in Togo therefore varies depending on the region and the knowledge that people have with this history. Still, apart from the political and commercial instrumentalisation, there is a clear divide between nostalgia bordering on 'Germanophilia' and a palpable bitterness when it comes to German colonial rule.[187]

In the northern province around Mango, the chief of station Gaston Thierry plundered several thousand tokens of African cultural property from local populations. As our colleagues from the Field Museum have shown, the sources point at looting during military expeditions rather than purchases. In late 1897, Thierry also ordered the murder of the former chief of Mango, Na Biema Asabiè, after he protested Thierry's reign of terror.[188] Since then, Na Biema has been one of the rare historical figures who are very popular among the Togolese people.[189] He is largely recognised as a hero of the resistance to German colonisation, and there is widespread knowledge of the fact that the German colonialists beheaded him to set an example. The Anufo (or Tchokossi) community has been looking for their ancestor's remains to this day, and many people suggest that his head was taken away by the Germans to be shown to neighbouring communities as a threat, to deter potential anti-colonial movements. Whatever can be said about the seizure of his possessions and the cultural assets of his community, the mystery surrounding the disappearance of his head is what makes this figure so popular. In fact, after Na Biema's murder, Thierry not only made profit by selling the chief's golden jewellery to the Linden Museum in Stuttgart, he also suspiciously sent dozens of ancestral remains to the Berlin Ethnological Museum, remains that he had taken from local graves in the region.[190] While the colonial government criticised Thierry' violence and machinations, this internal affair remained confidential until other colonial scandals broke out years later, in 1904.

Concerning the meaning of these spoils, over and above the German colonial ideology that considered the populations of Togoland and other former colonies as 'primitive' people, I argue that some of these belongings represent the spiritual and traditional power of their owners. They were symbols of sovereignty and, for a chief, losing them meant losing authority over and among his people. By extension, entire kingdoms and communities found themselves humiliated and weakened by colonial domination. These are spoils of war that, for their former custodians and for their descendants, form the very basis of their culture, the bearings, if you like, of their cultural orientation. To take it away from them reflected a determination to divert the population from its points of reference and to erase a cultural reality. In this scheme, taking all these possessions away through looting was not just theft for profit, but also a method of cultural aggression and violation, a way of weakening a community to the point of forcing them to wipe out their history.

These cultural assets are not mere 'objects' or collections, but witnesses of the past and bearers of complex identities. They are representations of the multiple self-definitions and histories of local communities. Make no mistake about it, Togo is a multilingual and multicultural society, a complex one, with community movements and lots of exchanges. At the same time, taking historical symbols of our identity away from us has made our lives difficult. How can we move towards development if we don't have a solid background? That's why I've been campaigning to this day for the return of these cultural assets because, to a certain extent, it would mean restoring our broken self. Europe too has evolved on the solid foundation of its cultures and narratives of identity formation, some of them racist and colonial. If a nation or community does not necessarily know where it is going, it should at least know where it comes from.

For a long time, our educational system has suffered from a lack of knowledge about our history because most schoolbooks were written and published in France, the former colonial metropole. These contested cultural assets can be mobilised against this, for another writing of history and the commemoration of anti-colonial resistance.[191] There is still a plethora of landmarks and periods of our history that we can't tie together because we don't have all the elements at our disposal to reconstruct this history. As symbols of West African chronology and epistemology, of the application of traditional knowledge, of the implementation of cultural practices, of an ancient system of rules and societal norms, these possessions which, in the meantime, became war booty, are for us sources for rewriting, reconstituting, if not even reconstructing our history. What we lack today is the chance to know that these belongings still exist and where they are, as well as the conviction that the history of these spoils can help us regain our dignity by teaching our children history from our own perspective. This is the very reason why these collections are being contested today. It is not a question of merely leaving them in a museum, as is done elsewhere, but of exploiting their potential, making use of them for educational purposes to teach history.

Transnational Cooperation, Intercultural Dialogue and a New Ethics between Europe and Africa

The presence of this war cloak in a North American collection comes as no surprise to me, considering the history of transatlantic colonial crossings. These spoils of war were commodified and used for commercial and scientific – that is, anthropological – purposes. They were therefore subject to massive and permanent circulation. Whether ethnographic collections, statues sold on the art market or even ancestral remains, collections in the USA are the result of various collecting practices in the field that were not always morally acceptable; they are also the result of transfers of both material culture and colonial ideas from Europe. The fact that, after the death of a colonial officer, his brother sold his loot to a North American museum, is a prime example of both the very familial and transnational nature of colonial heritage.

The future of these cultural assets depends on transnational dialogue. It is a complex question, which our colleagues at the Field Museum have addressed in their text – one that requires openness and intercultural exchange. I believe that, today, we are in the first phase of a long process that is not necessarily a process of restitution, but rather one of repertory. In other words, to draw up an inventory of everything that may have ended up anywhere through illegal, dishonest or unethical means. Museums form an important part of these diverse repositories. It is therefore essential that these institutions recognise that, if they want to learn or discuss the status of these cultural assets, only the original communities to which they belong can decide on their fate or inform on the appropriate ways to look, gaze at, display, care for, or, simply treat this heritage. Allow me to repeat that these cultural assets are not just mere aesthetic 'objects', but are intimately linked to people's souls, destinies and identities. Until now, I have the feeling that they have not been considered for their true value. For that, we need to talk to the communities and place them in social contexts. It is as if one of Mozart's musical instruments were in a Togolese museum. Would it then be considered as a dynamic 'object'? Would it allow a spirited vision of the history of European music? I don't think so. These collections must facilitate relational exchanges. They should be at the centre of intercultural contact between museums and communities and become the subject of serious discussions to understand not only their deep meaning, but also the living cultures of peoples who have been for too long considered as peoples without culture. It is in this sense that we speak of dynamism.

For us, academics, cultural workers, but also for the broader public, the key method is open-mindedness, not only towards foreign institutions implicated in the conservation of this heritage, but above all openness to setting up collaborative projects that will enable us to finally exchange on equal footing. The 'Legba-Dzoka Project', of which Sela Adjei and myself are a part, is one example of such partnership.[192] I believe that such projects can result in better understanding between people and diverse cultural spheres. Healthy contexts of humble exchange could lead to resolving the question of restitution or repatriation of this heritage, or could even help find out what this war cloak means for the various people of Mango. This exchange could also include other fields of study in the equation, for instance, people who, for too long, have erroneously considered these cultural assets to be 'primitive art'. It is essential to cast a critical light on disciplines such as art history and anthropology. A whole vocabulary needs to be changed; a new terminology needs to emerge. It would be a chance for the scientific community to develop a post- and decolonial perspective on concepts that have influenced social habits until today, to pursue a debate that has an impact on public opinion. These concepts were indeed at the origin of persistent colonial phenomena such as the racism we still experience today, especially in Western societies. Collaboration between universities and foreign institutions interested in a critical history of these collections can become a salutary means of tackling several key social issues.

For this collaboration to be fully successful, it is desirable that the political sphere refrains from interfering in the debate.[193] The risk at hand is that political stakeholders seek to exploit arguments and take advantage of the discussion. It is essential to allow scholars and universities to work freely and to bring together communities who inherited various colonial pasts for a genuine and sincere intercultural dialogue. In the end, I believe that the results and recommendations that emanate from these partnerships will enable politicians to take action. Another risk that requires caution is the capacity of conservative minds to jeopardise dialogue. Academics should strive towards agreeing or compromising on working methods, whatever the difficulties or the various objectives of such cooperation. Post-colonial acknowledgement of colonial inheritance will make scientific collaboration more dynamic and more adapted to multiple perspectives, especially if methods move away from Eurocentric theories. Terminologies that refer to exoticism, art, the sacred and anthropology, among others, deserve to be redefined and adjusted to transcultural milieux and perspectives.

To conclude, I would be delighted if, tomorrow, museums in the USA took the initiative of contacting us, the Togolese scientific community, and informing us of the presence of belongings from northern Togo in their collections. This could lead to the development of future projects that aim at understanding their provenance and recontextualising them. For the Field Museum, I think it would be important to address the presence of this war cloak which, since its arrival in the USA, has been folded and unfolded in storage rooms, and which, in its current status, bears only one meaning: a token of anthropological science, of material culture, detached from those who had worn it before it was taken away from Mango. By making inventories and repositories more accessible to the communities of origin, the institution and its audiences could get a better understanding of the plural meanings of these cultural assets. The museum would be the better for it, and the Togolese would emerge dignified.

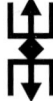

PART II

THE ROYAL PALACE

Part II engages with symbols of power and central elements of social life in African communities. They were coveted both by officers of the colonial troops as well as anthropologists and were most often taken away after the violent subjection of local rulers took place. Some of them have been returned, some are on their way back home, while the presence of others in museums has been so far unbeknown to their communities.

'The Royal Palace' will show how punitive expeditions were inextricably linked with the idea of submitting sovereign nations and communities to colonial rule, and how artefacts and symbols of African sovereignty can contribute to processes of empowerment and restoration of dignity to communities and their traditional leaders today. At the same time, the chapters also touch upon the political value of these symbols of power in the post-colonial African state. They advocate for caution when assessing the achievement of restitution. Is it still a process of reparation when power dynamics are still at play, and when certain communities and stakeholders are still marginalised in international debates, as well as within African countries and their political structures?

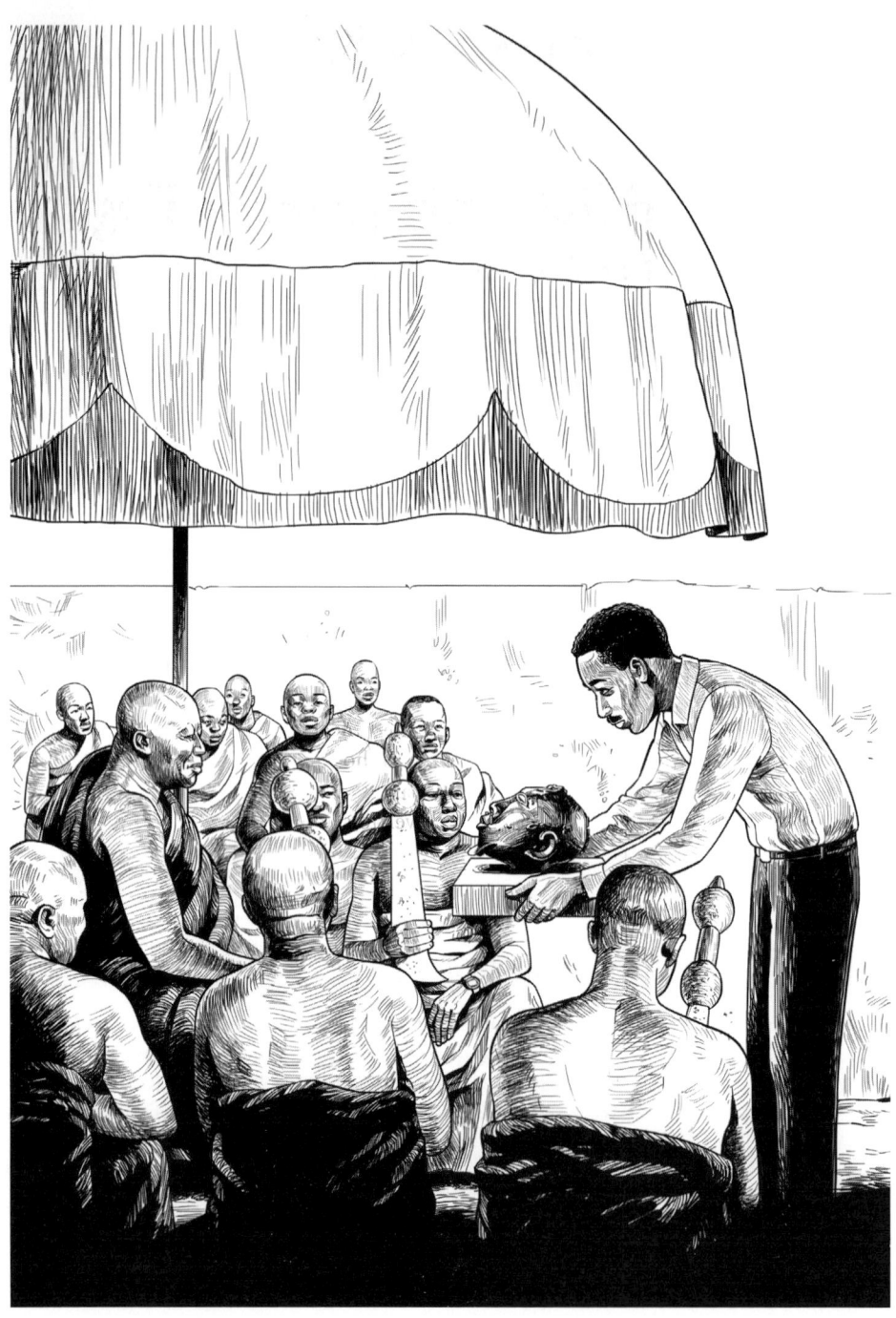

Artist: El Carna Mpesum

CHAPTER 6

Hiding and Returning Asante Regalia
The Journey of an Ancestral Messenger (1970–2024)

Nii Kwate Owoo

I was in Kumasi on 8 February 2024, when the Fowler Museum from Los Angeles, California, returned seven Asante regalia to the Asantehene Otumfuo Nana Osei Tutu II, 'some of which were looted from the palace in 1874, and others that were part of the indemnity that the Asante were forced to pay to the British at the end of the Sagrenti war'.[194] I am very privileged to have been part of such a historic landmark, and to have been physically present at this momentous occasion. Standing among the hundreds who had gathered there, I recalled the unique experience I had had fifty-three years earlier, when I got the chance to shoot a film in the basement of the British Museum. Like an ancestral messenger supposed to ensure that the story of our stolen cultural heritage languishing abroad is well told to the world, I have waited over half a century for an earnest conversation on the decolonisation of African art and museum collections to take place globally. I am conscious that I belong to a very small constituency of Africans who have ever laid eyes on these historical gems since they were violently removed, let alone to touch them. I will here recall the story of this film, before discussing the most recent developments in terms of restitution from Britain to Ghana.

From the Black Power Movement to Franz Fanon's 'White Mask'

I was born into a political and artistic family in the Gold Coast before independence. My father was a political activist, chairman of the Tudu branch of the Convention People's Party (CPP), to which the first President of Ghana, Dr Kwame Nkrumah, belonged. Already at the age of four, he used to carry me on his shoulders to take me to rallies where Nkrumah and other political activists would hold speeches. I remember hearing people shouting: 'Freedom, freedom, freedom!' I didn't understand what was happening, but it was obviously being inscribed subconsciously into my system. As I grew up, I also realised that my father was a movie fanatic. The Globe Cinema stood about five minutes away from our house. My father used to go there on Fridays, Saturdays and Sundays. He would often take us with him and put me on his lap, and I would often fall asleep. That's how I was introduced to the seventh art.

Later, I attended high school in Cape Coast. Cape Coast is the area where most of the colonial powers, the Portuguese, the Dutch and the British, of course, had settled. There are many castles there. It is by visiting one of these castles, going into the dungeons where Africans were enslaved before being shipped across the Atlantic, that I began to become very agitated emotionally. All these elements contributed to the formation of my political ideas, to shaping the person I am today. Besides, at school in Ghana, my favourite subjects had always been art and history. So, when I enrolled at film school in London in the late 1960s, all these things culminated into exploring ideas and politics around African art through film.

In the first year, I shot a documentary on three African artists: one from Nigeria, one from South Africa and the last one from Sudan. At that time, in the African diaspora, the Caribbean community and in general the Black community in London, there was a lot going on to counter racism, police brutality and racial harassment. I was a member of the Black Unity and Freedom Party. As part of these political activities, I decided to take a walk to the British Museum, which was just about a quarter of a mile from the film school. Out of sheer curiosity, I was searching for a subject to make my final graduation film. When I walked into the museum, I went to the Africa section first. It was a huge room, filled with glass vitrines from the ground to the ceiling. I was amazed, because for the first time in my life I realised the amount of material that had been taken away, including exceptional pieces of Asante regalia, glimmering in the glass vitrines (Figure 6.1). I had never seen these things before; some of them were very sacred cultural assets, works of art created by our ancestors that had only been meant for religious veneration in sacred shrines, not for public exhibition. Suddenly it clicked: this is the subject I was looking for! I should make a film about this.

The next issue was: How can I get closer? Which strategy should I use to access these collections? So, I made some inquiries at the information office of the British Museum to find out who the curator or the director of the Africa section was. I was told that it was headed by a man called William Fagg. He was famous. He had written many books on African art. But I wasn't deterred. I wanted to make an appointment to go and see him. You must realise that, in those days, I used to be part of the Black Power movement, so I was always dressed in black, with a black beret and a leather jacket. I would never have gotten an appointment with this dressing style. So, I rented a three-piece suit from the West End of London, a very impressive suit, the ones which come with a pocket watch and a chain. On the day of the appointment, I looked in the mirror and did not recognise myself. I walked to the museum and knocked on Fagg's door. When he opened, he looked quite impressed. He probably thought, 'This must be one of the colonised Africans, the ones we have vetted'. Fagg got up from his desk, welcoming me warmly. From then on, I put on my 'White mask', as Franz Fanon would say.

I wasn't overconfident though. 'What can I do for you?' William Fagg asked. I replied:

> Well, I'm here to congratulate you. It was my first visit to the Africa section of the museum. I saw some fantastic works of art. If there weren't people like you who were so generous to collect and look after them, and who've done incredible efforts to preserve them, they would have vanished in Africa. Nobody would have been able to see this heritage at all.

'Thank you,' he replied. He was very pleased. I added: 'Sir, if you please, I would like to make a film to promote the fantastic job that you are doing here.' Fagg fell for it. He remarked: 'You know, what you saw in the Africa session is only 2 per cent of what we have in our vast collection. The rest is below me. Come with me.'

I followed him to a door which opened to an iron spiral staircase. We descended about 50 feet, down to the basement. When we hit the basement, it was like a time machine. There was an aroma that smelled of aged wood of different sorts. I was no longer in the twentieth century but had zoomed back in history. The storage was a city under London, so vast, with small lanes instead of streets, and hundreds of thousands of boxes and plastic bags lined up on shelves on both sides of these secret vaults. There were also many employees riding electric trolleys, moving collections from here to there. It was unbelievable. Something hit me spiritually. There was an unmistakable energy down there. I felt some kind of euphoric sadness, as if my ancestors were saying: 'Welcome, son. It's good to see you here.'

We went back to his office and discussed the logistics. Fagg told me:

> It's going to cost you some money. You will have to pay a fee to get permission to come and shoot. Are you aware that you will be the first external camera ever to be allowed in these vaults? Besides, you will only be allowed to be on site from 9am to 5pm.

Fifteen Colonial Thefts

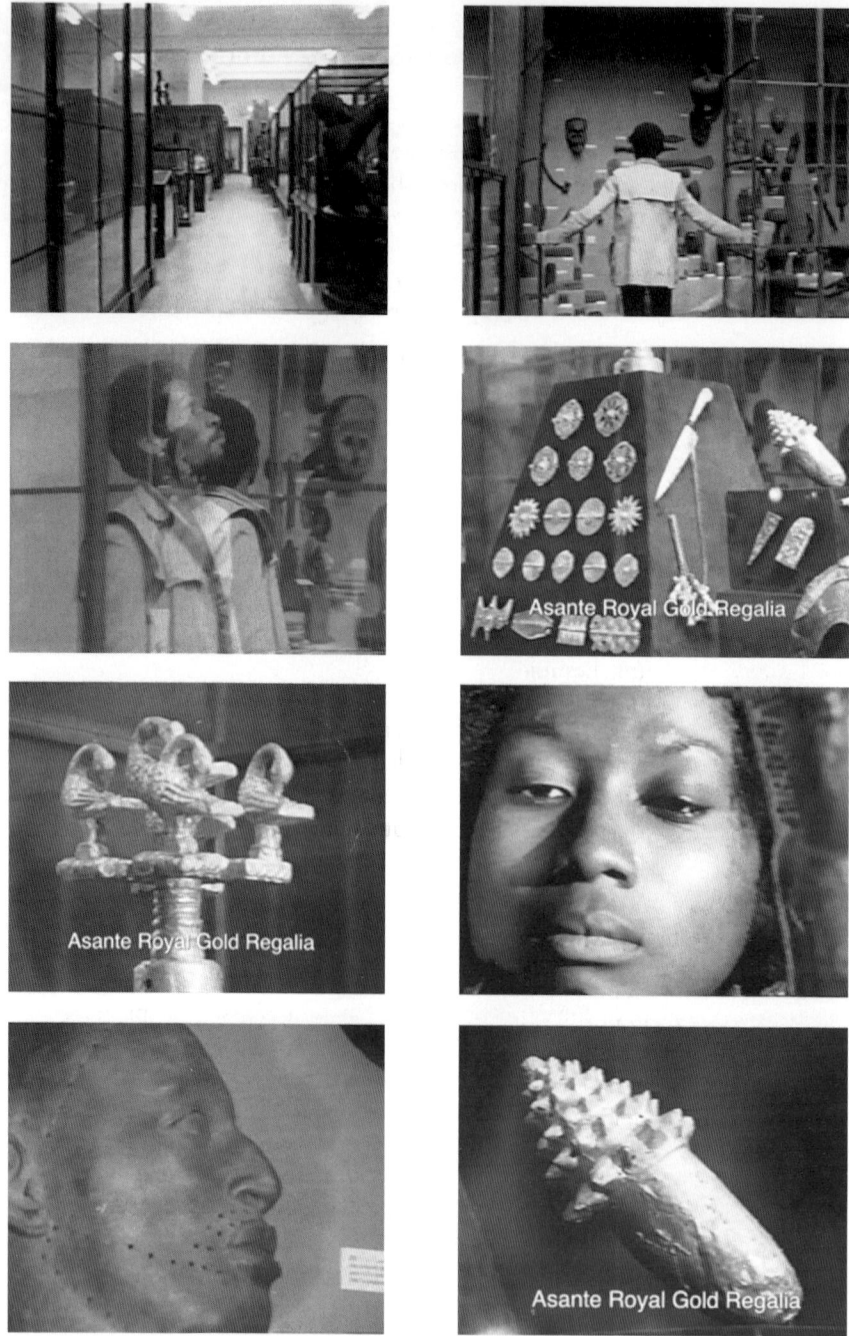

Figure 6.1: Stills of the film *You Hide Me*, showing the display of Asante regalia at the British Museum in 1970.

I was therefore compelled to shoot the film in one day. They were going to charge me £250. In 1970, this was a lot of money. I told him I would be able to raise the money and come back in a month's time. Soon after that, I got a job as a delivery man for a bakery, dashing from one restaurant to the other all over the West End of London. I also told my friends in the Caribbean community about what I had discovered hidden in the secret vaults of the basement of the British Museum. They all mobilised and supported the idea of my film unearthing what was kept hidden there for centuries.

The Message

Thanks to their support and financial contributions, I was able to raise the £250 and re-enter the museum storage. When the museum finally gave me the green light to enter the basement, I thought I should not go alone so I told one of my Ghanaian sisters about this opportunity. Margaret Akua Prah, who studied law in London at the time, was thrilled about the idea and accompanied me. On the day we entered the museum, she was sporting this big Afro. I was wearing a brown khaki trench coat. We had a camera crew of two. All the staff and security officers at the museum were mesmerised. They probably thought: 'How did you get the permission to come down here?' I mean, it was unbelievable!

Fifteen security officers were specially assigned to monitor and watch us, to make sure that we didn't steal any of the things that they had stolen from us. When we finally entered the basement storage, my sister was awestruck by some of the things she saw. We were both emotionally overwhelmed. It was certainly a good decision not to have come alone. On that day, we spent about a quarter of the time carried away, not filming at all but simply opening boxes, rediscovering powerful African cultural assets, admiring the excellent craftsmanship of their makers. It was incredible just to touch these sculptures, carvings, textiles and pieces of jewellery created by our ancestors (Figure 6.2). I had to unravel the fact that I was taking out figures and drums that had not been touched for almost a century. It was so emotional. It would have taken us weeks to explore different sections from the African storage alone. The commentary for my film was born in this basement, and when I came out of the museum storage, I knew precisely what the title and the message was going to be: *You Hide Me*.

After shooting the film, I got the raw negatives processed and printed into rushes ready for editing. The late German filmmaker Schlacke Lamche and his organisation Cinema Action Film Collective were so elated by the quality of the rush prints of the shots in the British Museum's basement that they generously donated the use of their professional 16mm Steenbeck editing suite. After the final cut was done, I approached the director of the Africa Centre in London to seek permission for organising the première screening of *You Hide Me*. This British woman managed the centre as a free

Fifteen Colonial Thefts

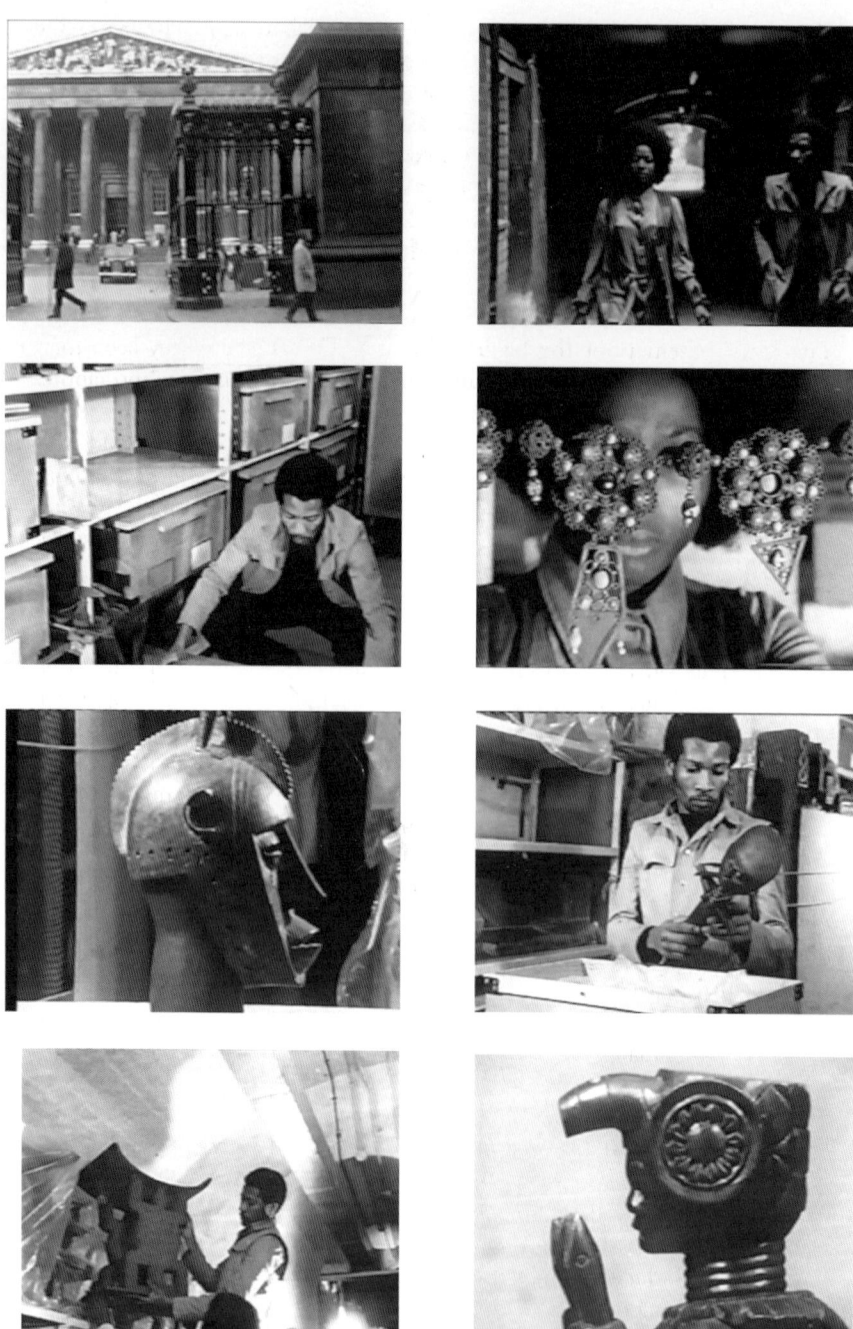

Figure 6.2: Stills from the film *You Hide Me*, showing Nii Kwate Owoo and Margaret Akua Prah in the storage of the British Museum.

venue for the African community to organise cultural and political events. She was very supportive of the idea behind the film and decided not only to host the première but also to publicise it widely across all major academic institutions in the UK, sending out invitation letters to university professors and academics, including to Oxford and Cambridge. I also sent a personal invitation to the British Museum and its staff. They sent four of their representatives. When they arrived at the venue, I offered them front row seats. They politely declined and went all the way to the seats at the back of the auditorium. Yet, I was curious at their reaction, so I watched them closely. The film started and the commentary kicked in:

> This is the basement of the British Museum. This is where they keep their vast collections of African Art, tools, furniture, musical instruments and clothes. We are going to have a look at what they have in their collections. Similar collections can be found in museums in all former colonial powers in Europe and America. The main part of these collections was acquired during the period of colonial rule. The objects were brought back to Europe by officers, tradesmen, missionaries and the colonial specialists called 'ethnographers'. On the whole, the collections represent the looting of a conquering army.

This tone was very radical at the time. After less than a minute, they put on the overcoats they had just taken off and vanished from the hall. Thus, I knew the message had been well received. The screening ended with a standing ovation and people from the audience donating money to finance the process of converting the film into the final married print. This helped me avoid being always compelled to use a special double bond projector, where the sound is played from one reel with the picture on another reel.

The second challenge was to show my film in the UK. I went to several distribution companies, carrying the film under my arm from one office to the next. They didn't want to touch it. I became so depressed, so I decided to take the film to Ghana, to show it to the people of my country. Upon my arrival, I went straight to the Ghana Broadcasting Corporation to inform the managing director at the time that I had just shot a film on African art kept at the British Museum, exposing all the stolen and looted artefacts hidden in their secret vaults. I asked him whether they would be interested in showing it on Ghanaian TV channels. The director of the station lectured me: 'Listen young man, you just can't come here with some rubbish. We have got more important and quality programmes, like Tom Jones and Bonanza' (i.e. the epic cowboy series). I retorted: 'I'm a Ghanaian citizen and have a right to put my work on screen.' He replied: 'Okay, then organise a preview of your film and I will send one of my representatives to come and vet it.' Luckily, the German Friedrich Ebert Foundation office in Accra agreed to lend their premises for this screening. I invited Ghanaians I knew from the film and television industry to come to the event. After they saw the film, they gave me a standing ovation. The rep from Ghana TV walked out without a word or comment. The following day, there was a long editorial promoting and supporting the film in the *Daily Graphic*, a national daily newspaper. I took a copy of the editorial and went once again to the director of Ghana Broadcast Corporation's office, but he was undeterred. He reprimanded me again: 'If I were you, I would be careful. You can't come here and destroy the good and cordial relationship between the Ghanaian government and British authorities. You are a troublemaker, so you better not start some foolishness here.'

When I got back to London, I realised that the *West Africa Magazine* had published a review of the film. This review reported that *You Hide Me* had been banned in Ghana. That made the film very popular. People were writing to me about this punitive ban by Ghana TV, wanting to know more about the controversy. The director of the Nigerian National Museum in Lagos, Dr Ekpo Eyo, expressed a keen interest in the film. In fact, he ordered and paid for the first copy I ever made. I was really delighted that at least one African country had placed an order for the film.

As none of the British distributors were interested, I decided to try my luck in the USA. An African-American organisation called the Philadelphia Filmmakers Workshop planned a series of lectures and screenings for me. I was constantly moving from one state to the next, going to high schools and colleges all over the East Coast. Everywhere I went, the response confirmed that my film was addressing something taboo, a topic some institutions were trying to suppress. When I came back to Ghana, I visited the University of Ghana at Legon in Accra and after some enquiries, the famous playwright Professor Efua Sutherland, who had read the article on my film in the *West Africa Magazine*, introduced me to the director of the Institute of African Studies, the late Professor Emeritus Kwabena Nketia. After I arranged a private screening of the film for him, he became emotionally charged and excited, and immediately offered me a position at the Institute as a research fellow with the responsibility of setting up a film department. It was an amazing experience. I got a job right there, on the spot! Subsequently, I developed a Media Research Unit with a mandate to explore how research materials produced by the fellows of the institute could be transformed into educational documentary series. At this point, I was compelled to put *You Hide Me* on the shelf because I had to deal with other projects. I even almost forgot about it. I had moved on to something new and exciting.

The Surreal Afterlife of *You Hide Me*

In 2020, more than two decades after my official retirement from the institute, I got a call from my eldest son Kweku Nii Owoo who lives in the USA. This was shortly after George Floyd was killed by US policeman Derek Chauvin. He said: 'Hey, Pop, there is a festival in Philadelphia, the BlackStar Film Festival, and somebody who saw

You Hide Me back in the seventies said that I should convince you to send the film for screening at this festival.' My response was: 'It's more than half a century old, so it cannot compete at any festival. It could only be shown in the information category.' Still, Kweku convinced me, so I uploaded a digital version of the film and sent it to him. One week later, he called me again, yelling at the top of his voice:

> Hey Pop, guess what! The audience gave you a standing ovation and now the directors of the Paris Short Film Festival, who were part of the audience in Philadelphia, have made a strong request for the film! They want to make it into their competition for a prize in the category Best Short Documentary!

When I shot and developed the film in 1970, I was driven by an incredible passion, because something was burning inside me, but then, everything had gone quiet. Now, suddenly the film was living a second life. One thing leading to another, *You Hide Me* was awarded the prize of Best Short Documentary at the September 2020 Paris Short Film Festival. What a shock! I didn't know whether to laugh or cry, with my son in a protracted jubilation mood. I couldn't believe it. From then on, the film went viral. I was getting phone calls from Europe, from Japan. Suddenly, *You Hide Me* was taking a walk, together with many global voices calling loudly for the restitution of looted African cultural heritage. The whole thing was becoming quite a bit surreal to me.

Apart from Ghana (and potentially Nigeria), *You Hide Me* has in fact never been broadcast publicly anywhere in Africa. This is a journey that needs to take place. Now that it is receiving attention, even spawning international debates and political reforms, my dream is to translate it and make it available in African languages, in other words, to decolonise *You Hide Me*, free it from the English language. It should begin with my country, making a version in my mother tongue, Ga, but also in Akan Twi, Hausa or Ewe and showing it on local Ghanaian television stations so that people can hold debates about this issue in their indigenous languages. I will then follow up with versions in Swahili, Yoruba, Igbo, isiZulu, isiXhosa… This is my vision for the future.

In 2022, I met with some officials at the Ghanaian Ministry of Creative Arts and Culture and showed them the film. With other researchers and officials, we then discussed the issue of restitution, and the ministry subsequently played an active role in a government decision to set up a Focal Group in charge of this matter. It was the first time the Ghanaian government officially entered campaigns for restitution, confronting British authorities and trying to convince them to return looted African heritage. Unfortunately, things have been moving very slowly. Nations in the Global North do not really understand that they hold the key to the essence and meaning of the restitution debate. It is about them coming to terms with the fact that they oppressed African societies and looted their political, cultural and spiritual symbols. They didn't pay for these cultural assets, nor were they given as gifts. Europeans desecrated graves and sanctuaries. They looted and burnt down palaces, like the one of the Asantehene in 1874. Colonialists even often forced Africans to carry these treasures on their backs for hundreds of miles, from the hinterland to the ships waiting on the Atlantic coast. Europe needs to be serious and undertake sincere self-reflection. And European institutions should remind themselves that action speaks louder than words.

The (Disappointing) Era of Restitution

In January 2024, the British Museum and the Victoria and Albert Museum (V&A) announced they had agreed to loan, respectively, fifteen and seventeen Asante cultural assets to the Manhyia Palace for three years. Among them, '13 pieces of Asante Royal regalia acquired by the [V&A] at an auction … of gold looted by the British army during the raid on and destruction of the royal palace on 4th–6th February' 1874, as well as looted 'regalia of respective Asantehenes, Kofi Karikari (c.1837–1884) and Prempeh I (1870–1931)' in the collection of the British Museum.[195] This was the result of months of negotiations with representatives of the Asantehene who felt that, 150 years after the infamous Sagrenti War of 1874, something symbolic must happen. This is, at least, a start.

Nevertheless, as a proud African, well aware of the invaluable contributions of our ancestors in areas like the arts, engineering, agriculture and medicine, this loan is quite disappointing. Restitution must prick the conscience of humanity, so that people realise when the right thing must be done. No school of thought should seek to justify that stolen goods can be loaned back to their original owners or custodians. I use the word 'custodian' in this context because these rare historical assets also belong to future generations, regardless of how 'special' we think our generation is. Restitution touches upon many disciplines, like history, the arts, cultural heritage, but also geopolitics and law. Even before shooting *You Hide Me*, I was aware of the global political relevance of restitution claims. I think British citizens must hold their government accountable for having set up laws that are so draconian, to say the least, and for not engaging to reform them. As Kwame Opoku wrote, 'The British have had enough time since the petition *The Call for the Return of the Asante Regalia* in 1974, and could have worked at a new legislation.'[196] It is utterly shocking that the government and institutions like the British Museum can still give the pretext that legislation of theirs makes restitution of stolen goods illegal, and that loans seem to be the only alternative.[197]

Besides, two golden trophy heads of King Kofi Karikari, looted in 1874, then described by none other than William Fagg as 'the largest gold work known from Ashanti or indeed from anywhere in Africa outside Egypt', are not part of this deal.[198] They are today exhibited at the Wallace Collection and at Windsor Castle, the second one being part of the Royal Collections Trust. It seems that double standards apply between Asante cultural assets that were not so prominently exhibited or kept in storage, and exceptional pieces that gleam in permanent exhibitions related to the British Crown or aristocracy. Again, this is disappointing. While it is good news that a few regalia are being returned, this should certainly fuel debates on the appropriateness of terms set by former colonial powers in these negotiations.

Even if restitutions take place, a lot remains to be done. In this context, filmmakers have a unique opportunity to use their skills to engage the public visually and with sound, and spark interest for this issue across generations, as the latest film by Mati Diop on the return of the treasures of Dahomey has shown. Not only can we recreate historic events, but we can develop parallel universes for the public to engage in political issues. As an African, it is my prerogative to tell stories that have been silenced because of their sensitivity. One should not shy away from the truth just because it is a shortcut. Africa was plundered and looted for centuries, and we cannot expect people who benefited from colonialism to tell our story as it should be told. I hope that the initiative I took to as twenty-six-year-old man, making this rare film that today stands as a witness of a dark period in the history of decolonial justice, can inspire African filmmakers, artists and, in general, citizens of the world to break taboos and express their radical ideas through their medium of preference.

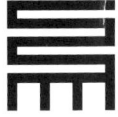

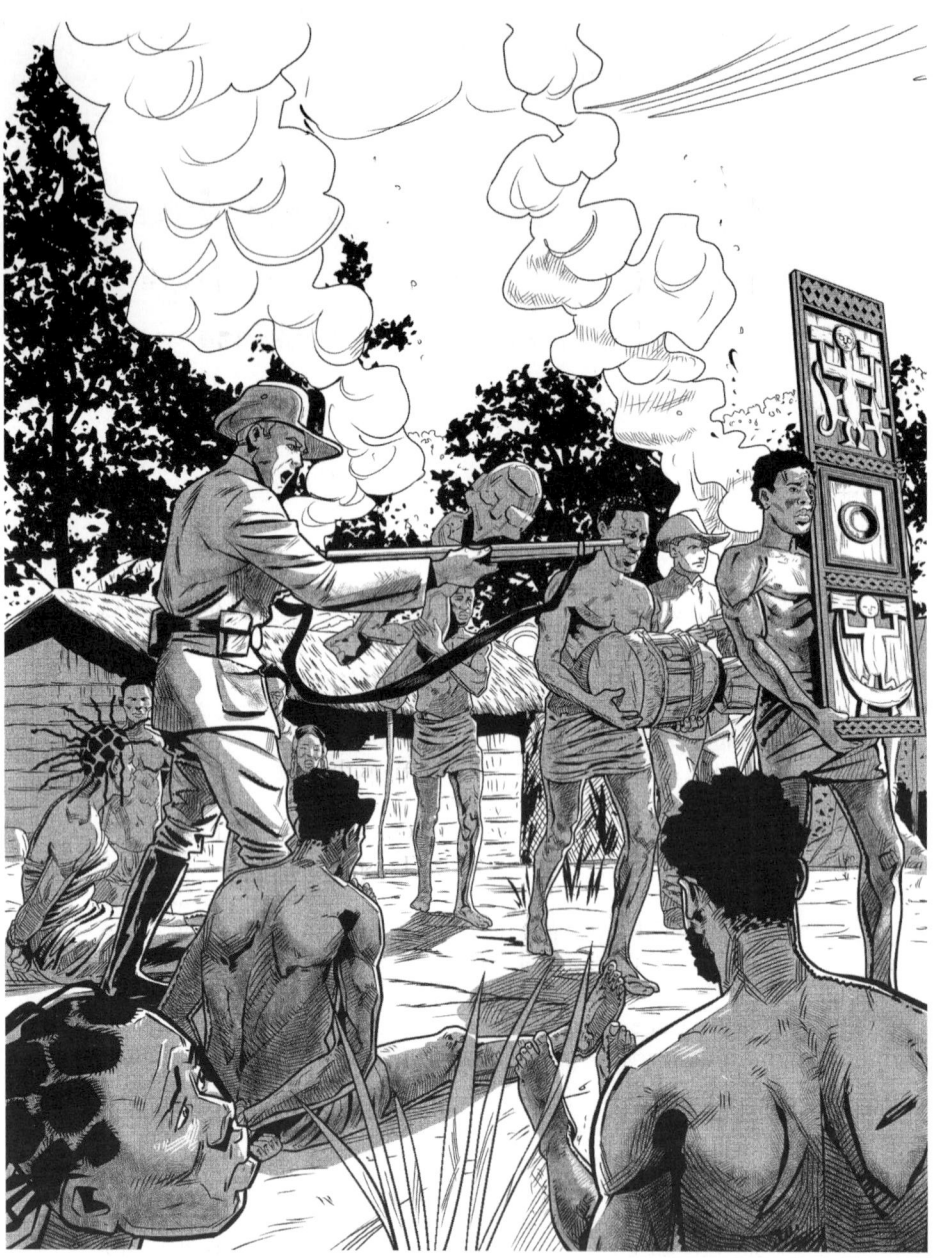

Artist: Franky Mindja

CHAPTER 7

A Plaque from an Ngolo *Etana*
The Looting of Architectural Heritage as a Token of Colonial Violence

Richard Tsogang Fossi and Jeanne-Ange Wagne

Since the German attack against the Duala king Kum´a M'Bape Bele (alias Lock Priso) in Bonabéri in 1884, and up until the First World War, the various communities and different kingdoms in the central African region today subsumed under the Republic of Cameroon witnessed almost uninterruptedly the terror of German's colonial regime. Subjugation, occupation and exploitation were the leading leitmotifs behind the numerous battles, combats and strike campaigns that German colonial troops (so-called 'protection forces') initiated against local communities and their leaders. Detailed military reports provide enough information about the large number of casualties and plundering of the attacked local communities. These archives repeatedly mention the intentional burning of peoples' villages, but such sentences were often censored by the apparatus of colonial propaganda. Together with the large-scale destruction of infrastructure and the confiscation of livestock came the looting not only of artefacts but also of fragments of architectural buildings that were vital for local societies and their inhabitants. As Robert Bevan fittingly observed in his book on the concomitant destruction of architecture in wars, 'the link between erasing any physical reminder of a people and its collective memory and the killing of the people themselves is ineluctable'.[199] A public report on the Ngolo expedition of 1901, written and published by Lieutenant Paul Franz Adolf Lessner, illustrates this sweeping destruction and the pillaging of cultural heritage, in particular local architectural elements, some of which are found today in the collection of the Linden Museum in Stuttgart, Germany.[200]

The Ngolo are part of the larger ethnic group known as the Oroko. They spread around thirty-five villages found in the Meme and Ndian Divisions, of which Ikoy, stronghold of former king Nakeli Nw'embeli, has been the political hub of the community.[201] Like many other Cameroonian communities, the Ngolo and their paramount chief Nakeli experienced the violence of German colonial conquest and occupation, with three military expeditions led against them by the commander of the so-called 'protection forces' Oltwig von Kamptz, the colonial chancellor Theodor Seitz, and several other officers, including Paul Lessner.[202]

Nakeli Nw'embeli, who opposed German intrusion until his capture and execution in 1901, can be considered today as an outstanding figure of anti-colonial resistance. Yet, his story remains largely unknown, both in Germany and Cameroon. Despite Lessner's reports, a few oral recollections, and two articles by African studies scholar Doreen Mekunda and historian Joseph B. Ebune, neither Nakeli's heroic confrontation with the colonial intruders, nor the destruction and plundering of Ngolo heritage and architecture have been the subject of critical analyses.[203] In this chapter, we recall what was termed *Bila ba Nakeli* (Nakeli's war) and examine the political meaning of the translocation of Ngolo architectural heritage, including the dismantling and looting of Ngolo houses of assembly (*etana*) and the involvement of anthropologists and museums in this colonial aggression.

Bila ba Nakeli (Nakeli's War)

In 1896, colonialists reported that the Ngolo had attacked a caravan loaded with rubber and ivory extracted by the Swedish firm Knutson, Waldau & Heilborn. Around 160 non-European carriers were allegedly killed and eaten by the assailants, presumably led by King Nakeli.[204] In addition, the Germans accused the 'ever insubordinate' Nakeli of blocking the path of a platoon of colonial officers and soldiers on their way to the station Johann-Albrechts-Höhe (today's town of Kumba). Allegations of cannibalism and rudeness towards colonial agents, of potential danger for Europeans, and of obstructing trade routes were frequently used by the colonial regime to justify the swift dispatch of military expeditions against local populations. This was the case for the subjugation of Neyon (1898), Simeko'o alias Angoula (1902), Fontem Asunganyi (1900–1901), the Maka and the Omvang (1910), among many others in German Cameroon.[205] Cannibalism in particular was a powerful gear in the well-oiled machine of colonial rhetoric, a pretext for teaching a civilising lesson in retaliation against a deed that only the blood of those who allegedly perpetuated it could atone for.

Oltwig von Kamptz commanded the first military campaign against the Ngolo in March–April 1897. Although the governor, Jesko von Puttkamer, was satisfied with the results, he admitted the shortcomings of the expedition when he wrote that 'a lot of blood would have to be shed before this part of the protectorate came to a definitive rest'.[206] The first campaign was in fact unable to dispute Nakeli's standing among the various Oroko communities and the impact of his shrewd politics in the region.

The second expedition, led by Theodor Seitz and Lieutenant Albrecht von

Arnim, was dispatched in 1898 and locked the whole region down, from the Rey Estuary to Kumba. It was once again driven by a rhetoric of punishment and strove to subjugate the Ngolo people once and for all. Due to the resilience of Nakeli and his followers and a lack of available troops – from March to September, the Germans led a whopping seven other military expeditions in the colony – this second campaign again failed in breaking Nakeli's power. These two ventures even had the contrary effect: his reputation and authority over neighbouring chiefs and their communities had increased.

Despite these failures, the officers did not come back empty-handed. Kamptz shipped around fifty Ngolo cultural assets to the ethnological museum in Berlin in July 1897.[207] These consisted mainly of anthropomorphic and zoomorphic sculptures, masks, bells, spears, gunpowder and iron bars. Parallel to that, he brought in 'a large quantity of plundered livestock', which the governor 'welcomed as a boon for our stocks of meat'.[208] These expeditions were also an opportunity for colonial agents to confiscate sacred artefacts and ancestral heirlooms. During the second expedition, Seitz arrested the Ekombe chief of the Bakundu-ba-Kake region for refusing to hand over his religious and sacred property.[209] At all levels of the colonial system, booty was in fact eagerly awaited. Even the Berlin museum's assistant director, Felix von Luschan, was in good spirits when he heard that a second expedition was in preparation. In a letter to a colleague, he disclosed the high hopes he had in one of his former protégés:

> [O]ne of my students, Lieutenant von Arnim, will join a renewed and large punitive expedition against the Ngolo in October (top secret!!). We can expect brilliant things. Mr. v. Arnim has been well informed on what we need ... The costs will likely be zero.[210]

This quote gives explicit insight into the active participation of museums in colonial plunder by showing how their staff encouraged and planned the looting of colonised people's heritage.

The last expedition, which stands in our focus, was the largest of the three and brought about even greater numbers of looted cultural assets, most of which are now in the collection of the Linden Museum in Stuttgart. In February 1901, after years of resistance to colonial occupation, three officers – Captain Franz Guse, Lieutenants Heinrich Umber and Paul Lessner – five non-commissioned officers, the military doctor Maxmilian Zupitza, 134 soldiers and 154 porters were dispatched to Ngolo country for a third campaign destined to bring Nakeli's defiance to an end. The operation was split into two columns, with Guse leading the eastern one via Kenge-Lobe, and Lessner the western one via Mufako-Kuma from Kirrekirre. The two columns re-united at the end of the month.[211] The discrepancies between Lessner's various reports and writings indicate that these (colonial) documents should always be read with caution, cross-referenced, and evaluated critically.

In Lessner's reports, the reason for the invasion and the submission of Oroko communities is clear: just like in other forest regions, the Germans had since 1885 coveted the abundant natural resources in Oroko land, especially gum. The German colonialist Eugen Zintgraff had also earlier remarked that the flow of trade in Nigeria justified the exploitation of the area for German trade, praising the colonial entrepreneurial spirit of the Swedes Knutson, Waldau and Heilborn. Because of a high population density, the Germans considered Oroko territory as a potential source of labour for colonial plantations, but also for tax and customs income in favour of the colony. It was in fact in this part of the territory that the concessionary company Gesellschaft Nordwest-Kamerun was established in 1899. With an economically operating German minority – about 550 in 1905, 1,000 in 1908 – oppressing a local majority of more than 2 million inhabitants according to a census of the colony in 1908, the brutish subjugation of local populations and the execution of their leaders during so-called 'punitive' expeditions set the course for a widespread exploitation of forced labour that, in the eyes of German colonialists, would solve the emerging workforce issue.[212] Under the guise of so-called 'peace negotiations' – which included the confiscation of land for colonial plantations, the supply of elephant tusks, sacred and royal symbols, crops, and grain – the colonial regime imposed humiliating conditions of servitude, dependence and extortion. In one instance, Lessner summoned the leaders of the Batanga communities and, under the threat of punitive violence, stripped them of their authority over political matters by ordering them to break bonds with Nakeli and the Ngolo.[213]

The humiliation of defeated leaders took many forms, ranging from having them lying down in front of the colonial officer, to chaining them up, floggings, deportation, forced exile or sentencing them to death. The Ngolo also witnessed such humiliating acts when some of their leaders surrendered to Lessner: the local rulers were forced to rub oneself with sand, ashes or whitewash as a sign of submission, to take off their clothes in front of their peers and lie flat on the ground.[214] By the way, this was the position that the colonialists affectioned when they whipped those who defied them. The fate of local women and children in colonial wars should also not remain unmentioned. The oppressors captured them to exert pressure on the rest of the community, and renowned German colonial administrators and officers, such as Eugen Zintgraff or Hans Dominik, admitted motivating their troops by telling them they would be able to rape local women with impunity.[215]

To refuse the passive role that such accounts of physical violence tend to impose on colonised peoples, it is essential to highlight their agency against colonial oppression and the multiple acts of solidarity that took place between the different groups. Generally, Africans did not simply accept the imposing of rules by European invaders. On the contrary, even though the wars may have been marked by asymmetrical weaponry, anti-colonial struggles were well-organised and undermined the might of imperial troops with direct or surprise attacks, something Joseph Ebune has termed 'primary resistance'.²¹⁶ Instead of complying with Lessner's demand for the surrender of Nakeli, the Oroko – and specifically the Ngolo – took advantage of their known surroundings and laid all kinds of mantraps on the marching paths of the troops, firing at them from various hiding places unbeknown to the invaders. They also weakened colonial soldiers by burning down their food source, namely, local farms that the colonialists seized and used as food storage.²¹⁷

According to Doreen Mekunda's work on Oroko societies and traditional shrines, the history of Oroko people 'has no substantial traces of tribal wars'. She describes these societies as 'hospitable' and their communal life before the colonial era as revolving primarily around agriculture.²¹⁸ Abiding by the maxim 'divide and rule', the colonialists obviously sought to tear down this peaceful social fabric between clans. Still, acts of solidarity in the face of colonial aggression occurred, which are one more instance of primary resistance. The Batangas offered sanctuary to the Ngolos and hid them from the German troops.²¹⁹ Even Nakeli, who had been oscillating between fighting and fleeing since the expeditions began in 1897, could rely on both his own hideouts as well as shelter offered from neighbouring communities who even provided him and his followers with food.²²⁰ The colonialists in fact offered a bounty of 500 Reichsmarks for his head, as they believed that the Ngolo could only be pacified once Nakeli had been 'taken care of' (literally 'rendered harmless'). Nakeli, 'an elderly, stately man, close to 50, with greyish hair, and energetic features',²²¹ was considered the wealthiest of the Oroko chiefs and correspondingly enjoyed the highest political position in the region.²²² Some of the communities audaciously refused to cooperate with the German *Schutztruppe* in their tracking down Nakeli. Others cleverly acted as spies and simulated cooperation.²²³ The Itoki, who are part of Bakundu societies, paid a heavy price for siding with Nakeli and supposedly affording him protection by way of a hide-out. When word circulated about Nakeli's apparent whereabouts, Lessner and his entourage entered Itoki and set fire to the *etana* – the political and spiritual centre of Oroko villages – where Lessner believed that the Itoki had hidden Nakeli. 500 Itoki men barricaded inside and forcibly prevented from escaping by German soldiers were reported to have died in agony in this massacre.²²⁴

Such monstrous acts of retaliation often aimed at discouraging local rulers from supporting Nakeli: the Bakundu chief, Dibuma, was compelled to change sides and help the colonialists in their chase against this so-called 'rebel', assisting Lessner in clearing an Ngolo hideout between Jumbo and Likume.²²⁵ A few weeks later, on 27 September 1901, Lessner summoned twenty-seven local chiefs to a gathering and forced them to renounce their alliance with Nakeli and to help handing him over to the colonial troops if occasion presented itself.²²⁶ The subjugation of the various Oroko chiefs to this terror regime was a watershed in the Ngolo anti-colonial struggle that ultimately led to Nakeli's defeat.

One of his sons, Mbire, and five accomplices contrived a plan to capture him.

Cornered, Nakeli still managed to kill four of them as he tried to escape. Despite years of 'fierce resistance', during which more than half of the colonial troops were wounded, he was finally overpowered and brought by a hundred or so of his compatriots to the colonial station in Rio-del-Rey and later to Douala.[227] The colonial administration sentenced him to death by hanging in his headquarters at Ikoy, 150 miles away from Douala. Lessner, who was accompanied by only thirty soldiers and a White non-commissioned officer, was appointed to carry out the sentence. In a last gesture of resistance, Nakeli refused to walk from the encampment to the gallows and Lessner ordered his men to carry him. The intent behind this cruel decision to hang Nakeli at his birthplace and own headquarters goes alongside the colonial strategy to confront resisting communities with their powerlessness and prevent further resistance. On 31 December 1901, Lessner hanged Nakeli in front of the Ngolo community. The officer presents the public execution as an act of triumph, but also hints at Nakeli's imperturbability, a steadfast man who 'died … without fear and without forgiveness'.[228] The only source that gives us insight into Nakeli's attitude at his execution is the colonialist's report. Despite the problematic nature of this document, Lessner acknowledges Nakeli's uncompromising resistance:

> [H]e declared it was a good thing that he was being executed now, for he would have never kept peace with the white man; … With a firm step he climbed the ladder that led to the gallows and put his head in the noose himself. This chief died like a hero.[229]

Lessner's words describing Nakeli as a hero are rare in the colonial situation. For military officers, local leaders and their people had no choice but to become 'friends' with the coloniser. A 'friendly' local, in the colonial view, was not an equal being, but, as Lessner himself wrote, an 'obedient vassal of the Kaiser'; this was the only condition for being granted life. An enemy of the colonial regime was therefore an 'enemy of civilisation' and needed to be annihilated.

Destruction and Loot of Architecture in the German Conquest of Cameroon

Alongside humiliation, executions, oppression and war, colonial conquest and the so-called 'civilising mission' included the looting of cultural assets and architectural elements. The colonial system was a very efficient system of extraction, and the confiscation of economic and cultural wealth generally considered as 'compensation for the war'.[230] Lessner engaged heavily in the violent practice of looting and collecting;

by 1902, he had assembled a huge number of noteworthy artefacts which he took with him on his return to Germany and sent to the Linden Museum in Stuttgart shortly after. With Lessner's 'collection' at the Linden Museum, we get to witness what Robert Bevan described as 'cultural cleansing with architecture and artefacts as its mediums'.[231] This 'cleansing', committed by officials of the German 'protection forces', European merchants, missionaries and scientists, was supported by cultural and political institutions in the German metropole, namely, museums and the Foreign Office.

In the nineteenth century and with the advancement of colonisation, the argument was raised that by collecting cultural artefacts, Europeans would save them from demise and from their doomed societies of origin. This claim was the basis for the establishment of ethnology as a discipline. Collecting and preservation were declared to be the guiding principles of the emerging ethnological museums and their respective collections.[232] The oppressive, violent and destructive colonial forces, with their so-called 'punitive expeditions', which swept through communities with death, suffering and devastation, elevated their frantic looting and collection of war booty to a humanistic-scientific act of pre-emptive care by way of this pretence. In what Rebekka Habermas has called a 'collecting fury', German museums received or purchased about 39,000 belongings from the colony 'Kamerun' from 1884 to 1919.[233] This enormous amount does not even include those that had been looted during those years but landed in museum collections after Germany had lost its colonies to Britain, France and Belgium after the Versailles Treaty.[234] During colonial times, military campaigns were often seen as the best way for museums to lay their hands on local art and architecture. When offering cultural assets from German Cameroon for sale to museums, one of the most prolific German art dealers during colonial times, the family business J.F.G. Umlauff, admitted that 'only in times of war or in the case of great expeditions [were] conditions more favourable' for the acquisition of African belongings.[235] Paul Lessner also praised his soldiers for their particular flair for looting, observing that they could uncover every cultural asset that the local population had hidden from them.[236] This relentless search for valuables was partly driven by a superiority complex manifest in trophy-hunting, partly by greed, for they usually served as an additional source of income, and partly by pride in glory and prestige. Upon his return to Germany, Lessner was awarded a war medal by Kaiser Wilhelm II in 1902 and received requests to hold lectures for economic, scientific and political elites.[237] Besides, many of his acolytes in Cameroon were awarded distinctions for their massive contribution to anthropological science and their efforts to satiate the gluttony of museums.

What about the specific looting of Ngolo architecture and cultural assets? All German members of the 1901 expedition sent Ngolo belongings to various museums in the European metropole.[238] In August, Captain Friedrich Wilhelm Langheld shipped 'a beautifully carved door' and a number of belongings from the town of Ikoy to the Berlin Ethnological Museum, including two drums and 'three staffs of Ngolo-chiefs'.[239]

The current museum database does not mention this door, which means that it was probably lost or destroyed in the meantime. Other architectural elements of Ngolo buildings can be found at the Linden Museum in the southern German city of Stuttgart. This museum, which holds the biggest collection of Cameroonian cultural heritage in the world (8,871 database entries), houses Lessner's 1901 collection, a shipment that originally contained more than a hundred Ngolo belongings. Only half of them are still in storage today.[240] Among them are three carved architectural wall plates and other artefacts taken from what Lessner described as a 'house for palaver'. After examination of the plates, cross-referencing with literature on Okoro cultures and architecture, we argue that, before Lessner took them away, the plates had been part of a sacred and political sanctuary known in Ngolo country as an *etana*.[241]

The *etana* is to be understood as an institution, a place of assembly that regulates society and embodies its collective identity. It is a political centre within Oroko communities, analogous to a House of Parliament or a Court of Justice in Western societies. At the time, only initiated men were allowed to enter an *etana*. There, all sorts of legal questions were debated, and important decisions were passed to assure peaceful social coexistence.[242] In other regions of the Grasslands, these places are known as *pah'ghoue*, *pah'tsueh* or *pah'keup*. These are places where calm and concentration are needed to commune with the ancestors, where initiates meet to discuss very specific matters relating to the spiritual life of the family or community. It is not a place for quarrelling, as the misleading and erroneous expressions 'palaver house' or 'juju house' suggest, but rather a place where people seek solutions or protection in difficult times. Through the magic of words, libations and offerings, the eldest member of the family, the *ngwala* or the priest of the kingdom, or the *fo* ('king' or 'chief') himself, utters words and performs rites to invoke the ancestors.[243] In the forest area, these shrines were usually placed at the middle of the village or the main entrance, as means of protecting the community or families against all evil.[244] The façade decorations of the sacred architectural structures in the forest regions of the north-west and south-west, such as the lands of Ngolo, Bakundu, Balong and Bafo, are of elaborate nature. Carved frames, doorposts or pillars usually made of special woods such as ebony, padouk, bibinga, etc. are not only viewed as cultural symbols of political authority, but also as sacred entities to which supernatural powers are attributed. In addition, they can be placed both indoors and outdoors of the sacred houses. They featured a rich variety of accessories and motifs, which were far from innocent given the powers attributed to certain carved animals.[245]

In his public report, Lessner devoted an entire section to the 'house of palaver' and its cultural and political significance. He discussed the wall panels, idols and carvings, showing off photographs and comparing them to Western concepts of art and architecture, such as 'relief' and 'wall panelling', thereby ascribing them aesthetic value. To his eye, the architectural structure of the *etana* was 'characterised by a more careful style of construction'; he admitted that the architectural elements belonging to it were not merely the material products of a vanishing 'primitive' people, but rather representative constituents of meaningful buildings and valuable cultural assets. This allows us to highlight another dimension of colonial violence: the targeted destruction and dismantling of representative architecture of subjugated societies, as well as the appropriation and transfer of central architectural fragments to one's own homeland, illustrates a strategic form of attack that destabilised those societies or nations in the context of war and, sometimes, went as far as to erase entire cultural histories through alleged scientific discourse.

It is regrettable that contemporary research on the relationship between war and the destruction of architecture rarely discusses colonial contexts, let alone the presence of looted architecture in colonial collections in museums. For the targeted attack on architecture in the course of German colonial warfare was, at the latest after 1901, not a rare phenomenon, and a context in which museums were inextricably involved. Local architecture was important to museums, partly because it enabled them to set up what they viewed as authentic setting for dioramas and their 'exhibitionary complex'.[246] Examples include industrial installations such as smelting furnaces and sculpted architectural pieces from sanctuaries and royal palaces.[247] Museum directors frequently and explicitly encouraged various officers to supply them directly with such valuable and culturally significant architectural fragments, sometimes even to take the whole structure apart and relocate it entirely in the cold halls of their institutions. In 1902, the assistant director of the ethnographic museum in Berlin, Felix von Luschan, wrote to Captain Bernhard von Besser, urging him, in the event of a 'punitive expedition', to first remove the impressive architecture of the palace of the Bangwa *fon* Fontem Assunganyi before potentially burning down the rest of the palace.[248] In 1905, the head of the colonial station in Bamenda, Hans Glauning, led a large and violent expedition into the southern zone of the station, during which he burnt the houses of the chiefs at Baham and Bamenom (today Bamena) and looted numerous *mbom die* and *ntok*, carved pillars that are now on display at the Humboldt Forum in Berlin.[249]

The dismantling of an *etana* in the course of the Ngolo expedition is also exemplary of the loss of significant historical heritage for the Oroko people. What remains of the damaged buildings are fragments and artefacts locked away in the depots of the Linden Museum, subject to foreign attributions. Through musealisation, these fragments were transformed into symbols of colonial domination, even though the museum's director Graf von Linden particularly lauded the carvings on the wooden plates for the elevated cultural status he believed they possessed, compared to other artefacts from the same collection.[250]

The correspondence file between Lessner and von Linden, indicates that Lessner sent seven boxes and five packages of ethnographic material from the Ngolo to the Museum für Völkerkunde in Stuttgart, after he had spent 'eight months [in the Rumpi Mountains] warring as the leader of a military expedition'.[251] In an explanatory list,

Lessner directly links some of the items to Nakeli or the *etana*: first, three 'idols from the palaver houses of Lifunga (Batanga), Ndoi I (Ngolo) and Kuwa (Ngolo)', three villages that his troops definitely attacked. Then, the list mentions '3 staffs of chief Nakelli from Ikoi, the one who was hanged on 31.12.01'. It is important to note that such precise description of the former owner and his dreadful fate is extremely rare in museum archives. Lessner thereby unambiguously stamps the staffs as war booty confiscated from the Ngolo king. The archival folder also informs on three 'drums from the palaver houses of Kuma and Bevoka, where the fleeing population left them behind'. This description is evidence of the Germans' rapid and violent invasion of people's villages; it also confirms the infringement of political and sacred spaces of Ngolo society. The colonial troops did not only rummage about in the *etanas*, but they also tore the buildings to pieces and returned to Germany with ornamented panels, one from the 'palaver house in Lakundu bei Lagua', which the troops had set ablaze, and two 'idols that formed a mural panel from the palaver house in Mbueme(?)'. This list of spoils contained in the archival folder about Lessner provides us with the indisputable proof of the violent provenance of these looted artefacts and architectural elements.

Our contribution has shown how military conquest went hand in hand with the looting of artefacts and architecture that belonged to African communities. Although fantasised as a means of saving so-called 'primitive art' threatened with extinction because of imminent contact with the so-called 'civilised world', the appetite of museums for African cultural assets and sacred belongings, combined with the violence perpetuated in the colonies, in fact precipitated the loss of priceless heritage through its appropriation and translocation to the metropole. Local architecture also suffered, as the colonialists burnt down the palaces of heroes of anti-colonial resistance, or systematically looted and dismantled them, taking away sculpted floor tiles, low-reliefs, doors, doorframes and wall panels. Because of their motifs and the wood used, these elements highly coveted by museums weren't – and still aren't – trivial. They are 'powerful cultural representations'[252] and, in the forest zone and the Grasslands, part of royal and sacred art. They were found only in the chieftaincies or on the houses of important notables. The removal of these elements and sacred entities was therefore an attempt to render local leaders physically, psychologically and spiritually powerless. What colonialists perpetuated, in particular Lessner – who in the 1930s became later a fervent supporter of the Nazis' expansionist and revisionist plan to recover German colonies – was pure and simple desecration and dislocation of a meaningful cultural and political system. Today, it is essential to oppose this enduring state of disempowerment, for instance, by remembering the long-standing resistance of many African leaders like Nakeli Nw'embeli.

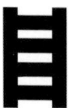

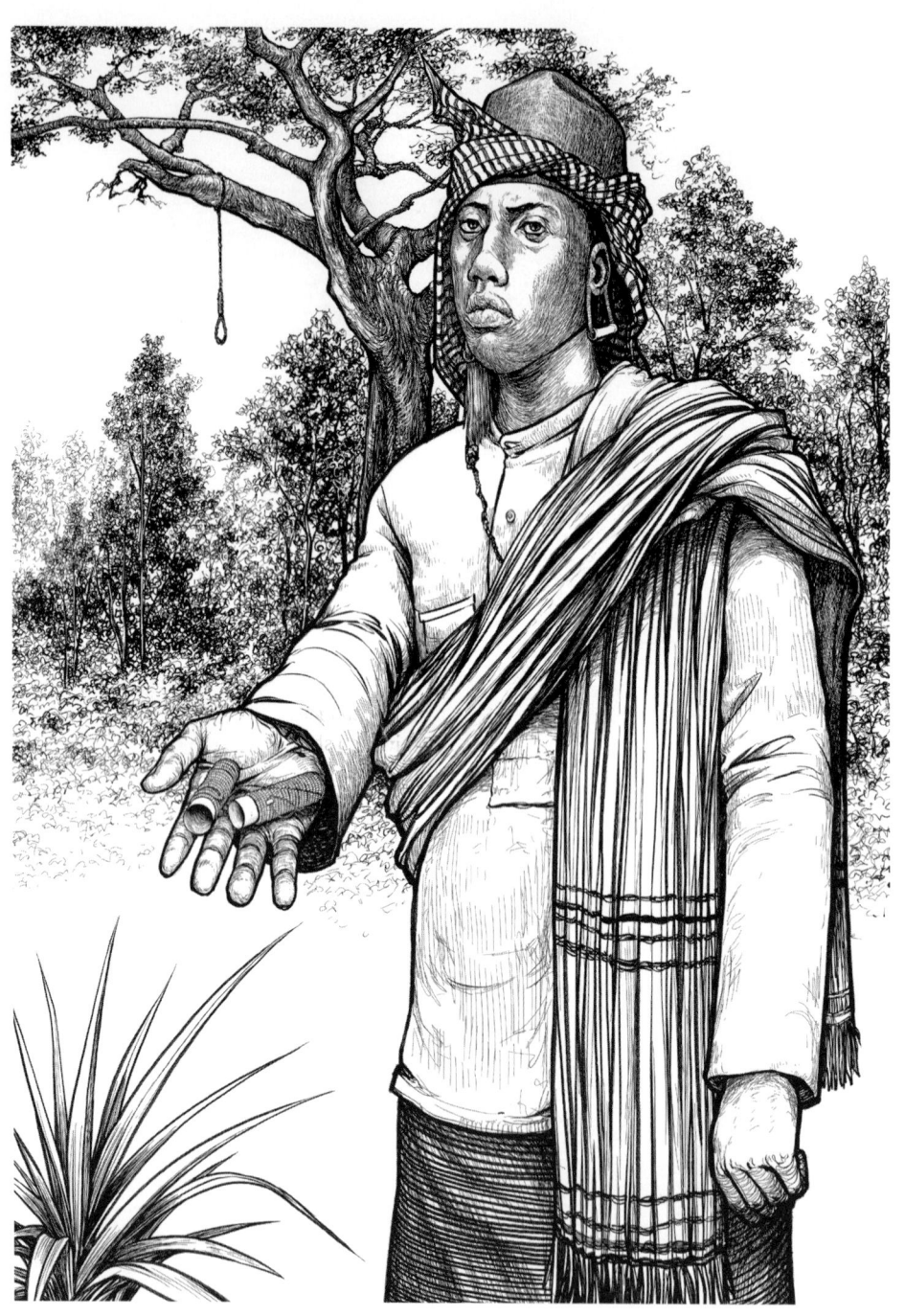

Artist: Bright Toh

CHAPTER 8

Conversation

Subverting Firepower
A German Cartridge Upcycled as a Snuffbox, a Symbol of Chagga Resistance

Konradin Kunze, Sarita Lydia Mamseri, Gabriel Mzei Orio and Mnyaka Sururu Mboro

The interdisciplinary research project *Marejesho asili mila utamaduni* (literally, 'The Return of Our Cultural Heritage' in Swahili) was conceived to share knowledge in Tanzania of ancestral remains and cultural belongings stolen through systematic German colonial violence.[253] The project enabled a way for intergenerational conversations and research to take place, crossing many localities in Tanzania and Germany. This exchange resulted in an exhibition that travelled to six villages in Kilimanjaro and Meru in 2022, stopping on open lawns or near historical sites of the respective chiefdoms in northern Tanzania.[254]

Marejesho has been steeped in acts of repair, supporting the present-day struggle for restorative justice fought by Chagga and Meru communities for decades. The objective of the struggle is the repatriation of ancestral family and community members back to the homeland, back home. This involved the identifying of missing ancestral remains from Kilimanjaro and Meru in museum depots at the Museum of Early and Prehistory in Berlin and at the American Museum of Natural History in New York. Through DNA testing, matches were made with living descendants. The *Marejesho* team also identified individual belongings that could be linked to places and people from the Kilimanjaro and Meru regions in the collections of the Ethnological Museum Berlin, the GRASSI Museum für Völkerkunde in Leipzig and the Linden Museum in Stuttgart.

The Exhibition

Placemaking was a significant aspect in conceptualising *Marejesho* as travelling temporary exhibition structure. Inspiration was taken from the familiar Swahili architecture of the *baraza*, which is an open terrace for social gatherings and local meetings, therefore, a space that is easily accessible.

The exhibition showcased a video installation called 'Mangi Meli Remains', featuring an animation on the life and legacy of chief Meli's stolen remains.[255] There were also archive-sourced historical photographs of *Mangis* (chiefs), and banners with pictures of cultural belongings from the Kilimanjaro and Meru region. An audio station with 120-year-old recordings of local Chagga songs and a video display of the team's visit to a German museum depot were also set up. Filmmakers from the film collective *bafico* had conducted video interviews with members of the communities and edited them on the spot to display them in the exhibition. Tanzanian visual artists Amani Abeid, Cloud Chatanda and Massana also joined *Marejesho*, creating live site-responsive drawings and paintings of reimagined pasts and futures. The artwork served as medium for connecting spaces in time, where people could reminisce and talk about ancestral histories and their relevance today. This was expressed through a public programme of discussions, film screenings, dance performances and the traditional sharing of *mbege* (locally made banana beer), in the spirit of a *baraza*.[256]

Of the multitude of archive photographs on display, one item that embodied complex histories of warfare, resistance, ownership, beauty and remembrance was a repurposed tobacco container, formally a German colonial military cartridge case (see Figure 8.1). It was repeatedly of interest during *Marejesho*'s sojourns and forms the basis of the discussion in this chapter.

The following dialogue took place in May 2023 between *Marejesho* team members: Konradin Kunze, artistic director and curator of the project, a member of the arts company Flinn Works; Mnyaka Sururu Mboro, activist and co-founder of Berlin Postkolonial in Germany; Gabriel Mzei Orio, researcher, cultural producer and founder of Old Moshi Cultural Tourism in Tanzania. The transcript was then edited by *Marejesho* curators Konradin Kunze and Sarita Lydia Mamseri.

In the spirit of recognising the validity of community-generated knowledge through oral traditions to piece together an understanding of dismembered histories, this dialogue contains both written and oral history source material.

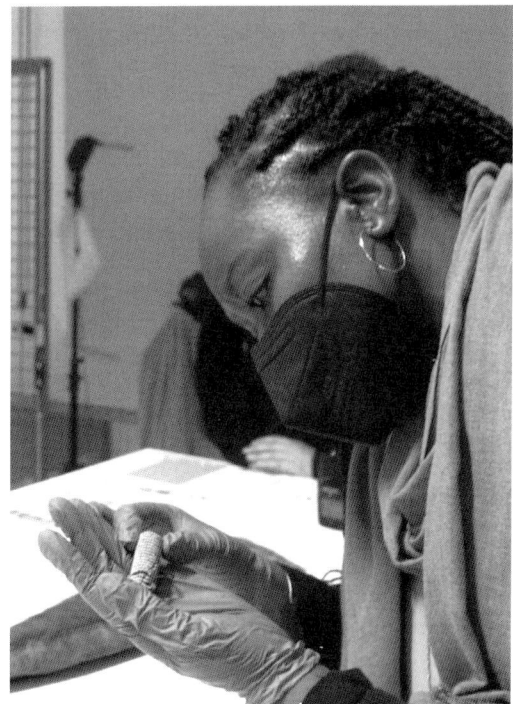

Figure 8.1: Curator Sarita L. Mamseri examines one of the beaded snuffboxes that allegedly belonged to Mangi Meli in the storage of the Grassi Museum in Leipzig. Photo: Bagamoyo Film Collective, Thomas Rotsching.

Dialogue

Konradin Kunze: Gabriel, you spoke with Isaria Meli, the grandson of Mangi Meli and showed him again the picture of this tobacco container, which the Grassi Museum in Leipzig labels as being one of the personal belongings of his grandfather. Does he remember it from the *Marejesho* exhibition?

Gabriel M. Orio: Yes, I showed him, and he remembers it vividly.

Konradin: I wondered when tobacco was introduced in East Africa. Originally, the plant comes from South America. I found that it was most likely brought in the sixteenth century – before the arrival of the German colonialists – by the Portuguese and then probably via the caravans to Kilimanjaro.[257]

Mnyaka S. Mboro: It seems it has been used in the region for centuries. I could be wrong, but I believe the plant was in the forests and was not necessarily brought. My grandmother used to take the tobacco leaves on a banana leaf and cover it to ferment for some three or four days. When it turns brown, you dry it. After that, you take the layers of the banana stem, wrap it in and hang it inside the traditional Chagga houses, below the roof, where the smoke from the cooking disperses, thus making the tobacco much stronger. Then, you need to grind it. I used to help her do that. We would add a little bit of bone marrow to the tobacco, so that it becomes smooth. Still, I am unaware of how my people learnt this technical process. Were this practice and knowledge imported to the region? If yes, by whom? I still ask myself.

Konradin: In preparation for the *Marejesho* exhibition, we visited the depots of ethnographic museums in Berlin, Leipzig and Stuttgart, and saw many kinds of containers. Some of them were explicitly labelled as being used for tobacco, but we cannot know for sure whether this was their unique purpose. I read that they could be used for gunpowder and matches for muzzle-loader rifles.[258]

Mboro: Yes, or poison for the arrows. You don't walk with the arrows when there is poison on them because, after some time, the poison dries out and disappears. So, you need to keep it somewhere in a sealed receptacle that you can carry with you. They also used small calabashes to keep tobacco, gunpowder or poison. The shape is quite similar.

Konradin: This container, however, is very special, because, according to the archival material attached to it, it is a cartridge from a German bullet decorated with blue beads. A handwritten note by the 'donor' indicates that this bullet was fired by the so-called *Schutztruppe*, the German colonial army, and was used against Mangi Meli and his people during the war of 1892. What do you know about this conflict?

Mboro: Before I come to this war, we need to go back to Hermann von Wissmann. As early as 1888, along the East African coastline, local people opposed German colonial rule. Only three years after the end of the Berlin Conference, there was strong resistance to Germans coming as settlers or plantation owners. So, Chancellor Otto von Bismarck told Wissmann: 'Go down there and try to stop this uprising.' This is when he formed the *Schutztruppe* ('protection forces'), which consisted of soldiers from Mozambique, AmaZulu from South Africa and Nubians from South Sudan. The resistance led, among others, by Abushiri, was brutally crushed by Wissmann's troops. He earned a nickname: Mr *Maafa*, which means 'great catastrophe' in Kiswahili, a term that besides is also used to describe the slave trade. The colonial troops pushed the border towards Mount Kilimanjaro, but *Mangi* Sina of Kibosho did not feel like submitting and raising the German Kaiser's flag, so he burnt it. After silencing the resistance at the coast, the Germans under Wissmann came to Kibosho. On the way, they met *Mangi* Rindi Mandara, the father of Meli. The German officers said to him: 'Support us by letting us enrol some of your warriors in our troops. They know the local language and know the way to Kibosho, so they will be useful to us as *askaris* (soldiers). For this, we will treat you as a good friend and, in exchange, we will help you expand your area of influence.' So Mandara assisted them. But the Germans suffered losses before they took Kibosho, because they didn't know about the furrows that Sina had erected around the town to protect his *boma* (fort). Mandara's warriors knew about them, but I think they didn't want to tell the Germans. Anyway, by that time, Meli was young and not yet *Mangi*. Still, my grandmother used to say of him, that even though his father decided to assist the Germans, Meli had already sworn: 'when I come to power, I'm going to get revenge, because my father's decision was not right.' At that time, the Germans had already set foot in Old Moshi, but they had not really settled yet.

Konradin: The Germans had erected a small station but then decided to shift the centre of their power in the region to Marangu. This is when two very important figures, a German officer and a Chagga chief, enter the scene: Carl Peters and *Mangi* Mareale of Marangu.

Mboro: Carl Peters was already based there: he had been appointed governor of the Kilimanjaro district after the colony was founded. To his dismay, he was never promoted to governor of German East Africa because politicians in Berlin knew how brutal he was, always using force, not diplomacy. Anyway, they still had to reward him with something, since he was regarded as the founder of the colony, the one who had collected the so-called 'treaties of protection' to support German claims on this territory during the Berlin Conference in 1884–1885.

Konradin: The way Carl Peters ruled, how he mistreated the people in Kilimanjaro with arbitrary hangings and so on, did this also add to *Mangi* Meli's strong opposition to the Germans?

Mboro: I am 100 per cent sure of that.

Konradin: But in 1892 Carl Peters was not in Marangu anymore. He was on a mission to negotiate the border with the British.

Mboro: This is what I know: Peters hanged a house boy who was accused of having a relationship with one of his concubines. But the girl, Jagodjo (sometimes also named Ndekodyo) was clever. She ran to the neighbouring village of Mamba and *Mangi* Malamia hid her there. Peters ordered that she be brought back, but Malamia refused. From that point on, Peters started burning down local houses.[259] In Kilimanjaro, our old houses are made of dry grass from the top to the bottom. So, they were compelled to hand the girl over and Peters hanged her. In Tanzania, Peters is known as *Mkono wa Damu*, which means 'The Bloody Hand'. In fact, all these events were known in Germany. In the national parliament, a representative from the Social Democratic Party, August Bebel, advocated publicly for Peters' dismissal. As a result, *Mkono wa Damu* was ordered to go back to Germany and was finally removed from all his posts.

Konradin: His successor was von Bülow, the head of the station in Marangu. Together with another German officer called Wolfrum, they planned to attack Meli because, when he came to power after Rindi Mandara's death in 1891, he was clearly opposed to German rule. So, they aimed to teach him a lesson. In 1892, they marched from Marangu to Old Moshi to attack him. It was in this war that this cartridge was probably fired. The Germans tried to attack by climbing up from the valley, but just like Kibosho, Old Moshi was protected by defence furrows and obstacles. And the Chagga people were equipped with rifles.

Mboro: Yes, which they had purchased from the Arab caravans.

Konradin: This battle was another disaster for the Germans. Both German officers died as a result of this battle. Von Bülow suffered from a wound, and then, when his troops tried to escort him back, he succumbed. The Chagga warriors killed Wolfrum on the spot. A British missionary who had settled nearby, just across the valley, witnessed the battle.

Gabriel: In Kitimbirihu, where the first Chagga Christian was baptised by the Lutheran church.

Konradin: Yes. It was a British mission called Church Mission Society. The young missionary, called Stegall, observed the battle from above, treated wounded Moshi warriors and wrote a report about it. And when he came down into the valley after the battle was over, he found the bodies of many soldiers, most of them African *askaris* from the *Schutztruppe*, but also that of Wolfrum. He described the place as one covered with empty cartridges like this one. This was probably one of the reasons that convinced the colonial troops to surrender and flee to the coast: they didn't have any ammunition left. With hindsight, we can assume that somebody picked up one of those cartridges and turned it into something beautiful like this beaded tobacco container. Today, you would call it upcycling.

Mboro: There is also a symbolic value: the Wachagga had won and picking up these cartridges which were lying around could have been a way to remind themselves that they had won this battle, as evidence. This was the proof! I also think that re-appropriating the weak bullets of the enemy could have been linked with some kind of belief in victory and good fortune.

Gabriel: Yes, Isaria Meli said this too – it is definitely a sign of victory. The Germans thought they were stronger because they had rifles and bullets. But we won, so we pick up the cartridges that belonged to them, apply beads and make use of them. It's a sign of victory and maybe also evidence that the German had rifles, but still lost, and this was what was left after they ran away.

Mboro: Also, if I remember well, when old people used to tell stories about what happened, they usually had something as proof. Not only for younger generations to see, but also simply when exchanging stories around a pint of *mbege*. They would recall past events and would show such a historical relic to the others, to tell them: 'You see, I still have one of those!'

Gabriel: Unfortunately, Isaria Meli does not have any belonging that was passed on from his grandfather to remember him. Only the stories, the history.

Konradin: What I find very interesting is that the cartridge was repurposed. The artist, whoever that was, attached the beads and upcycled it very nicely. I have read that such beads were probably imported from India and Sri Lanka and came to Kilimanjaro long before the Europeans, again through the caravan traders.[260]

Mboro: I strongly believe that the person who did the beading was a woman. Until today, women pass on the knowledge and expertise on beading practices. The beading for this cartridge was perhaps done by one of Meli's wives, an aunt, or another lady: When he came back with the piece and told how they had won the battle, she attached the beads.

Konradin: And this small metal chain tethered to many personal belongings from that time was not only used to fasten items, but often as an ornament as well, as witnessed in earrings. They were made from iron or copper…

Mboro: …by the goldsmiths.

Konradin: Yes. These were in fact original production from the Kilimanjaro region.[261] So, we know that there were – and still are – very skilled metalworkers in Kilimanjaro, both for weapons and for jewellery.

Gabriel: People have actually kept on melting iron in the villages up until today. They don't do it for tourists, but for the locals who pay a visit to the blacksmith to get their tools for their daily work in the fields.

Konradin: Coming back to Mangi Meli and the battle: the Germans had to flee and, for a few months, the Kilimanjaro region was free from foreign military presence. They dared to come back, but only to Marangu, and it took them one year to launch another attack against Meli.[262] This time they brought a lot of machine guns and soldiers from the coast under the command of Governor Friedrich von Schele.[263] When the expedition arrived in the region, they attacked Meli once again in August 1893. They had help from his rival, *Mangi* Mareale. And this time, unfortunately, they won, although four *askaris* and a German officer were killed.[264] We should mention that the graves of those Germans who died in the war are still there in Old Moshi. And we know that Meli had to surrender, to spare the lives of many more people.[265] So, it was on this day after the war in August 1893 that the owner of the cartridge changed for the second time. From the archival documents in the Grassi Museum, we can assume that *Mangi* Meli had worn, or at least owned, it. However, the note in the museum's archive claims that Meli had offered it as a gift on the day of his defeat. The person who then loaned it to the Grassi Museum was the German Officer Schrenck von Notzing, adjutant to Governor Schele.[266]

Mboro: I think the Germans just took it away from Meli. I strongly doubt that he gave it away.

Konradin: I mean, even if the Germans claim it was a gift, we need to take into account that Meli had just been defeated. He was compelled to agree to the conditions imposed by the Governor, who ordered him to deliver all their firearms, and to supply workers for the colonial administration. He also had to deliver elephant tusks and other supplies.[267]

Mboro: Those elephant tusks were like money, tribute. But you know, if you are a warrior, there are some things that you just don't give away. The cartridge might have been hidden somewhere.

Konradin: Or he wore it around his neck on a chain or necklace…

Mboro: Yes, and the Germans saw it…

Konradin: …and took it. Is this something that you would call a gift?

Gabriel: I don't think it was a gift. You know, a gift is something that you give from your heart. Meli might have given it to them, but even then, it cannot be called a gift. Meli's grandson, Isaria, believes that the Germans took it by force or by theft. Because at that moment of surrender, *Mangi* Meli had no say whatsoever.

Konradin: So, just like we assumed this upcycled cartridge was a sign of victory for Meli, can we also suggest that it became some kind of trophy for this German officer? He took away Meli's prize, because now they had won.

Mboro: It must have been a sign of victory for Meli. Perhaps intended for the people who would come after him, so that they would remember and continue fighting for what he fought.

Konradin: Besides, we know that Officer Schrenck von Notzing looted so many other things during that war.

Gabriel: In the collections of the Grassi Museum, we saw shields riddled with bullet holes. He even grabbed some belongings from the bodies of fallen Chagga warriors.

Konradin: And he mentioned this in the list of his collection. How can you claim you received gifts on the same day when you took away war booty? Now, what happened after the war? Meli did not die in this battle. He was allowed to remain *Mangi* in what is today Old Moshi. But the conditions, of course, were different.

Mboro: Totally different. The Germans ordered the people of Old Moshi to build them a military station on the site of Meli's destroyed *boma*. He could build new houses for himself, but without protection, and a little further up the hill.

Konradin: This is also the place where we set up our *Marejesho* exhibition when we made our stop in Old Moshi (see Figure 8.2). And there are still the ruins of a stone house, which supposedly was built by Meli, but he also had the traditional Moshi houses which Mboro described earlier. But then, he was executed on order of the German officers for allegedly conspiring against them, together with other leaders from Kilimanjaro and Meru. On 2 March 1900, the Germans hanged nineteen leaders from a tree outside the *boma*, a tree that still stands today.

Mboro: My grandmother was present at this hanging. Not because she wanted to be. Everyone, even people from neighbouring villages, had been summoned to witness the hangings. It was meant as a warning: if you do anything against the Germans, you will end up like these chiefs.

Konradin: Isaria told me that, after his hanging, *Mangi* Meli's head was chopped off and transported to the coast. From there, he was likely sent to Germany by ship. And until today, the head is missing and *Mangi* Meli has not been buried properly.

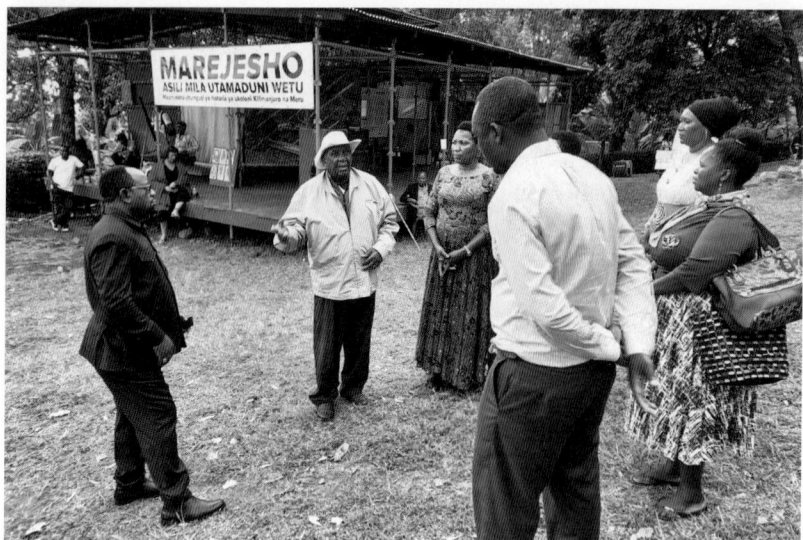

Figure 8.2: Isaria Meli (wearing a hat) relates the history of his grandfather to local officials. On the left, Morris Makoi, chairman of the Moshi district Council; next to Isaria Meli, the Old Moshi ward councillor, Jane Mandara. The exhibition was shown in Old Moshi, on the site of Meli's former *boma*, in front of the former German colonial station. Photo: Konradin Kunze.

Mboro: Yes, at that time, in every homestead, we used to have a place in the banana groves where our dead were buried. And when the missionaries came in, they forbade burials at home. They claimed the dead should be buried at the parish graves. It was not up for discussion but became an order of the colonial administration. The German Christian missionaries in Kilimanjaro, both Catholics and Lutherans, they really wanted to colonise us, break our traditions. And this went on until we got independence in 1961. Nowadays, we bury the dead at home again.

Gabriel: According to Isaria Meli, the Germans buried the bodies of *Mangi* Meli and his sub-chiefs just under the tree they used to hang them. This way, they prevented the relatives to get access to their remains.

Konradin: And today we know, that not only Meli's head was taken, but the remains of other hanged leaders, too. Possibly, they were exhumed later and then send to the Ethnological Museum in Berlin.[268] Which reasons were behind the theft of Meli's head?

Mboro: Racist – and so-called 'scientific' – research. And I mean really racist, because what the German scientists wanted to prove with our ancestors' heads was that we, Africans, were less human than the Europeans.

Gabriel: Isaria also thinks that they took Meli's head as a remembrance of how skilled he was at fighting, a worthy opponent who won a battle, but not the war.

Konradin: Finding and repatriating the head of *Mangi* Meli remains the main task and the main demand of many people, not only Isaria's and yours, Mboro, but of many others in the region. Unfortunately, we could not find any trace of it until today, although we are quite sure that his head was sent to Germany by the same people who also took many belongings, like this tobacco cartridge: German officers. Anyway, what do you think about Meli's personal belongings in the Grassi Museum? And all the other collections from Kilimanjaro and Meru that we have seen in the depots and featured in our exhibition, like the blanket and the headgear of *Mangi* Molelia or *Mangi* Sina of Kibosho at the Linden Museum in Stuttgart, or the ear jewellery of *Mangi* Mareale of Marangu at the Ethnological Museum in Berlin? Almost all of them have never even been exhibited. They have just been lying in storage rooms for more than 100 years. For whom are these belongings most important today? Is it the families? The descendants? For the village or the entire Kilimanjaro region? And what do you think should be done with them?

Gabriel: For me, this tobacco cartridge is really connected to Meli. And since no information has been found on the whereabouts of his head so far, I think this tobacco cartridge, as a preserved token of the past, is important to people in the whole Kilimanjaro region, perhaps even to Tanzanians in general, because of the history behind it. It is a contrast to the misery caused by the disappearance of his head. So maybe this heritage should belong to the whole Kilimanjaro region, because it is part of our history. And maybe, one day, we will have a museum: Kilimanjaro Museum. These belongings should be shown there. Even Isaria maintains they should be kept in a museum for Kilimanjaro people to see the valuable belongings of his grandfather and remember that he fought bravely.

Mboro: These chiefs, the *Mangis*, they were our governments. We didn't have a national centralised government like today. The *Mangi* was responsible not just for a family, but for a whole area. So those belongings should be there for the descendants of people from the Kilimanjaro region, not only for Meli's, Sina's or Mareale' descendants. As for the head of *Mangi* Meli, if we find it – and I still believe we will find it – he belongs with his descendants, it belongs to the family. And if they decide to bury him in the family grave, it is their right.

Together, we went to the old Kilimanjaro District Council building in Moshi town, which is empty now. You remember? It could become a regional museum, to host and care for the belongings after they return. Outside the building, there is an open space which lends itself for a potential site of remembrance. There, we could have the graves of those ancestors who were dehumanised, whose names were not recorded and who can no longer be identified as belonging to a family, but who belong to the Chagga community. If the search for Meli's head is successful, his descendants might even decide to bury him there as well, together with those who accompanied him to Germany. But concerning the belongings, I really believe that they belong to the whole area of Kilimanjaro. Maybe some few special ones can go to the families – that can be discussed.

Gabriel: Isaria told me that all the ancestral remains from Kilimanjaro leaders should return, also their personal belongings, because they are part of our history. And if *Mangi* Meli's head returns, he, his family and the people in Kilimanjaro would be very happy about it.

Konradin: With *Marejesho*, we have shown pictures of some of the belongings, historical photographs of the *Mangis*, and our video installation *Mangi Meli Remains*. Do you recall any reactions from our visitors?

Mboro: I think most of them were overexcited about the belongings. They knew personal belongings were taken away, but they did not know what they looked like. I talked with them about what should happen, and I think it will be the council of elders who decide what should be done with the belongings once they return home.

Gabriel: Yes, people came, visited the exhibition and they looked at photos of the belongings. Some were really keen, examining them one by one. Some even had emotional responses. I think it triggered deep thoughts on history, on the conditions in which those things were taken, on the process ahead to get them back. Others, especially older people, were just standing quietly, looking at these pictures, this history, the whole exhibition. But all the same, the encounter was carved in their memory. Other people learnt about it too late, as we were already moving to the next village. In fact, some people came to different villages to see it, to get precious information about the belongings and the ancestral remains. You know, I have got so many calls ever since. People ask: 'When are you going to show *Marejesho* again?' I have to tell them: 'Oh, we are done already.' People were hoping that exhibition would be done yearly, because it was a very short span of time, just one week per village. That wasn't enough. This also means that some people start doubting the promise of restitution. They start asking me: 'Are you really sure these belongings will be brought back?' I can recall quite a lot of different emotions – scepticism, impatience – but most of them are hopeful. They would celebrate if they could see those belongings return to their homeland in the future.

Mboro: People were not only looking at the pictures, but also trying to recall history, the things they knew, the atrocities that the colonialists committed, how prominent figures were killed and so on. And, of course, the belongings and the pictures are telling dreadful stories. What happened under German colonial rule – the wars, the killings, the military expeditions – they are well known in Tanzania. They are part of school curricula and related in books. So, people visiting the exhibition told me: 'Oh, what I heard or what I read about the past is true.' The truth is partly in those belongings. The youth and even children were keen to learn, especially thanks to the animated film on *Mangi* Meli's resistance. Some of them watched it over and over again; I don't know how many times. When, after having looked at the pictures, we told visitors about the possibility that some of these belongings could come back, they started believing in restitution. But I emphasised the fact that museums, in spite of their willingness, ask for the cooperation of the Tanzanian government. So, I told the people that, even if we are advocating for returns in Germany, they also need to do advocacy work in Tanzania, so that governmental bodies send official claims. Indeed, this procedure can also be an obstacle here, in Tanzania.

***

As of February 2024, the work to identify Tanzanian ancestral remains stolen through colonial plunder and kept in German museums and institutions in the USA and France continues, led by civil society groups and activists. In addition, cultural belongings such as body adornments, weapons of defence and even the tobacco cartridge, demonstrate the entangled nature of this history stemming from an asymmetric power imbalance that still leaves a tangible legacy up to today. The *Marejesho* team advocate that the research and labour to address this must be funded and supported by the German state as part of reparative action towards restitution.

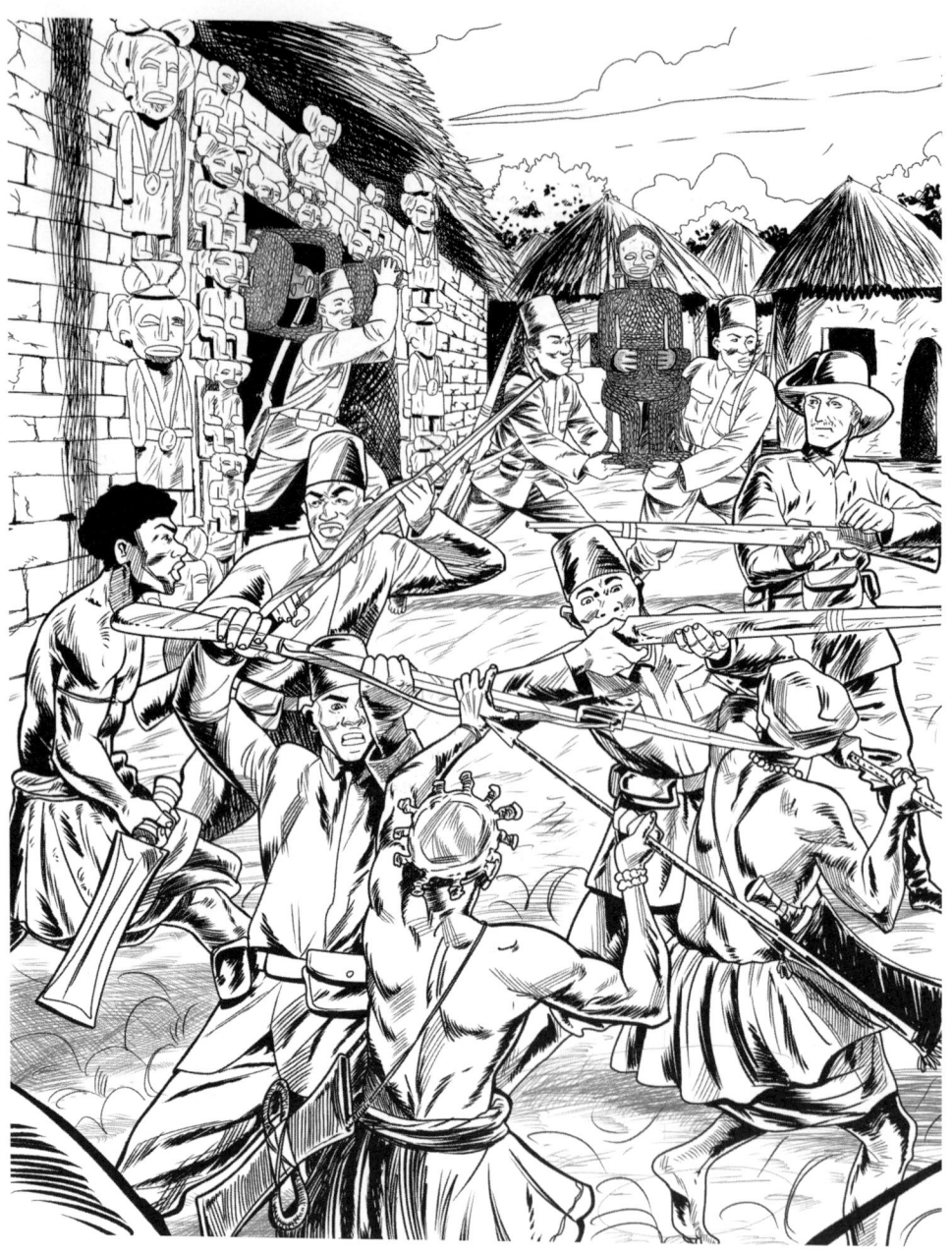

Artist: Yves Heles Toum

CHAPTER 9

In Defence of Theft?
On the Theft and Restitution of Ngonnso' and Punitive Exhibitions

Godfrey B. Tangwa and Fogha MC Cornilius Refem, alias Wan wo Layir

The story of the restitution of Ngonnso' began in the early 1990s at the behest of the *Fon* (ruler) of Nso'. Since then, it has been pursued by various volunteers and stakeholders. Today, that story cannot be told without mentioning *Walengon Nso'* Sylvie Njobati and Chimamanda Ngozi Adichie, the renowned Nigerian African writer. Through her organisation, Sysy House of Fame, and thanks to the skilful use of social media, Sylvie Njobati propelled the Nso' campaign for the restitution of Ngonnso' to hit the headlines. She can even be credited with obtaining the decision of the German detainers to return the effigy to its rightful owners.[269] Adichie, in turn, delivered one of the most memorable speeches for the restitution of Ngonnso' at the opening of the Humboldt Forum in Berlin in 2021. She drew an apt parallel between Ngonnso' for the Nso' and the Ikenga for an Igbo person, an ordinary-looking piece of wood but in fact a most precious possession.[270] Anyone who needs convincing reasons for the return of looted African heritage should listen carefully to Chimamanda Ngozi Adichie. Her speech evoked many of the ironies, contradictions and questions related to museums' involvement in putative acts of decolonisation, like restitution. In what follows, we reflect further on some of these incongruities and wonder if a process of decolonisation initiated by the coloniser and beneficiaries of colonialism may not in fact be aimed at consolidating privilege.

Who/What Is/Was Ngonnso'?

The effigy of Ngonnso', the matriarchal initiator of the Nso' dynasty and monarchical state, is a carving of a seated young woman with a bowl-like utensil on her lap. As a historical figure, according to oral tradition and historical accounts, Ngonnso' was one of the children of *Fon* Tinki of Rifem in Tikari (present-day Adamawa region in Cameroon). The death of *Fon* Tinki circa 1387 occasioned a succession dispute that resulted in the dispersal of the family. Ngonnso' migrated with a band of followers, who eventually settled in present-day Kimbo. Her effigy is completely beaded with cowries (*mbam se Nso'*) and was evidently used as the stand and receptacle of the royal palm wine dispenser (*nngiv melu'*). It was looted from the palace of the paramount Fondom of Nso', most likely by Hans Houben and his colonial troops in 1902.[271] This was in the context of a German military expedition aimed at subjecting the people of Nso' to German colonial rule.

It should be recalled that in Nso' culture, palm wine – a drink taped from the raffia palm – and kolanuts hold significant cultural and traditional importance. Raffia palm bushes and kolanut trees are the most visible vegetation on the landscape all over Nso' land, the latter being an important economic cash crop while the former supplies materials for building, furniture, artistic works, decoration, and mat-, bag- and basket-making. Ngonnso' was likely used during ceremonial or important events in the Nso' culture. The intricate beading adds decorative and ceremonial value to the carving. Cowrie shells have been used as ornaments and as a currency of economic exchange in Nso' culture, symbolising wealth, fertility and power. For this carving, the shells would have enhanced its visual appeal and reflected its cultural significance and importance as the guiding spirit of the people and dynasty she founded. The sculpture of Ngonnso' thus held great significance within the Nso' community, connecting them to their history, ancestral traditions and spiritual practices. The looting of the effigy and the ensuing longing for it resulted in the sculpture acquiring extra meaning for the Nso' people, as the calls for its restitution also invite a reckoning with colonial history.

In the different scenarios envisaged for recovering Ngonnso' once her whereabouts became known, one of the most compelling was to simply steal it back from the thief, based on the reasoning that the owner who steals back from the thief is not stealing but rather rightfully reclaiming what was stolen. This possibility, however, was greatly limited in its operability considering the power, intelligence, cleverness and protective facilities of the thief. Still, conceptually speaking, counter-theft remains a legitimate option, perhaps even an appropriate approach to decolonising a museum. Thus, while the title of our chapter – 'In Defence of Theft' – may appear provocative, we chose it quite deliberately. We are aware that it might be misconstrued as an attempt to vindicate the smashing of windowpanes in museums for the removal of 'objects', but that is not the point we want to make.[272] The point – if stretched to its logical limits – is that there should be no ethno-colonial museums; then, there would be no need for the smashing of windowpanes or the glass vitrines within them. In the same way, those who defend the theft and retention of artefacts, which were looted during colonisation for display in what we call 'punitive exhibitions' in Western museums, need to be reminded of the context of colonial plunder. These artefacts are often incorrectly labelled in their 'context of acquisition' as if they had been free gifts or articles bargained for in an exchange; instead, most have been looted, often violently, with resultant human suffering. So, when we speak of the museums' act of theft here, we are not speaking literally and casually. Restitution in this regard would also not be a simple question of logistics – it is a deeply moral issue. So much so that, if we had we been able, despite the tight security, incessant alarms and restrictions, to steal back Ngonnso' when she was exhibited at the Berlin Ethnological Museum and later at the Humboldt Forum, that heist, spectacular as it may have been, would have betrayed and trivialised the deep motive and intentions behind trying to right these historical wrongs. It would have reduced the act to a mere question of transport with theft being the *means* that made it possible.

In this chapter, we examine various agents and examples of colonial theft, including the military, museums, language, conservation work and narratives. We wish to do away with colonial and museal understandings of this effigy and concentrate on her relevance for the Nso' people, especially taking into consideration their relentless efforts for her restitution. Based on this premise, we propose to re-signify Ngonnso' by highlighting the fact that cultural artefacts and objects are not just symbols of a distant past but are living and meaningful parts of a community's identity, history and their future aspirations. By reclaiming her meaning and recognising the possibility of stealing her back as a decolonial move, there is potential for a powerful act of mental resistance against the effects of colonialism and coloniality. The looting of culturally significant objects and subjects has caused immense suffering and loss to its victims. In addition, theft (i.e. the mere act of taking without consent or permission) can have different moral implications depending on the context and details. In some cases, theft can be a means of decolonisation and restitution, while in others it can perpetuate harmful power dynamics and marginalisation of oppressed communities. Careful consideration and reflection are needed when evaluating the morality of theft as a colonial or decolonial move.

We recognise the deep injustice and suffering that often underlie the acquisition and display of cultural artefacts and objects in a museum, a concept which, at the time of the theft, was completely alien to the culture from which the artefact was stolen. This recognition is a crucial starting point for any decolonial critique of museums. It highlights the need to acknowledge and redress the historical and ongoing misunderstandings and harms inflicted on colonised/marginalised communities. We draw attention to how museums have contributed to the ongoing erasure of indigenous cultures and identities through the use of language and other forms of [mis]representation. Therefore, in proposing a resignification of Ngonnso' based on its meaning and relevance to the Nso' people, we also suggest the importance of centring the perspectives and experiences of marginalised communities in the display and interpretation of cultural assets. In this way, we aim and hope to challenge the dominance of Western perspectives and knowledge systems that support and perpetuate colonialism and to foreground the voices and agency of those who historically have been colonised, dispossessed, harmed and marginalised.

The Theft of Ngonnso' from the Nso' Palace

The first contact of German colonial soldiers with the Nso' occurred in 1902. The German expedition, led by Lieutenant-Colonel Kurt Pavel, was heading to Banyo in the present-day Adamawa region of Cameroon. They were well received by the Nso' and generously supplied with necessary victuals for their onward journey. The reigning *Fon* (King) of Nso' at this time was Sehm II (1880–1907), grandson of Sehm I, only son of Taamanjo, the greatest expansionist of the Nso' Fondom, and Lirfee, a noblewoman of the Mntar Nso' clan from Kitukela' in the Dzeng area.[273]

Even though the Nso' people had welcomed the Germans in a friendly fashion into their land, providing them essential supplies for their onward journey, their profession of friendship was not pleasing to the Germans who deduced from it a claim and an attitude of equality. At the time, Germans could not conceive of being considered equal with the Nso', and certainly would not allow them to believe in any way that they were. The Germans required a public act of humiliating submission and subordination. To make matters worse, Sehm II was an extremely proud person who also happened to be recklessly belligerent and overbearingly self-confident. It is in this context that Lieutenant Hans Houben led an expeditionary force to Kimbo in June 1902, and set camp right in front of the Nso' Palace (*Ntoh Nso'*).[274]

Here, we are confronted by the very crux of the matter. Moral reasoning is anchored on the simple postulate that a human being is a human being simply by being a human being and not for any other reason. This implies equality and imposes equity and fair consideration as procedural norms in dealing with all human beings. To ignore this is to discard the moral dimension or perspective in life. West European cultures, in general, might present some lessons which other cultures could learn from, especially in the domains of science, technology and commerce, but they do not have the prerogative of teaching lessons to other cultures in the domain of morality. Their insistence on doing so, by using their power and influence in the world, is one of the reasons why the world is in such a deplorable state. Colonialism may indeed be considered one of the most horrendous crimes against humanity ever committed.

Let's return to Houben. After several induced skirmishes around the Nso' Palace, leading to significant human losses, he was able to loot the palace and then set it on fire. The spoils included the effigy of Ngonnso', the *Ntara'* (royal ceremonial headwear), and the *Kava'* (the Fon's throne), both exhibited at the Linden Museum in Stuttgart as we write this chapter, as well as countless other items like stools, ornaments, ivories, guns, bowls, leopard skins and buffalo horns.

Another group of Germans returned to Nso' in 1905 under Captain Glauning, head of the Bamenda district. The colonial military force would first make what could fittingly be described by the Latin expression *argumentum ad baculum*, that is, an appeal to force. Glauning led a show of force through all the neighbouring states surrounding Nso' which aimed to demonstrate the strength of German colonial rule and deter defiance from the local population. Essentially, this marching army conveyed the message that resistance would be futile. The Germans sought not to establish friendly relations with the Nso' but to exert full control over them to consolidate their power in the region. However, the *Fon* of Nso', confident in the military strength and numerical superiority of his people, was determined not to surrender or be subdued by the Germans. He symbolically threw a handful of finger millet in the air while making the statement: '*M'fan ka'aiy? A mo Nso' wom dze'en ben*' ('What need I fear? This is how numerous the Nso' are'). Finger millet is a crop known for its small grain size and, by comparing the Nso' population to this tiny grain, the *Fon* emphasised that their numbers were vast and formidable.[275]

Sehm II, however, was unaware of, or simply ignored, the fact that the Germans had gone into a strong alliance with rival kingdoms of the Grassfields, particularly with the Bamum. The latter saw here a golden opportunity to recover the skull of their late King Saanguv, beheaded by the Nso' in an earlier war between the two fondoms, and to avenge themselves against the Nso'. Glauning and his allies invaded Nso' in April 1906. The war lasted about forty days. The Nso' were greatly unmatched, suffered heavy casualties – 700 to 800 according to the colonialists –, surrendered the skull of Saanguv, and capitulated to the Germans.

Yet, the violence described here was only the tip of the iceberg. Houben not only looted culturally significant objects from Nso', but there is also still profound silence on what happened to the elephant tusks – in other words, the wealth of the kingdom – that he took away from the Nso' Palace along with Ngonnso'. In addition, the military doctor Wilhelm Eckhardt and Lieutenant Karl von Wenckstern, both serving under Glauning's command, took away twenty-three skulls that the Nso' had been hanging as war trophies on the walls of one of their buildings, including the remains of Bamum warriors. They sent these to the Berlin Ethnological Museum to be measured and studied for racist theories, thereby doing harm even to the Germans' allies.[276] The presence of human remains in German museums also recalls the undocumented fate of the Germans' prisoners of war. In his forty-day war with the Nso', Glauning estimates his troops arrested 1,000 people, including women and children.[277] Only one princess – Yeefon, the young Queen-mother, later Yaa wo Faa – is known to have been ransomed.

Language, 'Punitive' Expeditions and Other Colonial Continuities

Amid the excitement, fears and anxieties that surround the restitution of Ngonnso', an interesting question arose within the Nso' community: When she finally returns, what language will she speak or understand for that matter? At first, this might seem a trivial question. But considering that Ngonnso' has lived in Germany for more than 120 years now, that she was spoken to/about only in German or other European languages, and has only heard Lamnso' again addressed to her during the visit of the *Fon* of Nso' in November 2022, does Ngonnso' still understand Lamnso'?

Language is an important tool of colonial theft. The violent expeditions that led to the killing, pillage and rape of Nso' society and other societies were given a pretentious moral impetus by being called 'punitive'. The suggestion was that indigenous people must have committed some crime by virtue of which the colonial expedition was a justified retaliatory move. Colonial conquest, plunder and theft were also repeatedly described as 'pacification'. In 1963, Franz Fanon unveiled this rhetoric. He wrote, in the colonies,

> the soldier ... does not lighten the oppression, nor seek to hide the domination. He shows them up and puts them into practice with the clear conscience of an upholder of the peace; yet he is the bringer of violence into the home and into the mind of the native.[278]

In the case under scrutiny, the crime committed might well have been the Nso's audacity to offer friendship, to assume they were equal to the Germans. Colonisers have employed language to incentivise colonial conquest and justify their horrendous deeds. In this way, language played an important role in exploitation and violence. This violence was first and foremost epistemic before being corporeal. 'Give the dog a bad name and you can kill it.'

Language has also been used to justify museums' continuous holding of the looted objects: by (mis)labelling them; by calling colonial loot 'ethnographic objects'; and by referring to colonial officers as 'amateur ethnographers', which is how the Humboldt Forum describes Glauning in their room dedicated to 'Colonial Cameroon'. In this way, museums have successfully whitewashed colonial crimes and hidden them in plain sight. What makes an 'ethnographic object'? Does the act of driving a knife into a skull, as one would drive a shovel into the sand, qualify one as an amateur ethnographer? Looting cultural assets in so-called 'punitive' wars has been euphemised as 'collecting ethnographic material', turning soldiers involved in the dispossession and killing of people into specialists in material culture and contributors to science.

Language has equally been manipulated to alienate people or things from the natural order of things or their environment. The suggestion, for example, that the theft of Ngonnso' could be considered a 'blessing in disguise', a suggestion that the Humboldt Forum peddles, demonstrates that even when violent pasts are acknowledged, the preservation of the artefact for so many decades could somehow a posteriori justify the means for its appropriation. Opponents of restitution have often suggested that African cultural heritage would long have been destroyed if not for the museums' efforts at preserving it. This pattern of reasoning was even expressed by some, like Sally Chilver, who at various times had joined the Nso' recovery campaign team.[279] Even today, it persists among some Nso' people who are currently involved in the campaign for restitution, especially those with little knowledge of the history, significance and stakes involved, but who are poised to reap personal economic benefit, celebrity or power in this highly mediatised process. Of course, given the eco-bio-communitarian worldview of the Nso', it would be perfectly acceptable if, long ago, Ngonnso' had been eaten by ants and termites in Kimbo, as the ants and termites in question are seamlessly a part of their life and their world. The epistemic violence engendered in this colonial violence is materialised by the complicity between the army and the museum. In their claim to protect the stolen object, museums take it out of its context, smear toxic chemicals on it, and render it devoid of use in the very context where it had purpose. The act of preservation here, therefore, becomes the very place where Ngonnso' finds her death, a disconnection from her life source.

The colonial army was a central instrument in the institutionalisation of theft. The theft was not restricted to the act of taking something from its rightful owner, either forcefully or without their knowledge. It included the violence that came before, during and after this act of unjust appropriation. This violence was, for the Nso', apparent in several ways, including the death toll and the hundreds of prisoners of war. These numbers, in fact, do not capture the magnitude of the atrocities committed. The colonial platoons that descended upon Nso' were mostly made up of Black people, recruited from West Africa or among Nso's neighbours. German colonial archives reveal that, in order to convince local men to join their recruits, several officers promised them that they would be allowed to rape women with impunity under their command.[280] The racist, gender-based and material violence inflicted upon the Nso' people was not even limited to these acts alone. If we consider the multifaceted nature of colonial violence and its extension beyond immediate physical harm, encompassing various forms of exploitation, coercion and cultural destruction, we should perhaps consider how the bodies of the colonised were used as tools for the colonial project, forcibly becoming the agents of colonial violence. Decolonisation means structural change and must not be reduced to mere questions of diversity and inclusion, as currently preached by museums.[281] With such histories, it also means addressing the complex, intricate and sometimes painful layers of colonial domination, those that turned victims into perpetrators and forced neighbours to fight against each other.

Punitive Exhibitions

The so-called 'punitive' measures, like the one that led to the looting of Ngonnso', have consequences beyond the specific moments of linear history within which they happened. It is necessary to examine not just the context in which the objects were looted, but also the enduring coloniality that frames the way they have been displayed in museums and how the 'punishment' continues to rob them of any subjectivity. The exhibition of loot perpetuates the suffering of the Nso' people and other affected communities at the hands of colonisation. It reiterates the power dynamics of colonialism, wherein the colonisers exert control over the narratives and representations of indigenous cultures. This brutal removal of objects from their original contexts and their relegation to museum displays has robbed them of their subjectivity and dynamic life. Visiting the museum becomes an act of participating in that punishment. The dislocated objects, constantly trapped in storage rooms and the glass vitrines, emphasise not only their disconnection from cultural contexts, but the separation of the object from subjects, that is, the onlookers, who thereby become implicated in this colonial punishment.

The cultural knowledge and stories that should accompany these objects are frequently overlooked or misrepresented/misinterpreted in favour of simplified cataloguing and labelling. This fails to capture their true value and sanctity. The meaning and agency of a subject like Ngonnso' is indeed not innate, but relational. In a museum, Ngonnso' and other cultural assets, despite their dynamic lives before the theft, are reduced to mislabelled pieces that feed the banalities of visual curiosity. Visitors are deprived of the opportunity to engage with these objects in a culturally meaningful or sensitive way. At the same time, the object is deprived of the relations that engender its agency, beyond being presented as distinct from White European cultures. Instead of fostering appreciation for the richness of African cultural histories, the museum often reinforces a voyeuristic and superficial curiosity, further perpetuating stereotypes and misunderstandings. Behind the glass, the sanctity of Ngonnso' is lost. In front of the glass, the visitor is complicit to the ongoing punishment of the Nso' people. This also holds true for ethical displays in the museum. Thus, what we call for is an acknowledgement of the mutilation inherent in exhibiting looted cultural assets, and an acknowledgement that 'show and tell' is not the (only) way to give meaning to non-European cultures. Besides, we contend that meaningfulness is subjective, so every culture defines for itself what these effigies are for them, and what the best ethics of care might be.

Colonial ethnographic museums have perpetuated a static and detached representation of African cultures, contributing to a narrative that presents certain civilisations as relics of the past. In doing so, they fail to engage actively with communities and do not contribute to the revitalisation and empowerment of those cultures. Yet again, to say that they 'fail' would even suggest that the role of these museums was to engage with communities when, by design, their mission has always been the contrary. Perhaps we must just acknowledge the fact that this is exactly how the structure was conceived: to mutilate, detach and uproot cultures. Nevertheless, if we were to consider that the role of museums today has shifted, that they truly seek to revitalise objects, and that some cultures would not have survived without them, this would bring us to another question: which cultures are in fact museum cultures? Which cultures own the museum and which cultures do museums claim to own? Which cultures end up in museums and which ones do not? This raises complex issues. Historically, museums have collected artefacts from cultures that they deemed exotic, foreign or dying because of colonial conquest and European contact. This biased selection process resulted in the underrepresentation, non-representation and misrepresentation of certain people, while prioritising the perspectives of colonisers and anthropologists.

A prime example of this enduring primacy of Western perspectives took place during the visit of the *Fon* of Nso' to Berlin in November 2022. HRH Sehm Mbinglo II performed a ritual of reintroduction on Ngonnso' (see Figure 9.1). Standing on soil brought from the Nso' Palace specifically for this ritual, he sprinkled water on the effigy of Ngonnso'. This gesture left the museum conservationist red-faced. She would later confess in a private conversation with one of us that she was horrified at the act of throwing water on the object because that was the best way of destroying it. She exclaimed that our people do not appreciate what this country (Germany) has done for us. Do we know how much money has gone into the preservation of this artefact? Do we know how much time she would have to spend cleaning it after this?

But what use is Ngonnso' to the Nso' people if she is not first and foremost a ritual object? In the interest of preservation, the Berlin Ethnological Museum has doused Ngonnso' with toxic chemicals for over a century. Its effective preservation practice in fact poisoned her. Not only was she denied life because unable to participate her people's cultural traditions, but she was also denied death by incessant cosmetic treatment with chemicals.

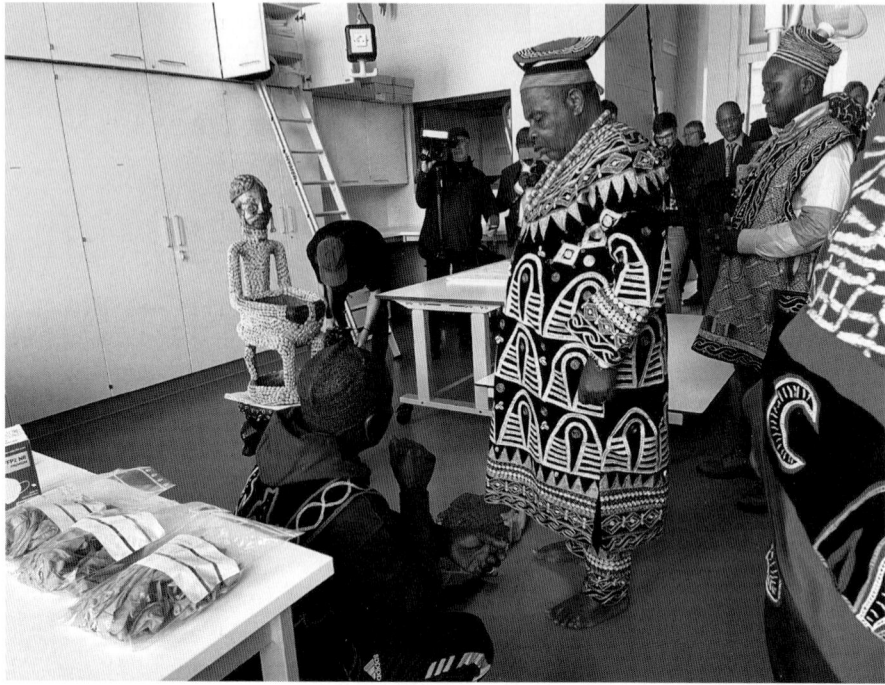

Figure 9.1: On 12 November 2022, His Royal Highness Sehm Mbinglo II paid a visit to Ngonnso' at the Humboldt Forum in 2023. It was the first time since the moment of theft that the Fon of Nso' met physically with the effigy and could initiate a ritual. Photo: courtesy of Sylvie Njobati and the Nso' Royal Palace.

The [Im]Possibility of Restitution

Restitution is impossible. Some human actions are irreparable. They may be regretful afterwards, confessed, atoned and forgiven, but they cannot be absolved away or repaired. For example, if on one of those glorious daybreak mornings, you come across an African lily, flourishing under the rising sun, and you deliberately step on it with your boots, crush it to the ground, and stampede on it repeatedly, you cannot subsequently repair the damage no matter how much you might regret it.

Restitution implies, above all, an honest admission and confession of the theft and the violence and damage that surrounded it, followed by repentance, amendment and reparation. In the 120 years since the theft of Ngonnso', how could the damages due ever be calculated, let alone paid in an act of restitution? Anything done along these lines could only be feebly symbolic. Is it surprising that Germany has firmly turned its back and shut its ears to any discussion about reparations or compensation? What about the Foundation Prussian Cultural Heritage presenting the return of Ngonnso' as the result of a positive evolution in European thinking? Colonial restitution efforts even go as far as trying to impose conditions, such as establishing suitable museums in the receiving country or making the returned assets available for public viewing. This is none of their business, seriously. Restitution of stolen property is restitution of stolen property. And it is absurd – even scandalous – for a repentant thief to impose conditions on the process.

After more than 120 years of museumification in Germany, it is high time Ngonnso' was considered for her true meaning. No one should dare ask 'what museum will she be going back to?' She was not stolen from a museum. Her fate after recovery should be left to the Nso' people. And for the Nso', as for other African peoples, the significance and use of such artefacts are far different from what Europeans do with their cultural heritage. Nso' people do not hang up artefacts just to be looked at and admired; they use them for whatever purpose they were made. Where museums exist in Africa, they are likely to be colonial remnants initiated, financed and controlled by former colonial powers or their African stooges and apprentices.

In the ongoing discussion among the Nso' regarding what should be done with Ngonnso' once she is finally back at *Ntoh Nso'*, the palace from where she was stolen, one of us suggested that she should be ritually, deeply buried in the open courtyard (*Maandze Ngaiy*). Part of the argument for this suggestion is that, apart from being the foundress of the kingdom, she was a stubborn, adventurous and erratic character compared to her two siblings, Nchari Yen, founder of the Foumban dynasty, and Nfoumbam, founder of the Bafia dynasty. Ngonnso' has troubled her descendants in profound ways, leaving them in the wilderness for over 120 years, during which many horrible things have happened to them: conquest, massive migration out of the kingdom and, most recently, her current dynastic successor's self-exile out of the kingdom, owing to a civil war raging in Cameroon, whose causes are rooted in the German colonisation of that part of Africa. Furthermore, burying her after performing a ritual would remove the worry about a befitting museum, as well as the possibility of her being stolen again. And, of course, as is the case with other departed ancestors, she will regularly be consulted, supplicated, questioned, praised or admonished at the spot where she is buried – cultural rituals that would enrich the ones that are still performed regularly in Nso': the yearly Ngonnso' cultural festival and the songs sung in her memory.

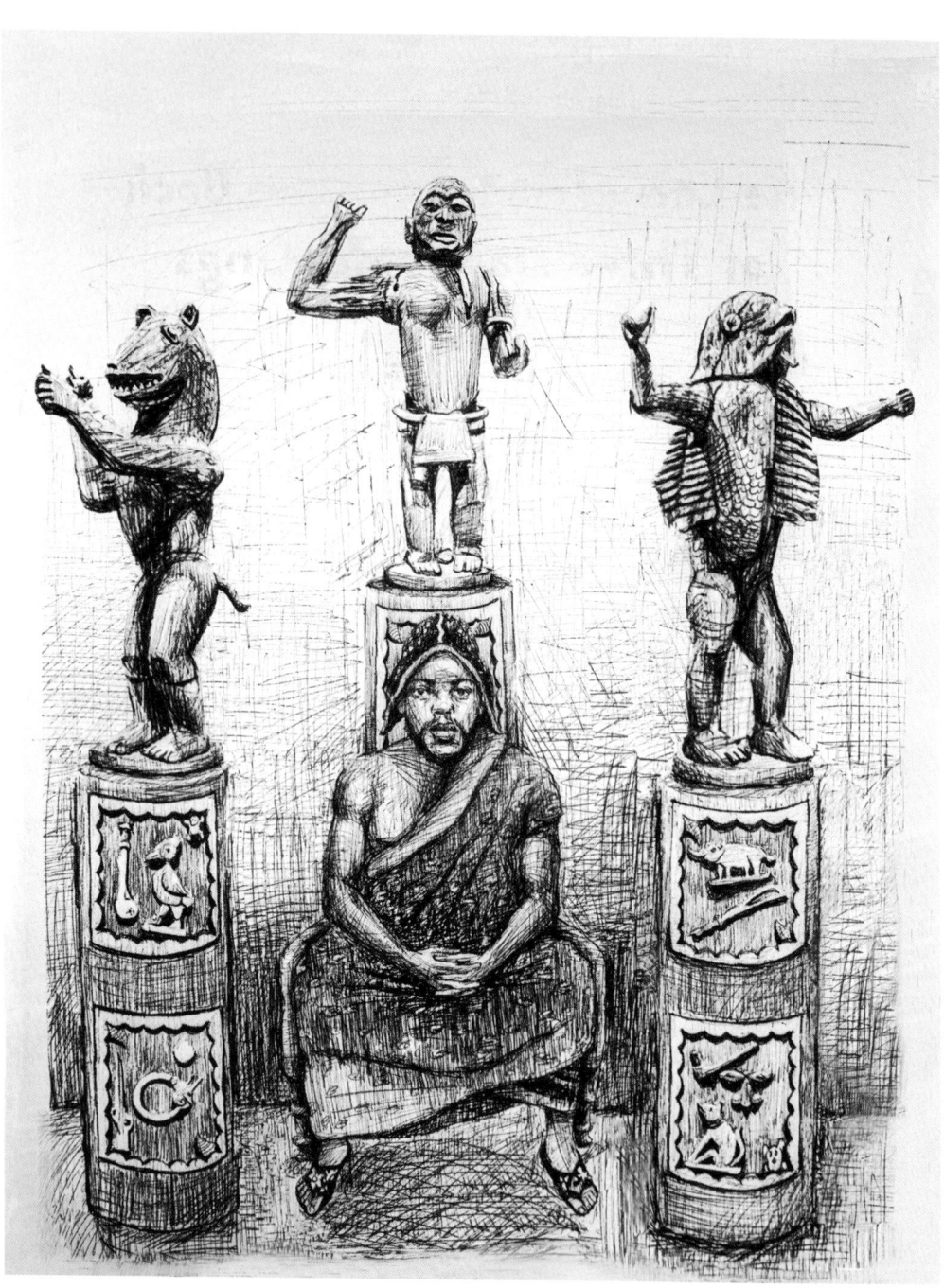

Artist: Chigozie Obi

CHAPTER 10

The Long Journey of the *Bocio* of Three Danxomè Kings

Didier Houénoudé and Gaëlle Beaujean

In 2021, the French Republic returned twenty-six cultural assets to the Republic of Benin. Three of them have been marked by political imagery from the moment they were conceived. Their story is a complex one to unravel. We are talking here about three human-sized statues, at least two of which are allegorical portraits of the kings of Danxomè, formerly the colonial territory of Dahomey, today Benin in West Africa.

The kings resided in Abomey, the kingdom's capital, and had been trading with Europeans – and Paris in particular – since the eighteenth century, first, in the context of the slave trade, and later, in agricultural goods. In 1885, at the Berlin Conference, fourteen European countries signed a treaty initiating the almost complete colonisation of the African continent, drawing new borders. The new Dahomey thus became part of the French colonial empire and colonisation was carried out by force in certain parts of the territory, in particular against the kingdom of Danxomè during the entire reign of Béhanzin (1890–1894). Under the orders of General Alfred-Amédée Dodds, the French conquered the capital on 17 November 1892. A few months later, the general handed over some of his personal booty to the Musée d'Ethnographie du Trocadéro, including three royal statues of Ghézo, Béhanzin and Glèlè, which remained in Paris for more than 120 years. When followed carefully, the journey of these *bocio*,[282] a local term that the West only recently adopted for these statues, enables us to examine the richness and variety of cultural value systems, as well as their strong religious, historical and political implications.

The *Bocio* in Vodun and Fon Culture: Meanings, Symbolism and Purposes

The literal meaning of *bocio* confers to this particular item the status of a receptacle of energy, a catalyst, or a device to counter bad luck. *Bocio* (pronounced 'bow-chee-aw' in English and 'bochio' in French) indeed translates as the corpse of the *bo*, an artefact made from vegetal and animal matter to which other kind of organic matter is sometimes added. The *bo* is used to defend oneself or attack an enemy in a mystical manner and is often improperly translated in European languages as 'talisman', 'amulet', '(lucky) charm' or '*gris-gris*'.

The typology of *bocio* reveals different forms: the *bocio bo*, a receptacle for a *bo* that the owner must always carry with them. In this case, the *bocio* is hollow and serves as a container or hiding place for the *bo*. This type of *bocio* only undergoes one ritual of purification that prepares it to receive and host the *bo*. Sometimes, in order to conceal the *bocio*'s function from the public eye, it is used as an armrest, seat back or fly chaser. The *bocio* itself can even be the *bo*. In this case, the plant species is chosen accordingly. If, for example, the function of the *bocio* is to provide protection for an individual, it is chosen from among the species that are most resistant to the vagaries of the weather and the most robust ones, those that already have great significance in Vodun spirituality and cosmogony. Once completed, the *bocio* undergoes rituals and becomes *bo*, and therefore sacred. There are also *bocio* that represent vodun, *bocio atínmɛ̀sɔ́* or *àtínkpàví*, and nowadays *bocio* that have an artistic function that includes simple contemplation. Special mention must be made of the *bocio atínmɛ̀sɔ́* and *àtínkpàví*, which are used to make the *kúɖyɔ̀*, a ritual that consists of replacing a sick person who is dying with a *bocio* and burying the *bocio* to rescue the individual's life. Here, the *bocio* acts as a substitute, taking on the ills that are supposed to afflict the individual and thus intervening in a form of medicine that Western culture equates with obscurantism.

The *bocio* have various meanings and are multifunctional. A single *bocio* might have several functions, and it is the function that determines the plant species used to carve the *bocio*. The *bocio* of kings are symbols representing the grandeur, invulnerability or the demiurge-like status of the sovereign. They can be zoomorphic, anthropomorphic or both at the same time. This is the case for the three *bocio* that France returned to Benin in 2021. They also serve as reminders of the monarch's authority in the minds of his subjects.[283] These statues, some of which can be moved, go wherever the king goes. Other *bocio* are moved only on rare occasions, for wars, for annual ceremonies such as the purification of the city (*tòkplɔ́kplɔ́*) or the annual *gandahi* ceremony. During this ceremony, which sees the king leave the palace to go to the market, he shows his people his power and ability to protect them. On this occasion, the *bocio* are carried on the head or on platforms or plinths pushed by some members of the palace court.

Other *bocio*, however, must not be moved because of their highly sacred nature. These ones stand in royal headquarters and represent the king's vulnerable body, so that he can take part in military battles without being affected by enemy attacks.[284] Lastly, some of them seem to have a metempsychosis function: in other words, they served as living quarters for deceased relatives or ancestors whose role was to advise the sovereign in the management of power. Through dedicated rituals, the souls of the dead are recalled.

The *Bocio* in Western Knowledge

'Devil', 'idol', 'fetish', 'amulet', 'talisman', 'charm' or even 'evil spirit', 'misshapen monster', '*magot*' (ugly figure) or '*marmouset*' (grotesque statuette) are the terms that were used to describe the Danxomean *bocio* in Western literature from the eighteenth to the early twentieth century.[285] The vernacular name *bo*, in the Fongbè language, appeared for the first time in the writings of British diplomat Richard Burton and those of zoologist Alfred Skertchly.[286] But the precise and complex meaning of *bo* and its sculpted version, the *bocio*, was only finally clarified at the end of the twentieth century in publications by the American art historian Suzanne Preston Blier. Her literal translation splits the word between *bo*, identified as medicine, power, and *cio*, the corpse, made present through sculpture.[287] In other words, it is thanks to specific care work that repels the dangers of death that the carved figure becomes effective.[288] The agency of the *bocio* depends on a combination of skills, people, gestures, words, products and manipulations dispensed by various specialists from the Vodun religion and the geomancy of the *Fa*. In the latter case, the royal diviners (*bokonɔ*) instructed the kings that military victory came with the *bocio*, such as those of Glèlè and Béhanzin.[289] The *bokonɔ* would then intervene to activate and deactivate them. In the 2000s, the king of Abomey Houedogni Béhanzin explained to the French anthropologist and author Galia Tapiero: 'when the king [Béhanzin's *bocio*] left, the statue had already been neutralised. Which means that what you have [in Paris] is just a piece of wood.'[290] Once cared for, these 'Kingly *Fa bociɔ*' were therefore reduced in the museum in Paris to a mere token of material culture, being detached from the *Fa*'s care.

However, it seems difficult on the Western side not to associate these figures with monuments of world sculpture. In this context, French ethnologists based in the French colony of Dahomey conducted studies of the artists of Abomey in 1959.[291] These have been followed up until this day, reaching an international scale. We know that the kings were careful to choose artists associated with the royal court, who were capable of developing original and exceptional forms.[292] In 1938, the North American anthropologist Melville J. Herskovits described the special status of the sculptor recognised as an artist, who is clearly distinguished from the craftsman in Fongbè language. To carry out his work, the sculptor isolates himself and chisels hard wood, sometimes with a small axe, a knife, a chisel and abrasive sheets.[293] In 1985, art historian Robert Farris Thompson identified Sosandande Likohin Kankanhau as the author of the royal *bocio* statue of Glèlè, to which we can also relate the *bocio* with the emblems of Béhanzin.[294] Over time, the artist's name became Sossa Dede in Western sources, whose most complete biography was written by the Beninese historian Bachalou 'Ba' Nondichao.[295]

As far as scientific studies of the *bocio* are concerned, the French anthropologist and colonial administrator Maurice Delafosse published the first article on the three polychrome *bocio* statues as soon as they arrived in Paris. Seeing 'in these works the beginning of an art, capable of being perfected', he recounts in his own way the departure of these sculptures 'that could be saved from the Abomé fire'. He goes on to describe each carving in detail and is able to clearly identify each of the three kings thanks to their emblems in the construction of hybrid effigies: the bird-man (Ghézo), the lion-man (Glèlè), and the shark-man (Béhanzin).[296]

The figure of Ghézo, however, raises more questions regarding its attribution to a royal figure. His body was covered with twisted iron blades fixed into the wood, which Delafosse immediately associated with the feathers of the ghé bird, one of King Ghézo's emblems. This is the only element that makes it possible to link the figure to a hybrid effigy. Although Maurice Delafosse does not mention it, the engraving in his article shows a human face for Ghézo's *bocio*, not a zoomorphic one like the other two. This face seems to have been reworked: the wood is clear, rough, unfinished, unlike the rest of the sculpture. What is more, considering the socle supporting the figure attributed to Ghézo, it seems to match other types of popular monochrome *bocio* sculptures planted in front of houses or at crossroads, which, for a long time, the French thought were the sole manifestations of *bocio*. This is why, in 1926, Georges Emmanuel Waterlot believed that the royal statue had been incorrectly attributed. For him, the socle demonstrated that it was a *bocio* that could in no way be linked to the king.[297] Following Waterlot's recommendations, the Musée du Trocadéro decided to 'separate' the statue of Ghézo from the others. We noted above the difficulty of defining or translating the term *bocio* in Western epistemology. After the Parisian museum initially associated them with so-called 'popular magic cults', an idea that was reinforced by the acquisition of more than fifty anthropomorphic *bocio* in 1930,[298] it took more than a century to understand the meaning of the term, the range of their functions, and the power of the *bocio*, including these royal embodiments. In spite of this, the museum side-lined Ghézo's effigy until 2009.

However, Delafosse's eye did not miss the dynamic arms, the presence of a weapon in the hand of the iron-bladed *bocio* of Ghézo, or the cartridge belts hanging on the hips of the lion Glèlè and the shark Béhanzin. He interprets in those details the representation of royal figures linked to war. It is entirely possible that the *bocio* of the three kings had brandished one or more weapons in the past. During a parade of wealth that took place under the reign of Glèlè (1858–1889), the British naturalist Alfred Skertchly noticed a figure reminiscent of the lion-shaped *bocio*: 'a gang of twelve man … appeared dragging a dray of native manufacture, upon which was the wooden figure of a very heraldic lion, rampant, and carrying a sword in either hand.'[299] This rampant lion could have been Glèlè's *bocio*, presented as lying down during the procession. Suzanne Preston Blier went deeper in 1986 when she learned from Sagbadju, son of Glèlè and *bokonɔ*, that the statues moved and spoke. Moreover, a descendant of King Glèlè and historian called Agbidinukun shared with her two songs dedicated to the *bocio* of Glèlè and Béhanzin.[300] In 1997, the North American art historian completed her knowledge on the use of these royal, magical and military *bocio*, pointing out that they bore 'talismanic materials' in cavities inside the figure or on the surface. She went on: 'as a royal war sculpture, it was brought in to help to change the course of events for the benefit of the king'.[301] According to anthropologist Galia Tapiero, at least two of the three were displayed at the parade of wealth and kept the rest of the time 'high on a platform in front of the private residence of the king'.[302] Her source, however, referred to deified royal ancestors, not kings.[303] Another hypothesis put forward in 2006 and 2008 comes from Beninese historiographers Gabin Djimassé and Ba Bachalou Nondichao. According to them, the *bocio* occupied a special covered space called *adanjeho* in the official palace, where they received promises of victory.[304]

From Appropriation to Restitution

The sign *du* of the Fa of Béhanzin insisted that the biggest threat would come from the ocean. In response, the king chose the strong name and the emblem of the shark, which announced his determination to preserve his territory from intrusions from the coast, in particular Ouidah and Cotonou. Barely enthroned in 1890, Béhanzin mobilised his army in Cotonou against the annexation of this city by the French army. Already effective in Porto Novo, French colonial occupation of the region intensified when, in August 1892, the French government decided to send an expeditionary column of over 3,000 soldiers led by Lieutenant-Colonel Alfred-Amédée Dodds to 'Dahomey'.[305] On 17 November 1892, the French army seized Abomey and planted the flag in the royal palaces. Before leaving his capital, King Béhanzin ordered all the treasures to be gathered and kept away in underground tunnels, and the palaces to be burnt down. The day after the capture of Abomey and the extinction of the fire, the French searched for the weapons still preserved in the city. They discovered underground hideaways where they found weapons, alcohol, textiles, as well as European and

local goods and possessions. An engraving published by eyewitness Alexandre d'Albéca shows some of the spoils of war (see QR code). He commented: 'After a few days, in front of the general's tent, there was a veritable bazaar.'[306] Nevertheless, images and representations of this loot are rare and details of the French spoils in Abomey are difficult to assess, even today.[307] Soldiers and non-commissioned officers testified to the opaque management and distribution of loot in Abomey. Information on the places where they were collected is scarce as well.

On his return to France in 1893, Dodds decided to donate eight royal assets to the Musée d'Ethnographie du Trocadéro.[308] After they were each assigned an inventory number and thereby became inalienable property under French national ownership, the *bocio* were transformed into royal statues through a succinct label and museal description. Delafosse reported the degraded state of the statues of Béhanzin and Glèlè, the former having lost its lower jaw and the latter with 'a broken arm and a piece of snout removed'.[309] After the museum's cabinetmaker 'repaired' them, the *bocio* returned to the museum's public area, displayed for a few decades on a pedestal as war trophies. Among the visitors in 1908, the young architect Charles-Edouard Jeanneret, more commonly known as Le Corbusier, sketched the *bocio* from different angles.[310] Whether appropriation or inspiration, Le Corbusier reproduced the photographs of the three *bocio* in one of the very first multimedia works titled 'Poème électronique', produced together with the composers Iannis Xénakis and Edgar Varèse, and shown at the 1958 Brussels World Fair. The *bocio* are shown in a sequence on men and war that plays on the ambiguity of the Danxomean and colonial wars, and features a shot of a sacred *nkisi nkonde* sculpture (see Chapter 12).[311]

From 1937 to 2003, the *bocio* were forced to act as 'ethnographic objects' at the Musée de l'Homme. Ghézo's *bocio* was placed in the background of the display case labelled 'Religion', and those of Glèlè and Béhanzin behind a display on Dahomey, before being later associated with African royalty.[312] The new curation of the works at the Musée de l'Homme was also accompanied by a gradual absence of information on the link between colonial conquest and the presence of these statues. Even though their transfer to the Musée du Quai Branly in 2006 meant that they were assigned the status of works of art, the display of the *bocio* included a multimedia broadcast on spoils of war. In 2009, a collaborative project between the museum and a Beninese team examined in greater depth the role of artists in Abomey, in particular that of Sossa Dede. It brought about conversations and debates on the biography of these courtly cultural assets, which researchers had until then largely neglected. In this respect, it is important to add that while the *bocio* of Glèlè and Béhanzin temporarily left both the Musée de l'Homme and the Musée du Quai Branly for exhibitions in Paris and New York, they did not join other loans from those two institutions to the Republic of Benin, neither for the exhibition dedicated to Glèlè at the palaces of Abomey in 1989, nor for the 'Béhanzin' exhibition at the Fondation Zinsou in Cotonou in 2009, for all its popular success.

The Long Journey of the *Bocio*

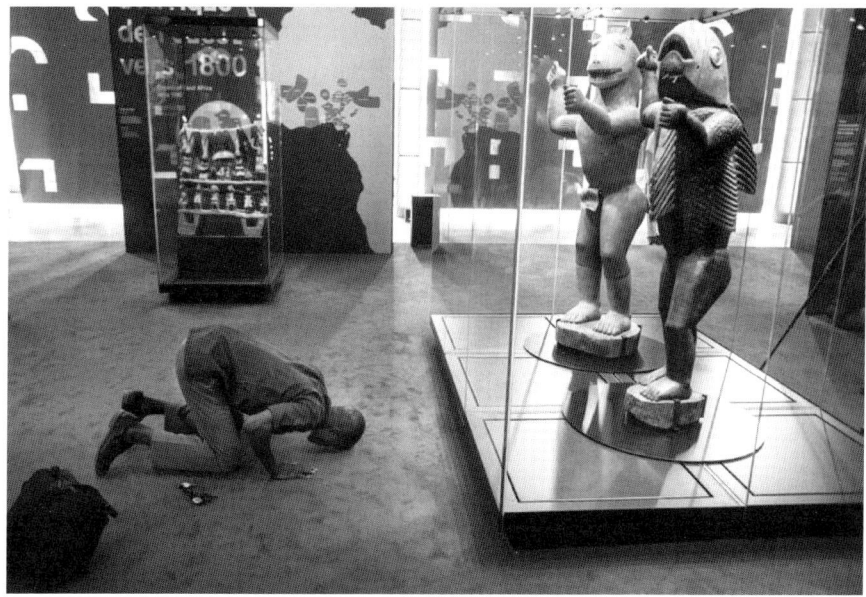

Figure 10.1: In 2022, after the return of the Danxomean treasures, a man kneels in front of the *bocio* of Béhanzin at the opening of the exhibition in Cotonou, Benin. Photo: Patrick Zachmann, © Magnum Photos.

Barely elected as President of the Republic of Benin, Patrice Talon openly supported his government in their request for the return of the Abomey treasures, a claim first made in July 2016. The French government initially refused, citing the Heritage Code and the inalienability of collections.[313] In 2017, newly elected President Emmanuel Macron announced at the University of Ouagadogou his intention to return African cultural assets to their countries of origin and facilitate their circulation. Felwine Sarr and Bénédicte Savoy submitted a report to the French presidential office on this issue in 2018.[314] In conjunction with the Ministry of Culture and its operators, such as the Musée du Quai Branly – Jacques Chirac, the French government proposed a bill for the restitution of twenty-seven African cultural assets, including twenty-six from Abomey, and their subsequent removal from the inventory.[315] After expert appraisals and discussions in the National Assembly and Senate, the bill was unanimously adopted by the National Assembly on 17 December 2020 and promulgated by the Head of State on 24 December 2020. The three *bocio*, along with 23 other assets looted from the Abomey court, were returned in November 2021.

The Return of the *Bocio* to Benin: Political and Popular Re-Appropriation

From the rejection of the French airline Air France and the chartering of a special plane by the Beninese government, to the pomp and circumstance when showcasing the crates containing the works, up until the parade of the convoy through the city of Cotonou which began at the airport and ended at the Palais de la Marina, the seat of the Beninese president, the staging of the return of the twenty-six treasures of Abomey was destined to restore Benin's besmirched honour and dignity. It also aimed to build a common Beninese identity around the regalia. Beninese cultural heritage could not travel back with an airline from the country that had despoiled Benin 129 years ago. Any support from France could have been interpreted as a condescending gesture from the former coloniser and was therefore turned down. The end of exile and the recovery of a freedom of decision on the fate of these treasures was not to be granted by the spoliator but won by the victim.

The route of the crates containing the works to the presidency was marked out so that the public could experience the event of their return. The ensuing welcoming ceremony took place in the gardens of the presidency, one of the central symbols of power. Leading figures from politics, civil society, the arts, culture and academia, as well as traditional figures, kings, dignitaries, religious and spiritual leaders were all on hand to celebrate the return of the twenty-six works.[316] The ceremony aimed to create a link in the public psyche between the success of the restitution process and the valued and laudable action of the Presidential Office, especially emphasising the commitment of its current occupant. It was also intended to prepare people to accept the fact that the works first housed in the presidential palace would subsequently be shown to all Beninese in the same space, without running the risk of giving the impression that the current government was monopolising these Danxomean cultural assets.

The exhibition, which was organised with some haste and excitement by a conglomerate of institutions (including the National Gallery, the National Agency for Heritage and Tourism, the Ministry of Culture, Tourism and the Arts, and the Presidential Office of the Republic of Benin), was intended to show the world that the Beninese are indeed capable of taking charge of their own cultural heritage and, above all, of complying with international standards in the exhibition process. The enthusiastic response to the exhibition from the large number of visitors – over 400,000 according to figures provided by the Ministry of Culture – seems to confirm the organisers' belief that the event was the right way to enable Beninese people from all walks of life to discover and/or be united around these treasures from their past.

The underlying idea for this exhibition was also to help the people of Benin reclaim their heritage, a heritage most of them were unaware of or, at least, unfamiliar with. The works in question had been absent from the land where they were born for 129 years, the equivalent of about five generations of Beninese. The question some commentators were asking was how Beninese people would go about reappropriating the works, and how long it would take for them to be adopted by the nation as a whole. In the end, the exhibition achieved what it set out to do: to unite the people of Benin around the important need to return Beninese heritage to its rightful owners (all the people of Benin, of course) and create a buzz around the 'royal treasures of Benin', which had once been the 'royal treasures' of Béhanzin, before colonial history made them 'war trophies'.[317] Today, they are elevated to the status of 'national heroes'.[318]

Many visitors to the exhibition were keen to reclaim these cultural assets from another era and saw them as the first steps towards the mass restitution of other cultural assets still held in Western museums. The president and a large section of the population have asked for the return of the sculpture of the god Gou, attributed to Akati Ekplekendo and exhibited at the Pavillon des Sessions near the Louvre, as well as the Fa tablet of Guèdégbé, the diviner appointed by King Béhanzin, still in the custody of the Musée du Quai Branly – Jacques Chirac.[319] Regardless of the emotions that arose in each and every Beninese when they visited the exhibition, a large majority felt that it is legitimate to continue to reclaim and take back cultural belongings to which they feel more or less attached.[320] The challenges facing Benin's and Africa's museum institutions will undoubtedly be: how to ensure that the people of Benin take ownership of this returning heritage; how to ensure that it is properly discussed; and how to nurture the new relationships that will be forged between these treasures and their communities of origin, and indeed Benin as a whole.

In the context of the restitution to Benin, these twenty-six cultural assets – but primarily the *bocio* and the thrones – have become a seductive asset, a pledge for reconciliation with an idealised past, that of the powerful kingdom of Danxomè.[321] The construction of the Museum of the Kings and Amazons of Danxomè (MuRAD) in Abomey, which will be the twenty-six cultural assets' final destination, is part of this desire to recreate the kingdom's glorious past. Although national discourse identifies them as part of 'the treasure of Béhanzin', Benin's national and African hero, the kings and amazons' feats of arms in the kingdom have been widely criticised by certain populations who have retained, until today, a terrifying memory of the Danxomean military conquests. To reconcile diverse perspectives and follow the rhetoric of national unity, it is essential to recall that this 'Treasure of Benin' around which the Beninese should build a new common identity was the result of various cultural and artistic influences brought by the many captives of the Danxomè army that led to the perennial establishment of a unique court art.

Creating unity among the people of Benin around assets whose link with their communities has been severed for 129 years is a colossal challenge. The successful re-appropriation of cultural heritage by the people of Benin should involve the contribution of these communities of people who hold the knowledge and know-how, however fragmentary, and should include the perspectives of women, minorities, curators, teachers and researchers.

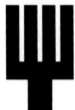

PART III

THE SACRED

Colonial conquest and missionary efforts went hand in hand with the destruction of shrines and the looting of religious symbols, from ancestor guardian figures to the sacred *tabots* of the Christian Ethiopian Orthodox Church. Practising what is often called iconoclasm, colonialists took away or even willingly destroyed sacred sculptures and medicine. These were then sent to museums who studied them and thereby perpetuated the colonial discourse on 'primitivism' and the argument for spreading European civilisation.

Items of an intimate character were also taken away. Prior to being snatched away, these personal possessions of family heritage such as protective effigies and grave ornaments had been a part of people's everyday life and daily rituals. This section will foreground the realm of the sacred, where spiritual knowledge was guarded, where taking these things away meant transgressing religious beliefs and violating someone's dignity. What did the theft of an ancestor, a guardian figure or a sacred drum imply? What about the execution of spiritual mediums in front of their people before purloining their remains away, preventing the proper burial rituals? What is the extent of the gaps which have been left in the spiritual knowledge and religious practices ever since the colonial profanation and desecration of sacred heritage?

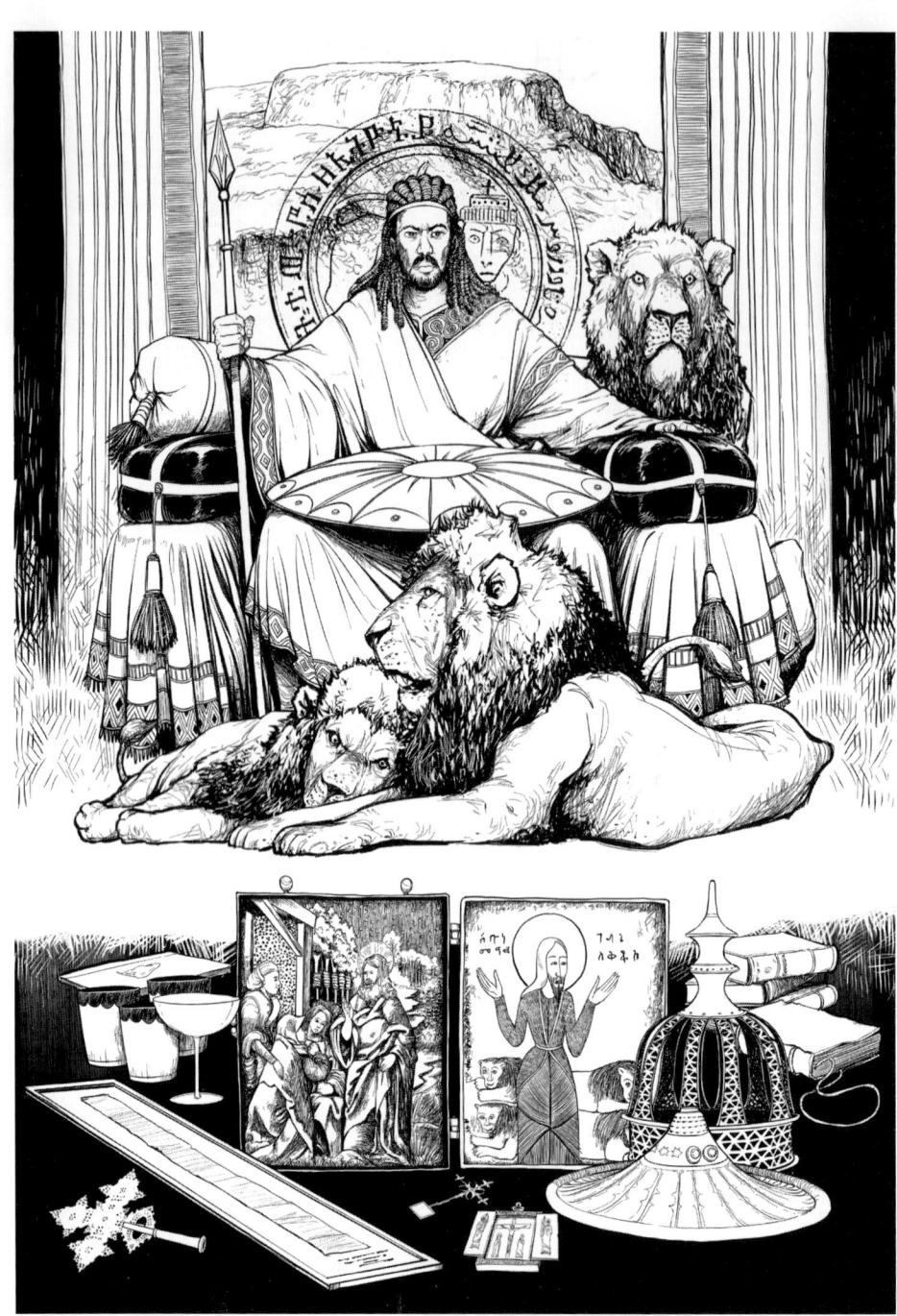

Artist: Bright Toh

CHAPTER 11

Degodding Maqdala

Emanuel Admassu and Eyob Derillo

Restitution

Euphemistically known as the British Expedition to Abyssinia, the brutal invasion of the Horn of Africa that took place in 1867–1868 is justified in the colonial record books through two recurring narratives: 1) freeing British hostages imprisoned by emperor Tewodros II; and 2) punishing the Ethiopian emperor for his malicious acts.[322] Neither argument accounts for the caravan of elephants that were used to extract countless cultural assets and sacred manuscripts.[323] The theft of 'ceremonial crosses, chalices, processional umbrella tops, weapons, textiles, jewellery and archeological materials, as well as *tabots*', was rendered as the collateral result of a tactical military operation.[324] There is minimal accounting of the reasons that brought British missionaries and explorers to Ethiopia in the first place; why they might have been perceived as potential threats by Tewodros II and how they were serving the interests of the British Empire, preceding and during the military action.

The invasion was not an anomaly. There have been others – before and after it – throughout Africa and Asia.[325] It was not a spontaneous response, but a predictable event forged by a world order that had been structured through theft and slavery. Therefore, a critical discussion around questions of restitution in the twenty-first century is a confrontation with the impossibility of return. Over the past few decades, scholars, artists and activists have opened up space to imagine what museums could become if they cease to be afterimages of colonialism. Ongoing protests, strikes and direct actions at museums are producing counterpoints to the ossification of Western art institutions.[326] These interventions are unveiling the conditions through which cultural assets have been acquired, interpreted and displayed.

Questioning the authority of museums prompts consideration of practices that remain beyond their purview. For example, the late poet and literary critic Harry

Garuba has written about African oral and literary traditions that project spirituality onto everyday items. He described embedding metaphorical meaning within cultural assets as practices of 'animist materialism' that lead to the 'continual re-enchantment of the world'.[327] These layers of meaning remain invisible to the uninitiated while offering catharsis to their practitioners, absorbing shifts in culture, politics and technology, into existing belief systems. Garuba argues that 'animist materialism' is a prudent response to social and environmental change. But it can also be understood as a nuanced form of cultural preservation that contextualises new spatial and material conditions within familiar origin stories. Therefore, the landscapes and cultural assets that were destroyed and looted by colonial forces are enveloped with mythological and spiritual significances that overflow and overwhelm their current ethnographic enclosures. Notions of non-human aliveness – often problematically stamped as 'animism' – are critical to restitution debates because they articulate how the museums displaying looted items from the African continent fail to register their vitality.[328]

After the British invasion, *tabot*s and manuscripts that were used in everyday liturgies and teachings were pilfered and transformed into rarefied artefacts; they have since been locked in the storage rooms and vitrines of Europe. This trajectory emblematises a process of desacralisation that is built on a long history of 'degodding/de-supernaturalizing' as a tool of empire.[329] The armies, scholars, curators and conservators, committed to the museological project of containment, have claimed that these cultural assets need to be kept in Europe, 'in the hope that some light might be thrown by them' on a continent characterised as dark.[330] Thus, the hallowed books and tablets that held communities together in the Horn of Africa were eclipsed by the promise of a universalising episteme: a quest to make *all* knowledge systems and cultures invariably transparent.

The British Museum and the British Library, two institutions that have historically weaponised their collections to exclude Africans from their conceptions of the human, currently hold manuscripts and *tabot*s that were looted from Maqdala in 1868.[331] The architecture of these archives, along with the documents that legitimise their existence in perpetuity, maintain the ambiance, as Achille Mbembe notes, of 'temples and cemeteries'.[332] The construct of the museum offers platforms for European experts of African art to argue that the regions these cultural assets come from are not modern, that Africans do not have the appropriate infrastructure or qualified personnel to preserve and maintain invaluable human heritage. We are told that knowledge can only be transferred across generations through processes that freeze and encapsulate material heritage. This belief system has an incongruous relation to the primary role of *tabot*s and manuscripts as activators of collective and solitary rituals, linking material and spiritual worlds. Thus, the interpretive frameworks and methods of valuation that frame these looted items are demonstrations of the West's inability to conceive other 'modes of being human'.[333]

Maqdala was invaded and destroyed two decades prior to the Berlin Conference of 1884–1885. It foreshadowed the colonial borders that have imposed regimes of commodity, extraction and immobility on Black life. The juridical abstractions of property that allow multinational corporations to speculate on Africa's resources today were measured, tested and built through 'expeditions' like the one that took place in Abyssinia. This is precisely why there is an urgent need to imagine methods of restitution that challenge nation-state formations. By outlining the intersections of architecture, heritage and migration, we could begin to unsettle the hegemonic role of Western museums as sites that construct, taxonomise and preserve racial hierarchies. By understanding Ethiopian history up to the Abyssinian Expedition through the looted *tabot*s and manuscripts, we aim to counter the carceral logics enacted by the edifice of the museum.

Tabots and Manuscripts

The profound spiritual, cultural and political significance of *tabot*s comes from the belief that the Ark of the Covenant – one of the most sacred relics of Judeo-Christian religious traditions – was brought from Jerusalem to Aksum by Menelik I, the son of Queen Sheba and King Solomon, in around the tenth century BCE. The Solomonic dynasty of Ethiopian monarchy traces its lineage back to this event. The *tabot*s found throughout Ethiopia are replicas of the tablets that were housed within the Ark of the Covenant onto which the biblical Ten Commandments were inscribed. Every Ethiopian Orthodox Tewahedo church is consecrated by housing a *tabot* at its centre, in a room called the *Bete Mek'des* (the inner sanctuary), where it remains concealed from the laity. On patronal feast days, *tabot*s are draped in ornate textiles, carried on the heads of priests, and paraded around cities and villages. The significance of the day is marked by the departure of the *tabot* from the *Bete Mek'des*. On *Timket* (feast of the Epiphany, 19 January), *tabot*s from several churches are followed by thousands of people marching in unison. Public thoroughfares become extensions of the sanctuary, as the processions move from the church to an open field for an overnight celebration. The following day, the parade follows the *tabot*s back to their respective churches.

A thousand years after the arrival of the Ark, Aksum became a powerful kingdom. Its socio-political influence spanned from the north-eastern coast of Africa across the Red Sea to the southern tip of the Arabian Peninsula. Facilitated by maritime trade and military might, Aksum's territorial dominance lasted several centuries before the era of European imperial expansion. Historian Bahru Zewde writes,

> the conversion of Aksumite King Ezana to Christianity in 330s [CE] ushered in a new chapter in the country's history. The creed, in its Orthodox form, came to express the cultural identity of a large section of its highland population.

Ideologically and diplomatically, the Ethiopian church and state were thenceforth tied up with the Alexandrian patriarchate in Egypt, who had sole authority to consecrate a bishop for the Ethiopian church, the *abun*.[334]

Thus, the official acceptance of Christianity happened in conjunction with the formation of an African empire. This means that people living in the region that is now known as Ethiopia (formerly known as Abyssinia) have been practising an indigenised creed of Orthodox Christianity for almost 2,000 years. Entanglements between religion, culture and politics were shaped through geographic proximities to the Red Sea, the Indian Ocean and the Nile River. Such proximities offered various sites of flow where power was negotiated between vast populations as they migrated from different parts of Africa, the Arabian Peninsula, southern Europe and South Asia.

Tabots functioned as the gravitational centres of the roving royal camps that came after Aksum. They anchored people to place.[335] Even the current capital of Ethiopia, established in the late nineteenth century, was settled around a *tabot* for Entoto Mariyam. Traditional Ethiopian Orthodox churches are circular or octagonal in plan, typically surrounded by forests and positioned within *ghebbi*s (fenced-in areas). The fence, the dense foliage and the *Bete Mek'des* serve as buffers between the *tabot* and its surrounding environment, offering concentric zones of worship and gathering. In popular Amharic parlance, the construction of a new church is described as the 'planting of a *tabot*', acknowledging its role as the seed that sprouts actual vegetation and a new community.[336]

Today, *tabots* continue to choreograph trans-scalar migration and stasis. People across Ethiopia make yearly pilgrimages to be in close proximity with specific *tabots* that are believed to possess healing powers, while farmers abstain from harvesting and ploughing their fields during the monthly celebration of their local *tabot*.[337] Feared, guarded and considered transcendent, the enigma of *tabots* is augmented by the fact that they are kept out of sight.

Yet throughout the history of the Orthodox church in Ethiopia, the invisible presence of *tabots* was coupled with the hyper-visible images and calligraphy of sacred manuscripts. These bound books have been held and carefully read by untold generations of people. The oldest surviving manuscripts, the Garima Gospels, date back to around 390–570 CE. Written by anonymous scribes in the ancient Semitic language of Ge'ez, a language now confined to ecclesiastical use, the sacred manuscripts register shifting aesthetic, spiritual and philosophical traditions. Most of the books were inscribed on parchment made from goat or sheep skin, then marked with margins, columns and text lines before writing. The parchment pages are bound using 'link stitch' to sew the quires together, then attached to decorated wood boards using the same thread. The volumes encompass a wide range of literature: gospel books, apocrypha, hymns, liturgy, ecclesiastical and civil law, psalters, patristic literature, lives of saints, letters, medicine and philology. Scribes used reed pens and various pigments made from carbon, stones, soil and plants. Put differently, the manuscripts were textured by the material specificities of the region, recording the movements of people and ideas along with shifts in flora and fauna.

Empire

In the seventeenth century, Emperor Fasilides (1632–1667) established Gondar as the new and seemingly permanent centre of the Solomonic dynasty. The city became a hub for transnational experiments in education and architecture. A formidable set of stone churches and castles were built to house an impressive collection of manuscripts and *tabot*s. A few decades later, during the reign of Emperor Iyasu I (1682–1706), the royal court of Gondar fostered a vibrant cultural environment for nuanced theological debates, cultivating an exchange of ideas in calligraphy, illustration and book-making methods from other regions, and resulting in the production of exquisite manuscripts. But the concentration of power in Gondar was an aberration within the long history of migration and annexation that had defined the northern kingdoms of Ethiopia. The sedentary nature of the new capital limited the frequency of direct oversight from emperors, emboldening regional lords and sparking one of the most chaotic periods in recent Ethiopian history: *Zamana Mesafint* (the 'age of princes'). From the mid-eighteenth to the mid-nineteenth century, political power was chipped away from the emperors in Gondar and distributed to nobles who had stronger armies and tax bases.

In the midst of this fragmentation, a distant relative of one of the regional lords – 'Maru of Dambya (south-west Gondar)' – named Kasa Haylu began to incrementally amass territory and influence.[338] Not having a clear hereditary path to power, and disenchanted by the infighting of the nobles, he 'became a *shefta* (rebel)' and 'soon came to head a group of bandits composed of other disgruntled persons and ordinary robbers'.[339] Kasa Haylu was crowned Emperor Tewodros II in 1855. He paved his path to the throne by staging and winning battles against regional kings, who did not consider him to be a legitimate heir to any dominion, let alone the title *negusa negast* ('king of kings'). During his short reign as emperor (1855–1868), Tewodros was preoccupied with attempts to stabilise a region that had been embroiled in territorial battles for more than a century. He was determined to reinstate the centrality of the Solomonic dynasty, conceptualising the new seat of his throne, according to his chronicler Alaqa Walda Maryam, as 'a new Gondar'.[340]

A belief in the inseparability of church and state fed Tewodros's indefatigable efforts of collecting ancient manuscripts, *tabot*s and treasures from numerous churches and castles in northern and central parts of Abyssinia.[341] Each victory in the battlefield presented an opportunity to move religious and political signifiers of power to Debra Tabor, where he had initially anchored his capital and, eventually, to his fortress in

Maqdala. There, Tewodros was planning to build a church named *Medhane Alam* ('Saviour of the World') along with a treasury and a national library. An exceptional collection of close to 1,000 manuscripts was assembled with the aim of establishing Maqdala as an 'centre of study as well as of worship'.[342] But Maqdala never achieved the monumentality of Gondar. Its architecture remained provisional. The construction of the fortress was perpetually interrupted by regional and transnational threats, the ripple effects of *Zamana Mesafint*. For Tewodros, the mounting tensions and hostility with neighbouring kings would eventually prove fatal when one of his northern rivals, the future Emperor Yohannes IV, aided the British in their Abyssinian invasion.

Tewodros's growing sense of isolation led to an obsession with modern artillery. Because he gained power almost exclusively through military action, the role of warfare remained central to his idea of leadership.[343] European artisans were recruited to make weapons for his army, and his correspondence with European monarchs was laden with requests for weaponry.[344] An attempted consolidation, from fragmented kingdoms to an empire with a national army, drove most of the political manoeuvrings of his reign. He initiated the larger project of nation-state formation – a project which Menelik II achieved a few decades later. But Tewodros was not only determined to fortify his control over northern Ethiopia, he also wished to expand his territory across the Red Sea to Jerusalem. During the latter half of his reign, this monumental vision shifted Tewodros's focus from the highlands to the coast. Freeing the holy city from the Ottoman Empire would have recuperated the ancestral claims of the Solomonic dynasty and legitimised his place within that lineage. But these aspirations of domination and expansion ultimately led to his demise. As they have done elsewhere, the machinations of European imperialism were able to exploit regional conflicts by fashioning relationships that interchangeably used guns and crosses, armies and spies camouflaged as missionaries.

Tewodros II's diplomatic relations with Britain were based on an assumed solidarity between Christian peoples. He was concerned, like the emperors before him, about the growing Egyptian encroachment from the north. This concern had been intensifying ever since Egypt absorbed Sudan in the 1820s. Thus, Tewodros wrote a letter requesting help from Queen Victoria. The letter articulated his underlying belief that the British Empire would not hesitate to defend a Christian sovereign from the threat of Islam. But his reliance on religious affiliations did not anticipate the fact that 'Judeo-Christian/Latin-Christian Europe [...] was in the process of reinstituting itself as the secular imperial entity', a process of 'degodding' that replaced Christianity with whiteness,[345] solidifying race over religion as the primary signifier that draws borders and kinships between different geographies and genres of the human.[346] It is difficult to decipher why the letter sent to Queen Victoria in 1863 did not reach her, but it is safe to assume that it was not given the level of importance that Tewodros had expected it to garner. Feeling slighted by the lack of response, the emperor grew suspicious that the British might be conspiring with Egypt. This growing suspicion eventually led to his infamous decision to imprison the British consul and other European envoys, sparking the outrage of the British public. From a geopolitical standpoint, Britain of course had other interests: protecting its route to India, maintaining diplomatic relations with the Ottoman Empire, and keeping a close watch on the growing power of Egypt.[347] Ultimately, the British might have been 'indifferent to his demands for assistance, but not to his imprisonment of Europeans'.[348]

Loot

Thirteen thousand soldiers were enlisted by the British Indian Army to board ships in Mumbai and sail across the Arabian and Red Sea, reaching the Gulf of Zula in October 1867. This trajectory serves as a tacit reminder of the global reach of Britain's imperial power in the nineteenth century. Hundreds of Ethiopians were killed, and thousands were wounded and displaced – lives that barely show up in the historical records, whether they be diaries, official military records or newspaper articles. The truth is, we will always fail to fully represent the scale and scope of destruction unleashed by the expeditionary force that was assembled to supposedly rescue nine European hostages. Predictably, most accounts lionise General Robert Napier, emphasising his talents as a military leader and his abilities as an engineer who was able to plan and construct the necessary infrastructure to carry out the devastating attack on Maqdala. The journalists, artists, translators and museum officials who accompanied the troops had been carefully selected to record the campaign, positioning the British Indian Army within a lineage of Roman and Greek armies that had passed through and, at times, dominated the Horn of Africa.

On 13 April 1868, Napier's troops stormed, destroyed and pillaged Maqdala. Much has been written about the irony in Tewodros II's use of a pistol that had been gifted to him by Queen Victoria to commit suicide; and the tragedy surrounding the abduction and premature death of his seven-year-old son, Prince Alemayehu.[349] The prince died of pleurisy after an insufferable eleven-year period of racist abuse in England, and his remains are buried outside St. George's chapel in Windsor.[350]

Shortly after the attack, a massive auction was held, lasting two days. The loot that was auctioned off to the men who participated in the raid required '15 elephants and nearly 200 mules' to carry it away.[351] Journalists who arrived at the scene before it was burned down have written about the simplicity of the architecture within the fortress – the tents that made up the treasury and the huts that housed the manuscripts.[352] These seemingly innocuous descriptions of the built environment in Maqdala have fuelled the justifications that have been repeatedly deployed over the ensuing 156 years (and counting) to defend the displacement of cultural assets from porous, temporary structures in Africa to climate-controlled rooms in Europe. But plunder always serves a larger agenda: making cultural and spiritual artefacts from different parts of the planet readily accessible to the British public, and thus, solidifying the Empire's conception of itself as the centre of the world.[353]

In 1867, shortly after the Abyssinian expedition was announced, trustees of the British Museum agreed to send Richard Rivington Holmes, an assistant in the Department of Manuscripts, to accompany the expedition.[354] His expertise in 'prints and manuscripts' influenced the sheer volume of books that were stolen from Maqdala. An orientalist fascination with the Christian emperor from Africa – constructed through newspaper articles and travel accounts by Europeans who had been visiting the region since the sixteenth century – set the stage for the feverish scramble between soldiers, museum officials and collectors:

> Mr. Holmes, as the worthy representative of the British Museum, was in his full glory. Armed with ample funds, he outbid all in most things; but Colonel Frazer ran him hard because he was buying for a wealthy regimental mess… and when anything belonging personally to [Tewodros] was offered for sale, there were private gentlemen who outbid both.[355]

European 'competition about antiquities and art works was not just about possessing them, but about "having the historical *right* to do so"'.[356] These were direct investments in a planetary project, constructing distinctions between those that the West considers to be 'human, not-quite-human, and non-human'.[357] Furthermore, Sylvia Wynter's formulation elucidates how modes of being human are inscribed through descriptive statements between people purported to be 'possessors of reason' and those that 'remain enslaved to the lack of reason'.[358] The official record books are riddled with conflicting desires to simultaneously render Emperor Tewodros 'as an equal opponent for the British and British Indian Army' and a racialised subject with phenotypic differences that had to be exhibited in Europe:

> a 'lock of the late King Theodore's hair' [was displayed] as a war trophy in a shop in Plymouth. This lock had been cut from his head by Captain C.F. James and displayed in a shop window on George Street as a 'matter of curiosity'.[359]

There are obvious distinctions, but also clear overlaps, between debates for the restitution of human remains and cultural assets (see also Chapters 8 and 14). These two realms outline the complexities between identity formation through cultural production and self-fashioning through theft and narration. The preservation of racial thought and the maintenance of domination are at the core of the existential fears demonstrated by European museums and libraries, as they contemplate returning looted cultural assets to Africa.

Out of approximately 1,000 manuscripts that had been gathered by Tewodros for the library in Maqdala, the finest group of 400 manuscripts were stolen and dispersed across Europe.[360] The movement of these volumes illustrates the bureaucracies of extraction, and how these systems purportedly fragmented the loot. We argue that this sharing and scattering anticipates future demands for restitution by making the actual volume of the spoils, and by extension their incredible worth, all the more difficult to gauge. Most of the Maqdala manuscripts were formally transferred from the colony to the metropole by the Secretary of State for India in 1868. This collection constitutes the British Museum Library's largest single acquisition of Ethiopian manuscripts. As an added measure of legislative fortification, the volumes were transferred from the British Museum to the British Library under the terms of the British Library Act 1972, coming into force on 1 July 1973. This transfer from museum to library spatialised a rhetorical shift from collection to education, from vitrines to stacks. Thus, reframing theft as charity, and transferring the role of guardianship from curators to librarians.

In line with these gestures of stunted generosity, the British Museum has agreed to permanently remove the eleven *tabot*s from display. The museum states:

> In line with earlier agreements with the church, and in light of their sacred nature, the *tabots* from Maqdala are not on public display. They are housed in a location specifically set aside for the purpose, created and maintained in close consultation with the Ethiopian Orthodox Church.[361]

We are prompted to ask the obvious question: then why are they still kept in London? What does Britain gain from foreclosing their role in anchoring communities and framing rituals in Ethiopia?

In the United Kingdom, numerous institutions took notable collections of manuscripts from Maqdala. These repositories include the British Library and the Royal Library in London (Windsor Castle), the Bodleian Library (Oxford), the Cambridge University Library (Cambridge), the John Rylands Library (Manchester), the Wellcome Institute of the History of Medicine (London) and the National Museum of Antiquities (Edinburgh). A few volumes are dispersed across other institutions in Europe, including the Vatican Apostolic Library (Rome), the Bibliothèque Nationale de France (Paris) and the Deutsche Staatsbibliothek (Berlin). But the British Library still houses the most extensive collection of Maqdala manuscripts outside of Ethiopia.[362]

Placemaking

How does one tell stories of dispossession without resorting to nostalgia? How can we attend to the legacies of domination fashioned through the entanglements between the Ethiopian Empire and the Ethiopian Orthodox Tewahedo Church? Furthermore, how does one address coloniality without the desire to hide and sublimate regional forms of subjection? The tragedy of Ethiopia is not defined by the singular event that destroyed and looted Maqdala. But narrating these stories of violence illuminates how notions of the sacred mirror the vectors of empire. We have not addressed the multiplicity of religions, languages and ways of relating to land and spirituality that exist throughout the region. Instead, we have focused on colonial theft as a way to challenge Ethiopia's claims of unimpacted exceptionalism. We are interested in examining the ongoing conditions of duress produced by the demands of desacralisation. Specifically, how the state and its aspirations of power produce fragmentation and exploitation, near and far.

Restitution means access. Beyond the obvious economic and juridical constraints that police Africans' relation to ancestral heritage, there is a web of assumptions embedded within discourses currently promoted to reframe the relevance of Western museums. These arguments articulate the potential for cultural institutions to function as counterpoints to the fascistic and nationalist politics that have been brewing across Europe and North America. We are expected to believe that an engagement with non-Western culture and aesthetics could soften borders and eradicate the 'antiblack weather' that engulfs our lives in the diaspora.[363] But how can these arguments incorporate the perspectives of Black people living in Africa? How does restitution attend to the demands made by scholars struggling to teach liturgy and philology without manuscripts in the monasteries and schools dispersed throughout rural Ethiopia? These are the people – not the emperors and leaders of the church – who have historically made and cared for the *tabots* and manuscripts. The very people who continue to be subjected to hegemonic interventions crafted by Euro-American cultural workers and politicians.

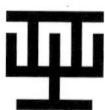

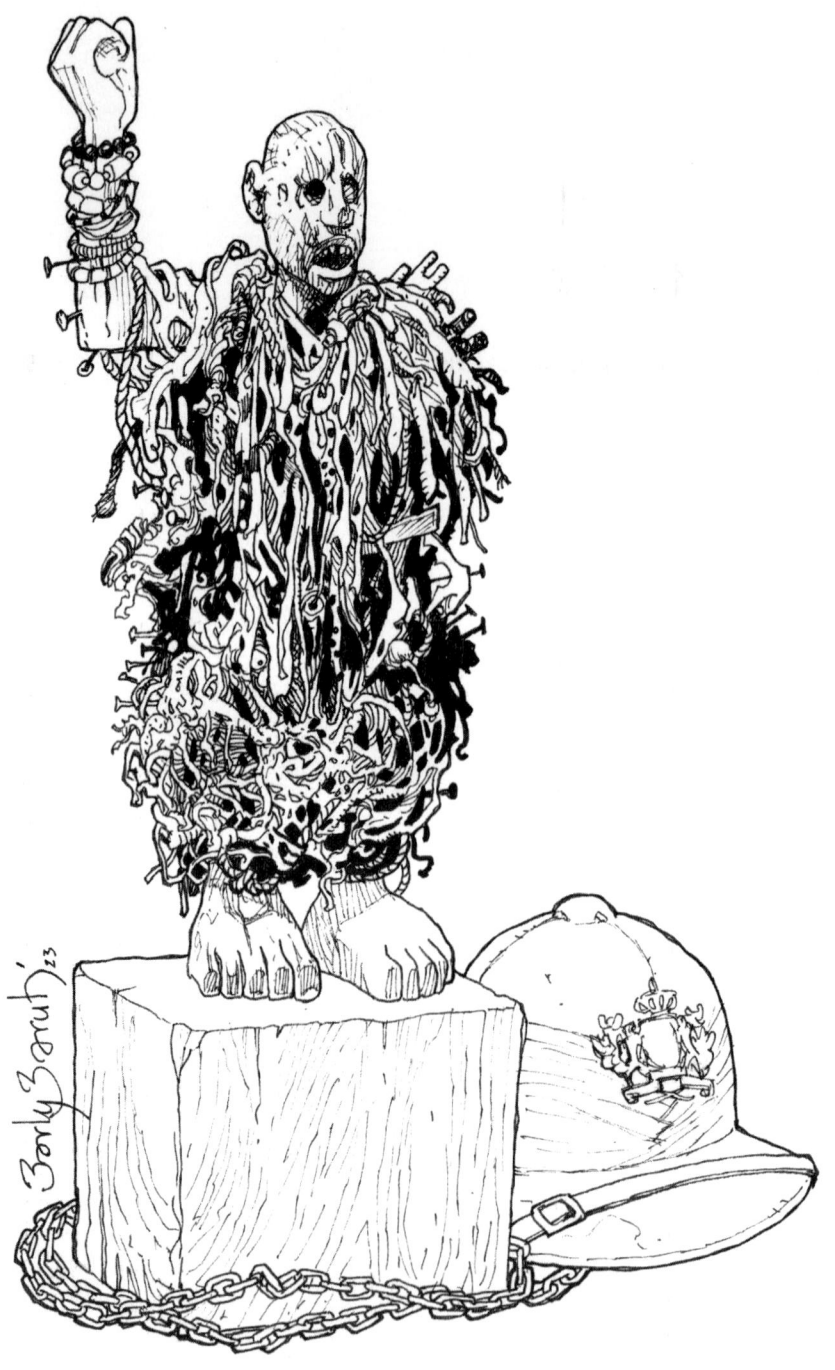

Artist: Barly Baruti

CHAPTER 12

Nkisi nkonde of Chief Ne Kuko of Boma
The Tragic Spoliation of a Sacred Sculpture

Placide Mumbembele Sanger

European colonisation in Africa, and especially the autocratic administration of Leopold II in the Congo, was anything but a philanthropic enterprise. It was characterised by acts of violence by military officers and other colonial officials against local populations. The Belgian historian and anthropologist Jan Vansina stressed that terror and violations of people's rights were widespread, even by the low standards of the time. Violence was the rule, not the exception. For even if indigenous people were regarded as human beings, the colonisers treated them as subhuman. We must therefore continue to refute the slogan and the lie that the conquest of the Congo was rather peaceful. It was bloody. Colonial occupation, Vansina reminded us as early as 1985, was based on the motto 'the might makes right' and the claim of a 'civilising mission', both of which were essentially supported by the use of violence as the norm.[364]

While the frequency of violent deeds increased during the colonial period, one should also acknowledge that before the colonisation in Africa and the Congo, other forms of violence existed and were often found in secretive societies or initiation ceremonies. Still, they had neither the same scope, nor the same consequences as the colonial violence exerted during the era of Leopold II. Historian Stephen Ellis demonstrated that, in the vast Congo Basin as in other parts of Africa before colonisation, the establishment of violence as a norm was linked to the trade of enslaved Africans, Africa having served for centuries as a reservoir for slaves.[365] It was in the international context of shackles and exploitation that the final division of the century took place, that is, at the Berlin Conference (1884–1885). Ellis maintains that history is replete with cases of carefully organised violence for motives that no one would legitimise today, and which, even at the time, posed a moral problem. But one must admit that the monopoly of violence imposed by the colonial order – fallaciously labelled as 'colonial peace' – did not eradicate the violence that already existed in Africa; it simply revamped it and took advantage of the established systems of coercion, using them for its own ends.

This is the *raison d'être* of this chapter, which examines the story of *nkisi nkonde*, a sacred Kongo sculpture endowed with spiritual power seized by the Belgian colonial agent Alexandre Delcommune during a punitive expedition in late 1878. Here, I differentiate between the Kongo people, a diverse group of people and cultures connected by a common language known as Kikongo, and the Congo, a territory spreading around the basin of the eponymous river that, since colonial conquest, has born many different names, from Congo Free State (1885–1908), to Belgian Congo (1908–1960), Congo-Léopoldville (1960–1966), Zaire (1971–1997) and the DRC (1997–present day). This chapter also attempts to explain how this looted cultural asset is perceived today in its community of origin, namely, among the Yombe in central Congo. Can it still be used by Congolese people? How can its original community be reconnected with both their history and this sacred sculpture, currently preserved at the AfricaMuseum in Tervuren, Belgium? How does the request for restitution made by the descendants of Ne Kuko sit vis-à-vis recent developments in Belgian law, namely, the recognition of the alienable nature of goods linked to the colonial past of the Belgian state and the new legal framework preparing the ground for restitution and returns? How does the Congolese decree that established a national commission in charge of the repatriation of cultural property, archives and human remains removed from the Congolese cultural heritage address this restitution claim?

Taken Under Violence

Colonial power relations have played a central role in the establishment of collections from the Congo currently held in Belgium.[366] In most cases, these cultural assets were spoils of war taken away during military raids and 'punitive' expeditions, acting as trophies to illustrate the conquest of the new territory. But it was mainly during the Leopoldian era (*r.*1878–1908) that the exploration of the territory and the search for raw material was characterised by a heightened brutality associated with the extraction of rubber. During this period, many military and civil servants stationed in the Congo committed atrocities against local populations, while sending collections of plants, animals, minerals, cut stones and anthropological material to Belgium, the most emblematic case being that of Chief Lusinga and the shipment of his head to the metropole.[367] Despite his resistance to colonial rule, Lusinga was killed during a 'punitive' expedition commanded by Belgian Lieutenant Émile Storms in the Tanganyika province on 4 December 1884. The Belgian colonial soldiers, together with local soldiers/warriors from communities who opposed Lusinga and had rallied to Storms' troops, decapitated the traditional leader on the battlefield. They came back to the military camp at Mpala with his head as a war trophy. On this occasion, Émile Storms 'collected' the belongings of the deceased Tabwa chief, an authentic instance of war booty notably composed of sculptures, one of which depicted Lusinga's ancestors.[368] Other Belgian officers used the same brutal methods to snatch, loot and appropriate what would later become substantial collections. Such was the case of Oscar Isidore Joseph Michaux, who gathered some 716 cultural assets during his military career in the Congo from 1889 to 1897. His collection was acquired by the Musée du Congo Belge in Tervuren on 18 April 1919, part of which is still considered as 'unmatched', 'marvellous' masterpieces.[369]

From 1886 to 1923, under the reign of Leopold II, the colonial capital, Boma, was notorious for being a city of violence. In a letter dated 18 September 1911, addressed to his father, the agricultural engineer Emile Chardome, director of the plantation office in Boma, described the dramatic way in which 'Matundu' – the powerful god revered by the indigenous population represented by a statue the size of a three-year-old child – was abducted. 'There's every reason to believe,' Chardome ventured, 'that the Whites recognized a certain power in native fetishes, or in the psychological impact they imagined those figures could have on the natives.'[370] This letter informs us that the Whites would leave the sacred sculptures to Black populations when they considered them harmless. The 'Matundu' effigy, however, was not harmless at all. For this reason, a European lieutenant was commissioned to remove it and, together with four Black soldiers, they set out on a mission. Matundu's owners resisted with firearms, wounding the lieutenant in the shoulder and a bullet pierced one of the soldier's buttocks. After being mistaken for the 'impregnable Matundu', the village chief was arrested, transferred to Boma, tried and sentenced to a public hanging. This is evidence of the fierce determination of Black people to safeguard their god and thereby their identity. It also shows the brutality of the methods used by the Whites to dispossess them of it. On learning of his death sentence, the chief replied: '*Jambove*' (*diambu ve*), meaning 'No problem' ('I don't care'). While the tragic execution of the chief led to a violent separation between the community and its sacred sculpture, a receptacle of spiritual power, it also subsequently desacralised the *nkisi nkonde* itself to the point where it became a mere aesthetic artwork and an object of curiosity.

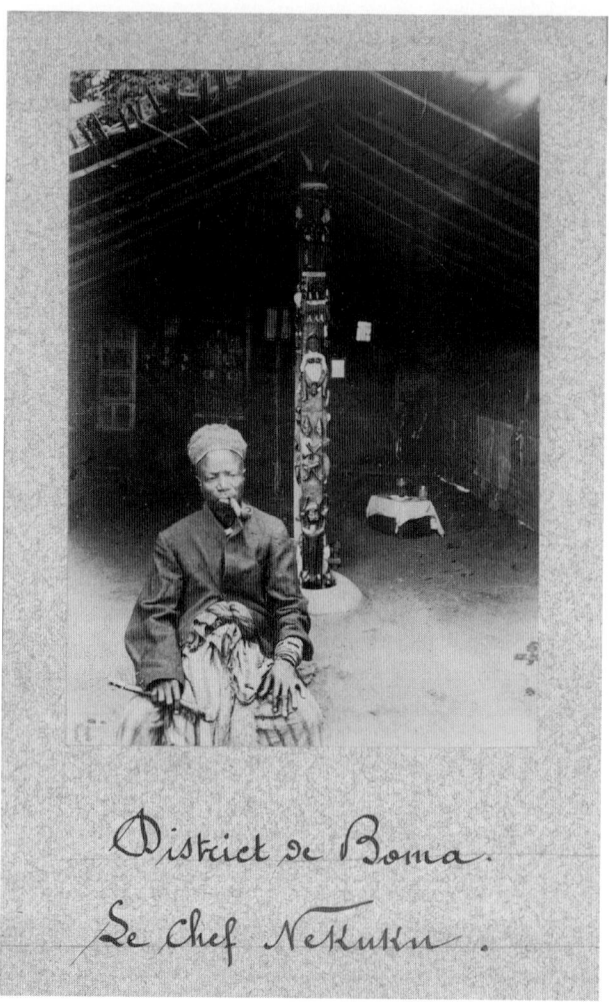

Figure 12.1:
Chief Ne Kuko of Boma.
This image taken by the
Yoruba photographer
and anti-violence activist
Herzekiah Andrew Shanu,
is part of an early tradition
of anti-colonial photography.
(HP.1961.74.53, collection
RMCA Tervuren; H.A. Shanu
[?], 1895–1905).

Ne Kuko, a Chief Determined to Reclaim his Coveted Sacred Sculpture

One of the major episodes of colonial violence in the town of Boma under Leopold II was the spoliation of *nkisi nkonde*, stolen by the manager of a factory there, Alexandre Delcommune, from a local chief called Ne Kuko. A large part of the historical information detailed in the following section comes from the research that art historian Agnès Lacaille led on the provenance of Ne Kuko's statue.[371]

From 1878 to 1884, numerous fights erupted between the kings of Boma and some of the traders who owned factories and trading posts in the Congo River estuary region. Armed conflicts even broke out whenever these kings dared to obstruct the caravans coming from the Mayombe river on their way to the Boma trading posts to sell their products. Local rulers often tried to make them pay a passage tax on their lands that was higher than the fee that had been fixed in 1872 after an alleged mutual agreement between the Whites and the kings. In those wars, the White traders led a force composed of only a few men but who were equipped with modern rifles, while the Boma kings, who led a far greater army, fought with stone rifles.[372]

European traders deemed the decision of the local chiefs to prevent the free movement of caravans through their territory unacceptable and considered it as a declaration of war.[373] In spite of the strong pressure exerted onto them, the chiefs upheld their decisions, even taunting the Europeans with courageous statements such as: 'the land belongs to us', 'we are the only masters in our own land', and 'if the Whites aren't satisfied, they can just go back to where they came from'. This is evidence of the climate of mistrust and injustice that reigned between local authorities and representatives of colonial authority at the time. Indeed, even before the Berlin Conference, most of the treaties signed between the two parties were not in favour of the indigenous populations. This led to frustration among the inhabitants of the region around Boma. Delcommune even gives evidence of this in his memoirs, admitting that he 'deceived the kings of Boma'.[374] The avowal goes on: 'it would be preposterous of me to assert that I made these kings aware of all the privileges that the rights of sovereignty entail.'[375]

To subjugate the chiefs who were 'recalcitrant' to colonial authority, European traders imposed a reign of terror. With the help of a few locally recruited mercenaries, they organised what they called a 'punitive expedition' against the local chiefs. During this fierce battle, the Belgian Delcommune, who had been in conflict with Ne Kuko, one of the great chiefs of Boma, got hold of his *nkisi nkonde*. This was a statue of Yombe power that the inhabitants of the village of Kikuku had left behind when forced to flee from the Belgian offensive. Among the Yombe, one of several linguistic subgroups among the Kongo people, *nkisi* means 'charm' and *nkonde* means 'hunter'. This famous figure was well known to the Belgian trader, for he had called upon it in the past: 'on the advice of a local official', Ne Kuko and Delcommune had agreed on a costly 'rental' of *nkisi nkonde* so that the trader could track down employees who had stolen money from him.[376] Delcommune admitted:

> I had known about this ~~fetish~~ for a long time, and I was aware of the great reputation it enjoyed twenty or thirty leagues around. I experienced it myself in curious circumstances that are worth being told, and which show the faith that the indigenous have in some of these gods.[377]

By willingly targeting this statue, the trader aimed to strike at the heart of the Kongo social system and weaken it from within. For this reason, Ne Kuko fought hard to recover his ancestor, who had been taken hostage and had become a precious trophy of war for the Belgian, but his efforts were in vain. With hindsight, the seizure of this trophy fits in perfectly with the regime of terror imposed by the various stakeholders involved in Leopold II's 'civilising mission' in the Congo, which sought to dehumanise and dominate local people to increase control over them and their resources. In his memoirs, Delcommune argued that this war 'shattered forever the prestige of the Boma kings and considerably strengthened the authority of the Europeans'.[378] Buoyed by this victory, Delcommune refrained from returning *nkisi nkonde* for the next four years, taking the figure with him on his return to Belgium in May 1883.[379]

In Brussels, Delcommune presented his trophy to Maximilien Strauch, Secretary General of the Association Internationale Africaine (AIA), an organisation founded by Leopold II himself, whose objective was to conquer territories in Africa. Before returning to the Congo in October 1883, on behalf of another organisation also created by Leopold II, the Association Internationale du Congo (AIC), Delcommune donated the statue to the AIA. The *nkisi nkonde* thereby became a real token of his commitment to the organisation and evidence of his efficiency on the ground. Above all, the statue was a valuable bargaining chip for his role into the new Leopoldian enterprise. Having tamed through violence the nine kings of Boma, the AIC entrusted the young Belgian trader with a new geopolitical ambition: obtaining sovereign rights over the territories concerned. In February 1884, Brussels dispatched the first confidential instructions, which Delcommune received in April and, according to him, 'la[id] the initial foundations of the future State, by securing the submission of the indigenous kinglets'.[380]

On his new mission, Delcommune renewed contact with the nine chiefs. On 19 April 1884, at the residence of King Ne Oro in the village of N'Eourou, he persuaded them to sign nine treaties in which they relinquished their sovereignty. Acting on behalf of the AIC, Alexandre Delcommune and Ne Kuko, his former enemy turned ally, agreed that the king would cede all rights of sovereignty over the entire territory under his authority to the AIC. This cession took place in return for payment of twenty pieces of cloth, two rifles and other gifts that Ne Kuko acknowledged having received. This second meeting between these two old enemies raises several questions that could not be answered by historiographical research so far: Why did Ne Kuko sign another treaty with Delcommune, the very one who had despoiled his cultural property and failed to return it to him? Among the Kongo, reconciliation is a central societal process between two conflicting parties. How could Ne Kuko agree to sign a treaty without first holding a reconciliation ceremony with Delcommune? Were the gifts offered by Delcommune to Ne Kuko counter-gifts that brought reconciliation between the two parties? Had Ne Kuko once again reclaimed his *nkisi nkonde* during those negotiations? Only in-depth field work among the communities of origin in Boma can fill this gap in this history of spoliation.

Meanwhile, in Belgium, Ne Kuko's *nkisi nkonde* was on the move from one institution to another, namely, from the AIC's collections to those of the État Indépendant du Congo (EIC, Independent State of the Congo, 1885–1908), which were for a period housed in the stables of the Royal Palace on the Place du Trône in Brussels.[381] Exhibited in 1885 at the Antwerp World Fair as a war trophy, it captivated the attention of visitors. In 1891, the EIC donated it to the Royal Museum of Antiquity, Armor, Artillery and Ethnology at the Porte de Hal. In 1906, *nkisi nkonde* found itself in the new premises of the museum in the Parc du Cinquantenaire. In the absence of space to house these collections (or rather, spoils of war) from the Congo, *nkisi nkonde* was kept in the cellar for several years, like most of the other Congolese belongings. It was not until 1912 that all the collections from the Congo, including the statue of Ne Kuko, landed at the Museum of Belgian Congo (Musée du Congo Belge) in Tervuren, today renamed AfricaMuseum.

To conclude, provenance research led by the AfricaMuseum on *nkisi nkonde* has made it possible to retrace and determine the chain of successive holders and owners of this statue of power, and to reconstruct most of the historical context of spoliation. However, it does not explain exactly how this change of ownership between former and later holder took place and how it ended up in the Tervuren museum. While written sources are relevant sources for provenance research, one should also resort to oral traditions and intergenerational narratives found among the living societies or communities of origin of this looted cultural heritage. In this case, research led by anthropologist Maarten Couttenier with the descendants of Ne Kuko in Boma has provided important information. But this study of *nkisi nkonde*'s relevance for the communities today can be expanded by identifying and involving people from neighbouring communities. Indeed, not all members of those labelled as 'source communities' by museums are able to relate well-founded accounts on the history of a given cultural asset. More inclusion in the research process would help avoid having competing and diverse interpretations.

Another problem that the AfricaMuesum in Tervuren has not seriously taken into account was the way the results of this research were communicated to source communities. For transparency reasons, the results of provenance research carried out in collaboration with descendants of the community of origin must be made known proactively not only to them, but also to the scientific or museum community in the countries concerned. In the face of this ethical requirement, Tervuren was however simply content to publish the provenance report of the *nkisi nkonde* online on its website without genuinely transmitting the results to the people in Boma. On 10 December 2023, in an interview I was able to conduct with the descendants of Ne Kuko, namely, Chief Alphonse Baku (whom Couttenier had already met in 2016) and his notable Jean Tsumba, the latter complained about not having had access to the results. Tsumba also explained:

> *Batu mawombo balutidi kuaku kasi me tukadi zaba biobi balembo sonika mudiambu di mikilu bietu mibuala. Betu biso tuisiko mbakusulu mosi mumambu mavioka mu ntama* (literally, 'Many researchers have passed through here, but we have little idea about what they will subsequently write about our ancestor. We don't all have the same understanding of what really happened').

For the AfricaMuseum, the international visibility of their report online enables this institution to maintain its positive 'image' as a century-old museum and justifies its policy of transparency concerning collections from colonial contexts. The presentation of *nkisi nkonde* as a masterpiece in the exhibition catalogue *Art sans pareil: Objets merveilleux du Musée royal de l'Afrique centrale Tervuren*, edited by curators at the museum and published in 2019, fits in perfectly with this new strategy in the era of the restitution of cultural property to African countries, something that has been labelled and criticised as 'strategic reflexivity' in the case of the Humboldt Forum in Berlin.[382]

What is the Future for Ne Kuko's *nkisi nkonde* at the AfricaMuseum?

For several years now, there has been debate, reflection and dialogue on the future of African collections acquired during the colonial era by certain former colonial powers in Africa. Most of this body of thought examines the contexts of acquisition of these thousands of artworks, traditional artefacts, cultural assets or sacred ancestors, as well as the conditions of their conservation in museums and private collections in Europe. Above all, the question around them is the envisaged return of this heritage to their countries of origin. While the restitution debate is not new, as Ne Kuko's claim in the wake of looting illustrates, it gained momentum in 2017 when French President Emmanuel Macron gave a speech in Ouagadougou, Burkina Faso, promising to set up the conditions for the restitution of African art kept in French collections.

Between Belgium and the Congo, the history of demands for restitution is as old as one can imagine. As a reminder, in 1960, it was already part of the negotiations for independence, when Congolese political leaders led by Joseph Kasa-Vubu and Patrice Émery Lumumba called for the return of the Tervuren museum collections. Faced with Belgium's refusal and the state wanting to retain a monopoly on the management and study of these collections, Congolese intellectuals and politicians continued to demand their restitution as part of the discussions on the Belgian–Congolese dispute. However, it was not until 1970 that the idea of repatriating cultural property crystallised because of two landmarks. First, the creation in the same year of the Institute of National Museums of Congo (IMNC), which largely resulted from the desire among Tervuren's management to suspend any return until the Congo had representative collections and adequate conditions for their conservation and study. Second, in 1973, during the Third Congress of the International Association of Art Critics (AICA) at N'Sele and also at the United Nations, President Mobutu asked 'the rich powers possessing works of art from poor countries to return some of them so that we can teach our children and grandchildren the history of their countries'.[383] Following these two seminal speeches, 8,923 cultural assets were 'transferred' by Belgium to Zaire (now the DRC, Democratic Republic of the Congo) over a period of six years from 1976 to 1982. While 'restitution' is a legal concept that implies reinstating their rights of ownership to the rightful owner, the Belgians have preferred talking about 'transfer' and 'donation': the first term helping them avoid the issue of reparation; and the second term being dependent on the good faith of both parties and dialogue between the museums involved.[384]

In recent years, other landmarks have stimulated debate and accelerated the restitution of cultural heritage acquired in colonial contexts, including the reopening of the AfricaMuseum in 2018. This vast renovation project promised the inauguration of a new, 'decolonising' approach to the collections, which would in part involve the perspective of the Congolese diaspora in what could be considered as a cathartic process. The murder of George Floyd and the subsequent Black Lives Matter (BLM) movement in Belgium, also tapped into social demands for a decolonisation of institutions. In several Belgian cities, activists targeted statues glorifying Leopold II, smearing them with red paint to symbolise the blood shed by colonialists.

The commemoration of the 60th anniversary of Congo's independence sparked and marked a gradual awakening of public opinion in Belgium, culminating in King Philippe officially expressing 'his deepest regrets' for the violence committed in the Belgian Congo, as well as the 'suffering and humiliations' that followed. In his letter to President Félix Tshisekedi, the King of Belgium admits that colonialists 'committed acts of violence and cruelty which still weigh heavily on our collective memory'. He also acknowledged that 'discrimination is still all too present in our society'.[385] This was a first avowal for the Belgian monarchy, even though the king refrained from apologising. The parliament set up a special commission to examine Belgium's colonial past in Africa. However, after two years of work, the commission also refused to issue apologies for the exactions committed in Congo, Burundi and Rwanda.

To exorcise the colonial past and make Belgium a model country in the era of restitution, the Belgian parliament passed a law in June 2022 that recognises the alienable nature of assets linked to the Belgian state's colonial past. This provides a legal framework for their restitution and return, and represents the apex in this new deal between the two countries. The DRC also promulgated two important legal texts: on 20 February 2023, a Prime Ministerial Decree fast tracked the creation of a national commission in charge of the repatriation of cultural property, archives and human remains removed from the Congolese cultural heritage, while a decree issued by the Ministry of Culture, Arts and Heritage on 26 June 2023 appointed its members.[386]

It is because of this favourable environment, and, above all, thanks to the work of a handful of people in Brussels that, in 2019–2020, descendants and representatives of the Tabwa community filed several requests for the restitution of the remains of Congolese chief Tabwa Lusinga, kept at the Brussels Museum of Natural Sciences.[387] However, to date, Belgium has taken no definite decision regarding Lusinga's repatriation. Another factor delaying his return is undoubtedly the establishment of the National Repatriation Commission mentioned earlier. According to its mission and its respective competencies, the Commission has the privilege to centralise all repatriation requests and forward them to third parties. According to Article 2 of the decree, one of the Commission's tasks is 'to identify, in collaboration with the countries concerned, the cultural goods, archives, and human remains removed from national cultural heritage and taken to the Schengen area before and after 1885'.[388] Consequently, no request for repatriation and restitution to the DRC that comes from an individual or community will be regarded as an official one if it is issued outside the jurisdiction of the Commission. Due to the very recent establishment of this Commission, Lusinga's descendants have yet to forward their request to the Commission's members in Kinshasa. Because its mission has not yet been properly explained to the population, this has brought about misunderstanding and delays.

As for Ne Kuko's statue, no official request has been made yet, either by the Congolese authorities, or by Ne Kuko's descendants. However, in an interview led by Maarten Couttenier in Boma in 2016, Ne Kuko's descendants – namely, Paramount Chief Madelaine Tsimba and the chief of the village of Kikuku, Alphonse Baku Kapita – expressed their intention to ask the Belgian state to return the *nkisi nkonde* to them, so that they could perform traditional ceremonies with this symbol of their traditional power. These include ceremonies linked to hunting, plant growth and agricultural harvests, among others. For Chief Alphonse Baku and the notable Jean Tsumba, whom I interviewed, the absence of the *nkisi nkonde* has had disastrous social and economic consequences in Kikuku. These include epidemics, drought and soil poverty, the disappearance of certain crops, the absence of game in the forests during the hunting season, and low agricultural yields, all of which have led to the desertion of the village. To this is added a systematic demonisation of the area by certain Christian churches who consider Kikuku a cursed village. It is for all these reasons that the descendants of Ne Kuko are demanding the return of the statue of their 'ancestor' so that they can exorcise the evil and continue to live normally.[389] According to them, the 'ancestor' can still be used, and traditional chiefs can revive its powers through appropriate rituals with other cultural assets.

However, while the request issued by Ne Kuko's descendants is justified insofar as all cultural assets still in use must be returned to their community of origin so that they can finally be used again or 're-socialised', it runs up against two difficulties: first, Congolese legislation prohibits any initiative for restitution that takes place outside the framework of the National Commission on Repatriation. Second, Belgian law on the alienability of goods linked to the state's colonial past stipulates that all illegally acquired goods must be returned to the state of origin. In Belgium's view, restitution and return can only take place on a state-to-state basis, and it is therefore up to the DRC to entrust the returned property to a specific person or community within its territory.

Epilogue

Far from being a 'civilising mission' in the heart of Africa, Belgian colonisation in the Congo was marked by military violence and the dispossession of symbols of the traditional and sacred power of local populations. These dehumanising raids were at the root of internal imbalances, the consequences of which are still being felt today within the communities affected by this history of violence. Hence, the need to reconnect these people with their cultural heritage, one that was looted and has been musealised in Western institutions for over a century. Although restitution is a long and complex process, it now appears to be the only alternative that could foster reconciliation between the former colonial powers and descendants of colonised people. Above all, it would restore the dignity of the dispossessed. The apology by King Philippe of Belgium for the violence and humiliation inflicted by Belgian colonial agents such as Delcommune was an important step towards reconciliation. But there can be no reconciliation without both the restitution of stolen property and reparations.

Between Belgium and the Congo, this important aspect is often tinged with great ambivalence and value judgements. It is therefore time to return the remains of Lusinga and other victims of colonialism, as well as the *nkisi nkonde* and other ancestors used in Kongo rituals and symbolism, to their communities of origin. This would allow them to mourn and reconnect with their deported ancestors.

At this point, it is worth recalling the merits of critical provenance studies, which make it possible to retrace, to a certain extent, the history of ownership of a cultural asset. But while provenance research is one of the fundamental missions of a museum, it should not be used as a pretext by cultural institutions and states to delay or prevent restitution requests from African countries. Provenance research only becomes effective when both written and oral sources are brought together, including the voices of members of communities and the diaspora. The contribution of the Congolese diaspora in Belgium to the debate on restitution and to the controversial renovation of the AfricaMuseum needs no further demonstration. However, it would be desirable to see members of this diaspora join forces with the communities that have remained in the country, so that they wage this struggle together. Besides, it is essential that the National Commission on Repatriation discuss with the Belgian state on an equal footing for a balanced restitution of cultural property. It was wishful thinking to see the Congolese diaspora represented on the National Commission on Repatriation. Regrettably, for reasons not explained by the Congolese authorities, they are absent.

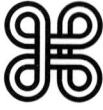

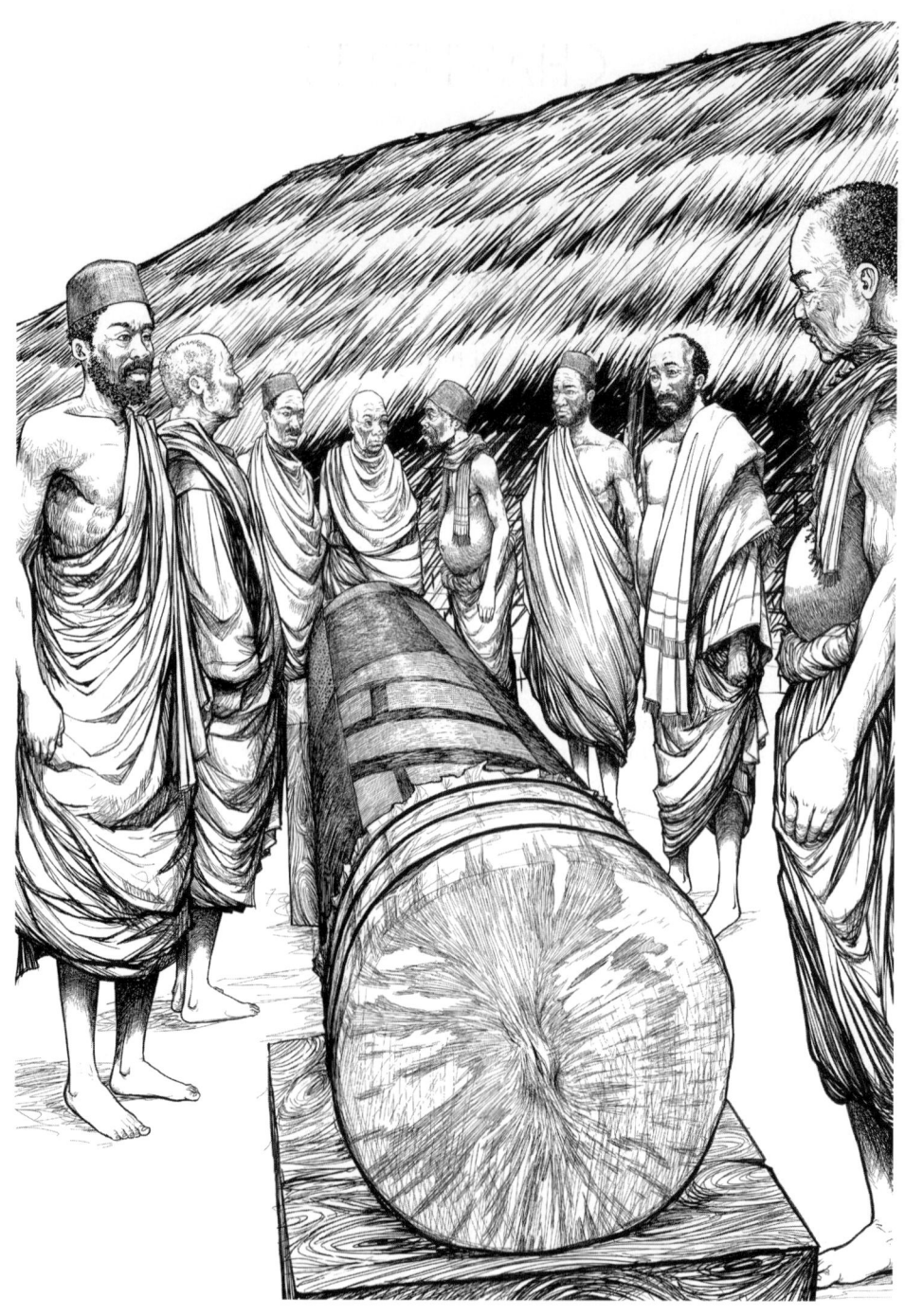

Artist: Bright Toh

CHAPTER 13

Conversation

The *Ngadji* of the Pokomo
On Revolutionary Responses, Release and Relationships

Njoki Ngumi and Adéọlá Adérẹ̀mí

This is a conversation between Adéọlá, a Yoruba writer, researcher and filmmaker, and Njoki, a Kikuyu writer, artist and strategist. The conversation focuses on the relationship between two important cultural spiritual assets that are currently held hostage far away from their homelands, because of the actions of the British during colonial rule, their imperial 'exploration' and violent domination of colonial territories.

The first of two specific cultural assets is the *Ngadji*, a tall drum of the Pokomo, a people who live by the East African Coast, within the borders of what is now the Republic of Kenya. It was used by elders in political and spiritual work, processes and rituals by the Pokomo community.[390] The second are the Benin Bronzes, a collective term for thousands of intricate plaques and sculptures made of bronze, brass and other materials, which are over five centuries old. They originally fulfilled a wide variety of functions in the Kingdom of Benin, which is now the Edo State within the Federal Republic of Nigeria. The *Ngadji* is currently in the possession of the British Museum, which also holds the largest collection of Benin Bronzes in the world (standing at over 900).[391]

This conversation will focus on the spiritual interaction and connection of both cultural assets with their communities and the Western museums that hold them.

***

Njoki: Greetings Adéọlá! It's beautiful to be able to hold space on this topic with you, talking to me from Nigeria, while I sit in Kenya, discussing the cultural heritage that belonged to our collective ancestors. Many of these assets are currently being held hostage by the descendants of those who took them away from our ancestors and retained them without our permission, but this heritage has never stopped belonging to us, and it belongs by right to future generations, regardless of where they are now.

One key point of this discussion is that we have to define the idea of *belonging* with a lot of flexibility. A cultural asset may be said to belong to the continent of Africa, and to Africans as a whole, but there are, of course, hierarchies of belonging. For example, the Benin Bronzes belong to Africans, nominally. But, in reality, they belong to the people of the Benin Kingdom. This is a fact even if in conversations about the Bronzes we might be forced to refer to the state as well – that is, the Federal Republic of Nigeria – when considering who claims them and who they belong to. The same with the *Ngadji*: it may be considered an African drum, but it primarily belongs to the Pokomo people.

Adéọlá: Greetings Njoki! Absolutely. It is imperative to make these distinctions when we speak of sacred belongings that were made by people whose ethnic groups and lineages have been co-opted into these newer political frameworks, such as the nation-state, in other words, republics with colonial origins, such as Kenya and Nigeria.

The over 5,000 sacred sculptures known collectively as the Benin Bronzes are spoken about in unison as though they were one entity, without proper understanding of just how many of these ancestral portrayals of Edo history and related sculptures were looted from the palace of the Benin Kingdom and from the Edo people.[392] It is easy to lose a sense of the scale of these thousands in the quiet plural of the word.

Regarding the *Ngadji* of the Pokomo people, it was crafted by people who communed with the world of the sacred unseen, as author and diviner Malidoma Somé recalled.[393] Thus, any renegotiation of its return must recognise it as such, not merely as a spectacle on display, an artwork or an inventory number in a storeroom. We can say the same of the Bronzes. Any return must centre on a dialogue with the spiritual custodians who know how to honour and engage with them.

Njoki: Anti-restitution proponents working in museums in the Global North, such as the British Museum, still maintain the erroneous position that returning African cultural assets like the *Ngadji* is an insurmountable, impossible task. Some, like representatives of the Museum of Ethnology in Vienna, Austria, have suggested that students from the African continent should come to Europe to look at this African heritage there. Friedrich Kussmaul, formerly of the Linden Museum in Stuttgart, trotted out the old prejudice that African museums are incapable of keeping cultural assets to global museum standards. Stefan Waetzoldt, former director-general of the Berlin State Museums, has called African demands for their cultural assets irrational and absurd.[394] Even those who seem nominally willing to consider restitution centre the challenged position of museums, with reduced funding and ongoing budget cuts, and consider the cost of substantive restitution too high to take on.[395]

But if we consider the idea of costs paid with even an iota of honesty – and I hate to have to argue rationally and calmly about infuriating subjects to counter ludicrous excuses from bullies – Africans have paid high costs since their cultural assets were taken, in multiple dimensions: emotional, mental, spiritual and social, beyond the trauma of dealing with physical absence. For example, the Pokomo people lost a sense of belonging, stability and centrality when rituals which require the *Ngadji*'s presence could no longer be performed.[396] They talk about their drum as a point of connection to solidify the governmental function shared by their chosen *Kĩdjo* (elders' council), the enforcers of their laws and their spiritual workers who maintained connection with the departed.[397] The *Ngadji* was so sacred that people were not supposed to look at it directly or talk about it if they were not members of the *Kĩdjo*. They were not allowed to accompany it when it was being moved. Messages would be sent to the villages located on the *Ngadji*'s route so people would know to not be nearby whenever the drum was passing there.[398]

And then one day, a Norwegian wood trader, Jens Anderssen – because thieves must be named in perpetuity, and violent ones more so – just came along and took it at gunpoint because he could.[399]

Adéọlá: It is despicable that someone can just pitch up and take the pivotal centre that connects you to your land, people and ancestors, just because they felt like it. It is ludicrous for those who come after to then dare ask how restitutive costs, such as those of couriers, packers and insurers, should be covered, as if these were the original sin.
I was once invited to attend an alleged 'decolonial' tour of the Royal Museum for Central Africa in Brussels, alongside a large group of Black activists and cultural workers. We'd seen the word 'decolonial' used on similar gatherings and we decided to be open about the potentials here, even though we were wary. During the walk-through, we were shocked to come across the remains of unnamed people as part of the exhibit, especially now with increased calls for review of the ethics of displaying them. We asked the guide why it was still acceptable to exhibit human remains in the museum. She bypassed this question and shared another piece of information: 'They were brought from the Congo, to show how different and barbaric the African skulls are from us Europeans.' She spoke like someone who was politely replying to a request for directions to the bathroom. The tour broke into pieces at that moment. Several people left the museum, furious. There were so many tears, so much anger, grief and pushback. I went home so broken. Many of us debriefed online and in person after that. We hated that we had been right about our initial wariness around the word 'decolonial' in that particular tour. In many ways, I am still wary of it now.

To use the words of Professor Kehinde Andrews, Whiteness is in this context truly a 'psychosis' with the inferiority it impresses upon everyone else. This multigenerational normalisation of White superiority frameworks, from the original collection through to the ongoing narrativisation, tells you that throwing the word 'decolonial' around is little more than a performance for many.[400]

Njoki: That sounds like it was a horrifying experience, my friend. I am hearing there that while the museum intended on preserving their relationship to these cultural assets, the tour guide was, in parallel, preserving racist and colonial narratives. Maybe for them 'decolonial' meant 'invite your Black neighbours into the museum to see Black cultural elements', which is extra cruel in retrospect.

Speaking of the ongoing obsession with the demises and remains of global majority citizens, there is another example of unethical exhibition of the paraphernalia of death. The memorial effigies known as *vigango* (singular, *kigango*) are anthropomorphic wood carvings with a totemic function, part of the culture of the Mijikenda people (who also live along the East African coast, like the Pokomo). They represent the soul of a departed loved one and are planted outside the family home to keep the connection between the living and the dead.[401] *Vigango* interact with the elements on purpose. Because they have a long minimalist shape and are sometimes curved, coloured and otherwise decorated, Europeans and North Americans decided they were decorative art pieces, and a robust trade in hundreds of these assets, brokered by unscrupulous art dealers, was thriving for a long time. Some *vigango* have been deaccessioned from museum collections and returned, like the Illinois State University Museum who agreed to handover thirty-seven of them to the National Museums of Kenya in July 2023. The California State University in Fullerton also famously returned their collection of twenty-seven *vigango* in a challenged, multi-year process fraught with bureaucracy on both ends, fearing poor publicity. It even lost federal funding after increased awareness of the problematics linked to these cultural assets. Some places like the Hampton University Museum and the British Museum still retain *vigango* in their collections.[402]

Besides, consider the wild decision that one person's grave markers can be another person's home decoration, or even art dealer's Ernie Wolfe's allegation that he only traded in 'deactivated' or pieces that were 'ritually obsolete',[403] and try to picture it from the *kigango*'s perspective: not only are you thousands of miles away from your family home, but you are now indoors, among strangers, thousands of miles apart from them. Beyond that, in museums, wood is subject to all kinds of processes of preservation, so you will never ever have the chance to go back and rejoin the earth in the way your family intended you to.

The current assumption is that these *vigango* will just be given back to a museum in their home country, and everything will miraculously be fine. However, the original role and place of *vigango* never required a museum. In addition, preserving can literally poison our cultural assets. I remember talking to a conservator-restorer in a prominent museum in Germany. She said that a couple of decades ago, doing museum preservation was very dangerous work, as the cultural assets were exposed to toxic chemicals to prevent them from being eaten by insects or deteriorating in storage. So, if your ancestors' belongings were preserved with the methods that were in play back then, any returned cultural asset would be a poisoned entity.[104] Imagine the implications of that, from a spiritual perspective.

But even if the *Ngadji* were to be returned in mint condition, how would the Pokomo people get back the time lost, the rituals undone and the unbroken societies? The fact that communities haven't led or participated in those rituals for decades, or even centuries, has repercussions. How would one invoice for that?

Adéọlá: The relationship with the asset is irreversibly changed. If you have a relative who went to live abroad when you were seven years old, and then they come home and you're thirty, they're no longer the same person, the one who left. Everyone has to do all of that work of getting to know each other again. The Bronzes were a physical manifestation of somebody who had a deep connection to you that remains even if they have travelled across the veil, away from the land of the living. They are a member of the Edo people's families, communities and histories, and so retaining proximity to the Bronzes is also about being close to their memory, and to the processes and rituals of keeping them near.

So, knowing that the Bronzes have been gone for multiple generations, how do we heal the faith elements and practices that were broken? We used to centre the awareness of our ancestors in everything we did, assisted by the existence of assets like the Bronzes and their parallels in other cultures, and now we are separated, intentionally from those realities and ways of being.

To prepare the people to receive some of these cultural assets, I believe that participatory conversations and research can be done to unpack where we are regarding this heritage, and where we would like to be. This is, I think, what museums should be doing: finding ways to help our ancient cultures meet us where we are today.

Njoki: What could the tangible steps after that be?

Adéọlá: We have to make it happen in this day and age. We must find the custodians, the griots, or their equivalents, of each region, to teach everyone in the community now, what these new relationships with our cultural heritage are, and to explore together how we can build new rituals. But this has to start from the very first step, determining how we would even come together to establish oneness of heart in these matters, so that we can start the long journey of learning these things together again. These conversations will also happen in the context of layered tensions with modern life, and so much plurality that we are living in: multiple points of faith and belief, intergenerational divides, changing gender roles and more. We would have to learn how to stop demonising indigenous faith practices because of current religious beliefs and opinions. How would we do that? That is really the true work, and it is a whole other universe of inquiry.

This is the true cost of reparative demands. It would also involve paying priests and priestesses, and facilitators to reconnect rituals with these cultural entities, if that is what is needed. We would need to make sure that these assets find their rightful owners, and not just go into any museum approved by White establishment.

Njoki: The other thing that is a challenge to the process of return are the borders of current nation-states, the ones that replaced communities or ethnic nations, to whom these cultural assets belong directly. There's a tension there. One of the biggest successes of colonial powers was breaking African communities apart, and then forcing us into taking on new national identities. The community – when not forcibly integrated into statist structures – finds itself existing as an isolated parallel, on its own, without the central support and validation that the nation-state gets. There are constant tensions and conflicts because of having to belong to both. We see these playing out every electoral cycle, in the form of electoral conflicts related to intranational diversity.

Adéọlá: Absolutely. This is also found in what is lazily called 'tribalism' in many African countries. I, for instance, always say, 'I'm Yoruba. I'm not Nigerian,' a lot, as a way of sitting with the reality of this tension. My grandfather always said that Nigeria is not his country because he was not born in Nigeria. Yes, he died in Nigeria, but that was never his home country. He was born a Yoruba man and died a Yoruba man. This second identity of a nation was forced on him and many Africans who do not feel a sense of duty or belonging to this new imposed national framework. We didn't get to opt in or out. The nation-state continues to exist because resources and value are forced to flow this way. So, the idea of coming together as communities also opposes the coloniality of national identity.

The Benin Bronzes are being returned to the Edo people of the Benin Empire, to the rightful palace of Omo N'Oba N'Edo Uku Akpolokpolo, Oba Ewuare II. It is good that the government recognised that they do not belong to the Nigerian Republic and handed them to their rightful owners.[405] This also reflects on the conversation around the *Ngadji*. It should not be returned to Kenya when it belongs to the Pokomo people.

There is a level of inhumanity and callousness in spending centuries stealing the creations of others, and then trying to justify that theft forever after. Colonial empires spent centuries watching indigenous people across the globe create magic, and they did nothing but steal that magic and build huge collections of it. Fast forward to now, when we often hear the dramatic, hypothetical argument of massive, emptied museum halls if all requested items were to be returned: 'but when everything goes back, we won't have anything…!'[406] Well, they should sit with that discomfort, the same way the people whose belongings were taken away from them had to sit with the absence of their stolen cultures. Sit with the knowledge that all your ancestors had to offer to the present day was violence, thuggery and genocide.

Speaking of thuggery, historian Manuela Bauche unveiled another messy story. In the Natural History Museum in Berlin, there's a coral diorama. In 1967, a team of German researchers from Berlin conducted an expedition to Cuba to collect coral and make casts of the fish that would form the centrepiece of this planned exhibit. They ended up taking six to ten tons (22,000 pounds) of coral reef back home. Can you picture 10,000 kilograms of anything? Six tons is about the weight of an African elephant and ten, that of a small military truck. Well, they took ten tons of coral, and then never built the thing that they wanted to build with it. They only managed a very small diorama, so tons of coral was taken from Cuba as a waste.[407] Can these people even see their own lives? How about taking two pieces, or even two kilograms? Why did it have to be 10,000 kilograms? This level of greed is disgusting.

Njoki: Keeping that heavy burden on Cuba's ecosystem in mind, let's cross over to the idea of release. I've been thinking about the idea of multigenerational struggle and the things that get passed on. That, for instance, the ways in which the people who first met the colonisers and fought them are completely different from the ways their children fought the colonisers' children, and are themselves completely different from the ways their children's children have continued to lead the struggle, because the people, the zeitgeist and the contexts of the conflicts are different now, and evolving every day.

When the colonisers first came to do what we now know was reconnaissance, many of our ancestors welcomed them as honoured guests from faraway places.[408] But they and the military invaders who came in their wake, had never considered us as human, and the violence and destruction that followed shows that. That is, in my opinion, one of the reasons why any claim of legitimate ownership is treated like a debate. We are still not human to them, so many are incapable of treating this like a conversation between equals.

Adéọlá: Absolutely. The website of the British Museum, for example, maintains that:

> the Museum also acknowledges difficult histories, including the contested means by which some collections have been acquired, such as through military action … The British Museum is actively engaged in re-examining the acquisition histories of such collections and caring for them with appropriate respect in close dialogue with African partners.[409]

Why do these African colleagues have to hold space and wait as the BM does the unending work of 'acknowledging difficult histories' and exploring 'contested means' as if the ancestors of our African colleagues were not living those histories as they were happening. Are we supposed to infer that these relationships are equitable, that these partners and the BM are walking together through these 'difficult histories', hand in hand?

Only one museum shop gets to sell an 'exclusive replica of the Head of Ife, cast and hand-finished in high-quality resin... based on the original which is now housed in the British Museum's collection', for £1,750. Only one museum gets to say that this original head 'was discovered in 1938 at the Wunmonije Compound in Ife, Nigeria', with the word 'discovered' doing some very heavy and euphemistic lifting, while claiming this replica as 'a fascinating and majestic home ornament celebrating African art'.[410] Only one museum has the power to grant permission, after years of requests, to a community representative to come and visit their sacred drum, as was given in 2016 to Mr Baiba Dhidha Mjidho, a representative of the Pokomo people, to unceremoniously spend a few minutes with the *Ngadji* in their East London storerooms, as if he was visiting it in a prison.[411] There can never be equity when one party holds this kind of power over another, regardless of any 'close and sustained dialogue with [African] partners', especially when these African parties have to plead on paper with letterheads for the chance to be heard.

It is unimaginable that Africans asking for the unconditional return of African cultural assets, taken without African permission, is viewed as complaining, or as a radical demand. It also implies that the people who are asking for these cultural assets to be returned are already labelled as being 'too much', which then means that the museums are buying time until the next group of moderates arise, so they can say, 'Now these are the people we can have a conversation with, not those aggressive ones.' Maybe reimagining the current exclusive and colonial relationship means that work has to be done to create a relationship with the people who own these cultural assets to decide if they want to share or loan them. In the case of the Benin Bronzes and the *Ngadji* that we're talking about, they are not just art. The *Ngadji*, for instance, was never meant to be on public display. That goes against everything it was intended for.

The one thing that the British Museum can do with the African department of their museum, if they want assets intended for display, is to directly commission African cultural workers. Not hoarding 'contested' cultural inheritances (surely the only point of the contest here is that they are refusing to return what is not theirs) or cultural assets taken through bloodshed and violence. They can reconsider ethnography entirely, from a new place, because ethnography does not have to be about taking away things from people. It could be establishing a structure like The Human Library, where people from different cultures share their knowledge through multiple media.[412] There are several other options available. Cultural openness and integration have to work both ways. If the British Museum is interested in maintaining that 'close dialogue with African partners', perpetuating the injustice that began with looting, and retaining things away in storage, must end immediately. No more assuming that you have the knowledge because you can study tons of 'contested' heritage whenever you want.

Njoki: Remember that the rationale behind military looting during the violent marauding expeditions they then called 'punitive' was about denying people their places of prayer, the sacred materials that they prayed with, and anything that they would use to reinforce their power. If they believed they had power, they would believe they could fight the coloniser and win. So, in refusing to answer restitution claims, museums are telling claimants to fully relinquish the claimants' own heritage, even as an idea.

It is the same way governments of countries that were active colonisers want the nations of those they colonised to release our memories of colonial times forever, and act like it didn't happen, and doesn't affect what is happening now. Our kinfolk in North and South America and the Caribbean have been asked to move on from slavery and colonialism,[413] an enduring sentiment despite the increased volume and force of the global Movement for Black Lives. Frank Wilderson III surmised that the material and psychic life of the human species is fuelled by Black Death, and as such, one can deduce that colonisers will always colonise, and their behaviour and intentions will remain colonial, always and eternally, to produce this outcome.[414]

But let's look at this from our perspective: if the British Museum says that they are a holder of British cultures, when there are long lines of non-British people, kilometres around the block, with requests in hand asking for their cultural assets back, then that means that the museum has created a scenario where British culture is defined by theft. This has even been strongly echoed by their own people – author and King's Counsel Geoffrey Robertson has called the museum's own trustees 'the world's largest receivers of stolen properties'.[415] Those items were not gifts. The *Ngadji* was not a gift. Their huge collection of Benin Bronzes was not a gift. Even if these assets landed in the museum after a series of fraught donations over several generations, the original transfer was not a gift, and laundering the process does not make it so.

Adéọlá: From a spiritual perspective, if we think about what release could mean for us, there are still a few options. Even though it is gut-wrenching to consider, our cultures remain, our people remain, and *the seeds of everything that is ours did not die, because we are still alive*. So, what would happen if we released the physical aspects of these stolen assets? With the Benin Bronzes and the *Ngadji* as examples, what if they were released in rituals that were led by those people? As we said, the *Ngadji* is a drum which, among other functions, harmonises intentions in both the physical and spiritual realms. What if the Pokomo people were to create another portal artefact, and called on the ancestors as they released the *Ngadji* currently being held hostage, and requested that the power that lies within it come back to us, as they release its physical representation in full?

The Benin Bronzes are not mere ancestral sculptures; they serve as visual representations of revered ancestors and are most often placed on altars for veneration. What if the people who come from their lineage were to say, 'We are our ancestors'? Indeed, we are physically, spiritually, energetically our ancestors. We could perhaps choose to say our ancestors do not reside in those bronzes anymore, and that they are with us in different ways now. We could perform rituals to call them back to us and consider destroying all connection with the British Museum through the items they hold in the physical world and the spiritual realm. We could also choose to connect directly with them spiritually, with intention, despite their physical absence.

One interesting example of this is the November 2023 performance of the Nigerian rapper and songwriter Divine Ikubor, popularly known as Rema, who chose to represent and venerate the image of the sixteenth-century ivory mask of Queen Mother Idia when performing for tens of thousands of his fans in London, and witnessed by millions more globally through social and digital media.[416] Rema himself said of his performance that it invoked a rebirth of the mask, despite it being physically away from him and his people. The actual mask is, like hundreds of others, held hostage in the British Museum. I think that while any insistence on return is forever valid, it reinforces the power of our ancestors when we request them to join us in artistic and cultural self-restitution, without waiting eternally for any performed benevolence by the coloniser to return physical things.

Njoki: Maybe our infinite grief fuels the museum's determination to retain our cultural assets, because it keeps them, and everything they stand for, relevant.

Adéọlá: In Yoruba culture, you can make an *Olugbohun* with different intentions for your family, and when you realise it's in danger, you can revoke its *Àṣẹ*.[417] That can be done for the bronzes too. I think that changes the conversation totally, where we're not even bargaining anymore as there is no reason to. And after that, it has no power or meaning because we do not claim it. It's like we're disowning it because you have defiled it by touching it when you were not invited to, by holding onto it for centuries against our will, allegedly 'preserving' it with toxic chemicals that have severed its spiritual energy.

Njoki: There is a foundational flaw in any iteration of justice that demands more of the aggrieved than of the aggressor. I believe that every path that people are taking on their journey back to themselves, in their fullest, most authentic forms, after centuries of violence, is right. Those who are in their seventh generation asking for their exact assets back and who will not quit? They are right. Those who are making decisions to release and find new ways forward? They are also right. To me, revolution and release means coming back to yourself after your enemies placed so many obstacles in your path and finding a way to do that together with other members of your communities, by blood and by intention.

Adéọlá: Recently, we've observed the British Museum beckon the public to help them locate the thousands or more illegally stolen and sold precious items from their inventory that were taken by their very own members of staff.[418] It shouldn't come as a shock that the aggrieved peoples of the world are all thinking about cultural heritage being held under lock and key there. We have seen the end of the claim of safety by that same museum. As they clearly cannot protect this massive inventory, they must surely return looted cultural assets to their rightful homes and owners, in the most healing and restorative ways, ways that dignify these assets and their recipients. That is one way museums can attempt to bridge these massive chasms between us.

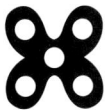

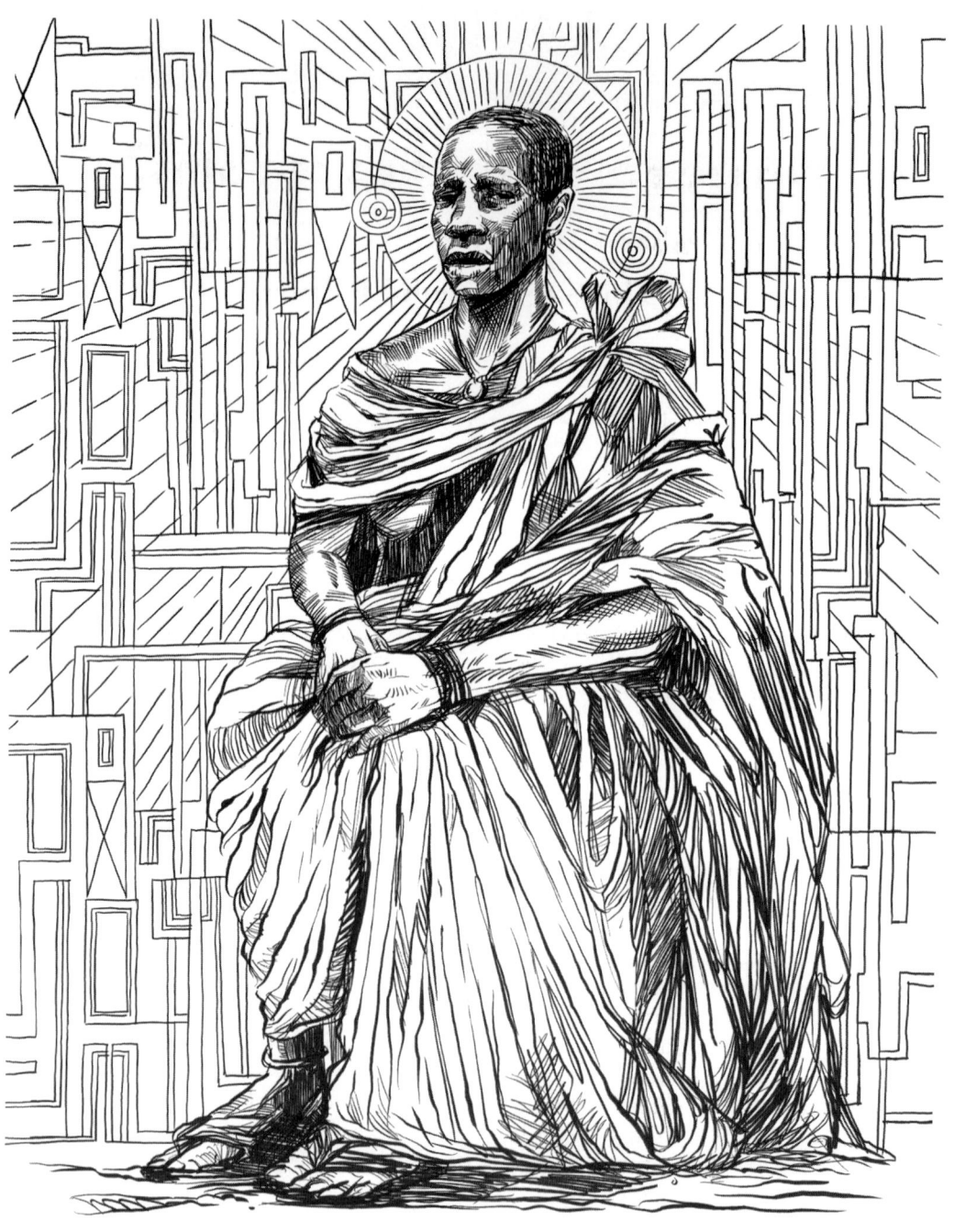

Artist: Sindiso Nyoni

CHAPTER 14

Where are Nehanda's remains?
A Zimbabwean Search in the Context of Shifting Museum Politics

Njabulo Chipangura, Farai Chabata and Lennon Mhishi

Mbuya Nehanda was a historical figure and as a spirit who became a symbolic driving force behind Zimbabwe's earliest war of anti-colonial resistance, known as the First Chimurenga (1896–1898). Because of her resistance, Justice John Philipp Watermeyer sentenced her to death in 1897 and the British captured and murdered her on 27 April 1898, together with her so-called 'accomplice', Sekuru Kaguvi Gumboreshumba. Her head is believed to have been taken to England as a trophy.

What makes Nehanda an interesting historical figure is that her story allows her to be both a historical and legendary figure in Zimbabwe. In 2015, during National Heroes Day commemorations in Harare, the then president Robert Mugabe called on the Natural History Museum in London to return Mbuya Nehanda and Sekuru Kaguvi's remains to Zimbabwe. He declared: 'surely, keeping decapitated heads as war trophies in this day and age in a national history museum must rank among the highest forms of racist moral decadence, sadism, and human insensitivity.'[419] Against the backdrop of ongoing debates on how to decolonise museums in Europe, especially those who house unethically acquired cultural assets and ancestral remains, this chapter zooms in on the recent search for Nehanda's remains undertaken by Zimbabwean authorities from the National Museums and Monuments of Zimbabwe (NMMZ) and National Archives of Zimbabwe (NAZ) in the UK. We address how violence in the settler colonial project silenced resistance by spirit mediums such as Nehanda, especially in the context of punitive and carceral measures in the colony of Southern Rhodesia, akin to what Patrick Wolfe has called the 'logic of elimination'.[420] This chapter also discusses what it means in practical and decolonial terms to 'rehumanise' remains as ancestors of living people through appropriate, ethical and unconditional repatriation.

A Historiography of Nehanda: Colonial Violence and Memory

Charwe Mbuya Nehanda is an icon of the protracted and arduous struggle against occupation of what Britain used to call 'Southern Rhodesia', a colonial territory named after Cecil John Rhodes who was credited for establishing the colony in 1890. According to feminist historian Ruramisai Charumbira:

> Charwe wokwa Hwata was a child of the Hwata dynasty (*dzinza/rudzi*) one of many such dynasties that formed in the late eighteenth and early nineteenth centuries as older Shona kingdoms dissolved, and smaller confederacies and dynasties emerged. [H]er people had migrated and settled in the Mazowe valley beginning in the late 1700s. Charwe became the medium of Nehanda in the Mazowe District around 1881. The district already had a history of Nehandas buried at Shaverunzi and a village known as Nehanda Village (*kwa Nehanda*). Charwe, therefore, is more popularly known by the nonhereditary politico-religious title of Nehanda (sometimes spelled Nyanda, Nahanda, or Nianda) rather than by her own name. Often mistaken as the only Nehanda, Charwe was one of many women who channeled the spirit of Nyamita (or Nyakasikana), a royal female spirit of the Mutapa dynasty (later a kingdom). Nyamita was believed to be a spirit of rain, land, and agricultural fertility. Once she became a medium of Nehanda (*homwe ye mhondoro ya Nehanda*) Charwe assumed the position of adviser not only to the holder of the Hwata title, but to a much larger constituency, as royal spirits were believed to transcend dynastic lines.[421]

The name Mbuya Nehanda has become almost synonymous with the First Chimurenga (aka *Chindunduma*) because of the outstanding role played by Charwe in coordinating the anti-colonial movement, thereby giving it the much-needed impetus and tenacity that it required against British colonial rule. The name 'Chimurenga' is derived from Murenga, a Shona ancestor and oracle who is believed to have spoken through the rocks to inspire the earliest attempts of anti-colonial resistance led by spirit mediums such as Nehanda, Kaguvi and Mashayamombe in 1896. These spirit mediums sometimes worked closely with chiefs, as witnessed by Kaguvi and Chinengundu Mashayamombe's cooperation, and Nehanda's influence on Chiefs Hwata and Chiweshe.

Ruramisai Charumbira further relates Nehanda's central role in the anti-colonial struggle in the following terms:

> As European settlement became permanent, Nehanda-Charwe, like many Africans, was unnerved, especially by what she perceived as the corrupting nature

of European culture. From 1896 into 1897 more robust resistance emerged in reaction to European settlement in the Mazowe valley and in the colony at large. Nehanda-Charwe was active in the organization and coordination of the war against imperial patrols deployed in the Mazowe, leading its commanding officer, Colonel Edwin A.H. Alderson, to remark that the district of Mazowe had fertile lands and a fertile resistance movement as it was the land of the celebrated Nehanda.[422]

The settlers had established strongholds in the area such as Fort Alderson and Fort Mazowe (both national monuments today), an indication of the spirited resistance to colonial rule in a territory that White settlers highly coveted for its rich soils, mineral wealth, flora and fauna. In response to the confiscation of cattle and land, among other forms of oppression and extraction by the settler colonial system, Shona and Ndebele people rose in resistance. In the violent response by the colonial regime, spiritual leaders were captured and publicly executed. This was the fate of Charwe in late 1897, when British colonial forces arrested her at Baradzanwa, a place in the Upper Mazowe Valley that local people call Gomba (i.e. 'hole') in reference to the separation of Charwe from her community. It took the mobilisation of reinforcements from Salisbury to suppress the African resistance in this region which resulted in the death of the infamous colonial administrator of the area, Native Commissioner Henry Polard, who was targeted because of his brutality towards local people. Charumbira notes that 'during her time in custody and her trial (December 1897 through April 1898), Nehanda-Charwe was defiant against Christian conversion right up to the day she was executed by hanging in Salisbury on 28 April 1898'. Her execution took place at a gaol that is believed to have been located where the Harare Central Police Station now stands. Father Francis Richartz of the Roman Catholic Church's Society of Jesus (Jesuits), who unsuccessfully tried to baptise her before her hanging, highlighted her stern courage. As happened with other leaders of the First Chimurenga – and many other African leaders in similar contexts of anti-colonial resistance – her remains were probably taken to England as trophies and are now widely believed to be stored in one of several museums in the UK. Zimbabwean history remembers that before the British hanged her, she prophesied: *'mapfupa angu achamuka'* ('my bones will rise again'), encouraging those struggling against colonial rule to find inspiration from her unwavering dedication to the movement in the face of imminent death.

Since the 1980s, debates on the precise role of indigenous spirituality, religion and their priests in the context of anti-colonial movements in Southern Africa have raged among historians. Two main schools of thought have spawned a relative bipolarism in academic circles. First, the 'absent priesthood' argument, from, for example, the British scholar Julian Cobbing and Zimbabwean historian David N. Beach, supporting the belief that the decision to resist or collaborate with the colonisers rested entirely on political leadership, that is, the chiefs, who, in this line of argument, represented secular leadership. Beach even published a controversial article titled 'Charwe: A Woman Unjustly Accused', which generated a heated debate and direct verbal exchanges between him and the renowned Zimbabwean poet and novelist Solomon Mutswairo.[423] Beach accused literary writers of ignoring historical facts, while Mutswairo retorted that even historians are biased and that Nehanda would remain a heroine of the people forever no matter how historians viewed her role in the First Chimurenga.[424]

Spearheaded by British historian Terence Ranger, the second main school of thought on the issue emphasises the role of religious leaders, particularly spirit mediums, in providing the impetus for the outbreak of resistance, bolstering connections between the 1890s and subsequent anti-colonial struggles in the twentieth century.[425] This continuity was further substantiated by gestures of intergenerational passing, as when ninety-year-old Nyamasoka Chinamhora, a veteran of the First Chimurenga, handed over a war axe, sword and knobkerrie to Robert Mugabe and Joshua Nkomo in 1962, proclaiming:

> Take this sword and these other weapons of war, and with them fight the enemy to the bitter end. Let the time be the same as those days when we used to keep as many cattle as we wanted. Also let it be that we shall plough wherever we like and as we like.[426]

Since her death, Zimbabweans have sought Nehanda both spiritually and physically for guidance and to fulfil her prophecy.[427] Many other veterans of Zimbabwe's colonial resistances of 1896–1898 invoked Nehanda's influence as the inspiration for the movement now referred to as the First Chimurenga/Umvukela or *Hondo yeChindunduma*, often including Gumboreshumba, the spirit medium of Sekuru Kaguvi. In addition, her famous, almost prophetic declaration that her bones would rise became a slogan of the struggle for Zimbabwe's independence in the 1970s.[428] Her statement encouraged future resistance against colonial rule and became the rallying point for the ultimate war of liberation from the shackles of colonialism, the Second Chimurenga (1964–1979), which led to the independence of Zimbabwe in 1980. As highlighted by historian and former Chief Secretary to the Zimbabwean president, Misheck Sibanda, the spirit of Nehanda was dominant in the Mazowe and Chiweshe areas of Mashonaland and 'in a fundamental way, the spirit mediums of Mkwati, Siginyamathse, Kaguvi and Nehanda provided the necessary religious ideological consensus for the anti-white struggle'.[429] Many veterans of Zimbabwe's liberation struggle recollect that Nehanda provided guidance to the freedom fighters.[430] For instance, the guerrillas baptised one of the liberation war zones 'Nehanda', namely, the north-east sector with areas bordering Mozambique. One of the most popular mediums of Nehanda's spirit at that time operated around Musengezi to Chifombo Camp on the Mozambique–Zambia border. Reports relate that she carried out a nine-day march to give inspiration and guidance to the new fighters.[431] She advised them to avoid touching women, eating certain types of relish, and fighting each other, if they wished their anti-colonial armed struggle to succeed. According to some senior members of the Zimbabwe African National Liberation Army, Mbuya Nehanda was their most important and most influential recruit. Josiah Tungamirai, one of the leading cadres of the liberation struggle, recalled that, once the young people knew that Nehanda had joined the war, they followed suit in large numbers. Although she died at Chifombo on 12 June 1973, the war continued up until a ceasefire was brokered in 1979 and eventual independence on 18 April 1980.[432]

The Search for Nehanda: British Museums and the Decolonial Question

What became of Nehanda-Charwe's body following her execution has been a subject of tremendous speculation. It is both a case of missing bones and that of missing or migrated archives. Due to the absence of eyewitness accounts of her death and the presence of gaps in the archival record at the National Archives and the Jesuit Archives in Zimbabwe, where some of Father Francis Richartz's notes and diaries were deposited, the whereabouts of the remains of Nehanda and many of her contemporaries remain unknown to historians and to her people. It is possible that British colonial authorities deliberately concealed what happened in an attempt close off any potential future insurgencies, thinking that Nehanda's grave would likely become a pilgrimage site. There is untested speculation that her body may have been interred in the African section of the Pioneer Cemetery in Harare, while her skull was taken to England as a war trophy.

In July 2022, a team of archaeologists from the National Museums and Monuments of Zimbabwe (NMMZ) and archivists from the National Archives (NAZ) was assembled by the government to visit various museums in the UK in search for remains of Nehanda. They visited the Natural History Museum in London, the British Museum, Cambridge University's Duckworth Laboratory, the Pitt Rivers Museum at Oxford University, and the Manchester University Museum, hoping to start a process of rehumanisation and repatriation that could ultimately pave the way for her dignified reburial back home. Cameroonian philosopher Achille Mbembe and South African historian Ciraj Rassool have both argued that, in addressing colonial history and starting processes of decolonisation, one should go against colonial mindsets that relegated these 'skeletons of empire' to the status of mere collections and stripped them from their names. In a nutshell, one should grant these ancestors their humanity again.[433]

A popular sentiment was that Nehanda's remains had been kept at the British Museum. This museum indeed holds a non-negligible number of ancestral remains from former British African colonies, as a list published on their website informs. It is on this basis that the Zimbabwean delegation premised its search there, but this was not conclusive. At the Pitt Rivers Museum, a display case informs visitors of the presence of human remains at the museum, in storage, but refrains from exhibiting them. According to the panel, the museum holds the remains of one individual from Zimbabwe, but this person apparently could not have been Nehanda. Yet, one of us was able to establish the existence of two additional hair samples from Mutare and Matebeleland in the collection. Further inquiries are ongoing.

The search for Nehanda's remains also took the Zimbabwean delegation to the Manchester Museum, which is part of the University of Manchester and has more than 25,000 entries in its ethnographic collection, ordered according to continents, of which a large part comes from the dispossession of indigenous communities outside Europe. Its African collection holds more than 10,000 cultural assets. Like most ethno-colonial museums, the Manchester Museum has been complicit in some of the worst practices of appropriation, such as looting, dislocation and the implementation of racist violence, visible in the stories attached to these imprisoned belongings. However, this museum has started rethinking colonial-knowledge production and is addressing the extent to which colonial violence was at the centre of its collecting practices. It has underlined its commitment to truth-telling, openness and disclosure by inviting source and diaspora communities to do collaborative provenance and biographical research.[434] Henceforth, the visit by officials from NMMZ and NAZ was another example of the proactive engagement approach that the museum has been undertaking with regard to the unconditional repatriation of collections acquired unethically. In September 2023, the Manchester Museum repatriated 143 cultural assets to the Anindilyakwa people of Groote Eylandt, Northern Australia.[435] Precedence to this unconditional repatriation had been laid out in 2019 when forty-three secret, sacred and ceremonial artefacts were returned to the Gangalidda and Garawa, Nyamal and Yawuru aboriginal communities in Australia.

Encyclopaedic museums like the Manchester Museum and the British Museum took shape as global repositories of extracted cultural assets, sites of ordering them according to colonial mindsets, and spaces where the public could acquire knowledge of (and control over) colonised peoples and cultures.[436] European colonialism was an epistemic project bound up with Enlightenment notions of reason, progress and modernity, which imagined Europe as the global site of scientific knowledge and which set about creating the non-Western world as its mirror.[437] Admittedly, the Manchester Museum has also been complicit in amassing African cultural heritage during the same period and perpetuating theories that supported colonisation.[438] Anthropology produced colonial practices of ordering African communities and their belongings in a grid that drew upon Linnaean classification and informed scientific racism, educational curricula, and legal and administrative frameworks.

In pursuit of this ordering of the world, material culture was extracted from colonised societies, deprived of its original and contextual meaning, and scrutinised through the lens of colonial knowledge and mindsets.[439] Although the Zimbabwean delegation's visit in Manchester did not help find the actual location of Nehanda's remains, it did open space for future collaborative provenance research on eighty-five cultural assets that are from today's Zimbabwe. These include ceremonial axes, snuff boxes, wooden bowls and clubs that were collected by the musician Phillip Godlee in the 1930s, as well as wooden baskets, beaded bags, beaded belts, bracelets and beaded gourds acquired by Ian Harrison in the 1960s. The information available is inadequate and museum staff – which includes one of us – are hoping to build a collaborative research partnership with communities in Zimbabwe to cater to this issue. Community engagement is a fundamental aspect of challenging colonial narratives and restoring the social biographies of living cultures represented in the collections.

The mere fact that the delegation was allowed to see all the 'living cultures' that came from Zimbabwe during British colonial rule is a testament of the openness and the decolonial directions that the Manchester Museum embraces. As anthropologist Bruno Brulon Soares argues,

> decolonisation cannot just be about restitution or giving back cultural heritage objects to communities – it is about inviting these communities to change our ways of thinking to rethink our own understanding of cultural heritage and to denounce the violence produced by museums.[440]

As curator of living cultures at the Manchester Museum, Njabulo Chipangura understands that the belongings he cares for are not just static, frozen and mundane 'ethnographic objects' but rather cultures that actively represent living people and their practices.[441] The anthropological category of 'objects' has until today anonymised the makers, users and owners and silenced the meanings behind these cultural assets.[442] But when one considers curatorship as a function of care, they can be viewed through a decolonial prism that emphasises their connection to people's beliefs and stories. Therefore, one cannot care for material culture at the expense of ignoring its social biography. Moreover, in African contexts, cultural assets have potency and are often treated by communities as living beings which they can use, touch, smell and taste. They have individual biographies and carry with them important meanings connected to their ritual and cultural functions located in societies of origin.[443]

Unconditional repatriation is a decolonial method based on open disclosure. It starts with identifying cultural assets that were looted as result of colonial violence and should be followed by a process of returning them back to the communities. Abiding by an ethics of truth-telling, the museum takes the initiative and no longer waits for claims from source communities, since they are often unaware of what is found in storage. Despite criticism against museums using and abusing of the term 'decolonial',[444] the

Manchester Museum paves the way for empirical decolonial work, not a method that is set in stone but rather a learning process.[445] In the hope that Nehanda's remains will be located, we regard the possible subsequent repatriation of her remains and those of her fellow spirit mediums to Zimbabwe not as a loss but rather as an opportunity for building active relationships between museums in the UK and their communities, be they Zimbabwean or diasporic. Building on decades of repatriation work in North America, Chip Colwell demonstrated that repatriation is not an end, but a new beginning, as each case gives birth to new struggles to come to terms with past colonial violence.[446]

Memorialisation and Commemorations

The memory of Nehanda-Charwe in post-independence Zimbabwe is intrinsically linked to the conundrum and the mystery surrounding her death and the fate of her head and body. Since Zimbabwean independence in 1980, squares, streets and buildings were named after her and several other prominent spirit mediums of the First Chimurenga, granting them national standing and honouring their achievements. In the case of Nehanda-Charwe, this memorialisation even extends to statues, poetry and songs.

Despite the absence of her remains, she commands a grandiose presence in a statue that was erected in 2021 in Harare's Central Business District (CBD). Statues as tangible forms of heritage shape the way identities are created and disputed, whether as individuals, groups or the nation-state.[447] Therefore, to understand the historical and embedded nature of heritage, one should go beyond treating it as a set of problems to be solved by calling for a deeper engagement with the production of identity, power and authority. Tinashe Mawere offered an insightful analysis of this monument and argued that 'the erection of the Nehanda statue and the narratives around it should invite us to question what history is (re)captured, what memory is (re)captured and (re)membered, what past, present and future is [sic] performed and for whose benefit'.[448] Nehanda's physical presence in the CBD is a powerful example of African cultural heritage occupying the citadel of socio-economic and political power. Located at the intersection of roads honouring two fathers of African independences – Julius Nyerere and Samora Machel – it demonstrates the paramount importance of this historical and legendary figure in the history of the anti-colonial movement and in shaping decolonial futures in Zimbabwe.

Liberation war edifices and other sites related to the First and Second Chimurenga enjoy a privileged position in heritage conservation and protection in Zimbabwe. However, the remains of liberation war fighters are still scattered around the country in mine shafts, mass graves and former detention centres such as the Butcher site, Hebert

Mine and Chibondo.[449] The search for Nehanda's bones has indeed been accompanied by the search for the remains of veterans of the liberation struggle who were buried in mass and, hitherto, unknown graves in Zimbabwe, Angola, Mozambique and Zambia. In the construction of the liberation heritage archive, what was also called Zimbabwe's 'memorial complex', exhumations have been heavily politicised.[450] In this 'complex', the lives of former anti-colonial fighters are remembered through monuments, public commemorations, and other memory practices controlled by the ruling ZANU–PF party at the national, provincial and district level, on sites designated as 'heroes' acres'. In other words, ZANU–PF has the power and authority to decide who qualifies as a hero of the successive anti-colonial struggles. Mbuya Nehanda was declared a national hero at independence and, although her remains were not interred on the National Heroes' Acre in Harare, a cenotaph known as the Tomb of the Unknown Soldier was erected in acknowledgement of her efforts and those of all liberation war fighters whose remains are still missing.

The urban landscape further demonstrates Nehanda's prominence in the national memory. Mbuya Nehanda Street, formerly Victoria Street, further symbolises Nehanda's victory in death following her sentencing to death by Justice Watermeyer, whose judgement was in fact sanctioned by Queen Victoria. Another Mbuya Nehanda Street near the Kopje area in Harare, formerly Salisbury's central business district, is one of the busiest streets occupied by local entrepreneurs. Mbuya Nehanda Maternity Hospital is a major maternity wing at Parirenyatwa, Zimbabwe's largest referral hospital. Finally, Mbuya Nehanda Children's Home on the outskirts of Harare takes care of orphaned children.

Furthermore, numerous songs during the liberation struggle made use of the legend of Nehanda, while Hosiah Chipanga, a contemporary musician and social satirist, pleaded with Nehanda to free people from Pharaoh – probably a metaphor for the socio-economic hardships. She is also an inspirational figure who symbolises the spirit of resistance against colonial domination in many influential works of Shona literature, art and song. In the poem *Soko Risinamusoro* (1958) by the nationalist Herbert Chitepo, Nehanda is venerated as the protector of the Zimbabwean country. Nehanda-Charwe became 'Mbuya Nehanda' (Grandmother Nehanda) and, as such, she was immortalised. She is depicted in the eponymous poetic novel by Yvonne Vera who was awarded the 1994 Commonwealth Literary award, as a well as in *Death Throes* by Charles Samupindi, in Shimmer Chinodya's *Harvest of Thorns*, in Garika Mutasa's *The Contact* and in Chenjerai Hove's *Bones*. By 1980, a majority of Zimbabweans had heard about her in song or poetry or seen her on posters and pictures.[451] The new government presented her to the public as the *mhondoro* (spirit) which protects the new state. The popular poem *Nehanda Nyakasikana* from Solomon Mutsvairo's novel *Feso*, published in 1957 and banned by the Rhodesian Front Government, was fondly recited by the late Vice-President Simon Muzenda on national television. A powerful and prolific oral tradition grew around Charwe's name, her part in the uprising, her refusal to convert to Christianity, her defiance on the scaffold and her prophesy '*Mapfupa Angu Achamuka*' to win back freedom taken away by the Europeans. In time, her political influence and the healing and protective powers associated with the spirit medium became intricately fused. In songs, poetry and in legendary narratives, Nehanda became a political and cultural icon in post-independent Zimbabwe. The listing of Upper Mazowe valley as a national monument in 2007, a landscape (*Gomba*) that Nehanda had traversed and influenced, the region where she was captured and killed, can be interpreted as the culmination of post-colonial efforts to recognise and celebrate Nehanda, while simultaneously protecting the land and its spiritual and symbolic value.

This speaks to one of the long-standing discussions in the management of heritage in Africa, particularly the tension between history and memory on sites officially regarded as liberation heritage sites while colonial symbols still stand in juxtaposition. Many African cities, including Zimbabwe's capital, Harare, have remained citadels of colonial symbols of power and privilege. Schools, streets, buildings and place names perpetuate the dominant position of colonial narratives, a past that has deliberately excluded some cultures and voices. Various attempts have been made to decolonise the urban landscape through renaming and the erection of statues in honour of liberation icons, notably Joshua Nkomo in Bulawayo and Nehanda in Harare. Cityscapes play a significant role in influencing the cosmological views of cit(y)zens, including their sense of belonging to the nation or the local community. Therefore, heritage and art interact in Zimbabwean urban landscapes not merely to influence the ambience of these spaces but to counter colonial and modernist conceptions of heritage. Public art is rarely art for art's sake but accompanies the city's emergence from a past that was dominated by colonial theft and violence. At another level, Nehanda's statue has the power to defy the limits of representation and meaning imposed by state patrons. Public art indeed encourages people to keep on asking questions on how to deal with this brutal colonial past while imagining decolonial futures for the city and the nation. The presence of the statue is also a constant reminder of the need to find Nehanda's remains, or at the very least, to find out what happened after her execution in 1898.

Conclusion

The case of Mbuya Nehanda, who spearheaded the First Chimurenga, was then publicly executed in 1898, and whose remains were probably taken as a trophy of conquest and are widely thought to have been shipped to England, epitomises the complexity of remembering anti-colonial leaders in the absence of closure. The search for Nehanda's remains, which started in prominent cultural institutions in the UK, underlines the importance of repatriation and the demands for rethinking the role of museums, away from places that incarcerate ancestors, towards the acknowledgement of living cultures that are sacred, spiritual and symbolic. Against the background of scientific racism, oppressive museum practices and enduring colonialities, Mbuya Nehanda stands once again as an important symbol of resistance and refusal. Her remains are not ensconced in storage, but they 'rise again' with these calls for repatriation to her home, today's Zimbabwe.

Recently, a delegation from NMMZ and NAZ visited several museums in the UK to search for Mbuya Nehanda's remains. In our piece, we zoomed in on the exchange at the Manchester Museum where one of us works as curator of Living Cultures. We demonstrated that even if this museum does not hold Nehanda's remains, there was an open engagement that allowed the delegation to see other cultural assets from Zimbabwe looted during British colonial rule. We argued that such an open-door policy and proactive engaging with different communities is one of the methods in the process of decolonisation of museums. Truth-telling, accountability, honest disclosure and genuine facilitation of unconditional repatriation are some of the strategies that have been adopted by the Manchester Museum regarding collections that stem from colonial contexts.

Nevertheless, we also underscored that decolonisation is not just be about the restitution of cultural heritage to communities. It begins with inviting these communities to change our ways of thinking and understandings of the biographical meanings of these cultural assets and to denounce the violence produced by museums and other dominant discourses. The chapter transitioned to the memory of Nehanda and how she has been monumentalised in Zimbabwe, especially her statue in Harare's CBD. To this end, we cast a critical eye on the politicisation of heritage in Zimbabwe by showing how Nehanda, despite all the good intentions of finding her remains and bringing her home, has been used and abused by ruling elites for political mileage. Liberation War Heritage sites are constructed through a careful and selective propagation of narratives promoted by ZANU–PF, the party in power since independence in 1980.

Where are Nehanda's remains? This is a question that Zimbabweans will continue to grapple with until all museums and universities in the UK come up with an answer. In 2021, the Natural History Museum in London stated that 'after extensive research we have found no evidence to suggest that remains of Mbuya Nehanda are held or have ever been held by the museum. We've shared all information we have with the authorities in Zimbabwe.'[452] Institutions with colonial collections must practise openness and accountability, not only in responding to claims, but equally in disclosing what they hold. Otherwise, communities in Africa, whose material is imprisoned in various collections, will never get to know of these holdings. Such proactive action must be regarded as the precursor to any form of repatriation.

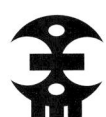

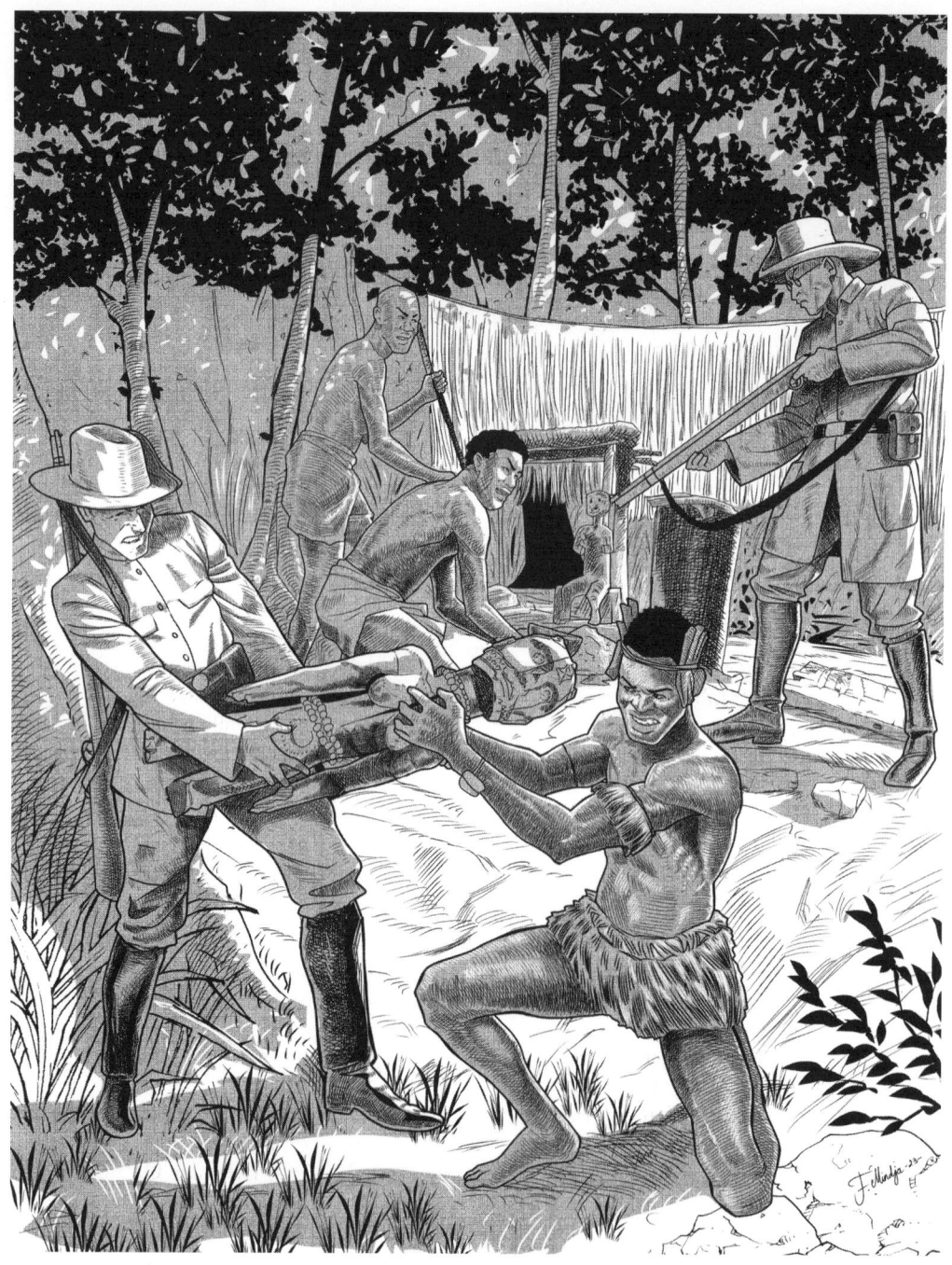

Artist: Franky Mindja

CHAPTER 15

Byéri

Ancestor Guardian Figures of the Kwasio People in Southern Cameroon

Yrine Matchinda and Sebastian-Manès Sprute

In memory of Jean-Baptiste Nzambi († 2022)

In 2014, an ancestral guardian ascribed to the Mabi[453] people of today's southern Cameroon (or 'Mabea' in colonial orthography) and dated to the early nineteenth century was sold by the auction house Sotheby's in Paris for €4.4 million (minus fees), 'well above its high estimate of €3.5 m'.[454] It climbed up to the third place on the podium of highest prices ever achieved for an auctioned African artwork, and constituted a record for this art-historical type of sculpture.[455] In keeping with their code of conduct, Sotheby's informs on the provenance of the figure, retracing it to the French artist Félix Fénéon, who has been described as a man 'at the forefront of aesthetic thought [including] about non-western material culture'.[456] However, the auction house was unable to provide any information on the unknown 'virtuoso artist' – as Sotheby's former Head of African & Oceanic Art put it – who carved this ancestral guardian figure. Their catalogue also failed to inform on Fénéon's potential suppliers of sacred African cultural heritage, or at least admit that their research on provenance could not retrieve any information regarding the context of acquisition – or the potential looting – of the ancestral guardian figure on the African continent.[457] Such incomplete provenance, research that in the case of auction houses aims at raising the price by retracing its prestigious former owners, tends to 'frame the production of value for African art as an exclusively Western process', as art historian Sylvester Okwunodu Ogbechie argued.[458] It willingly eclipses the conditions of production and acquisition of this worthy figure on the African continent.

In June 2023, a renewed auction of a *byéri* statuette – this time of the Fang in today's Gabon – took place at Sotheby's in Paris. On this occasion, Yannick Elydjah Meyo and other members of the transnational organisation Collectif Gabon-Occitanie and the Representative Council of Black Associations (CRAN, Conseil représentatif des associations noires, France) intervened, letting the auction house and potential buyers know that this relic was 'a sacred sculpture used in our *byéri* rituals. It represents our ancestors, belongs to our community, and must not be put on sale. At the very least, this cultural asset was wrongly acquired.'[459] Sotheby's ran the auction anyway. However, following this intervention, potential buyers got cold feet; no one bid at the auction, and so the relic was not sold. This was a small victory, but there is still a long way to go before private collections start consulting communities and ritual experts in cases of dubious acquisitions of sacred belongings.

In 1899, a similar 'female ancestral sculpture (Ngule malang)' of the Mbvumbo, a population group closely related to the Mabi and sharing the Kwasio language, was relegated to a museum 'object' by the owner of a colonial plantation in German Cameroon, Georg August Zenker (1855–1922).[460] As we speak, it sits in one of the largest holdings of Cameroonian cultural heritage, the collection of the Grassi Museum in Leipzig, under inventory number MAf 00643. Many other museums in continental Europe keep statuettes attributed to the Kwasio-speaking people (Mabi/Mabea, Mvumbo and Ngumba): the Ethnological Museum in Berlin, the Musée du Quai Branly in Paris, the Linden Museum in Stuttgart, the Museum Five Continents in Munich, the MARKK in Hamburg, the Ethnological Museum in Dresden, the Landesmuseum in Hanover and the Rietberg Museum in Zurich.[461] Often found as stand-alones, these sculptures made of wood represent the last remnant of so-called *byéri* reliquaries, sacred ensembles that, in addition to such statuettes, also contained the remains of esteemed ancestors, a container for their remains and funerary goods. In many cases, however, the original *byéri* ensembles were torn apart in the course of violent colonial processes of appropriation and extraction, so that only the ancestor guardian figures can be found in most German collections today, while some anthropological collections – like the one at the American Museum of Natural History – were tasked with amassing the remains of ancestors.[462] Reliquaries have always been highly coveted by European collectors, not least since the beginning of the intensified collecting activity of the colonial-modern era.[463] The ethnologist and art historian Louis Perrois – whose Eurocentric study of ancestral rites in central Africa always makes it in Sotheby's catalogue bibliographies every time such a statuette is auctioned off – contributed to this hype by elevating them to the status of archetypal masterpieces: he called them the pinnacle of African sculptural carving.[464]

In colonial times, practices of ancestor veneration involving the use of *byéri* reliquaries were still a widespread phenomenon in many of the population groups in Southern Cameroon, Equatorial Guinea and Gabon, which are also grouped under the ethnic umbrella term of 'Fang'.[465] The presence of *byéri* relics of the Kwasio-speaking Mbvumbo and Mabi people of Southern Cameroon (who are counted among the Fang) in numerous public and private collections worldwide is closely related to the violent invasion of their settlement area as a result of German colonial rule in Cameroon. German collection holdings in particular are often more or less directly linked to the crushing of the local resistance led by the Mabi against German colonial rule in 1893.

In this chapter, we discuss the case of the Mabi to illustrate the looting of sacred relics as part of a military regime that had for its foundation the exercise of colonial violence. We also examine the spiritual dimension of destruction and loss, as well as the resulting consequences for contemporary societies.

The German Campaign against the Mabi

The war waged against the Mabi was one of the first German military undertakings on the ground. Its purpose was to expand the sphere of colonial rule, which, until 1890, had been limited mainly to the coastal regions, and 'to pave the way for the increased economic exploitation of the colony by German capitalists'.[466] The war campaigns for the subjugation and exploitation of local populations like the Mabi in the years from 1891 to 1893 were generally characterised by a logic of war economy based on plunder and looting. In addition, colonial rule at that time was extremely brutal and exploitative. The draconian regime and despotic aegis of the then deputy governor and chancellor of the colony Karl Theodor Heinrich Leist (1859–1910) and his deputy, Vice-Chancellor Alwin Karl Wehlan (1860–?) was implemented through their primary instrument of terror: the so-called *Polizeitruppe* or police-force, a paramilitary formation consisting mainly of those whom Paulin Oloukpona-Yinnon has called slave mercenaries ('esclaves-mercenaires').[467]

According to Wehlan's report on the war campaign against the Mabi, the purpose of the military venture was not only to enforce the colonial trade monopoly but also to capture the leader of the Mabi resistance whom the Germans identified as 'King Benga from Majesse', who reportedly 'had declared war on the Europeans to the knife'.[468] However, while the archival sources only mention 'King Benga from Majesse', the oral tradition recalls three important leading figures whom Cameroonians remember today as 'national' heroes: the actual leader of the resistance, Biang Bwô Mbumbô alias 'King Mayessè', Nagyang Kwamba alias 'King Benga' and Biwèe Nagya alias 'King Massili' are all considered as central historical figures of the Mabi in the struggle against German colonial rule.[469] According to oral history, Biang Bwô Mbumbô (1833–1893) was originally not of royal descent, but was regarded as a free spirit and warrior of powerful stature who, in the face of German occupation, rose to become the leader of the armed resistance.[470]

The German campaign against the Mabi started on 15 March 1893 in Douala, from where Wehlan and his core force initially set out for Groß-Batanga on the steamer *Nachtigal*, a ship that bore the name of the man considered as founder of the colony Kamerun, Gustav Nachtigal. Under Wehlan's command stood 'drill sergeant Lewonig, the government official Nette, medical assistant Brückner …, 85 men of the police force and 30 porters' as well as a '3.7 cm rapid fire gun and a Maxim gun'. The hostilities began at night, on the coastal village of 'Ndumali', when the colonialists launched a surprise attack from the steamer. The next day, Wehlan recruited '600 Banoko and Bapuku, who were in dispute with the Mabeas … as auxiliary warriors' in order to advance further inland with their support and knowledge of the terrain. In the days that followed, the police force often clashed with 'heavy resistance', which they managed to put down due to superior weaponry, especially artillery.[471]

In many instances, Wehlan's wording and phrasing in his official report discloses the scale and extent of violence used against the Mabi. For example, in the case of the attack against 'Mbekaka', the troops 'wiped off [the village] from the face of the earth'; Wehlan also reports conquering 'Yeneka', 'only after a stubborn fight, in which there was a veritable melee …'. Further, 'Bandi, a prosperous village consisting of nine independent parts' was not only 'razed to the ground', but the Germans also hanged some of their prisoners, while committing a massacre by shooting the fleeing villagers. As the Vice-Chancellor shamelessly reported, part of the fleeing inhabitants found themselves trapped in a dead end in a ravine, which offered him and his troops 'the most effective ground': 'With the help of the Maxim gun, the enemy received heavier losses here than in any other place'.[472]

Later during the campaign against the Mabi, the expedition's extremely violent and demonstrative approach also led to further war crimes. Thus, after only two days, on 17 March 1893, the troops were able to capture the strongly fortified 'main centre of unrest', the town of Mayessè.[473] The war against the Mabi was then to continue for another two weeks until Wehlan returned to Douala with the police force on 31 March 1893. It had left a trail of devastation through the entire area of Mabi settlements.

The violence against the indigenous population, as well as the plundering of their material livelihoods and possessions, had been part of the colonial rulers' calculations from the outset, as the soldiers could make ends meet partly through the sale of war booty or the enslavement of prisoners.[474] Contrary to customary practice as the time, the police soldiers under Wehlan's leadership were not allowed to 'keep the spoils'.[475] As the soldier Akapo noted in this regard, the fact that Chancellor Leist had taken the loot 'not for the government but for his own person' incensed the soldiers dependent on the profit generated by the sale of looted goods.[476]

With regard to the treatment of the prisoners during the war campaign, the contemporary witness and station chief of the Mundame post, Wilhelm Vallentin (1862–?), reported that in one case, three prisoners were 'abandoned to the lust of the soldiers, ... and ... slaughtered ... [or] cut, hacked and mutilated with knives, since Assessor Wehlan had given the order not to use the rifles when killing'.[477] Or, as Wehlan reported directly to Vallentin when they shared dinner,

> Since [the prisoners] were all dying here, he had them beaten to death on the ship (literally: 'I had them beaten on the head'). Then he went on to say that the soldiers, especially one of them, had done an excellent job of pulling the skin off the enemies' skulls. A cut would be made on the lower jaw with the knife, then the teeth would be used to pull the whole scalp over the face and head. Is this not ideal warfare?[478]

In view of these statements, Vallentin wondered, not without reason, 'what other horrors might take place during such "campaigns", about which nobody finds out, [horrors] that the white members prefer to hush up out of a sense of shame'.[479]

In fact, Wehlan's official report is no exception. Not only was it written with considerable delay, weeks after the events, but the violent actions of the police force are hardly mentioned in it and, according to Dietrich von Oertzen (?–?), the district bailiff of Kribi, Wehlan deliberately concealed them with numerous 'inaccuracies'.[480] The thin and misleading archives also leave the question of fate of the Mabi's hero, Biang Bwô Mbumbô, partly unanswered, something that noticeably differs from the oral historical accounts that have survived among his descendants. Wehlan indeed reported that his troops were unable to apprehend Biang Bwô Mbumbô during the campaign, but that the Mabi, 'delivered up their previous ruler King Benga' after the fighting, since it was a prerequisite imposed by the Germans for peace negotiations. Subsequently, the Germans condemned him to death by hanging.[481] In stark contrast, oral history and the statements of Francois Mabvouer, a great-grandson of Biang Bwô Mbumbô, describe the course of events after his extradition in the following way:

> Biang was arrested by his peers and handed over to the Germans in Grand-Batanga, a district south of Mbèkaa in Kribi. Escorted by 25 soldiers, he was hanged. But hanging him would not have been easy, as the rope around his neck snapped three times. ... Once hanged, his body was decapitated, and his head shipped to Berlin in Germany. The Germans dumped his body on the high seas with heavy stones tied to his ankles. But to their surprise, when they returned, they found him lying on the beach. They buried his remains in Iyiguè Iyiguè or Iké Iké, a Batanga village between the left bank of the Kienké river and the right bank of the Lobé river, by the sea.[482]

False reports that obscured or glossed over the actual course of military operations remained unchallenged and the colonial government consciously endorsed and rewarded the cruel and aberrant behaviour of its representatives. The governor of the colony at the time, Eugen von Zimmerer (1843–1918), showered Wehlan and his military expedition against the Mabi with praise, describing it as a 'brilliant feat of arms of the police force'.[483] He even suggested that Wehlan should be awarded the prestigious Order of the Red Eagle with Swords.[484]

Genocide and the Loss of Knowledge of *Byéri* Ancestral Veneration

The Mabi, on the other hand, suffered hundreds of deaths, and many of their villages, farms and fields had been destroyed. To add insult to injury, the so-called 'peace negotiations' were in fact conditions of surrender that included paying penalties to the colonial government in the form of ivory or rubber and sending some of their people to the colonial station to work as forced labour. These conditions far exceeded what the war-torn Mabi society could deliver and further contributed to the impoverishment and decline of the community.[485] The war of 1893 thus marked the beginning of a vicious circle of colonial exploitation and cultural destruction that was to continue throughout the entire German colonial era.

Prestigious cultural assets, valuable artefacts and *byéri* relics that had not already been destroyed, looted or forcibly sold during this first wave of violence were largely taken out of the country during the German colonial period in the face of pressure from colonial authorities and missionaries who sought to delegitimise and ultimately destroy local faith because they considered the beliefs negatively as 'paganism' and pockets of resistance. The associated decline of *byéri* rites among the Mabi continued throughout the first half of the twentieth century under French colonial rule through a stigmatisation and cancelling of local religious practices. It was exacerbated by a non-negligible and increasing removal of *byéri* relics spearheaded by European art traders, as the sculptures gained international fame among experts of so-called 'primitive art'.[486] According to the local notable Jules Mana, a contemporary witness of this decline, the last official initiation ceremony in which *byéri* reliquaries were used took place in 1962.[487] Since then, the *byéri* rites have no longer been practised in their original form, but in private circles and under the strictest secrecy.

It is essential to understand that the loss and decline of knowledge about the *byéri* is a direct consequence of the war of 1893 and the subsequent colonial oppression. By 1916, '75 percent of the Mabi had been killed, especially adults and, in particular, the elites'.[488] To this can be added the loss of raw materials as tribute to the colonial government (e.g. ivory) and of religious possessions through extortion and looting. This left a long-term impact on the cultural and spiritual spheres that can still be witnessed today. This is what Jude S. Mboum labels as ethnocide, in his book titled *Les Mabi de*

Kribi: Du Génocide à Ethnocide, published in 2022, which retraces the history of the Mabi people. Mboum describes the consequences of colonial violence for the local culture from the perspective of a local historian. German colonial presence left indelible scars in the social fabric and cultural identity of the Mabi through forced assimilation, the gradual disappearance of sacred artefacts and the abandonment of religious practices. This assimilation is well documented in a few oral accounts that have been passed on from generation to generation. It manifests itself nowadays and above all in the Mabi's widespread lack of local knowledge about their own history. In this regard, the notable entrusted with all religious and spiritual matters of the contemporary Mabi society and self-described as a 'ritual expert', Jean Baptiste Nzambi (Figure 15.1), explained in an interview that 'it was the Germans and their missionaries who banned the Mabi rites and rituals performed with the reliquary, pretending it was "Satanism"' or even fanaticism'[489]. When one asks Mabi representatives about their cultural and spiritual life in the post-colonial era, as we did on the ground, a gap appears, accompanied at times by a demonisation of *byéri* ancestors' cult.

Today, only recent studies offer a rudimentary idea of the practices of ancestor veneration associated with the *byéri*. Nonetheless, existing research focuses much more on the studies of the German colonial researcher Günter Tessmann and the French art historian Louis Perrois, who convey discriminatory and Eurocentric perspectives in their work. However, our interviews with notables and elders among the Mabi enlightened us on the significance of the *byéri* as both a sacred sculpture and a cult. One of the most interesting descriptions came from Achille Dtoundgou, who underlined that the *byéri* is not a statuette per se, but a sacred sculpture imbued with spiritual potency that is worthy of veneration. He explained is as followed: 'This object of worship is the tool, the vehicle through which we come into contact with our ancestors. So, the Mabi cult is called *byéri* and it is the *byéri* which gave birth to these sculptures.' The cult in itself is the practice of ancestor veneration and constitutes the central element of the religiosity of the Mabi people. It consists of entering into direct contact with the ancestors through the statuette, which represents the ancestor and is a sign of the presence of the deceased among the living. The Mabi believe in the 'beyond', in the existence of two worlds: the visible ('*bopiara*'), where the living are; and the invisible ('*ngionom*'), where the ancestors live and provide their descendants with help and support in daily life.

The King Mayessè Foundation and the Revival of Ancestor Veneration

In 2017, the Mabi people founded the King Mayessè Foundation, an organisation rooted in a desire to know their own history, revive what has been forgotten, and make it known to the world. It was baptised in honour to Biang Bwô Mbumbô and primarily deals with historical and ancestral facts unknown to new generations. For the members of the organisation, it is also a question of promoting the cultural heritage of the peoples of the southern region and giving them back their lost identities. As one of the community leaders put it: 'The Mabi have remained in the heart of the land, in the heart of the people. The Mabi remained in fear for a long time. We could no longer speak out or defend ourselves because of the genocide. Now the people are starting to organise themselves.'[490] This foundation was born in a context of national remembrance of Biang Bwô Mbumbô: in 2014, the president of the Republic of Cameroon officially recognised him as a national hero and gave his name to the first tugboat of Cameroon's very first deep-water port in Kribi. The Mabi notable Adolphe Mingwuli commented: 'We are proud to have had such an illustrious ancestry. This is why we bless and wish long life to King Mayessè, the boat that bears his name and through which our ancestor lives again.' According to the chief of the Mabi Pfièbouri group, this baptism was a feat of the Mabi people, especially since they consider the sea as an important 'element in nature worthy of veneration'.[491]

For most of the people we interviewed, restitution of Mabi cultural and spiritual heritage is no longer just a wish, but it is already in action. According to the notable named Achille Ndtoungou, progress on the restitution issue should begin with the recognition of King Mayessè as 'a pioneer and a person who defended his people and said stop to the aggressor'.[492] Aware of the colonialists' intention to rid Africa of its so-called 'fetishes' by removing these religious tools from Cameroon, the King Mayessè Foundation is today fighting for cultural rearmament in this community, long mired in the trauma of extinction. It preserves cultural and spiritual elements to revive Mabi spirituality: the songs in the languages linked to the ancestors; the reintroduction of traditional practice of the *byéri* cult; and finally, the *Nguma Mabi* (Pride of the Mabi) festival, created in 2001 and elevated to the rank of one of Cameroon's major festivals by the Ministry of Arts and Culture of Cameroon (MINAC). This event is in fact understood as a 'traditional instance of strategic reflection, representation and supra-clan regulation, but also as the traditional festival of the Mabi people, celebrated every 15 December in Kribi'.

The main element of this celebration of tradition remains the rightful restitution of the emblematic *byéri* reliquaries to their communities of origin, those figures who have been called 'symbols of divinity'.[493] Sadly, among the numerous *byéri* reliquaries in German collections, only in rare cases do the items bear an undoubted 'ethnic'

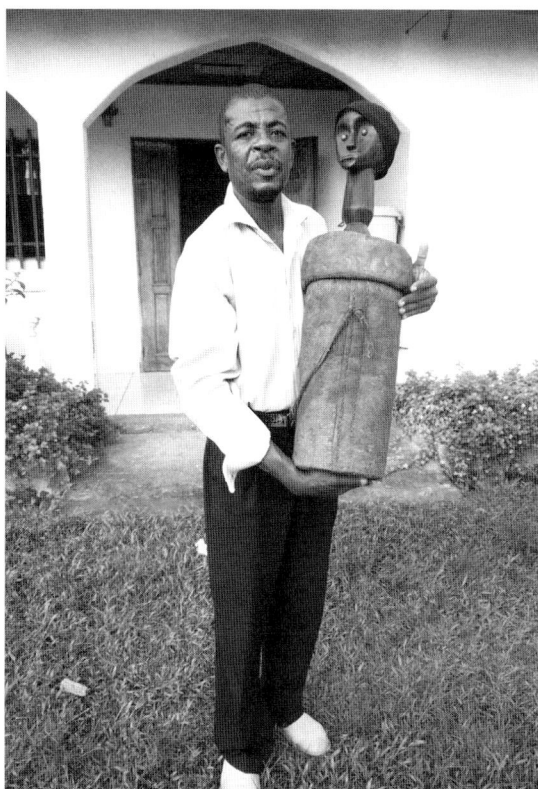

Figure 15.1: The ritual expert Jean-Baptiste Nzambi, carrying the *byéri* of Etienne Ntunga Mandtuo, descendant of Biang Bwô Mbumbô's, member of the Nti clan, and chief of the village Mpoergu. The *byéri* ensemble contains the remains of Ntunga Mandtuo's parents. Photo: Sebastian-Manès Sprute.

indication of origin referring to the Mabi. This is the case for one inventory entry (MAf 34108) at the Grassi-Museum für Völkerkunde in Leipzig, and three inventory entries at the Museum für Völkerkunde in Dresden (38421, 38659 and 38660).[494] The often illegitimate circumstances of appropriation and the lack of knowledge on the part of colonial officials documenting the translocation of African cultural assets mean that there are many other comparable sculptures in collections that could potentially be *byéri* reliquaries of the Mabi. Due to insufficient scientific documentation, some have no indication of provenance whatsoever. Many others are attributed to the group of Fang populations mentioned earlier, or to Pangwe populations (French 'pahouin'). Note that many other groups in the region can be subsumed under the overarching term 'Fang'.[495]

The existence of certain pieces of sacred artefacts known as *byéri* in the high chieftaincies of the Mabi today proves their deep attachment not only to this valuable ancestral sculpture, but also to their cultural heritage:

> In our religion, this statuette was very significant. There was a gap in the transmission of cultural elements. It was the elders who made these sacred sculptures, who carved them out of wood, who gave them a certain energy that enabled them to go, and who consulted them when there were concerns among the population and to bring back answers to the people.[496]

Attempts have been made over the years to reproduce these reliquaries, but they cannot act with the same force. This is why some informants, like Jean-Baptiste Nzambi, have tried to reappropriate these figures and initiate themselves spiritually:

> One of my missions as a notable and ritualist in the chiefdom is to bring back the practice of *Ngilmalende* [*byéri*] veneration to the village. We're ready, we're just waiting for the majesties to say 'go' [give their approval] and we'll put everything back together![497]

Restitution in this sense is not just about remembering ancestors, but also about reappropriating sacred sculptures and re-instituting them in time so that they can enjoy their original functions. The example we see today among this people shows us that the void left by the translocation of Mabi cultural assets is giving way to new practices through the design and sacralisation of new material culture, as well as the rehabilitation of ancestral rites to ensure the cultural and spiritual stability of the people.[498] As one of the notables put it:

> The project of reclaiming is first and foremost a spiritual project. It's about spirituality, identity, and culture. Our problem is that we need to wholly rehabilitate our people, we need to rehabilitate their identity, their culture, their spirituality. That's the first objective. It goes deeper than building a school or a museum. Schools are places of memory.[499]

In terms of memory, these accounts reveal a broad reconnection of the break between generations. They also call for the establishment and construction of places of memory like community museums for future generations, a mausoleum for King Mayessè, which should henceforth become a resting place for Mabi patriarchs of different generations who worked for the development of the people in their lifetimes, and the construction of a school that will enable history to be passed on to future generations in order to safeguard the memory of the Mabi in particular, and of Cameroonians in general. However, the question remains hanging: how will memory be passed on to future generations? In this case, the project takes on a material dimension, as Achille Ndtoungou, one of the Mabi notables, explains in an interview:

> [O]n the Mayessè site,[500] bringing back the bones means keeping them somewhere, building a mausoleum to house Biang Bwô Mbumbô's remains and burying people who have had a truly spiritual life. The ultimate aim is to create a memorial. There will be his mausoleum, but also a museum and a school for initiation into the art of worship. The village will also be designed in the spirit of Mabi architecture. We still don't know how the Mabi chiefdoms and societies were built. Above and beyond everything else, it's going to be in a place of remembrance. It's a project that goes beyond the Mabi people. It's a project that has a national dimension.[501]

Today, the site of Biang Bwô Mbumbô's headquarters is located on a palm oil plantation owned by the company Socapalm. Access is restricted and many other hurdles stand in the way of the Mabi's vision for a place of remembrance. As we write this chapter, negotiations with this company – repeatedly criticised for flouting environmental regulations and social rights of workers in Cameroon – are under way.

ABBREVIATIONS

AIA	Association Internationale Africaine
AIC	Association Internationale du Congo
AICA	International Association of Art Critics
BArch	German Federal Archives
BLM	Black Lives Matter
CBD	Central Business District
CPP	Convention People's Party
CRAN	Conseil représentatif des associations noires, France (Representative Council of Black Associations)
DRC	Democratic Republic of the Congo
EIC	État Indépendant du Congo (Independent State of the Congo)
IMNC	Institute of National Museums of Congo
MINAC	Ministry of Arts and Culture of Cameroon
MuRAD	Museum of the Kings and Amazons of Danxomè, Abomey
NAZ	National Archives of Zimbabwe, UK
NMMZ	National Museums and Monuments of Zimbabwe
SMB-ZA	Central Archives of the Berlin State Collections
V&A	Victoria and Albert Museum, London
ZANU–PF	Zimbabwe African National Union – Patriotic Front

NOTES ON EDITORS, CONTRIBUTORS AND ARTISTS

Foreword

Peju Layiwola is an artist, curator and professor of art history at the University of Lagos. She has built on the artistic tradition of her mother, Princess Elizabeth Olowu, who was the first female bronze caster in Nigeria, and works in a variety of media ranging from metalwork and pottery to textile and sculpture. Her research addresses diverse thrusts of the post-colonial African condition, including pillage, repatriation and restitution, memory, gender and the continually mutable processes of artistic production. She curated and co-curated several exhibitions, most notably *Benin 1897.com: Art and the Restitution Question* at the University of Lagos and of Ibadan (2010), *Whose Centenary?* in the streets of Benin City (2014), *Resist! The Art of Resistance* at the Rautenstrauch-Joest Museum in Cologne (2021) and *Body, Blue and Beyond* at the Thought Pyramid Art Centre in Lagos (2022).

Editors

Sela K. Adjei is an artist and researcher based in Ghana, and a lecturer at the University of Media, Arts and Communication (Institute of Film and Television), where he teaches philosophy, digital imaging, digital art and computer application design. He studied Communication Design and African Art at the Kwame Nkrumah University of Science and Technology in Kumasi and obtained his PhD in African Studies at the Institute of African Studies in University of Ghana in Legon. His PhD thesis investigates the philosophy of art in Vodu religion and criticises European conceptions of Vodu art and aesthetics. His research interests include West African spiritual epistemologies, transnational museum studies and the development of creative industries.

Yann LeGall is a postdoctoral researcher at the Institute for Art History of the Technical University in Berlin. He was a member of the project 'The Restitution of Knowledge', led in partnership with the University of Oxford. In his work, he investigates the enduring presence of colonial spoils of war from so-called 'punitive' expeditions in German museums. His PhD thesis, completed at the research training group *minor cosmopolitanisms* at the University of Potsdam, investigates memory cultures in and after the repatriation of ancestral remains to African countries and communities. As a member of the initiatives Berlin Postkolonial e.V. and Postcolonial Potsdam since 2014, he has led guided tours in both cities and developed a digital audio guide on traces of colonial history in Potsdam.

Authors

I. The Battlefield

Felwine Sarr is a humanist, philosopher, economist and musician, and is the Anne-Marie Bryan Chair in French and Francophone Studies at Duke University in Durham, NC. He is the author of the acclaimed book *Afrotopia*, in which he brings together various strands of Africa-based knowledge production and philosophy to develop reflections on the present condition and the future of African thought and ideals. Well-known for his ground-breaking report 'The Restitution of African Cultural Heritage: Toward a New Relational Ethics', co-written with Bénédicte Savoy, Sarr was dean of the Economics department at the University of Gaston-Berger in Saint Louis, Senegal. His research focuses on economic policies, epistemology, decolonial thought and the history of religious ideas. In addition to scholarly work, he has published the meditative essay '*Dahij*', a collection of short stories titled *105, rue Carnot*, as well as philosophical essays '*Méditations africaines*' and 'Habiter le monde'. Further, he is the co-founder of the Laboratory for the Analysis of Societies and Powers/Africa-Diasporas (LASPAD) in Saint Louis, the publishing company Jimsaan in Dakar, and the annual workshops *Ateliers de la pensée and the eponymous doctoral school*, which seek to stimulate a 'non-colonial' school of thought. In 2010, he was awarded the prize Abdoulaye Fadiga for research in economics. As a singer-songwriter, he has released three albums.

Bénédicte Savoy is professor of modern art history at the Institute for Art Studies at the Technical University in Berlin, and former professor for the cultural history of European art from the eighteenth to twentieth centuries at the Collège de France in Paris. As an art historian, she specialises in critical enquiry into the provenance of works of art, including looted art and other forms of illegally acquired cultural assets. Together with the economist and scholar Felwine Sarr, Savoy was commissioned by French President Emmanuel Macron to inquire in the prerequisites for the future restitution of African cultural heritage. Their report, titled *The Restitution of African Cultural Heritage: Toward a New Relational Ethics*, was published in 2018 and has been one of the most influential publications on looted art from the colonial era and the restitution debates. In her latest book, *Africa's Struggle for Its Art: History of a Post-Colonial Defeat*, Savoy documented the numerous endeavours by African nations and stakeholders to recover cultural heritage acquired under colonial circumstances during the 1970s and 1980s.

Osman Nusairi is a London-based Sudanese researcher, playwright and translator. **Fergus Nicoll** is a Research Associate in the Faculty of History at the University of Oxford. They have collaborated for more than twenty years in researching the rise of Muḥammad Aḥmad, the self-styled Mahdī. Together, they have compiled an English-language index of the Mahdī's writings and a bibliography of the Mahdīa featuring sources in Arabic, Ottoman Turkish and a variety of European languages. They are currently preparing a translation of ʿAli al-Mahdī's oral history of the Mahdīa. This research was undertaken as part of the University of Sussex project *Making African Connections: Decolonial Futures for Colonial Collections*, funded by the British government's Arts and Humanities Research Council project AH/S001271/1.

Mwelela Cele is an archivist, historian and cultural heritage expert who works at the Provincial Heritage Authority: KwaZulu-Natal Amafa and Research Institute. He was head of the archival department at the Albert Luthuli Museum and librarian at the Killie Campbell Africana Library in Durban. His research examines Zulu history and knowledge production, as well as the history of archives of the anti-apartheid struggle.

Alhaji Sulemana Alhassan Iddi is a master traditional court *gonje* fiddle musician and an oral musician by birth. He holds a master's degree in Peace and Development Studies from the University of Cape Coast and works as a civic educationist, mediator and a consultant for Northern Ghanaian history and cultural heritage. He is currently the Chief Executive Officer of the Yendi Heritage and Resource Center, a non-profit organisation that promotes heritage and tourism in Northern Ghana. In this capacity, he teaches the *gonje* fiddle music and narrates history to preserve and promote historical and cultural heritage sites in eastern Dagbon, hosting local and foreign anthropologists, historians and students on study tours.

Elias Aguigah is a postgraduate student of social anthropology and political science at Free University Berlin and the École des Hautes Études en Sciences Sociales (EHESS) in Paris. He was a research assistant in the DFG-AHRC-funded project 'The Restitution of Knowledge'. His research interests lie in the critique of neocolonialism, African liberation theory, political anthropology and the restitution of material heritage to Africa. He has published on the political economy of post-colonial restitution and on the plunder of African heritage from Ghana and Cameroon.

Michael A. Gyimah is a Ghanaian curator working with ANO Institute of Arts and Knowledge. **Marlena Barnstorf-Brandes** and **Ricarda Rivoir** are cultural anthropologists, members of the project 'Provenance of Colonial-Era Collections from Togo' at the Grassi Museum für Völkerkunde, Leipzig. Art historian **Jan König** works in the *Future Programme Reinventing Grassi.SKD*. After working collaboratively together at the museum, the four have teamed up to create a research collective dealing with colonial collections from Dagbon in close cooperation with Alhaji Sulemana Alhassan Iddi. The team combines experiences in post-colonial provenance research as well as artistic and archival research, international collaboration and community-based curating.

Julia Kennedy is a collections assistant at the Field Museum in Chicago, working with African, Pacific Islands and Latin American ethnographic material. Her current work focuses on co-curation and collaborative collections care with Pacific Islander communities in the USA and abroad. **Christopher J. Philipp** is the collections manager of the African, Pacific Islands and Latin American collections cared for by the Field Museum in Chicago. He has stewarded these collections in partnership with several communities for over twenty-five years. Chris's primary research interest is ethnomusicology. **Foreman Bandama** is an assistant curator of African anthropology at the Field Museum and a lecturer at the University of Illinois-Chicago. He obtained his PhD from the University of Cape Town. His thesis examined the archaeology and technology of metal production in late iron age settlements in southern Africa, a research topic on which he has published extensively in the past decade.

Kokou Azamede is professor at the Department of German Studies at the University of Lomé (Togo) and a scientific consultant and lecturer in German as a foreign language at the Goethe Institute. He is a leading scholar on German colonial photography and the history of the mission during the imperial era in West Africa. In 2022, he was awarded the prestigious Jacob & Wilhelm Grimm Prize of the German Academic Exchange Service (DAAD) for his contributions in research on German literature, identity, colonial history, transculturality and hybridity.

II. The Royal Palace

Nii Kwate Owoo is a Ghanaian academic and filmmaker. He studied direction, camera and editing at the London Film School and at Isleworth Polytechnic, London. He was the founder and head of the Media Research Unit at the Institute of African Studies (University of Ghana) from 1978 to 2002. His documentary film *You Hide Me* (1970) is considered the first by an English-speaking independent Africa. Owoo has been producer and director on a number of other notable film projects, such as the 1991 feature *Ama: An African Voyage of Discovery*, which he co-directed with Kwesi Owusu for Channel 4 television. Reviewed as 'the first African film set and shot in the UK', *Ama* broke box-office records in Accra and has been shown at Cannes, as well as at the New York African Film Festival.

Richard Tsogang Fossi is a postdoctoral researcher on the DFG-funded project 'Reverse History of Collections: An Annotated Atlas of Cameroon's Material Heritage in German Museums'. This project is a bi-national cooperation between the Technical University Berlin in Germany, and the University of Dschang in Cameroon. Tsogang Fossi was a visiting fellow and curator at the MARKK in Hamburg and co-curated the acclaimed exhibition *Hey Hamburg, Do You Know Manga Bell?* on the history of Cameroonian resistance to German colonialism. His PhD examined post-colonial Cameroonian literature and memory in the context of tri-national contact with European influences (British, German and French). He has extensively published on material culture, colonial history and post-colonial landscapes of memory.

Jeanne-Ange Wagne is an art historian, art mediator and creative worker based in Berlin. Her research and artistic practice deals with cultures of remembrance, colonial history and studies of provenance. She has developed and led critical workshops and tours for public programmes of cultural and art institutions in Berlin, such as KW Institute for Contemporary Art, the 12th Berlin Biennale, the Academy of Arts and the DEKOLONIALE. Former research assistant in the research project 'The Restitution of Knowledge' at the department of Art History at the Technical University in Berlin, she also co-curated and coordinated the event series 'KuK-Tuesdays: Dislocation', which dealt with the (re-)appropriation of cultural heritage in the era of restitution.

Sarita Lydia Mamseri is a British-Tanzanian curator and writer. She is the programming manager of the department for culture at University College London. She acted as artistic director of the transnational project 'Humboldt Lab Tanzania', which brought together the National Museum of Tanzania, the Berlin Ethnological Museum and a plethora of Tanzanian artists and researchers around the question of East African belongings in museum collections in Berlin. She worked as a curator with several prominent institutions, including the Smithsonian and the Liverpool Biennial. She wrote the screenplay of the acclaimed short film *Mangi Meli Remains* and has worked as head curator of the project *Marejesho asili mila utamaduni wetu* funded by the German Federal Cultural Foundation.

Mnyaka Sururu Mboro is a founding member of the NGO Berlin Postkolonial e.V. and consultant in the project 'DEKOLONIALE – Memory Cultures in the Berlin City'. Trained as an engineer, he is also a Kiswahili teacher and a Tanzanian activist who has lived in Berlin for more than thirty years. Mzee Mboro has been the driving force behind several NGO campaigns, including the *No Humboldt 21!* initiative, which criticised the opening of the Humboldt Forum in the rebuilt Berlin Palace. Since the 1980s, he has been an advocate for greater recognition of issues such as restitution, post-colonial justice, reparations and memory. He is a member of advisory boards in Berlin districts for the renaming of colonial street names and leads guided tours on traces of colonial history in Berlin in the so-called 'African Quarter'.

Konradin Kunze is an actor, stage director and independent researcher at the theatre company Flinn Works. He coordinated the project *Marejesho asili mila utamaduni wetu*, a partnership with **Gabriel Mzei Orio**, head of the Old Moshi Cultural Enterprise, and the Grassi Museum in Leipzig. This project brings material and immaterial culture back to local stakeholders and elders in the Kilimanjaro region and develops a practice of knowledge restitution before material restitution takes place. Kunze studied at the University of Music and Drama in Hanover and was a member of the Moks Theatre in Bremen and the Junges Schauspielhaus in Hamburg. With the company Flinn Works, he developed research-based transnational theatre projects such as *Maji Maji Flava*, a co-production with the Tanzanian theatre company Asedeva on German colonialism in East Africa. Recent productions on colonial history also include *Skull X*, *Kosa la Vita – Kriegsverbrechen*, *Fear&Fever* and, most recently, the exhibition *Mangi Meli Remains*.

Godfrey B. Tangwa is a senior fellow in governance and ethics at the Nkafu Policy Institute, and emeritus professor at the University of Yaoundé 1, Cameroon, where he was Head of the Department of Philosophy from 2004 to 2009. His PhD explored epistemology and metaphysics within the philosophy of science, with research interests firmly anchored in bioethics and African philosophy. He is a member of the International Association of Bioethics (IAB), the Cameroon Academy of Sciences (CAS), the African Academy of Sciences (AAS), Vice-Chairperson of the Cameroon Bioethics Initiative (CAMBIN) which he founded in 2005, and an executive committee member of the Pan-African Bioethics Initiative (PABIN). Professor Tangwa has published extensively on bioethics and African philosophy and contributed significantly to research ethics, regulation and governance and capacity-building in research on the African continent. His latest book, *African Perspectives on Some Contemporary Bioethics Problems*, was published in 2019.

Fogha MC Cornilius Refem, alias **Wan wo layir**, is a non-human, self-inflicted severe drapetomania patient, a *Kulturbanause* (cultural philistine), a trickster and a multi-award-winning troublemaker. Among his numerous awards and recognitions, he was the first person ever to receive the official and prestigious ban from the Humboldt Forum in Berlin. He is also a doctoral research fellow at the Research Training Group *minor cosmopolitanisms* at the University of Potsdam, Germany, and a visiting scholar at the Ecologies of Knowledges programme at Duke University in Durham, NC.

Didier Houénoudé is professor of art history at the Université Abomey-Calavi in Cotonou, Benin. He is an expert on West African contemporary art and cultural assets from Benin as well as on the restitution debate. He was a member of the official delegation that accompanied the 2021 restitution by France of cultural heritage from the kingdom of Danxomè to the Republic of Benin. Didier Houénoudé was also a visiting professor at the Technical University in Dresden, Germany, where he expanded the art history curriculum.

Gaëlle Beaujean is a museum curator and head of African collections at the Musée du Quai Branly – Jacques Chirac in Paris. She is the author of the book *L'Art de cour d' Abomey*, a critical and comprehensive study of Danxomean cultural heritage in French collections, the published form of her PhD in social anthropology defended in 2015 at the EHESS in Paris. She curated the exhibitions 'Artistes d'Abomey – Dialogue sur un royaume africain' (2009), 'L'Afrique des routes' (2017) and is the chief curator of 'Mission Dakar-Djibouti [1931–1933]: Contre-enquêtes' (2025).

III. The Sacred

Emanuel Admassu is an architect and assistant professor at Columbia University's Graduate School of Architecture, Planning and Preservation (GSAPP). His work focuses on spatial justice, design theory and contemporary African urbanism. Admassu is a co-founding and board member of the Black Reconstruction Collective. He is also co-founding principal of the art and architecture practice AD–WO, which casts a critical eye on how race and space are constructed in practices of visualising and measuring. Their work has been exhibited internationally, including at the Venice Biennale (2023) and the Chicago Architecture Biennial (2023). AD–WO's creations are part of the permanent collections at the Art Institute of Chicago and the High Museum of Art in Atlanta. Admassu co-edited the anthology *Where Is Africa* (2024), which challenges the traditional positioning of the arts in and on Africa through interviews, essays and artworks.

Eyob Derillo is a scholar specialising in Ethiopian manuscripts and literature. He holds degrees in art history, archaeology and film studies from Birkbeck and is currently completing his doctorate at the SOAS University of London. He currently serves as Project Officer for the Esmée Fairbairn Foundation 'Abyssinia Project' at the King's Own Royal Regiment Lancaster Museum, where he manages project activities focused on enhancing exhibitions and documenting collection items from the 1868 Abyssinian expedition. He is former curator for the Ethiopic and Ethiopian collections at the British Library, where he curated the exhibition 'African Scribes: Manuscript Culture of Ethiopia' in 2018. His research centres on Ethiopian spirituality within a Christian context, with interest in ancient manuscripts, contemporary Ethiopian literature, codicology and Ethiopian history.

Placide Mumbembele Sanger holds a PhD in Political and Social Sciences from the Université Libre de Bruxelles. His PhD thesis investigates cultural policy, in particular the role and the colonial history of museums in the Democratic Republic of Congo. He currently teaches museum studies at the University of Kinshasa. His research deals with the issue of cultural heritage in the African (post-)colonial context and included a residency at the AfricaMuseum in Tervuren, near Brussels. His current interest is in the issue of restitution of cultural assets between Belgium and the Democratic Republic of Congo.

Njoki Ngumi is a Kenyan artist, filmmaker, feminist thinker and non-practising medical doctor. In 2018, with The Nest Collective, she was co-creator of the International Inventories Programme, examining the history of Kenyan material and immaterial cultural heritage in museum collections, alongside Cologne's Rautenstrauch-Joest Museum, Frankfurt's Weltkulturen Museum and Kenya's National Museum in Nairobi. She co-hosted a podcast series with multi-hyphenate artist, musician, filmmaker and worldbuilder Jim Chuchu, styled 'Invisible Conversations', reflecting on looted cultural assets, and looking critically at the narrativised intentions and values of colonial thieves. Ngumi's multidisciplinary and multi-sectoral work currently focuses on her individual art practice, and high-level research and strategy in health, culture, youth and new/emerging economies. She is also part of several local, regional and international collaborations, about the old worlds that are dying and the new ones that are currently being born.

Adéọlá Naomi Adérẹ̀mí is a Yoruba Greek artist and curator passionately dedicated to reclaiming African narratives and advocating for social justice. Her groundbreaking debut documentary, *I am Afro Greek: Black Portraiture in Greece* (2021) stands as testament to her relentless commitment to spotlighting important stories, elevating marginalised narratives and confronting societal biases. Adéọlá's boundary-breaking artistic vision has led her to collaborations with esteemed artists all over the world that reshape narrative landscapes, such as her compelling project 'Ancestral Veneration: An Offering by Adéọlá Naomi Adérẹ̀mí', recently commissioned by the Nairobi-based Nest Collective. Adéọlá's work stands at the intersection of public health science and Yoruba healing heritages in art and storytelling, showing a decade's dedication to collaboration with displaced communities worldwide. Her journey embodies the creation of worlds where well-being is core to humanity's holistic wellness, as she fosters spaces where diverse voices thrive, and advocates for equitable and inclusive landscapes.

Njabulo Chipangura is an anthropologist and curator of living cultures at Manchester Museum (University of Manchester). Njabulo has an interest in the empirical ways that museum practice can be decolonised through epistemic and aesthetic disobedience, benchmarked by undoing earlier ways of knowledge production in collections and exhibition practices. He has published extensively on the coloniality of museums, associated knowledge production and representation practices, and the process of decolonising museums in Africa, most prominently in his recent volume titled *Museums as Agents for Social Change: Collaborative Programmes at the Mutare Museum* (2021). He is also a visiting lecturer and researcher at the Centre for Urbanism and Build Environment Studies (CUBES), University of the Witwatersrand, Johannesburg, South Africa.

Farai Chabata is a senior curator of ethnography at the Zimbabwe Museum of Human Sciences. A historian by training, Farai is responsible for the museum's ethnographic collection and has expertise in issues around intangible cultural heritage management, community liaison, curatorial practice and conservation. His research interests include indigenous knowledges, identities, museum futures, collections biographies, provenance and contemporary art, the latter being channelled through collaborations with young visual artists in Zimbabwe.

Lennon Mhishi is an anthropologist and postdoctoral researcher at the Pitt Rivers Museum, who is part of the transnational research project 'Reconnecting Objects: Epistemic Plurality and Transformative Practices in and Beyond Museums', led in Dakar, Dschang, Cape Town, Berlin and Oxford. His interdisciplinary work spans interests in Africa and its diasporas, the afterlives of slavery and colonialism, and the approaches to contemporary forms of exploitation, forced labour and human rights in different African countries. Lennon holds degrees from the University of Zimbabwe, Monash University (Australia) and SOAS, University of London. His PhD thesis focused on music and belonging as part of the genealogy of Zimbabwean and more generally Black expressive cultures in the UK. He was a member of the Antislavery Knowledge Network at the University of Liverpool, working on approaches to confronting oppression through art and creative media. In this context, he has collaborated with communities in Mali, Niger, Ghana, Uganda, Kenya, Nigeria, Sierra Leone and the DRC.

Yrine Matchinda is a doctoral candidate in German studies and cultural studies at the University of Dschang, Cameroon and a member of the project 'Reversed History of Collections: An Annotated Atlas of Cameroon's Material Heritage in German Museums', funded by the German Research Foundation. In her dissertation, she analyses Cameroonian ritual objects in colonial collections and the social consequences of their removal and translocation. For this, she has conducted more than fifty interviews with traditional and spiritual leaders in Cameroon.

Sebastian-Manès Sprute was a postdoctoral researcher on the research project 'Reverse History of Collections: An Annotated Atlas of Cameroon's Material Heritage in German Museums'. His PhD thesis, completed at the Humboldt University in Berlin, examined the coloniality of time and its imperial imposition in Senegal from 1880 to 1920. He worked as a curator at the Linden Museum in Stuttgart, where he pushed for a decolonial turn in the museum's practice. His fundamental research led to the exhibition 'Difficult Heritage: The Linden-Museum and Württemberg in the Colonial Period'. He has published on colonial and decolonial conceptions of time, as well as on the history of acquisition of Cameroon's cultural heritage by German museums, including high-profile artefacts such as the throne of Ibrahim Njoya, *Mandu Yenu*.

Artists

Assil Diab is Sudanese graffiti artist, graphic designer and visual artist who was born in Romania. Known as @Sudalove, she was the first female graffiti artist emerging from Sudan and Qatar dubbed by the programme 'She Leads Africa' in 2016. Assil graduated from Virginia Commonwealth University (VCU) in 2011 in Richmond, Virginia, with a Bachelor of Fine Arts in graphic design. In 2021 she received the '10 Under 10' Award and was recognized as being one of VCU's top ten graduates of the last decade for her noteworthy achievements in her career and the community.

Barly Baruti (a.k.a. Baruti Kandolo Lilela), born in 1959 in Kisangani, formerly known as Congo-Léopoldville, is a Congolese cartoonist. He is widely acknowledged as am internationally renowned Congolese illustrator. He wrote his first graphic novel *Le Temps d'agir* in 1982, which focuses on environmental issues. In 1984, he was invited to work at the renowned Studios Hergé in Brussels. Baruti later returned to Congo, where he published several albums before relocating to Belgium in 1992. In 1994, his graphic novel *Objectif Terre!*, an environmental manifesto, was published by the Cultural Centre in Kisangani. During the late 1990s, Baruti collaborated with Frank Giroud on the creation of comic series *Eva K* and *Mandrill*. In 2010, he participated in the first international exhibition of African comics held in Paris. Additionally, Baruti is one of the co-founders of the Atelier de Création et de l'Initiation à l'Art (Creative Workshop for an Initiation to Art) aimed at nurturing talented young individuals in Kinshasa.

Bright Toh is a self-taught visual artist who portrays the synergy between Africans, wildlife, and their common environment as a core aspect of African identity. In 2020, Toh won the UNHCR Global Youth with Refugee Art Contest and in 2023, his mini documentary *Unsung Hero* was awarded the PWEE Kenya Special Jury award. Besides, he participated in the 2023 Doul'art Collective exhibition and the 2022 'Last Picture Show' Lagos Collective exhibition. He has worked with international organizations such as WFP, WildAid, UNESCO, and IOM on art-based projects. In 2019, his works were published by the newspaper *The Guardian* on their Global Illustrated City series.

Chigozie Obi is a multidimensional artist who utilizes multiple materials and media to narrate stories influenced by personal and societal encounters. Her work reflects her interest and profound fascination with human life, the body, beauty standards, gender roles, mental health, self-acceptance and activism. Obi obtained a bachelor's degree of Visual Arts from the University of Lagos in 2017 and was a resident at Gasworks, London in 2022. Her work has been featured in several exhibitions, including 'Reverie' at the DADA Gallery in Lagos and 'Young Talents: Polymathic Nature' at the C+N Gallery CANEPANERI in Genoa (2023), 'Unity' at the Vollery Gallery in

Dubai (2022), 'Intersections' at the Gallery Affinity in Lagos (2021), and 'Real Life Is Fragile' at Thinkspace Projects in Los Angeles (2020). She was selected as Arthouse Contemporary's Artist of the month in July 2018 and was awarded the Access Bank 'Art X Prize' and the Future Awards Prize for Art in 2021.

Elkanah Kwadwo Mpesum, known popularly as El Carna, is a talented digital artist with a background in Communication Design. He received his education at Prempeh College and the Kwame Nkrumah University of Science and Technology before embarking on a successful career as a professional illustrator. Over the years, El Carna has worked on numerous projects, including children's book illustrations, and has collaborated with esteemed publishers such as Disney Books. In addition to his work as an illustrator, El Carna is also the Creative Director of El Carna Studios, an illustration agency he founded to nurture and support young artists in Ghana.

Franky Mindja (a.k.a. Mindja Mengouana Frank Edgard) is an illustrator and cartoonist who graduated in plastic arts from the Mbalmayo Institute of Artistic Training. Born in Yaoundé, he began his career in 2015 after obtaining his artistic baccalaureate. His expressive and colourful drawing style takes inspiration in African art and seeks to represent the richness and the multitude of African cultures. In collaboration with the civil society organisation Initiative Perspectivwechsel e.V. from Germany, he published illustrations in the graphic novel *Widerstand* which traces three generations of anti-colonial resistance in Cameroon. Franky also participated in the temporary exhibition *RESIST – Art of Resistance* curated and shown at the Rautenstrauch-Joest Museum in Cologne.

Sena Ahadji is a Ghanaian artist who graduated from Coventry University. Her artistic versatility shines through her adeptness in various mediums, including painting, sculpting, and illustrating, making her a dynamic force in the contemporary Ghanaian art scene who intertwines cultural influences from Togo. Sena's creative journey is marked by a commitment to sustainability. As project coordinator for The Longitudinal Dialogues in 2022, she spearheaded a transformative initiative, collaborating with six schools in Accra to create art from recycled and upcycled materials, a testament to her dedication to eco-conscious practices. In 2022, Sena's artistic exploration extended to an impactful residency at Osei Duro in Ghana, where she ingeniously repurposed scraps into functional products. Demonstrating a passion for community engagement, she conducted workshops with ten primary schools in Accra, culminating in an exhibition at FCA Ghana in early November 2023.

Sindiso Nyoni is a graphic artist, illustrator, activist, street-artist, and graphic designer born in Bulawayo (Zimbabwe) and based in Johannesburg. He graduated from the University of Johannesburg and has worked as an illustrator and art director in the

South African advertising sector ever since. Sindiso Nyoni tackles some of Africa's most pressing issues with his subversive 'street' style, a fusion of pencil, ink, pastels, gauche, acrylic, and digital media. Also known as R!OT, his work has been, among others, exhibited at the International Biennial Poster Exhibitions, and as far afield as New York, London, Amsterdam, Berlin, Madrid, Tenerife, Zagreb, The Vitra Design Museum, The Guggenheim Bilbao Museum, and The Museum of Modern Art in Mexico City. He has collaborated on projects awarded with the Cannes Lion award, sits on the South African Mint Design Advisory Panel, and was a member of the Loerie Awards Communication Design jury and the Botswana-based Ideas Expo judging jury. He was the African representative for Icograda's 50th World Communication Design Day.

Yves Heles Toum Armel from Dschang, Cameroon, embarked on his journey into the realm of digital art in 2021 as a self-taught artist. His artistic biography is characterized by his contribution to significant projects such as 'Au Secours' in collaboration with the ANLU Library organization and the NGO Glokal e.V. in their programme 'GLOBAL Erinnern'. These initiatives reflect his commitment to social and cultural causes, showcasing his creative talent in the service of engaged visual storytelling. Heles Toum continues to push the boundaries of digital art, leaving a distinctive mark in the artistic landscape with his unique perspective and dedication to positive change.

ENDNOTES

Foreword

1. The significant role of activists, scholars and other groups in promoting the narratives of repatriation and restitution is instantiated in how young people are being enabled to perceive history and appropriate its memory to make political and cultural statements. At a recent performance in the O2 Arena in London, Divine Ikubor, a Nigerian musician who hails from the ancient city of Benin and goes by the stage name of Rema, donned a performative Queen Idia Mask to perform his famous song, 'Calm Down'. After the show, he tweeted the following words: 'My Ancestors bronzes sit in the museum of this very city so I remade mine. Hence, Edo is redefined, the map reshaped, your minds awakened & the mask reborn. Thank you London!' The message is clear: value resides in these cultural materials, and the significance of their forced removal from Africa continue to resonate in the many new ways that Africans across generations relived them.
2. See Jessica Parker and Danai Nesta Kupemba, 'Germany asks Forgiveness for Tanzania Colonial Crimes', *BBC News*, 1 November 2023, https://www.bbc.com/news/world-africa-67285182 (accessed 10 January 2024).
3. Olufemi Taiwo, *Against Decolonisation: Taking African Agency Seriously* (London: C Hurst and Co, 2022).

Introduction

4. Dalya Alberge, 'British Museum is World's Largest Receiver of Stolen Goods, Says QC', *The Guardian*, 4 November 2019, www.theguardian.com/world/2019/nov/04/british-museum-is-worlds-largest-receiver-of-stolen-goods-says-qc (accessed 20 November 2023).
5. Sadiya Chowdury, 'Nigeria Demands Return of Benin Bronzes after Thefts from British Museum', *Sky News*, 24 August 2023, https://news.sky.com/story/nigeria-demands-return-of-benin-bronzes-after-thefts-from-british-museum-12946236 (accessed 20 November 2023).
6. Hartwig Fischer, quoted in Tim Hanlon, 'British Museum "Thief" is Curator of 35 Years "Who put Priceless Items on eBay"', *Mirror*, 14 August 2023, www.mirror.co.uk/news/uk-news/breaking-british-museum-thief-unmasked-30726527 (accessed 20 November 2023).
7. Dan Hicks, 'The Last Remaining Argument against Restitution has Now been Lost', *The Art Newspaper*, 29 August 2023, www.theartnewspaper.com/2023/08/29/the-last-remaining-argument-against-restitution-has-now-been-lost (accessed 31 January 2024).

8   See Helen Rees Leahy, *Museum Bodies: The Politics and Practices of Visiting and Viewing* (Farnham: Ashgate, 2012); Viv Golding and Wayne Modest (eds), *Museum and Communities: Curators, Collections and Collaboration* (London: Bloomsbury, 2013); Robert R. Janes and Richard Sandell (eds), *Museum Activism* (Abingdon: Routledge, 2019); Clémentine Deliss, *The Metabolic Museum* (Berlin: Hatje Cantz, 2020); and Laura Raicovich, *Culture Strike: Art and Museums in an Age of Protest* (London: Verso, 2021); Felicity Bodenstein, Damiana Otoiu and Eva-Maria Troelenberg (eds), *Contested Holdings: Museum Collections in Political, Epistemic and Artistic Processes of Return* (New York: Berghahn Books, 2022), among many others.

9   See Andrew Zimmerman, *Anthropology and Antihumanism in Imperial Germany* (Chicago, IL: University of Chicago Press, 2001), 155–157; and Felwine Sarr and Bénédicte Savoy, *The Restitution of African Cultural Heritage: Towards a New Relational Ethics*, French Ministry of Culture, November 2018, report N°2018-26, https://www.about-africa.de/images/sonstiges/2018/sarr_savoy_en.pdf.

10 Manuela Fischer, 'Multiple Suppliers in Permeable Spaces. Ethnographic Collecting at the End of the Nineteenth Century', *Journal of Art Market Studies* 6, no. 1 (2022), https://doi.org/10.23690/jams.v6i1.134.

11 J.F.G. Umlauff, 'Kurze Erklärung zu den Katalogen N° 222 und 223 der Kamerun Sammlung', May 1914, SMB-ZA, I/MV 753, E 1055/1914, 322–323.

12 Dan Hicks, *The Brutish Museums: The Benin Bronzes, Colonial Violence and Cultural Restitution* (London: Pluto, 2020); Barnaby Philipps, *Loot: Britain and the Benin Bronzes* (London: OneWorld Publications, 2021); Götz Aly, *Das Prachtboot: Wie deutsche die Kunstschätze der Südsee raubten* (Frankfurt am Main: S. Fischer, 2021); and Khadija von Zinnenburg Carroll, *The Contested Crown: Repatriation Politics between Europe and Mexico* (Chicago, IL: University of Chicago Press, 2022), 84–85.

13 Henrietta Lidchi and Stuart Allan (eds), *Dividing the Spoils: Perspectives on Military Collections and the British Empire* (Manchester: Manchester University Press, 2020).

14 Molemo Moiloa, Reclaiming Restitution: Centring and Contextualising the African Narrative (Open Restitution Africa, 2022).

15 Philologist Victor Klemperer lists 'punitive expedition' as the first term that he identified as 'specifically Nazi'. See Victor Klemperer, *The Language of the Third Reich – LTI Lingua Tertii Imperii: A Philologist's Notebook*, trans. Martin Brady (London: Bloomsbury, 2013 [1947]), 43. For contemporary use of the term in far-right groupuscules, see 'Expédition punitive à Crépol: Gérald Darmanin annonce la dissolution de trois groupuscules d'ultradroite', *Marianne*, 28 November 2023, https://www.marianne.net/politique/gouvernement/expedition-punitive-a-crepol-gerald-darmanin-annonce-la-dissolution-de-trois-groupuscules-d-ultradroite (accessed 3 March 2024).

16 Ariella Aïsha Azoulay, *Potential History: Unlearning Imperialism* (London: Verso, 2019), 19–23. See also Hicks, *The Brutish Museums*, 41–42.

17 Buluda Itandala, 'African Response to German Colonialism in East Africa: The Case of Usukuma, 1890–1918', *Ufahamu: A Journal of African Studies* 20, no. 1 (1992): 3–29, https://doi.org/10.5070/F7201016775. For a brilliant critique of colonial treaties in Africa, see Saadia Touval, 'Treaties, Borders, and the Partition of Africa', *The Journal of African History* 7, no. 2 (1966): 279–93, https://doi.org/10.1017/S0021853700006320.
18 Lidchi and Allan, *Dividing the Spoils*, 11.
19 We are conscious that this time-frame eclipses ongoing conditions of imperial neocolonial rule, most visible in settler colonial spaces in the Americas, the Pacific, South Africa and Namibia, as well as British, French and Dutch overseas territories. Colonialism is still a reality today.
20 Margareta von Oswald, *Working Through Colonial Collections: An Ethnography of the Ethnological Museum in Berlin* (Leuven: Leuven University Press, 2022), 54.
21 The editors would like to thank James Hamill at the British Museum and Lise Mesz at the Musée du Quai Branly for answering our questions on the evolution of holdings in these institutions.
22 British Museum, 'Collecting Histories: Conflict', www.britishmuseum.org/about-us/british-museum-story/collecting-histories (accessed 1 January 2024).
23 The head of Yao leader Hassan bin Omari (aka Makunganya) was part of Felix von Luschan's private teaching collection, a collection that Luschan's wife sold to the American Museum of Natural History after the anthropologist's death. Today, the head is listed as inventory number 4728 in the collections of the AMNH.
24 See Kate Brown '"The Idea Is Not to Empty Museums": Authors of France's Blockbuster Restitution Report Say Their Work has been Misrepresented', *The Art Newspaper*, 24 January 2019, https://news.artnet.com/art-world-archives/restitution-report-critics-1446934 (accessed 1 January 2024).
25 Two German colonialists in the colony of Kamerun admitted encouraging the rape of local women (see Chapters 8 and 9). For more insight on rape a tool of colonial domination, see Khedidja Adel, 'Le viol: humiliation et terreur', in *Colonialisations: Notre Histoire*, ed. Pierre Singaravélou (Paris: Seuil, 2023), 318–320.
26 For the project *Digital Benin*, see https://digitalbenin.org/ (accessed 1 January 2024).
27 Clémentine Deliss, 'Powerless Collections', Venice Biennale, Nordic Pavillon, 2009; and Azoulay, *Potential History*, 65.
28 Ekpo Eyo, Amadou Matar M'Bow, Bakari Kamian, among many others. See Bénédicte Savoy, *Africa's Struggle for its Art: History of a Postcolonial Defeat* (Princeton, NJ: Princeton University Press, 2022).
29 Hicks, *The Brutish Museums*, 4.
30 Nuno Domingos, Miguel Bandeira Jerónimo, and Ricardo Roque, 'Rethinking Resistance and Colonialism', in *Resistance and Colonialism: Insurgent Peoples in World History*, ed. Nuno Domingos, Miguel Bandeira Jerónimo and Ricardo Roque

(Cham: Palgrave Macmillan, 2019), 12.
31. See Oduor Obura, *Decolonising Childhoods in Eastern Africa: Literary and Cultural Representations* (London: Routledge, 2022).
32. Kwame Opoku, 'When will Britain Return Looted Ghanaian Artefacts? A History of British Looting of more than 100 Objects', *AfricAvenir*, 6 January 2011, www.africavenir.org/fr/kwame-opoku-when-will-britain-return-looted-ghanaian-artefacts-a-history-of-british-looting-of-more-than-100-objects/ (accessed 1 January 2023).
33. Ngũgĩ wa Thiong'o, 'The Language of African Literature', in *Decolonising the Mind: The Politics of Language in African Literature* (Nairobi: East African Educational Publishers, 1981; Woodbridge: James Currey, 1986), 4–33; Rowland Abiodun, *Yoruba Art and Language: Seeking the African in African Art* (New York: Cambridge University Press, 2014); and Achille Mbembe, *Critique of Black Reason*, trans. Laurent Dubois (Durham, NC: Duke University Press, 2017), 163–169.
34. Felwine Sarr, *Afrotopia*, trans. Drew S. Burk (Minneapolis, MN: University of Minnesota Press, 2019), 76.
35. See Peter Vergo (ed.). *The New Museology* (London: Reaktion Books, 1989), 3.
36. See Robin Boast's criticism of what he labelled as 'neocolonial collaboration' in museums' post-colonial turn: 'Neocolonial Collaboration: Museum as Contact Zone Revisited', *Museum Anthropology* 34, no. 1 (2011): 56–70, https://doi.org/10.1111/j.1548-1379.2010.01107.x.
37. See Laura Gibson and Rebecca Kahn, 'Digital Museums in the 21st Century: Global Microphones or Universal Mufflers?' *Museological Review* 20 (2016): 43.
38. See Gesa Grimme and Larissa Förster, 'Locating Namibian Cultural Heritage in Museums and Universities in German-Speaking Countries: A Finding Aid for Provenance Research', *Working Paper Deutsches Zentrum Kulturgutverluste* 6 (2024): 27–29, https://doi.org/10.25360/01-2024-00002.
39. See Adam Hochschild, *King Leopold's Ghost: A Story of Greed, Terror, and Heroism in Colonial Africa* (Boston, MA: Mariner Books, 1998), 176.
40. Hannah Turner, *Cataloguing Culture: Legacies of Colonialism in Museum Documentation* (Vancouver: University of British Columbia Press, 2020).
41. The Natural History Museum in London, the Foundation Prussian Cultural Heritage in Berlin, the University of Strasbourg, the Penn Museum in Philadelphia or the American Museum of Natural History in New York are just a few examples of institutions that hold remains acquired as a result of grave-robbing activities.
42. Quoted in Turner, *Cataloguing Culture*, 135.
43. For a critique on the discourse of primitivism see Gene Blocker, 'Is Primitive Art "Art"?', in *Philosophy from Africa: A Text with Readings*, ed. P.H. Coetzee (Oxford University Press, 2003), 411; and Abiodun, *Yoruba Art and Language*, 9.
44. Editors' note: In our pursuit to present a nuanced understanding of African

cultural heritage and its significance, we have consciously chosen to challenge the use of certain terms, notably 'fetish'. This decision stems from a principled stance against the colonial, racist and outdated connotations that have historically clouded the true value of African spirituality and knowledge systems to shift away from language that perpetuates misunderstanding, disrespect and exoticisation, and foster a respectful appreciation of African cultural assets. Throughout this volume, wherever the term is quoted from colonial archives or museum catalogues, it is deliberately struck out. This editorial choice aims to draw the reader's attention to its problematic nature and complex colonial history, and to distance ourselves from the negative implications associated with it, which unfairly links African spiritual values and art to pejorative perceptions. This approach was inspired by similar decisions in academic and research settings, as evidenced in Sela Adjei and Simon Kofi Appiah's work and the project report *Researching Colonial Provenances*. With this explanation, we wish to communicate transparently on those editorial choices and encourage readers to adopt critical approaches towards the power inherent in language and the representation of African knowledge in scholarly discourse.

For critique on the discourse around 'fetishism', see William Pietz, 'The Problem of Fetish', *Anthropology and Aesthetics* 9 (1985): 5–17, https://doi.org/10.1086/RESv9n1ms20166719; William Pietz, 'Bosman's Guinea: The Intercultural Roots of an Enlightenment Discourse', *Comparative Civilizations Review* 9, no. 9 (1982): 3, https://scholarsarchive.byu.edu/ccr/vol9/iss9/3; and R.C. Morris and D.H. Leonard, *The Returns of Fetishism: Charles de Brosses and the Afterlives of an Idea* (Chicago, IL: University of Chicago Press, 2017); Sela K. Adjei, 'Legba, Dzoka and Indigenous Knowledge Systems: Rethinking Vodu Epistemologies', *Conference Unpacking Missionary Collections*, Utrecht University, 19–21 September 2022; Simon Kofi Appiah, '*Fetish* Again? Southern Perspectives on the Material Approach to the Study of Religion', *Open Theology* 8, no. 1 (2022): 79–94, https://doi.org/10.1515/opth-2022-0197; and Marlena Barnstorf-Brandes et al. (eds), *Researching Colonial Provenances* (Dresden: Staatliche Ethnographische Sammlungen, 2024), https://doi.org/10.18452/27458.

45 See Jennifer Wilkinson, 'Using and Abusing Art', in *The African Philosophy Reader*, ed. P.H. Coetzee and A.P.J. Roux (London: Routledge, 2000), 388.

46 Statues and statuettes from Greek, Roman, Norse and Viking mythology (e.g. Zeus, Janus, Odin, Thor, Freyr etc.) were also considered as 'powerful figures' in the imagination of the Western world, yet they were (and are still) not classified as 'fetish-power objects' in Western museums and art history annals. For further discussions on the so-called crisis of representation in anthropology, see Sonia Silva, 'Art and Fetish in the Anthropology Museum', *Material Religion* 13, no. 1 (2017): 77–96, https://doi.org/10.1080/17432200.2016.1272782.

47 See Kyrah Malika Daniels, 'Mirror Mausoleums, Mortuary Arts, and Haitian Religious Unexceptionalism', *Journal of the American Academy of Religion* 85, no. 4 (2017): 959, https://doi.org/10.1093/jaarel/lfx012; and Paul Radin, *African Folktales and Sculpture* (New York: Pantheon Books, 1952), 330–331.

48 See Kwasi Wiredu, 'Decolonizing African Philosophy and Religion', in *Decolonizing African Religions: A Short History of African Religions in Western Scholarship*, ed. Okot P'Bitek (New York: Diasporic Africa Press, 2011), xi and xvi.

49 See Museums Association of Namibia, 'Press Conference: Confronting Colonial Pasts, Envisioning Creative Futures', 30 May 2022, Independence Memorial Museum, Windhoek, https://www.facebook.com/watch/live/?ref=watch_permalink&v=426332568999499 (accessed 5 March 2024); and Priya Basil, 'Necrography: Death-Writing in the Colonial Museum', *British Art Studies* 19 (February 2021), https://www.britishartstudies.ac.uk/issues/issue-index/issue-19/death-writing-in-the-colonial-museums (accessed 5 March 2024).

50 'Objects, cultural artifacts, African artifacts, restituted objects, ritual object, ethnographic object, piece of wood, effigy' etc. Kyrah Malika Daniels also pondered over a similar philosophical problem when she admitted that 'in hopes of highlighting such cultural nuances and imperfect linguistic translations, I will alternate between the use of the terms "ritual objects", "sacred art", and "ritual healing arts"'; see Daniels, 'Mirror Mausoleums', 959–960.

51 See, for instance, the work of Looty NFT and Cosmo Wenman's release of the scan of the Nefertiti bust in 2019.

52 For a critique of conservation photography in the context of Indigenous Australian curatorship, see Diana J.B. Young, 'What do Museum Objects Want? Re-Thinking Photographic Conventions in Ethnographic Museums', *Visual Anthropology Review* 38, no. 1 (2022): 60–84, https://doi.org/10.1111/var.12265.

PART I: THE BATTLEFIELD

53 For a comprehensive discussion of the case of the Gweagal shield, see Alice Procter, *The Whole Picture: The Colonial Story of the Art in Our Museums & Why We Need to Talk About It* (London: Cassell, 2020), 129–139.

54 For instance, French and German reports about East Africa accused British officials and missionaries of providing firearms to local populations in the Kilimanjaro region and training them.

1. The Treasure of Samori Touré

55 Général Gouraud, *Au Soudan: Souvenirs d'un africain* (Paris: Editions Pierre Tisné, 1939), 224.

56 Archival folder 'Visite du marabout Cheikh Ousmane Badji (objets Samory)',

Fonds Musée national des arts d'Afrique et d'Océanie – Série J: Relations avec les sections du musée, DA001498/61371, Archives of the Musée du Quai-Branly – Jacques Chirac.

57 Dan Hicks, *The Brutish Museums: The Benin Bronzes, Colonial Violence and Cultural Restitution* (London: Pluto, 2020), 53.

58 Albert Adu Boahen, 'New Trends and Processes in Africa in the Nineteenth Century', in *General History of Africa: Africa in the Nineteenth Century until the 1880s*, ed. J.F. Ade Ayaji, vol. 6 (Paris: UNESCO, 1989), 40–63.

59 Yves Person, 'States and Peoples of Senegambia and Upper Guinea', in *General History of Africa: Africa in the Nineteenth Century until the 1880s*, ed. J.F. Ade Ayaji (Paris: UNESCO, 1989), vol. 6, 636–661. Also from the same author: *Samori, une Révolution Dyula*, 3 vols (Dakar: IFAN, 1968–1975).

60 Mbaye Guèye and Albert Adu Boahen, 'African Initiatives and Resistance in West Africa, 1880–1914', in *General History of Africa: African under Colonial Domination 1880–1935*, ed. Albert Adu Boahen, vol. 7 (Paris: UNESCO, 1985), 114–148.

61 Elara Bertho, 'Photographies de Samori Touré: de la carte postale coloniale aux pochettes de vinyles. Le devenir d'une icône', *Cahiers d'études africaines* 58, no. 230/2 (2018), 301–322; see also Elara Bertho, 'Filmer la résistance à la colonisation: stratégies postcoloniales de mémoire et d'oubli. À propos du scénario Samori de Sembène Ousmane', *Cahiers d'études africaines* 56, no. 224 (2016), 875–890; Angie Epifano, 'Commerce and Colonialism in the Regalia of the Samorian State', *African Arts* 53, no. 2 (2020): 28–41, https://doi.org/10.1162/afar_a_00526; and Olivier Kodjalbaye Banguiam, *Les officiers français: constitution et devenir de leurs collections africaines issues de la conquête coloniale*, PhD thesis, Paris Ouest Nanterre La Défense, 2016, www.theses.fr/2016PA100045.

62 Quoted in Banguiam, *Les officiers français*, 264.

63 Quoted in Banguiam, *Les officiers français*, 489.

64 Musée du Quai Branly – Jacques Chirac, online collection: 71.1889.2.1.1-2, reportedly 'taken from a Samory warrior'; 71.1889.2.2, 'taken from a warrior in the Samory army'; 71.1889.2.4, simply 'from the Samory army'; and 71.1889.2.5 which was allegedly 'worn by a Samory warrior'.

65 Musée du Quai Branly – Jacques Chirac, online collection: respectively, 71.1882.24.1.1-2; 71.1889.146.1 and 71.1892.25.3; and 71.1892.25.10 and 71.1892.25.11.

66 Musée du Quai Branly – Jacques Chirac, online collection: respectively, 75.15215.5, 75.15215.6 and 75.15215.7; 75.15215.8; 75.15215.4; and 75.15212.

67 Gouraud, *Au Soudan*, 'The Spoils', 209–210; and 'The Treasure', 223–224.

68 Gouraud, *Au Soudan*, 224.

69 Telegram from Louis Archinard to the governor of Senegal, dated 12 April 1890, quoted in Daniel Foliard, 'Les vies du "trésor de Ségou"', *Revue historique*

4, no. 688 (2018): 879, https://doi.org/10.3917/rhis.184.0869.
70 See Foliard, 'Les vies du "trésor de Ségou"', 874.
71 Gouraud, *Au Soudan*, 209.
72 Person, *Samori, une Révolution Dyula*, vol. 3, 2014.
73 Auguste Jean Baptiste Chevalier, letter dated 28 May 1899, quoted in Bulletin de la Société linnéenne de Normandie 5, no. 3 (1899), 70.
74 Gouraud, *Au Soudan*, 224.
75 See Whitney Battle-Baptiste and Britt Rusert (eds), *W.E.B. Du Bois's Data Portraits: Visualizing Black America* (New York: Princeton Architectural Press, 2018).
76 Gaston de Wailly, *A travers l'exposition de 1900*, vol. 10 (Paris: Fayard frères, 1900), 91.
77 Jules Charles-Roux, *Les colonies françaises: L'organisation et le fonctionnement de l'exposition des colonies et pays de protectorat* (Paris: Imprimerie Nationale, 1902), 163–164.
78 See photographs of the 'Galerie des Conquêtes' of the Musée des Arts Africains et Océaniens taken before 1963: Jean Chuzeville, 'Sans titre [Trésor de Samory]', no. PF0092830 (avec couronne); 'Trésor de Samory', no. PP0132741 (sans couronne), Musée du Quai Branly – Jacques Chirac, Paris.
79 Georges Monmarché, 'Paris et sa proche banlieue', *Les Guides Bleus* (Paris: Hachette, 1957), 402.
80 'Tapis de selle du roi du Haut-Niger Samory Touré', PM82001549, Musée du terroir, Montauban. www.pop.culture.gouv.fr/notice/palissy/PM82001549.
81 Gouraud, *Au Soudan*, 211.
82 Label in front of the display case showing the 'trésor de Samori' at the Musée de l'Armée, Paris, Salle Afrique, 2021.
83 Epifano, 'Commerce and Colonialism in the Regalia of the Samorian State', 28.
84 Epifano, 'Commerce and Colonialism in the Regalia of the Samorian State', 31.
85 Ekpo Eyo, *Two Thousand Years of Nigerian Art* (Lagos: Federal Department of Antiquities Nigeria, 1977), 8.
86 'Visite du marabout Cheikh Ousmane Badji', DA001498/61371.

2. The Manifesto of the Sudanese Mahdī: Banners as Artefacts of Empire

87 No. 1.–The Khartoum Campaign, Sudan Intelligence Report No. 60, 1898, 8.
88 G.W. Steevens, *With Kitchener to Khartoum* (New York: Dodd, Mead and Co., 1898), 264.
89 Ernest N. Bennett, 'After Omdurman', *The Contemporary Review* 75 (January–June 1899): 20–23.
90 'What Happened at Omdurman?', *Launceston Examiner*, 11 March 1899, 14. Inclosure No. 1, Major-General Lord Kitchener to Lord Cromer, 1 February

1899, Egypt No. 1 (1899): Despatches from Her Majesty's Agent and Consul-General in Egypt respecting the Conduct of the British and Egyptian Troops after the Battle of Omdurman, 1. Ernest Bennett's allegations were also vigorously denied by other reporters who were present, including Bennet Burleigh, 'Conduct of Troops at Omdurman: Unfounded Charges of Cruelty: A Vindication', *The Daily Telegraph*, 2 January 1899, 5.

91 Sudan Archive, University of Durham, A. Hunter Papers, SAD.964/4/64–73. Hunter commanded Kitchener's Egyptian Army Division: Appendix 4: Staff and Composition of Nile Expedition, Sudan Intelligence Report No. 60, 29.

92 Bābikr Badrī, تاريخ حياتي [*History of My Life*], 3 vols (Omdurman: n.p., 1959–1961), vol. 2, 3. All translations by Osman Nusairi unless otherwise indicated.

93 The *jibba* (gibbeh) was a patched smock, worn by most if not all the fighters loyal to the Mahdī and his successor. It originated as an expression of an individual's rejection of material luxury, as the worn-out garment was patched and patched again. By the mid-1890s, it had evolved into a stylised, symmetrical and often colour-coded ensemble of appliquéd squares, of which the ones sent home by Tullibardine are fine examples.

94 Letter dated 9 April 1898, in John Murray (7th Earl of Atholl), *Chronicles of the Atholl and Tullibardine Families*, 5 vols (Edinburgh: Ballantyne Press, 1908), vol. 5, 10.

95 Letter dated 9 September 1898, in Murray, *Chronicles of the Atholl and Tullibardine Families*, vol. 5, 19. Lord Tullibardine eventually secured one finial, which the family history notes was 'pierced by a shrapnel bullet' (ibid., 23). It was mounted on the clock tower at Blair Castle in Scotland. After the clock tower's roof collapsed in a fire, it was replaced with a facsimile.

96 General Viscount Wolseley, *The Soldier's Pocket-Book for Field Service* (London: Macmillan, 1886), 165–166.

97 John Mack, 'The Agency of Objects: A Contrasting Choreography of Flags, Military Booty and Skulls from Late Nineteenth Century Africa', in *Dividing the Spoils: Perspectives on Military Collections and the British Empire*, ed. Henrietta Lidchi and Stuart Allan (Manchester: Manchester University Press, 2020), 44.

98 Fergus Nicoll and Osman Nusairi, 'The Tomb of the Sudanese Mahdī: Desecration, Dispersal and Rediscovery', *Third Text* (forthcoming).

99 Ernest N. Bennett, *Downfall of the Dervishes: Being a Sketch of the Final Sudan Campaign of 1898* (London: Methuen, 1899), 222.

100 British Museum, Windsor Castle, Guards Museum, National Army Museum, Royal Hospital Chelsea (London); Blair Castle (Pitlochry); Black Watch Castle and Museum (Perth); Brighton Museum & Art Gallery; Bristol Museum and Art Gallery; Great North Museum (Newcastle upon Tyne); Highlanders Museum (Inverness); Museum of Somerset (Taunton); Kelvingrove Art Gallery and Museum, Glasgow; Osbourne House (Isle of Wight); Rifles Berkshire and Wiltshire Museum (Salisbury); Royal Engineers Museum (Gillingham);

Royal Green Jackets (Rifles) Museum (Winchester); Royal Marines Museum (Portsmouth); Royal Regiment of Fusiliers Museum (Warwick); and Sir Hector Macdonald Museum (Dingwall). Also National Museum of African Art, Washington DC; State Hermitage, St Petersburg; and Sudan Archive, University of Durham.

101 *Navy and Army Illustrated*, vol. 7, no. 92, 5 November 1898, 165. The flag was apparently presented by Kitchener to Queen Victoria and remains in the possession of the Royal Collections Trust, see Mack, 'Agency of Objects', 48.

102 *The Times*, 21 November 1898, 12.

103 Ali Saleh Karrar, *The Sufi Brotherhoods in the Sudan* (London: Hurst, 1992), 129, 136, 158 and 162.

104 Highlanders' Museum, Fort George, Inverness: 356–668.

105 Lit. 'friend of Allah', a generic honorific for holy men and fraternity leaders.

106 ʿAbd-al-Qādir al-Jīlānī (1077–1166) was a conservative Sunni scholar whose lectures on Sufism were highly influential. Aḥmad ibn ʿAlī al-Rifāʿī was a twelfth-century scholar and Sufi leader, celebrated for his abstinence and charity, in what is now eastern Iraq. Ibrāhīm ibn ʿAbd-al-ʿAzīz ʿAbū-al-Magd was a thirteenth-century Sufi imam from Dasūq in the Egyptian Delta. Aḥmad al-Badawī was a thirteenth-century Sufi mystic born in North-West Africa who established his own fraternity, the Badawīa, after settling at Ṭanṭā in the Egyptian Delta.

107 Inks available at that time were made, variously, of soot from cooking pots mixed with gum arabic (from the acacia tree) or from dried fish scales. Dark blue (*nīla*) colouring came from a dye introduced by the Ottomans that was also used for women's dresses known as *al-zarāq*. Subsequently, the lettering on *anṣār* banners was usually traced in ink before being appliquéd in rough local cotton.

108 The Qur'an, 55:27 and 55:78, are the only references to this epithet of Allah. This is the most frequently reproduced formula on surviving Mahdist banners.

109 ʿAlī al-Mahdī, جهاد في سبيل الله [*Jihad in God's Cause*], ed. ʿAbdallah Muḥammad Aḥmad (Khartoum: Khartoum University Press, 1965), 13–14.

110 Highlanders' Museum, Fort George, Inverness: 356–667.

111 Col. The Hon. John Colborne, *With Hicks Pasha in the Soudan* (London: Smith, Elder & Co., 1884), 161.

112 Haim Shaked, *The Life of the Sudanese Mahdi: A Historical Study of Kitāb saʿadat al-mustahdī bi-sīrat al-Imām al-Mahdī by Ismāʿīl bin ʿAbd-al-Gādir* (New Brunswick, NJ: Transaction Books, 1978), 96–97.

113 Decree dated 14 Dhū al-Hijja 1300 (16 October 1993): Muḥammad Ibrāhīm Abū-Salīm (ed.), الآثار الكاملة للإمام المهدي [*The Collected Works of the Imām al-Mahdī*] (Khartoum: Khartoum University Press, 1990–1994), vol. 1, 393–394.

114 Letter to Gen. Yūsuf Ḥassan al-Shallālī, garrison commander at Fashoda: al-Mahdī, *Jihad in God's Cause*, 29–30.

115 Ibrāhīm Fawzī, السودان بين يدي غردون وكيتشنر [*Sudan Under Gordon and Kitchener*]

(Cairo: n.p., 1901), vol. 1, 92–93.

116 Letters dated 17 Rabīʿ I 1300 (27 January 1883), 13 Jumāda I 1300 (22 March 1883) among others, and 17 Dhū al-Hijja 1300 (19 October 1883) respectively: Abū-Salīm, *Collected Works of the Imām al-Mahdī*, vol. 1, 242–243, 265–267 and 397–398.

117 Letter to Mūsa Muḥammad al-Aḥmar, dated before the month of Shaʿbān ah 1298 (before 30 June 1881): Abū-Salīm, *Collected Works of the Imām al-Mahdī*, vol. 1, 75.

118 *Letter from the Khalīfa ʿAbdullāhī to members of the Tījānīa ṭarīqa* (Khartoum: Khartoum University Press, 1970), 45–48.

119 Peter M. Holt, 'Correspondence', *Sudan Notes and Records* 36/2 (1955), 205.

120 For a similar item, taken from colonialists and recycled by African rulers, see Chapter 8 on Mangi Meli's tobacco container.

121 For example, Sheikh Muḥammad ʿAbdallah al-Khojalī, one of the Mahdī's earliest teachers, established 17 religious schools between Khartoum and the White Nile; much earlier, Sheikh Arbāb al-ʿAqāʾid (died 1691) was reported to have had more than a thousand pupils: Muḥammad al-Nur ibn Deifallah, Kitāb al-ṭabaqāt fī khuṣūṣ al-awliyyāʾ wa'l-ʿulamāʾ wa'l-shuʿrāʾ fī al-Sūdān [*A Classification of Saints, Scholars, and Poets in Sudan*], ed. Yusuf Fadl Hassan (Khartoum: Khartoum University Press, 1985), 99, 136 and 163.

122 Reproduced as Plate IV in William Galloway, *The Battle of Tofrek* (London: W.H. Allen & Co., 1887), 76.

123 Muḥammad Ibrāhīm Abū-Salīm, تاريخ الخرطوم [*A History of Khartoum*] (Khartoum: Dār al-Arshād, 1971), 98.

124 Fr Joseph Ohrwalder, *Ten Years' Captivity in the Mahdi's Camp, 1882–1892* (London: Sampson Low Marston & Co., 1892), 63 and 94.

125 Letter dated 9 September 1898, in Murray, *Chronicles of the Atholl and Tullibardine Families*, vol. 5, 16.

126 ʿIṣmat Hassan Zulfū, كرري: تجليل عسكري لمعركة أم درمان [*Kararī: A Military Analysis of the Battle of Omdurman*] (Khartoum: Urban Press, 1978), 515–516.

127 Col. Sir Reginald Wingate, 'Report on the Death of Khalifa', dated 25 November 1899: Sudan Archive, University of Durham, SAD.867/6/1–11.

128 İsmail Hakkı Göksoy, 'Some Aspects of the Anglo-Egyptian Condominium Rule in Sudan (1899–1914)', n.p., 2019, 79.

129 Highlanders' Museum, Fort George, Inverness: 356–668.

130 J.A. Reid, 'Story of a Mahdist Emir', *Sudan Notes and Records* 9/2 (1926), 79–82.

3. *IsiHlangu* from the Anglo-Zulu War of 1879: 'We need to infuse African-ness in museums'

131 Yann LeGall would like to thank Corinne Sandwith warmly for facilitating this

exchange. Mwelela Cela is grateful to the KwaZulu-Natal Amafa and Research Institute for sharing precious material and photographs in the context of this publication.

132   Sir Henry Bartle Frere British High Commissioner from 1877 to 1880 had been sent to Southern Africa to implement the confederation of the colonies.
133   Sir Theophilus Shepstone, Secretary of Native Affairs for Natal up to 1877 and later Administrator of the Transvaal.
134   See Ron Lock, *The Anglo-Zulu War: Isandlwana, the Revelation of a Disaster* (Barnsley, South Yorkshire: Pen & Sword Military, 2017), 32–33.
135   S. Jabulani Maphalala, 'Zulu Relations with the Whites During the Nineteenth Century: A Broad Perspective', *Historia 25*, no. 1 (1980): 19–27.
136   C.T. Binns, *The Last Zulu King: The Life and Death of Cetshwayo* (London: Longmans, 1963), 119–120.
137   Inkosi Ntshingwayo kaMahole Khoza was second only to Inkosi Mnyamana kaNgqengelele on the King's council.
138   Mavumengwana kaNdlela Ntuli was the brother of Inkosi Godide. The Inkosi of the Ntuli. Both were sons of Ndlela kaSompisi, King Dingane's chief induna.
139   Binns, *The Last Zulu King*, 122.
140   See John Laband, *The Fall of Rorke's Drift* (Barnsley, South Yorkshire: Greenhill Books, 2019), 42–45.
141   Ian Knight, *Great Zulu Commanders* (London: Arms and Armour, 1999), 79.
142   Bhekizizwe Peterson, H.I.E. Dhlomo Memorial Lecture, University of KwaZulu-Natal, Campbell Collections, November 2012.
143   Jeff Guy, *The Destruction of the Zulu Kingdom: The Civil War in Zululand, 1879–1884* (Scottsville: University of kwaZulu-Natal Press, 1994), 59.
144   Accession number Z 28249 A.
145   Inventory number 1943.6.118.
146   Inventory numbers Af1954,03.1 (shield).; Af1954,03.3 (spear); Af1954,03.4.a-b (gunpower horn); Af1934,0712.8 (armlet); Af1934,0712.5 (axe); Af1934,0712.4 (ceremonial staff); Af1934,0712.9 (weapon or ceremonial equipment).
147   See Verne Harris, '"They Should Have Destroyed More": The Destruction of Public Records by the South African State in the Final Years of Apartheid, 1990–1994', *Transformation* 32 (2000): 29–56.
148   Sello Hatang and Sahm Venter (eds), *Nelson Mandela by Himself: The Authorised Book of Quotations* (Johannesburg: Pan Macmillan, 2011), 144.
149   Inventory numbers Af1950,18.1 and Af1963,15.2.
150   John Laband, *Historical Dictionary of the Zulu Wars* (Plymouth: Scarecrow Press, 2009), 133.
151   The Pitt Rivers Museum in Oxford holds a photograph showing a proud and well-dressed Cetshwayo during his time as an inmate at the Castle of Good Hope (inventory number 1998.54.50).

152   Lock, *The Anglo-Zulu War*, vii–viii.

153   Leandra Engelbrecht, 'Shaka iLembe Makes History as Best-Ever Performance for a MultiChoice Drama Series', *News24*, 24 June 2023, www.news24.com/life/arts-and-entertainment/tv/shaka-ilembe-makes-history-as-best-ever-performance-for-a-multichoice-drama-series-20230624-2 (accessed 4 December 2023).

4. The Plunder of '*Adibo Dali*' and Why Looted Cultural Goods Need to Return to Dagbon

154   The authors would like to thank Léontine Meijer-van-Mensch, Friedrich von Bose, Ohiniko Mawussé Toffa, Oussounou Abdel-Aziz Sandja, and the people of Yendi, without whom this contribution would not have been possible.

155   Alhaji Alhassan I. Sulemana, 'Ka Adibo Dali la? What of the Battle of Adibo? Interrogating German Rule in Dagbon', in *Germany and its West African Colonies: 'Excavations' of German Colonialism in Post-colonial Times*, ed. Wazi Apoh and Beatrice Lundt (Berlin: Lit Verlag, 2013), 173–183.

156   A focus on the cultural heritage from Dagbon held by the Grassi Museum has been pursued in the project 'Provenance of Colonial-Era Collections from Togo' (see Marlena Barnstorf-Brandes, Friedrich von Bose, Silvia Dolz, Ricarda Rivoir, Julia von Sigsfeld, Ohiniko M. Toffa for the State Ethnographic Collections Saxony, 'Researching Colonial Provenances', Final Report of the Project 'Provenance of Colonial-Era Collections from Togo in the Museum für Völkerkunde Dresden and the GRASSI Museum für Völkerkunde zu Leipzig' (Dresden: Staatliche Ethnographische Sammlungen Sachsen, 2023), in English: https://doi.org/10.18452/27458; in German: https://doi.org/10.18452/27457; and in French: https://doi.org/10.18452/27459.

157   Thomas Edward Bowdich, *Mission from Cape Coast to Ashantee* (London: John Murray, 1819), 178.

158   Letter from Hans Gruner to August Köhler, dated 4 November 1896, BArch R1001/4391, 76–77.

159   Peter Sebald, Togo 1884–1914 (Berlin: Akademie Verlag, 1988), 182; and Georg Trierenberg, *Togo, die Aufrichtung der deutschen Schutzherrschaft und die Erschließung des Landes* (Berlin: Ernst Siegfried Mittler und Sohn, 1914), 25.

160   For a more detailed account, see Elias Aguigah and Yann LeGall, 'Remnants of "Adibo Dali" and the Plunder of Yendi in German Museums', *History Workshop Journal* 96 (Autumn 2023): 71–95, https://doi.org/10.1093/hwj/dbad011.

161   Emmanuel F. Tamakloe, *A Brief History of the Dagbamba People* (Accra: Government Printing Office, 1931), 42.

162   John Chernoff and Alhaji Ibrahim Abdulai (eds), 'The Pre-Colonial and Colonial Period', in *A Drummer's Testament: Dagbamba Society and Culture in the*

       Twentieth Century, www.adrummerstestament.com/2/2-14_The_Pre-colonial_and_Colonial_Periods_web_chapter.html#2-14-8 (accessed 15 June 2023).
163   Chernoff and Abdulai, 'The Pre-Colonial and Colonial Period'.
164   More about this expedition in Sebald, Togo 1884–1914, 201–204; Tamakloe, *A Brief History of the Dagbamba People*, 43–44; and Chernoff and Abdulai, 'The Pre-Colonial and Colonial Period'.
165   Valentin von Massow, *Die Eroberung von Nordtogo 1896–1899*, ed. Peter Sebald (Bremen: Edition Falkenberg, 2014), 213. In his ignorance of local languages, Massow called Kambon Nakpem Ziblim Wag-biegu by the Hausa denomination for the Dagomba war leader.
166   MAf 03357 and MAf 03358.
167   Correspondence between the Berlin Museum für Völkerkunde, the Auswärtiges Amt, and the Grossherzogliche Sammlungen für Alterthümer und Völkerkunde, SMB-ZA, I/MV 725, E 1267/1901, 190–196.
168   III C 10646.
169   See Aguigah and LeGall, 'Remnants of "Adibo Dali"', 78.
170   Massow himself stated in his diary: 'and in addition the Babylonian confusion of languages: Haussa, Ewe, Anago, Mossi, Grussi, Tschi, Ashanti and several other languages, so that one absolutely cannot make oneself understood and always needs three to four interpreters'; and Massow, *Die Eroberung von Nordtogo*, 166.
171   Colonial archives also noted this massive depopulation of Yendi and its surroundings. For this reason, the German colonial government doubted the economic value of eastern Dagbon for the colony and even tried to exchange Yendi and Mango for a territory around the Volta estuary, but the British refused. See Sebald, *Togo 1884–1914*, 203–204.
172   For further information, see Barnstorf-Brandes et al., 'Researching Colonial Provenances'.
173   To contact the Yendi Heritage and Resource Center (YHRC), email: yendiheritage.rcenter@gmail.com.

5. A War Coat of the Anufo/Tchokossi: From Northern Togo to the Field Museum in Chicago

174   The 'war cloak' from Mango, Togo, Field Museum: catalogue number 104802. https://collections-anthropology.fieldmuseum.org/catalogue/1004973.
175   Marcela A. Garcia Probert and Petra M. Sijpesteijn, *Amulets and Talismans of the Middle East and North Africa in Context: Transmission, Efficacy and Collections* (Leiden: Brill, 2022).
176   Elias Aguigah, Yann LeGall and Jeanne-Ange Wagne, 'Colonial Violence in the North of Togo and the Plunder of Biema Asabiè's Belongings', *VOICES*, State

Collections in Saxony, 19 January 2023, https://voices.skd.museum/en/voices-mag/colonial-violence-in-the-north-of-togo-and-the-plunder-of-biema-asabies-belongings/ (accessed 6 December 2023).

177 Edward Graham Norris, 'Atakora Mountain Refuges Systems of Exploitation in Northern Togo', *Anthropos* 81, no. 1/3 (1986): 109–136.

178 August Köhler, Notes to K.A. 1035, dated 22 February 1901, BArch R1001/4393, 160.

179 Gaston Thierry, Letter to Felix von Luschan, dated 24 May 1905, SMB-ZA, I/MV 733, E 1009/1905, 40–41.

180 Otto Finsch, Letter to George Dorsey, dated 14 April 1905, Archives of the Field Museum.

181 Annual Report of the Director to the Board of Trustees for the year 1904–1905 2, no. 5 (October 1905): 350–350, https://doi.org/www.biodiversitylibrary.org/item/25572.

182 Matthias Erzberger, 'Der Fall Thierry', in *Die Kolonial-Bilanz* (U. Druck D. Germania, 1906), 81–82.

183 See, for instance, Kuassi A. Akakpo, *Discours et contre-discours au Togo allemand* (Paris: Le Manuscrit, 2014).

184 See Fanny Pigeaud, 'La France, suspect principal dans l'assassinat de Sylvanus Olympio', in *L'Empire qui ne veut pas mourir: Une histoire de la Françafrique*, ed. Thomas Borrel, Amzat Boukari-Yabara, Benoît Collombat and Thomas Deltombe (Paris: Seuil, 2021), 256–258.

185 In 1984, in Baguida-Lomé, the statute of German–Togolese Friendship was established to commemorate a hundred years of 'friendship', in reference to the centenary of German colonisation of Togo (1884–1984).

186 See Peter Sebald, *Auf deutschen Spuren in Lome: ein Stadtführer* (German Embassy in Togo, 1997).

187 See Dadja Halla-Kawa Simtaro, *Le Togo 'Musterkolonie'. Souvenir de l'Allemagne dans la Société Togolaise*, PhD thesis, Université Aix-Marseille, 1982.

188 Report by Gaston Thierry, dated 19 November 1897, BArch R1001/4392, 163.

189 See Nicoué L. Gayibor, *Des bâtisseurs du Togo: Biographies de quelques ancêtres, héros et précurseurs de l'histoire nationale* (Paris: Khartala, 2015).

190 See Gaston Thierry to Berlin Museum für Völkerkunde, dated 22 November 1902, SMB-ZA, I/MV 726, E 825/1905, 255–263.

191 Two new textbooks on the history of Togo published in 2015 by the Association of Historians and Archaeologists of Togo are being introduced in public schools to compensate for the shortcomings of the old ones. These textbooks could be further improved with the help of new references, such as museum archives and cultural heritage.

192 Birgit Meyer, 'The Legba-Dzoka Project: Tracking and Unpacking the "Collection Carl Spiess"', *Religious Matters in an Entangled World*, Utrecht

University, 25 October 2022, https://religiousmatters.nl/the-legba-dzoka-project-tracking-and-unpacking-the-collection-carl-spiess-ubersee-museum-bremen/ (accessed 27 November 2023).

193   See recommendations forwarded to the German Foreign Office by Kokou Azamede and Andreas Mehler: 'Restitution als Chance zum Dialog zwischen "Zentrum" und "Peripherie"', *Megatrends Afrika Blog Joint Futures* 13, 23 October 2023, www.megatrends-afrika.de/publikation/mta-joint-futures-13-restitution-als-change-zum-dialog (accessed 27 November 2023).

PART II: THE ROYAL PALACE

6. Hiding and Returning Asante Regalia (1970–2024): The Journey of an Ancestral Messenger

194   Silvia Forni, quoted in Opemsuo Radio, 'Fowler Museum Returns "Stolen" Asante Artefacts to Otumfuo', YouTube, 8 February 2024, https://www.youtube.com/watch?v=YZhbkJ8APww&ab_channel=OpemsuoRadio (accessed 18 February 2024). For more information on the looting of Kumasi in 1874, see, among others, Henry Brackenbury, *The Ashanti War: A Narrative*, vol. 2 (Edinburgh: William Blackwood & Sons, 1874); Henry Morton Stanley, *Coomasie & Magdala: The Story of Two British Campaigns in Africa* (New York: Harper & Brothers, 1874); Albert Adu Boahen, 'The Hundredth Anniversary of the Sagrenti War', in *Africa in the Twentieth Century*, ed. Toyin Falola (Trenton, NJ: Africa World Press, 2004), 277–285; and Kwame Opoku, 'When Will Britain Return Looted Golden Ghanaian Artefacts? A History of British Looting of More Than 100 Objects', *Modern Ghana*, 5 January 2011, https://www.modernghana.com/news/310930/when-will-britain-return-looted-golden-ghanaian-artefacts-a.html#google_vignette (accessed 18 February 2024).

195   Manhyia Palace Museum, British Museum and V&A Museum, 'Asante Regalia to be Displayed in Ghana for the First Time in 150 Years', press release, 25 January 2024, https://www.britishmuseum.org/sites/default/files/2024-01/Asante_regalia_to_be_displayed_in_Ghana_for_first_time_in_150_years.pdf (accessed 18 February 2024).

196   Kwame Opoku, 'British to Loan Looted Asante Gold Artefacts to Asante/Ghana?', *Modern Ghana*, 21 May 2023, https://www.modernghana.com/news/1232230/british-to-loan-looted-asante-gold-artefacts-to.html (accessed 24 February 2024).

197   Editors' note: In a quite baffling newspaper article accompanying the press release, the director of the V&A, Tristram Hunt, wrote:

> While a long-term loan and not a full, legal repatriation of these wondrous

examples of west African goldsmithing, this renewable cultural partnership offers a new paradigm for a broader sharing of contested colonial heritage, *while existing laws preventing restitution remain in place.* It might allow us to move beyond the limits of the Parthenon sculptures debate and think about a more equitable future for looted collections in so-called encyclopaedic, European museums. [our italics]

Legal scholars Petra Warrington and Sara Pridgeon, together with Samantha Knights from the Kings' Council, have hinted at a way to tackle the alleged unbending character of the British Museum Act (1963) or the National Heritage Act (1983). They advocate for a 'creative reading' or an updated 'interpretation of section 5(c) of the 1963 Act'. Why should national museums move 'beyond' legal restitution and circumvent ethical solutions for alleged 'equitable' ones, when neither they, nor the Department of Culture, Media, and Sports (which was ironically formerly called Department of National Heritage) have never ever genuinely attempted to reconsider these laws in depth? A law passed in 2022 that sought to grant museums and their trustees more leeway for de-accession was even updated in February 2024 to keep strict governmental approval for cases of restitution. See Tristram Hunt, 'V&A's "Return" of Looted Ghana Gold is a New Way to Tackle Britain's Painful Past', *The Guardian*, 27 January 2024, https://www.theguardian.com/culture/2024/jan/27/vas-return-of-looted-ghana-gold-is-a-new-way-to-tackle-britains-painful-past (accessed 26 February 2024); Petra Warrington and Sara Pridgeon, 'Restitution in the UK: Developments in Law and Practice', *International Bar Association*, 10 May 2022, https://www.ibanet.org/restitution-in-the-UK-developments-in-law-and-practice (accessed 26 February 2024); and Angelica Villa, 'UK Government Updates Restitution Law, Keeps Approval Process Intact for Museums', *Art News*, 5 February 2024, https://www.artnews.com/art-news/news/uk-government-updates-restitution-law-1234695085/ (accessed 26 February 2024).

198   Russell Chamberlin, *Loot: The Heritage of Plunder* (London: Thames and Hudson, 1983), 93.

7. A Plaque from an Ngolo *etana*:
The Looting of Architectural Heritage as a Token of Colonial Violence

199   Robert Bevan, *The Destruction of Memory: Architecture at War* (London: Reaktion Books, 2016), 19.

200   Paul Lessner, 'Die Baluë- oder Rumpi-Berge und ihre Bewohner', *Globus* 86 (1904): 273–278, 337–344 and 392–397.

201   Sometimes also spelled 'Nakelli' or 'Nakeri'. See Dan T. Friesen, *Oroko Orthography Development: Linguistic and Sociolinguistic Factors* (Grand Forks, ND: University of

North Dakota Press, 2002), 2–6; and Doreen Mekunda, 'Traditional Shrines and Artefacts in Oroko Land: The Judicial, Ethical and Social Significance', *International Journal of Linguistics, Literature and Culture* 5, no. 3 (2018): 76–90, http://dx.doi.org/10.19044/llc.v5no3a6. The following formerly self-governing communities make up the group labelled as Oroko: Bamusso, Bakoko, Ngolo, Batanga, Bima, Bakundu, Balondo, Mbonge, Ekombe and Balue.

202 Report by Oltwig von Kamptz to Foreign Office, dated 17 March 1897, BArch R1001/3345, 50–65; and Report by Theodor Seitz to Foreign Office, dated 16 August 1898, BArch R1001/3346, 36–51.

203 See Mekunda, 'Traditional Shrines and Artefacts in Oroko Land'; and Joseph Betoto Ebune, 'Nakeli-Wa-Embelle and the Ngolo Resistance to German Colonial Rule in Cameroon', *Epasa Moto: Multidisciplinary Journal of Arts, Letters and Humanities of the University of Buea* 2, no. 1 (2015): 89–102.

204 See Lessner, 'Die Baluë', 395.

205 See Richard Tsogang Fossi and Sebastian-Manès Sprute, 'Anhang: Exemplarische Biografien', in *Atlas der Abwesenheit: Kameruns Kulturerbe in Deutschland*, ed. Mikaél Assilkinga et al. (Berlin: Reimer, 2023), 372–428.

206 Jesko von Puttkamer, *Gouverneursjahre in Kamerun* (Berlin: Georg Stilke, 1912), 101.

207 Letter from Kamptz to Berlin Museum für Völkerkunde, SMB-ZA, I/MV 718, E 875/1897, 38.

208 Puttkamer, *Gouverneursjahre in Kamerun*, 102.

209 See Report by Seitz to Foreign Office, 48.

210 Luschan to Grünwedel, 25 July 1897, SMB-ZA, I/MV 764, E 437/1897, 26.

211 Report by Lessner to Foreign Office, dated 28 October 1901, BArch R1001/3349, 185.

212 Lessner to Foreign Office, 195–196.

213 Lessner to Foreign Office, 190–191.

214 Lessner, 'Die Baluë', 338.

215 Eugen Zintgraff, *Nord-Kamerun* (Berlin: Gebrüder Paetel, 1895), 138–139; and Hans Dominik to Colonial Government, dated 1 June 1910, BArch R 175-I/92, 102–103.

216 Ebune, 'Nakeli-Wa-Embelle', 89.

217 Lessner to Foreign Office, 188.

218 See Mekunda, 'Traditional Shrines and Artefacts in Oroko Land', 78.

219 See Lessner to Foreign Office, 190.

220 See Lessner, 'Die Baluë', 395.

221 Lessner, 'Aus meinen Kameruner Briefen', in *Auf weiter Fahrt: Selbsterlebnisse zur See und zu Lande. Deutsche Marine- und Kolonialbibliothek*, ed. Julius Lohmeyer and Georg Wislicenus (Leipzig: Wilhelm Weicher, 1907), 105–139, here 113.

222 See Lessner, 'Die Baluë', 393.

223 See Ebune, 'Nakeli-Wa-Embelle', 96.
224 See Ebune, 'Nakeli-Wa-Embelle', 99–100; and Mekunda, 'Traditional Shrines and Artefacts in Oroko Land', 86.
225 See Ebune, 'Nakeli-Wa-Embelle', 100; and Lessner to Foreign Office, 192.
226 See Lessner to Foreign Office, 192–193.
227 See Lessner, 'Die Baluë', 396; also, Wilhelm Langheld, *Zwanzig jahre deutsche Kolonien* (Berlin: Wilhelm Weicher, 1909), 300.
228 Lessner, 'Aus meinen Kameruner Briefen', 128 and 130.
229 Lessner, 'Die Baluë', 397.
230 Puttkamer, *Gouverneursjahre in Kamerun*, 265.
231 Bevan, *The Destruction of Memory*, 19.
232 Rebekka Habermas, 'Rettungsparadigma und Bewahrungsfetischismus: Oder was die Restitutionsdebatte mit der europäischen Moderne zu tun hat', in *Geschichtskultur durch Restitution? Ein Kunst-Historikerstreit*, ed. Thomas Sandkühler, Angelika Epple and Jürgen Zimmerer (Cologne: Böhlau Verlag, 2020), 80–81 and 85.
233 In German '*Sammelwut*' (see Habermas, 'Rettungsparadigma und Bewahrungsfetischismus', 87).
234 See Sebastian-Manès Sprute, 'Dislokation des kamerunischen Kulturerbes in Zahlen', in *Atlas der Abwesenheit: Kameruns Kulturerbe in Deutschland*, ed. Mikaél Assilkinga et al. (Berlin: Reimer, 2023), 44–45.
235 Johann F. G. Umlauff, 'Kurze Erklärung zu den Katalogen N°222 und 223 der Kamerun Sammlung', dated May 1914, SMB-ZA, I/MV 753, E 1055/1914, 322–323.
236 Lessner, 'Die Baluë', 337.
237 Lessner to Linden, dated 11 January 1903, Archives of the Linden Museum, Korrespondenzakte Lessner.
238 We found collections attributed to Captain Guse at the Berlin Ethnological Museum, the Grassi Museum in Leipzig, the University Georg August in Göttingen, and the Landesmuseum Natur und Mensch in Oldenburg; Lessner and Zupitza at the Linden Museum in Stuttgart; and Umber at the Georg August University in Göttingen.
239 Correspondence between Luschan and Langheld, 18 August–2 October 1901, SMB-ZA, I/MV 725, E 863/1901, 59–60.
240 Gesa Grimme found 99 items, see Grimme, *Provenienzforschung im Projekt 'Schwieriges Erbe'*, Linden Museum Stuttgart, 2018, 85, https://epub.ub.uni-muenchen.de/77792/ (accessed 27 November 2023).
241 Lessner to Linden, dated 3 October 1902, in Archives of the Linden Museum, Korrespondenzakte Lessner.
242 See Mekunda, 'Traditional Shrines and Artefacts in Oroko Land', 84.
243 See Louis Perrois and Jean Paul Notué, *Rois et Sculpteurs de l'Ouest Cameroun* (Paris:

Karthala, 1997), 48.
244 See Gustav Conrau, 'Einige Beiträge über die Völker zwischen Mpundu und Bali', BArch R1001/3298, 196–197; Max Buchner, *Aurora colonialis* (Munich: Piloty & Loehle, 1914), 276; and Lessner, 'Die Baluë', 394.
245 See Buchner, *Aurora colonialis*, 276; Zintgraff, *Nord-Kamerun*, 46; Ernst Vollbehr, *Mit Pinsel und Palette durch Kamerun* (Leipzig: List und von Bressensdorf, 1912), 150; Friedrich Autenrieth, *Ins Innerhochland von Kamerun* (Stuttgart: Holland & Josenhaus, 1900), 60; Ute Röschenthaler, 'Max Esser's "Bakundu Fetishes"', *African Arts* 32, no. 4 (1999): 76–80, https://doi.org/10.2307/3337670; and Rosalinde Wilcox, 'Elephants, Ivory and Art: Duala Objects of Persuasion', in *Elephant: The Animal and Its Ivory in African Culture*, ed. Doran H. Ross (Los Angeles, CA: Fowler Museum of Cultural History, University of California, 1992), 260–273.
246 See the sculpted pillars removed and taken to the Museum Five Continents in Munich by Thomas Berké around 1905 or those sent to the Landesmuseum Hanover by Wilko von Frese in 1910. Pierre Harter, *Arts anciens du Cameroun* (Arnouville: Arts d'Afrique noire, 1986), 93.
247 See the description of those shrines in Conrau, 'Einige Beiträge', 196–197.
248 Felix von Luschan to Imperial Government in Kamerun, dated 10 February 1900, SMB-ZA, I/MV 722, E 74/1900.
249 See Bernhard Ankermann to Wilko von Frese, dated 20 December 1910, SMB-ZA, I/MV 750, E 2484/10, 54; also Harter, *Arts anciens du Cameroun*, 93–96.
250 Linden to Lesser, dated 21 October 1902, Archives of the Linden Museum, Korrespondenzakte Lessner.
251 Lessner to Linden, dated 11 August 1902, Archives of the Linden Museum, Korrespondenzakte Lessner.
252 See Machtobjekte ('objects of power') in Mikaél Assilkinga, 'Verkannt, Vermisst, begehrt: Machtobjekte aus Kamerun in Deutschland', in *Atlas der Abwesenheit: Kameruns Kulturerbe in Deutschland*, ed. Mikaél Assilkinga et al. (Berlin: Reimer, 2023), 157–171.

8. Subverting Firepower: A German Cartridge Upcycled as a Snuffbox, a Symbol of Chagga Resistance

253 The project is a collaboration between the Germany-based arts and theatre company Flinn Works, the non-governmental organisation Berlin Postkolonial, and the Old Moshi Cultural Tourism enterprise based in Moshi, Tanzania.
254 *Marejesho* was shown in Keni, Rombo; Marangu; Old Moshi; Kibosho; Machame and Poli, Meru.
255 'Mangi Meli Remains' (2018) was a collaborative research project and exhibition focusing on the resistance of Chagga chief Meli against German colonial rule,

his subsequent execution, and the ongoing search led by his grandson Isaria Meli for his missing remains. For more information, see www.flinnworks.de/en/project/mangi-meli-remains (accessed 6 July 2023).

256 *Marejesho* was also shown in Germany from October 2023 to June 2024 at the Tieranatomisches Theater in Berlin. The German iteration focused on the voices of the descendants and community members.

257 For a comprehensive study of the introduction of tobacco in pre-colonial Africa, see Chris S. Duvall, 'Cannabis and Tobacco in Precolonial and Colonial Africa', in *Oxford Research Encyclopaedia of African History* (Oxford: Oxford University Press, 2017), https://doi.org/10.1093/acrefore/9780190277734.013.44 (accessed 6 November 2023).

258 August Widenmann, *Die Kilimandscharo-Bevölkerung* (Gotha: Justus Perthes, 1899), 59. In this book, the German colonial military doctor, August Widenmann, also mentions the use of cartridges for tobacco (68).

259 Testimony by Mangi Marealle transcribed by German colonial officer St. Paul, dated 18 August 1892, BArch R1001/281, 97–100.

260 Marilee Wood, 'Divergent Patterns in Indian Ocean Trade to East Africa and Southern Africa between the 7th and 17th Centuries CE: The Glass Bead Evidence', *Afriques* 06 (2015), https://doi.org/10.4000/afriques.1782 (accessed 28 October 2023).

261 Georg Volkens, *Der Kilimandscharo* (Berlin: Reimer, 1897), 222.

262 Governor Julius von Soden intended to launch what he called 'a war of revenge and extermination', a term that flirts with genocidal vocabulary (see Report by Soden to Foreign Office, dated 2 October 1892, BArch R1001/281, 113).

263 According to the report, the attacking 'Schutztruppe' consisted of 5 companies with a total of 23 German officers and 566 African *askaris* (see Report from Schele to Foreign Office, dated 13 August 1893, BArch R1001/283, 80).

264 See Telegram by Ernst von Manteuffel, undated, BArch R1001/283, 63.

265 The German military doctor Alexander Becker reports that, according to the Moshi people, they had suffered 135 deaths in the battle. Alexander Becker, *Aus Deutsch-Ostafrikas Sturm- und Drangperiode* (Halle: Hendel, 1911).

266 Index card MAf 27686, catalogue Grassi Museum für Völkerkunde Leipzig, State Collections Dresden (SKD). Schrenck von Notzing gave the cartridge and other belongings to the museum under 'reservation of ownership'. In 1925, after Notzing's death, the museum bought these loaned belongings.

267 Report by Governor Schele to Foreign Office, dated 21 August 1893, BArch R1001/283, 138–144.

268 As part of the *Marejesho* project, several ancestral remains from the leaders hanged by the Germans could be identified, either by DNA matching with living descendants or thanks to historical research. Among them are Mangi Molelia of Kibosho and his brother, Mangi Meli's akida (minister) Sindato

Kiutesha Kiwelu, all held by the Foundation Prussian Cultural Heritage (SPK) in Berlin, as well as Mangi Lobulu of Meru, held by the American Museum of Natural History (AMNH) in New York. See also Erin L. Thompson, 'A New York Museum's House of Bones', *Hyperallergic*, 15 October 2023, https://hyperallergic.com/850350/a-new-york-museums-house-of-bones/ (accessed 6 November 2023).

9. In Defence of Theft?
On the Theft and Restitution of Ngonnso' and Punitive Exhibitions

269   Kim Chakanetsa, 'Cameroon's Ngonnso: "My fight to bring our sacred stolen statue home"', BBC, 17 June 2023, www.bbc.com/news/world-africa-65746910 (accessed 4 January 2024).

270   Humboldt Forum, 'Festrede von Chimamanda Adichie', YouTube, 29 September 2021, https://youtu.be/gMRv5xhMCo4 (accessed 4 January 2024).

271   Despite several sources claiming that Kurt Pavel acquired Ngonnso' peacefully during his visit to Kimbo at the beginning of 1902, we contest that the Nso' would never have willingly relinquished Ngonnso', and argue that Houben's attack and destruction of the palace offers the most plausible scenario. A military doctor under Pavel's command also describes how, 'as commander of the troops, Pavel naturally got the lion's share and carried off the best things, a large part of which he had to donate to the Berlin museum', evidence that further supports the theory of Houben looting Ngonnso' and Pavel claiming it before sending it to the Ethnological Museum (Maximilian Zupitza, Letter to Karl von Linden, dated 13 June 1903, Korrespondenzakte Zupitza, Archives of the Linden Museum Stuttgart).

272   In this chapter, following other writers on Ngonnso', we use the terms 'object', 'artefact', 'effigy', 'statue', 'carving', 'sculpture', interchangeably. We are aware that this is contentious and even controversial. We do so while acknowledging that these terms do not represent the agency or the cultural significance of Ngonnso' to the Nso' people, but are rather based on colonial and anthropological categories. While not necessarily translating the real essence of Ngonnso', the interchangeable use of these terms reflects the fact that Ngonnso''s agency and essence is relational. The presence of Ngonnso' in a museum has reduced her to an 'object', a central impetus for the fight for her restitution. There is therefore no resignification without restitution, and we refrain from performing a linguistic resignification when the reality does not reflect it. In other words, as long as Ngonnso' is in a museum, she is reduced to an object.

273   For more information on the Nso' dynasty and their Fondom, see Paul N. Mzeka, *Four Fons of Nso': Nineteenth and Early Twentieth Century Kingship in the Western Grassfields* (Bamenda: Spider Publishing Enterprise, 1990), 77.

274 See Hans Houben, Bericht über das Gefecht bei Kumbo, dated 20 June 1902, BArch R175-I/112, 34–35.
275 For more information on Nso'–German relations, see V.G. Fanso and E.M. Chilver, 'Nso' and the Germans: The First Encounters in Contemporary Documents and in Oral Tradition', in *Nso' and its Neighbours: Readings in Social History*, ed. B. Chem-Langhëë and V.G. Fanso (Amherst, MA: Amherst College, 1996), 102–131.
276 See Letter from Eckhardt to Luschan, dated 19 June 1907, SMB-ZA, I/MV 446, E 1581/1907; and Letter from Wenckstern to Luschan, dated 27 February 1908, SMB-ZA, I/MV 446, E 2264/1907.
277 Hans Glauning, Bericht über die Bannso-Expedition, BArch R1001/3353, 139.
278 Franz Fanon, *The Wretched of the Earth*, trans. Constance Farrington (New York: Grove Press, 1963 [1961]), 38.
279 Sally Chilver, one of the earliest campaigners on the Nso' side for restitution of Ngonnso', in a personal communication with one of us, had made the observation that perhaps the theft of Ngonnso' could be seen as a 'blessing in disguise', because had she remained in Kimbo, she would have long been eaten by ants and termites.
280 When reporting on his expedition against the Omwang and Maka in 1910, Major Hans Dominik wrote:

> Captain Marschner had long had to recruit auxiliary forces and thereby promised them a share of the female booty, … on the one hand because the people would not risk their lives without a share of female booty, and on the other hand because, without the prospect of getting one or the other transferred [*überwiesen*] to them, they would never spare the lives of those females but would cut them down and eat them up. … I, as an officer, am always aware that I have to stand for my orders. Besides, as a human being, I have carried out in this campaign only deeds for which I am ready to take responsibility and answer to myself. In any case, regardless of the military sentence that may be passed on me by a court martial … I would hereby like to convince my superior authorities that I acted correctly when I used auxiliary warriors and left a certain number of female prisoners to them.

(Hans Dominik to Imperial Government, dated 1 June 1910, BArch R175-I/92, 102–103).

281 See Rossila Goussanou and Fogha MC Refem, 'Des objets en excès et des [im]possibilités à décoloniser les musées', *Trouble dans les Collections*, 10 April 2023, https://troublesdanslescollections.fr/2023/04/10/4320/ (accessed 5 January 2024).

10. The Long Journey of the *Bocio* of Three Danxomè Kings

282   According to the alphabet used for the transcription of Fon language and its concept, *bocio* is spelled *bòcyɔ́*. In this text, we have retained the usual French spelling to facilitate reading.

283   According to our interlocutors, Gabin Djimassè, Bachalou Nondichao and Sébastien Davo, this type of *bocio* is subject to rituals called *wújì* that bestows onto it some special abilities, such as inspiring respect of authority and awe everywhere the king is present.

284   According to our sources, this type of *bocio* was created after the tragic death of King Ghézo during a military expedition.

285   Susan Preston Blier, *African Vodun: Art, Psychology, and Power* (Chicago, IL: University of Chicago Press, 1995), 7.

286   See Richard Francis Burton, *A Mission to Gelele, king of Dahome* (London: Tinsley Brothers, 1864), vol. 2, 4, quoted in Melville Jean Herskovits, *Dahomey, an Ancient West African Kingdom* (New York: J.J. Augustin, 1938), vol. 2, 368; and J. Alfred Skertchly, *Dahomey As It Is: Being a Narrative of Eight Months' Residence in that Country* (London: Chapman and Hall, 1874), 139 and 469.

287   Suzanne Preston Blier, 'Bocio: Arts du Pouvoir', in *Dieux, rois et peuples du Bénin*, ed. Christophe Vital and Hélène Joubert (Paris: Musée du Quai Branly; La Roche-sur-Yon: Somogy, 2008), 38.

288   Suzanne Preston Blier, *Royal Arts of Africa: The Majesty of Form* (London: Laurence King Publishing, 1998), 122.

289   Blier, 'Bocio: Arts du Pouvoir', 41.

290   Galia Tapiero, 'An Object Exhibited', in *Artistes d'Abomey / Artists from Abomey*, ed. Gaëlle Beaujean-Baltzer (Cotonou: Fondation Zinsou; Paris: Musée du Quai Branly, 2009), 317.

291   Jacques Lombard and Paul Mercier, *Guide du Musée d'Abomey* (Porto-Novo: IFAN, 1959).

292   Gaëlle Beaujean-Baltzer (ed.), *Artistes d'Abomey / Artists from Abomey* (Cotonou: Fondation Zinsou; Paris: Musée du Quai Branly, 2009).

293   Herskovits, *Dahomey, an Ancient African Kingdom*, 364–366.

294   Robert Farris Thompson, *Flash of the Spirit: African and Afro American Art and Philosophy* (New York: Random House, 1983), 169.

295   Bachalou Nondichao, 'Sossa Dede', *Artistes d'Abomey/Artists from Abomey* (Cotonou: Fondation Zinsou; Paris: Musée du Quai Branly, 2009), 161.

296   Maurice Delafosse, 'Statues du roi de Dahomé au Musée ethnographique du Trocadéro', *La Nature* (no. 1086, 1894), 262.

297   Emmanuel Georges Waterlot, *Les bas-reliefs des bâtiments royaux d'Abomey, Dahomey* (Paris: Institut d'ethnologie, 1926), 8.

298	In 1930, colonial administrator Christian Merlo offered more than fifty anthropomorphic *bocio* from Abomey to the Musée d'Ethnographie du Trocadéro, which today are in the collection of the Musée du Quai Branly – Jacques Chirac, inventory number 71.1930.21.3 to 71.1930.21.57.
299	Skertchly, *Dahomey As It Is*, 254.
300	Blier, *African Vodun*, 336, 333 and 348 [translation from French].
301	Blier, *Royal Arts of Africa*, 121.
302	Tapiero, 'An Object Exhibited', 317.
303	Alexandre d'Albéca noticed these particular dispositions and wrote about them. Nevertheless, the *bocio* mentioned there did not refer to the kings but to deceased ancestors elevated to the status of divine figures and to vodun related to the establishment of the royal family. See Alexandre L. d'Albéca, *La France au Dahomey* (Paris: Hachette et Cie, 1895), 109.
304	Gaëlle Beaujean-Baltzer, 'Du trophée à l'œuvre: parcours de cinq artefacts du royaume d'Abomey', *Gradhiva* 6 (2007): 76, https://doi.org/10.4000/gradhiva.987.
305	For more on the colonial war, the expedition, and the spoils of war, see Gaëlle Beaujean, *L'Art de Cour d'Abomey: Le Sens des Objets* (Dijon: Les Presses du Réel, 2019), 223–258.
306	D'Albéca, *La France au Dahomey*, 111. The derogatory term 'bazaar' in French comes for the neutral Persian word بازار which means 'market'. This negative connotation is the result of decades of Francophone colonial and racist discourse that shaped the historical semantics of the term.
307	Gaëlle Beaujean, 'L'Art de Cour d'Abomey: Le Sens des Objets', PhD thesis (Paris: EHESS, 2015).
308	In 1895, the same general donated another series of looted assets that he had received from the expeditionary force under this command.
309	Delafosse, 'Statues du roi de Dahomé', 263.
310	Christine Mengin (ed.), *Le Corbusier et les arts dits «primitifs»* (Paris: Éditions de la Villette, 2019), 321. These sketches are kept by the Fondation Le Corbusier in Paris, archive number FLC3864, FLC 4061, FLC6338 and FLC5850.
311	Veronique Boone, '*Le Poème électronique*: De l'art primitif au multimédia', *Le Corbusier et les arts dits «primitifs»*, ed. Christine Mengin (Paris: Éditions de la Villette, 2019), 221 and 229.
312	See photograph number PV0057919, Musée du Quai Branly – Jacques Chirac.
313	See Loi n° 2002-5 du 4 janvier 2002 relative aux musées de France, in particular, article 11.
314	Felwine Sarr and Bénédicte Savoy, *Restituer le patrimoine africain* (Paris: Philippe Rey, Seuil, 2018).
315	The sabre known as that of El Hadj Omar Tall, formerly in the Musée de l'Armée, was returned to Senegal. The twenty-six cultural assets from Benin

all come from Abomey. They had all been seized by General Dodds on site and then donated to the Musée d'Ethnographie du Trocadéro. The assets include regalia in various materials, including three thrones; an engraved stool, portable metal altars, one bearing the emblem of Béhanzin and the other the emblem of the ancestor of the Agassou dynasty (the panther), four palace doors and the three *bocio*; a series of portable metal altars and 'ethnographic objects' such as an engraved calabash, a weaving loom, a leather bag and other items associated with the army, including 'recade' sticks and a soldier's uniform.

316 Among others, guests included the late King of Abomey, Dada Sagbadju Glèlè, the King of Nikki, the King of Savalou and the King of Kétou (kingdom of former foes of Abomey).

317 In fact, the exhibition of the twenty-six treasures overshadowed the contemporary art exhibition was organised at the same time. Referred to as a 'diptych exhibition' by the organisers, that is, a combination of two exhibitions into one, the curatorial venture is difficult to apprehend. One of the impressions left on the visitor is that the contemporary art exhibition serves at times as a foil to the exhibition of the twenty-six restituted works.

318 The real hero, however, seems to be the head of executive power, since he succeeded in bringing back the royal treasures despite the difficulties that made this return seem impossible. In the eyes of tradition and in the consciousness of the Beninese people, the Head of State thus became the worthy successor to the kings of Danxomè, whose struggle he is completing.

319 Benin President Patrice Talon himself alluded to this in his speech at the reception of the 26 works at the Élysée Palace on 9 November 2021:

> Mr Chairman, it is regrettable that this act of restitution, so appreciable as it is, does not give us complete satisfaction. Indeed, how can you expect me to be so enthusiastic when I leave here with the 26 works, while the Gou god, an emblematic work representing the god of metals and the forge, and the Fa tablet, a mythical work of divination by the famous diviner Gèdègbé, and many others, continue to be held here in France to the great displeasure of their rightful owners?

Patrice Talon, 'Allocution de Patrice TALON à l'occasion de la cérémonie de restitution de 26 oeuvres du patrimoine culturel du Bénin', *Les Trésors Royaux du Bénin*, https://tresorsroyaux.bj/article/9/allocution-patrice-talon-occasion-ceremonie-restitution-oeuvres-patrimoine-culturel-benin/ (accessed 6 March 2024).

320 The authors of this chapter visited the exhibition seven times and conducted interviews with visitors on site. Such responses from students and scholars are also visible in Mati Diop's film *Dahomey*, which was awarded the Golden Bear at the Berlin Film Festival in 2024.

321 In the scenography of the exhibition *Art of Benin. D'hier à aujourd'hui: de la restitution à la révélation* the thrones and *bocio* stand under the brightest spotlight, thereby showing the extent of the power of the kings of Danxomè.

PART III: THE SACRED

11. Degodding Maqdala

322 Trevenen J. Holland and Henry M. Hozier, *Record of the Expedition to Abyssinia* (London: Her Majesty's Stationary Office, 1870).
323 Rita Pankhurst, 'The Library of Emperor Tewodros II at Mäqdäla (Magdala)', *Bulletin of the School of Oriental and African Studies* 36, no. 1 (1973): 19, https://doi.org/10.1017/S0041977X00097974.
324 'Maqdala Collection', British Museum, https://www.britishmuseum.org/about-us/british-museum-story/contested-objects-collection/maqdala-collection (accessed 11 February 2024); see also, Holland and Hozier, *Record of the Expedition to Abyssinia*.
325 'In China (1860), in Korea (1866), in Ethiopia (1868), in the Asante Kingdom (1874), in Cameroon (1884), in the Tanganyika Lake region, and the future Belgian Congo (1884), in the current region of Mali (1890), at Dahomey (1892), in the Kingdom of Benin (1897), in present-day Guinea (1898), in Indonesia (1906), in Tanzania (1907), the military raids and so-called punitive expeditions conducted by England, Belgium, Germany, Holland, and France, during the 19th century became occasions for unprecedented pillaging'; see Felwine Sarr and Bénédicte Savoy, *The Restitution of African Cultural Heritage: Toward a New Relational Ethics* (Berlin: Matthes & Seitz, 2019), 10.
326 See, for example, the campaign Strike MoMA (International Imagination of Anti-National, Anti-Imperialist Feelings, *Strike MoMa Reader* [New York, 2022]); the interventions by pan-African activist Mwazulu Diyabanza at the Musée du Quai Branly – Jacques Chirac in Paris, the Musée d'Arts Africains, Océaniens et Amérindiens in Marseille (France) and the Africa Museum in Berg en Dal (The Netherlands); the work of Chidi Nwaubani and the artistic collective LOOTY; the campaign No Humboldt 21! and the subsequent protests against the erection of the Humboldt Forum; as well as protests at the British Museum like the one staged by the activist collective BP or not BP? in 2020 (BP or not BP?, 'Victory at the British Museum!', 20 August 2020, https://bp-or-not-bp.org/2023/08/20/victory-at-the-british-museum/ [accessed 2 April 2024]).
327 See Harry Garuba, 'Explorations in Animist Materialism: Notes on Reading/Writing African Literature, Culture, and Society', *Public Culture* 15, no. 2 (2003): 261–286, https://doi.org/10.1215/08992363-15-2-261.
328 For further reading on the question of animism and its problematic nature in African spiritual contexts, see Stephen Owoahene-Acheampong, *Inculturation*

and *African Religion: Indigenous and Western Approaches to Medical Practice* (New York: Peter Land Publishing, 1998), 49–54; and J.S. Mbiti, African Religions and Philosophy (New York: Frederick Praeger, 1969), 7–9.

329 Sylvia Wynter, 'Unsettling the Coloniality of Being/Power/Truth/Freedom: Towards the Human, after Man, Its Overrepresentation – An Argument', CR: *The New Centennial Review* 3, no. 3 (Fall 2003): 273, https://doi.org/10.1353/ncr.2004.0015.

330 Pankhurst, 'The Library of Emperor Tewodros II at Mäqdäla (Magdala)', 23.

331 Holger Hoock, *Empires of the Imagination: Politics, War and the Arts in the British World, 1750–1850* (London: Profile Books, 2010), 7.

332 'The status and power of the archive derive from this entanglement of building and documents. The archive has neither status nor power without an architectural dimension, which encompasses the physical space of the site of the building, its motifs and columns, the arrangement of rooms, the organization of "files", the labyrinth of corridors, and the degree of discipline, half-light and austerity that gives the place something of a nature of a temple and a cemetery: a religious space because a set of rituals is constantly taking place there, rituals that […] are quasi-magical in nature, and a cemetery in the sense that fragments of lives and pieces of time are interred there, their shadows and footprints inscribed on paper and preserved like so many relics.' See Achille Mbembe, 'The Power of the Archive and its Limits', in *Refiguring the Archive*, ed. Carolyn Hamilton et al. (Dordrecht: Springer, 2002), 19–27.

333 Wynter, 'Unsettling the Coloniality of Being/Power/Truth/Freedom', 269.

334 Bahru Zewde, *A History of Modern Ethiopia, 1855–1974* (London: James Currey; Athens, GA: Ohio University Press; Addis Ababa: Addis Ababa University Press, 1991), 8.

335 Yirga Gelaw Woldeyes and Tekletsadik Belachew, 'Decolonizing the Environment through African Epistemologies: Descolonización ambiental mediante epistemologías africanas', *Gestión y Ambiente* 24, no. 1 (July 2021): 73, https://doi.org/10.15446/ga.v24nsupl1.91881.

336 For the implication of this concept in the diaspora, see Joachim Person, 'Planting of the *Tabot* on European Soil: The Trajectory of Ethiopian Orthodox Involvement with European Continent', *Studies in World Christianity* 16, no. 3 (December 2010): 320–340, https://doi.org/10.3366/swc.2010.0107.

337 Woldeyes and Belachew, 'Decolonizing the Environment', 73.

338 Zewde, *A History of Modern Ethiopia*, 27.

339 Zewde, *A History of Modern Ethiopia*, 28.

340 Pankhurst, 'The Library of Emperor Tewodros II at Mäqdäla (Magdala)', 16.

341 Pankhurst, 'The Library of Emperor Tewodros II at Mäqdäla (Magdala)', 20.

342 Pankhurst, 'The Library of Emperor Tewodros II at Mäqdäla (Magdala)', 15.

343 Zewde, *A History of Modern Ethiopia*, 32.

344 Zewde, *A History of Modern Ethiopia*, 34.
345 We understand that the capitalisation of 'whiteness' is an issue that remains contested: some people do, and some people don't. To us, capitalising 'Black' is not simply an acknowledgement of the construction of race, but also an intervention against anti-Blackness. Therefore, capitalisation of 'white' presents a false equivalence between the ongoing construction of whiteness and Blackness. For further reading, see Mike Law, 'Why We Capitalize 'Black' (and Not 'white')', *Columbia Journalism Review*, 16 June 2020, https://www.cjr.org/analysis/capital-b-black-styleguide.php (accessed 4 April 2024); and Julia Craven, 'Capitalizing *White* Won't Fix the Media's Racism Problem', *Slate*, 5 August 2020, https://slate.com/news-and-politics/2020/08/capitalizing-white.html (accessed 4 April 2024).
346 Wynter, 'Unsettling the Coloniality of Being/Power/Truth/Freedom', 300.
347 Lucia Patrizio Gunning and Debbie Challis, 'Planned Plunder, the British Museum, and the 1868 Maqdala Expedition', *The Historical Journal* 66, no. 3 (2023): 554, https://doi.org/10.1017/S0018246X2200036X.
348 Zewde, *A History of Modern Ethiopia*, 39.
349 Andrew Heavens, *The Prince and the Plunder: How Britain took One Small Boy and Hundreds of Treasures from Ethiopia* (Cheltenham: The History Press, 2023).
350 Gunning and Challis, 'Planned Plunder, the British Museum, and the 1868 Maqdala Expedition', 565.
351 Pankhurst, 'The Library of Emperor Tewodros II at Mäqdäla (Magdala)', 19.
352 Pankhurst, 'The Library of Emperor Tewodros II at Mäqdäla (Magdala)', 16.
353 Mabel O. Wilson, 'They Once were Somewhere Else: The Transplantations of *The Histories (Le Mancenillier)*', in *David Hartt: The Histories*, ed. Cole Akers (Los Angeles, CA: Inventory Press, 2022), 100.
354 Gunning and Challis, 'Planned Plunder, the British Museum, and the 1868 Maqdala Expedition', 560–561.
355 Henry M. Stanley, *Coomassie and Magdala: The Story of Two British Campaigns in Africa* (New York: Harper & Brothers, 1874), 470.
356 Gunning and Challis, 'Planned Plunder, the British Museum, and the 1868 Maqdala Expedition', 561
357 Alexander G. Weheliye, *Habeas Viscus: Racializing Assemblages, Biopolitics, and Black Feminist Theories of the Human* (Durham, NC: Duke University Press, 2014), 40.
358 Wynter, 'Unsettling the Coloniality of Being/Power/Truth/Freedom', 304.
359 Gunning and Challis, 'Planned Plunder, the British Museum, and the 1868 Maqdala Expedition', 564.
360 Pankhurst, 'The Library of Emperor Tewodros II at Mäqdäla (Magdala)', 40.
361 'Maqdala Collection', British Museum.
362 Pankhurst, 'The Library of Emperor Tewodros II at Mäqdäla (Magdala)', 40. For a more recent accounting of the manuscripts, see 'The Looted Library', *The*

Prince and the Plunder: https://www.theprinceandtheplunder.com/the-looted-library/ (accessed 22 February 2024).

363 Christina Sharpe, 'Antiblack Weather vs. Black Microclimates', *The Funambulist* 14 (3 November 2017), https://thefunambulist.net/magazine/14-toxic-atmospheres/32058-2 (accessed 2 April 2024).

12. *Nkisi nkonde* of Chief Ne Kuko of Boma: The Tragic Spoliation of a Sacred Sculpture

364 Jan Vansina, 'Préface', in *Du Sang sur les Lianes. Léopold II et son Congo*, ed. Daniël Vangroenweghe (Brussels: Didier Hatier, 1985), 9–12.

365 Stephen Ellis, 'La violence dans l'histoire de l'Afrique', in *La mémoire du Congo: Le temps colonial*, ed. Jean-Luc Vellut (Ghent: Snoeck/MRAC, 2005), 37–42.

366 See Jean-Luc Vellut, 'Réflexions sur la violence dans l'histoire de l'État indépendant du Congo', in *La Nouvelle Histoire du Congo. Mélanges eurafricains offerts à Frans Bontick*, c.i.c.m, ed. Mabiala Mantuba-Ngoma (Tervuren: Musée Royal d'Afrique Centrale; Paris: L'Harmattan, 2004), 269–287; and Sara Van Beurden et al., 'Provenance, politique et possession d'objets africains: une introduction', in *(Re)making Collections: Origins, Trajectories & Reconnections*, ed. Sarah Van Beurden, Didier Gondola and Agnès Lacaille (Tervuren: Africamuseum, 2023), 47–80.

367 Sarah Van Beurden, *Congo en vitrine. Art africain, Muséologie et politique. Les Musées de Kinshasa et de Tervuren* (Tervuren: AfricaMuseum, 2021), 38.

368 Boris Wastiau, 'The Violence of Collecting: Objects, Images, and People from Colonial Congo' (MRAC, 2010). Also presented at the panel discussion 'History, Museums, and the Politics of Memory: The Congo in Belgium after King Leopold's Ghost' of the American Historical Association's annual meeting in New York, 4 January 2009.

369 Julien Volper and Philippe de Moerloose, *Art sans pareil: Objets merveilleux du Musée royal de l'Afrique centrale* (Tervuren: AfricaMuseum, 2019), 135.

370 Pamphile Mabiala Mantuba-Ngoma, 'Violence dans une capitale coloniale: Boma 1886–1923', in *Histoire, conscience nationale congolaise et africaine*, ed. Stanislas Bucyalimwe Marro and Emmanuel Murhula A. Nashi (Brussels: Scribes, 2015), 162.

371 Agnès Lacaille, 'Statue Nkisi Nkonde', AfricaMuseum, 8 October 2021, www.africamuseum.be/fr/learn/provenance/nkisi-nkonde (accessed 12 December 2023).

372 Alexandre Delcommune, *Vingt années de vie africaine au Congo Belge (1874–1893): récits de voyages, d'aventures et d'exploration*, vol. I (Brussels: Ferdinand Larcier, 1922), 90.

373 Delcommune, *Vingt années de vie africaine au Congo Belge*, 93.

374 Delcommune, *Vingt années de vie africaine au Congo Belge*, 163.

375 Delcommune, *Vingt années de vie africaine au Congo Belge*, 165.
376 Julien Volper, 'Statue anthropomorphe nkisi nkonde', in *Art sans pareil: Objets merveilleux du Musée royal de l'Afrique centrale*, ed. Julien Volper (Tervuren: Musée Royal de l'Afrique Centrale, 2019), 15.
377 Delcommune, *Vingt années de vie africaine au Congo Belge*, 96.
378 Delcommune, *Vingt années de vie africaine au Congo Belge*, 103.
379 Maarten Couttenier, 'EO.0.0.7943', BMGN: *Low Countries Historical Review* 133, no. 2 (2018): 79–90, https://doi.org/10.18352/bmgn-lchr.10553.
380 Delcommune, *Vingt années de vie africaine au Congo Belge*, 160.
381 Patricia Van Schuylenbergh, *Faune sauvage et colonisation. Une histoire de destruction et de protection de la nature congolaise* (1885–1960) (Brussels: PIE Peter Lang; Berlin: Collection Outre-Mers, 2020), 130.
382 See Friedrich von Bose, 'Strategische Reflexivität: Das Berliner Humboldt Forum und die postkoloniale Kritik', in *Historische Anthropologie: Kultur, Gesellschaft, Alltag*, ed. Rebekka Habermas and Susanna Burghartz (Cologne: Böhlau, 2017), 409–417.
383 See, for instance, Bénédicte Savoy, *Africa's Struggle for Its Art: History of a Postcolonial Defeat*, trans. Susanne Meyer-Abich (Princeton, NJ: Princeton University Press, 2022), 29–34.
384 Placide Mumbembele Sanger, 'Le retour du masque kakuungu en République Démocratique du Congo: Au-delà du geste', in *(Re)making Collections: Origins, Trajectories & Reconnections*, ed. Sarah Van Beurden, Didier Gondola and Agnès Lacaille (Tervuren: AfricaMuseum, 2023), 277–287.
385 'Voici la lettre du roi Philippe à Félix Tshisekedi', *L'Echo*, 30 June 2020, https://www.lecho.be/economie-politique/belgique/general/voici-la-lettre-du-roi-philippe-a-felix-tshisekedi/10236172.html (accessed 12 March 2024).
386 The decree issued by the Ministry of Culture, Arts and Heritage: CAB/MIN/CAP/JJM/JLM/022/2023.
387 For example, in 2018, the journalist Michel Bouffiaux published a two-part investigative article in *Paris Match Belgique* in which he revealed the presence of the skull of the Tabwa chief Lusinga at the Museum of Natural Sciences in Brussels and denounced its retention. Since then, he has been campaigning for its repatriation to the Congo. See Michel Bouffiaux, 'Lusinga… Et 300 autres crânes d'Africains conservés à Bruxelles (partie 1): Un vieux registre du Musée du Congo', *Paris Match Belgique*, 23 May 2018, https://tinyurl.com/yupnqpnh; and 'Lusinga… Et 300 autres crânes d'Africains conservés à Bruxelles (partie 2): Le «pauvre diable» de l'ULB', *Paris Match Belgique*, 24 May 2018, https://tinyurl.com/ykgug2z3 (accessed 3 March 2024).
388 Article 2 of Decree no. 23/06 of 20 February 2023 on the creation, organisation and operation of a National Commission responsible for the repatriation of cultural property, archives and human remains removed from the Congolese

cultural heritage, p.2.
389 Couttenier, 'EO.0.0.7943'.

13. The *Ngadji* of the Pokomo:
On Revolutionary Responses, Release and Relationships

390 Annabelle Steffes-Halmer, 'Looted Art from Kenya: Empty Display Cases', *DW*, 6 March 2021, www.dw.com/en/looted-art-from-kenya-when-the-display-cases-remain-empty/a-57735942 (accessed 4 January 2024).
391 Alex Greenberger, 'The Benin Bronzes, Explained: Why a Group of Plundered Artworks Continues to Generate Controversy', *ArtNews*, 2 April 2021, www.artnews.com/feature/benin-bronzes-explained-repatriation-british-museum-humboldt-forum-1234588588/ (accessed 4 January 2024).
392 Eva L.R. Meyerowitz, 'Ancient Bronzes in the Royal Palace at Benin', *The Burlington Magazine for Connoisseurs* 83, no. 487 (1943): 248–253.
393 Malidoma Patrice Somé, *Of Water and the Spirit: Ritual, Magic, and Initiation in the Life of an African Shaman* (New York: TarcherPerigee, Penguin, 1995), 175.
394 See Nosmot Gbadamosi, 'Africa's Stolen Art Debate Is Frozen in Time', *Foreign Policy*, 15 May 2022, https://foreignpolicy.com/2022/05/15/africa-art-museum-europe-restitution-debate-book-colonialism-artifacts/ (accessed 4 January 2024).
395 Kristin Hausler, 'On International Museum Day: A Call to Increase Funding for Return & Restitution', *British Institute of International and Comparative Law*, 18 May 2023, www.biicl.org/blog/59/on-international-museum-day-a-call-to-increase-funding-for-return-restitution (accessed 4 January 2024).
396 Editors' note: the case of the sacred drum of the Tchaman *djidji ayôkwe*, which in 2024 was in the process of being returned to Côte d'Ivoire, after having been kept at the Musée de l'Homme and the Musée du Quai Branly – Jacques Chirac in Paris, offers an interesting parallel from West Africa. The Ivorian anthropologist Georges Niangoran-Bouah recounts that, after presenting photographs of the slit drum to community members in Adjamé in 1958 as part of his research, the population reacted heavily to these images: 'elders shouted war cries, lamentations were heard and many young people wanted to obtain an image of the object they only knew by name'; see Julien Volper, 'Divergent Accounts and Grey Areas Surrounding the Ivorian Drum Known as *djidji ayôkwe*', Varia 19 (2023): 101–118, https://doi.org/10.4000/aaa.5036.
397 Jasmine Atieno, 'Why the Revered Ngadji Still Beats in the Heart of the Pokomo', *The People Daily*, 21 July 2021, www.pd.co.ke/lifestyle/why-the-revered-ngadji-still-beats-in-the-heart-of-the-pokomo-86301/ (accessed 11 January 2024).
398 Max Bearak, 'Kenya's Pokomo People Ask the British to Return What was Stolen: Their Source of Power', *The Washington Post*, 9 August 2019, www.

washingtonpost.com/world/2019/08/09/kenyas-pokomo-people-ask-british-return-what-was-stolen-their-source-power/ (accessed 11 January 2024).
399 Bearak, 'Kenya's Pokomo'.
400 Kehinde Andrews, 'The Psychosis of Whiteness: The Celluloid Hallucinations of *Amazing Grace and Belle*', *The Journal of Black Studies* 47, no. 5 (2016): 435–453, https://doi.org/10.1177/0021934716638802.
401 Monica L. Udvardy, Linda L. Giles and John B. Mitsanze, 'The Transatlantic Trade in African Ancestors: Mijikenda Memorial Statues (Vigango) and the Ethics of Collecting and Curating Non-Western Cultural Property', *American Anthropologist* 105, no. 3 (2003): 566–580, https://doi.org/10.1525/aa.2003.105.3.566.
402 Joseph Nevadomsky, 'The Vigango Affair: The Enterprise of Repatriating Mijikenda Memorial Figures to Kenya', *African Arts* 51, no. 2 (2018): 58–69, https://doi.org/10.1162/afar_a_00403. In the online collection of the British Museum, inventory numbers Af1908,0723.89, Af1908,0723.90, Af1908,0723.91 and Af1908,0723.92 are *vigango* labelled as 'grave markers'.
403 Marc Lacey, quoted in Nevadomsky, 'The Vigango Affair', 62.
404 Lotte Arndt, 'Poisonous Heritage: Chemical Conservation, Monitored Collections, and the Threshold of Ethnological Museums', *Museum and Society* 20, no. 2 (2022): 282–301, https://doi.org/10.29311/mas.v20i2.4031.
405 Gareth Harris, 'Nigeria Transfers Ownership of Benin Bronzes to Royal Ruler – Confusing European Museums' Plans to Return Artefacts', *The Art Newspaper*, 26 April 2023, www.theartnewspaper.com/2023/04/26/who-will-museums-partner-with-over-benin-bronzes-now-eyebrows-raised-as-latest-nigerian-government-announcement-makes-oba-owner-of-artefacts (accessed 11 January 2024).
406 See David Cameron's statement on an 'unworkable precedent' ('Koh-i-Noor diamond 'staying put' in UK says Cameron', *BBC*, 29 July 2010, www.bbc.com/news/uk-politics-10802469 (accessed 11 January 2024).
407 Manuela Bauche, 'Cuban Corals in East Berlin's Natural History Museum, 1967–74', Representations, 28 March 2018, www.representations.org/cuban-corals-in-east-berlins-natural-history-museum-1967-74/ (accessed 11 January 2024).
408 Kwame Gyekye, 'African Ethics', *The Stanford Encyclopaedia of Philosophy*, ed. N. Zalta (Fall 2011 edn), https://plato.stanford.edu/archives/fall2011/entries/african-ethics/ (accessed 11 January 2024).
409 'Conflict', *British Museum*, www.britishmuseum.org/about-us/british-museum-story/collecting-histories (accessed 11 January 2024).
410 'The Head of Ife Replica', *The British Museum Shop*, www.britishmuseumshoponline.org/the-head-of-ife-replica.html (accessed 11 January 2024).
411 Etsey Atisu, 'Here's Why the Pokomo of Kenya want Britain to Return their

Sacred "Ngadji" Drum Stolen 111 Years Ago', *Face2Face Africa*, 13 August 2019, https://face2faceafrica.com/article/heres-why-the-pokomo-of-kenya-want-britain-to-return-their-sacred-ngadji-drum-stolen-111-years-ago (accessed 11 January 2024).

412   See *The Human Library Organisation*, https://humanlibrary.org/ (accessed 11 January 2024).

413   Rowena Mason, 'Jamaica Should "Move On from Painful Legacy of Slavery", Says Cameron', *The Guardian*, 30 September 2015, www.theguardian.com/world/2015/sep/30/jamaica-should-move-on-from-painful-legacy-of-slavery-says-cameron (accessed 11 January 2024).

414   See Gloria Wekker, 'Afropessimism', *European Journal of Women's Studies* 28, no. 1 (2021): 86–97, https://doi.org/10.1177/1350506820971224.

415   Dalya Alberge, 'British Museum is World's Largest Receiver of Stolen Goods, Says QC', *Guardian*, 4 November 2019, www.theguardian.com/world/2019/nov/04/british-museum-is-worlds-largest-receiver-of-stolen-goods-says-qc (accessed 11 January 2024).

416   Divine Ikubor alias @heisrema, tweet on 16 November 2023, *Twitter/X*, https://twitter.com/heisrema/status/1725112280008827051.

417   Aderemi S. Ajala, et al, 'Conceptualization of Traditional Healing System in Yoruba Worldviews', *Anthropology and Ethnology Open Access Journal* 2, no. 2 (2019): 000126, https://doi.org/10.23880/aeoaj-16000126.

418   Oscar Holland and Martin Goillandeau, 'British Museum Asks Public to Help Recover Stolen treasures', CNN, 27 September 2023, https://edition.cnn.com/style/british-museum-public-hotline-stolen-treasures-intl/index.html (accessed 11 January 2024).

14. Where are Nehanda's Remains?
A Zimbabwean Search in the Context of Shifting Museum Politics

419   David Smith, 'Robert Mugabe tells Natural History Museum to Return Human Skulls', *Guardian*, 13 August 2015, www.theguardian.com/world/2015/aug/13/mugabe-demands-return-of-skulls-from-londons-natural-history-museum (accessed 4 January 2024).

420   Patrick Wolfe, 'Settler Colonialism and the Elimination of the Native', *Journal of Genocide Research* 8, no. 4 (2006): 387–409, https://doi.org/10.1080/14623520601056240.

421   Ruramisai Charumbira, 'Nehanda (d. c.1460)', in *The Dictionary of African Biography*, ed. Henry Louis Gates, Emmanuel Akyeampong and Steven J. Niven (Oxford University Press, 2012), 5.

422   Ruramisai Charumbira, 'Charwe (c.1862–1898)', in *The Dictionary of African Biography*, ed. Henry Louis Gates, Emmanuel Akyeampong and Steven J. Niven (Oxford University Press, 2012).

423 David Beach, *A Zimbabwean Past: Shona Dynastic Histories and Oral Traditions* (Gweru: Mambo Press, 1994), 10–18.
424 Conference presentation attended by Farai Chabata at the Department of History of the University of Zimbabwe in 1995.
425 Terence Ranger, Revolt in *Southern Rhodesia, 1896–7: A Study in African Resistance* (Evanston, IL: Northwestern University Press, 1967), 1–11.
426 Daily News, 30 July 1962, quoted in Sabelo J. Ndlovu-Gatsheni, *Do 'Zimbabweans' Exist?* (Bern: Peter Lang, 2009), 80.
427 Panashe Chigumadzi, *These Bones Will Rise Again* (London: Indigo Press, 2018), 12.
428 Tabona Shoko, *'My Bones shall Rise Again': War Veterans, Spirits and Land Reform in Zimbabwe* (Leiden: African Studies Centre, 2006), 1–17.
429 Misheck Sibanda, 'Early Foundations of Africa Nationalism', in *Turmoil and Tenacity: Zimbabwe 1890–1990*, ed. Canaan Banana (Harare: College Press, 1989), 25–49.
430 Cara Krmpotich, Joost Fontein and John Harries, 'The Substance of Bones: The Emotive Materiality and Affective Presence of Human Remains', *Journal of Material Culture* 15, no. 4 (2010): 371–384, https://doi.org/10.1177/1359183510382965.
431 Terence Ranger, 'Nationalist Historiography, Patriotic History and the History of the Nation: The Struggle over the Past in Zimbabwe', *Journal of Southern African Studies* 30, no. 2 (2004): 215–234, https://doi.org/10.1080/0305707042000215338.
432 See Sibanda, 'Early Foundations of Africa Nationalism', 27.
433 Achille Mbembe, 'Decolonizing Knowledge and the Question of the Archive', lecture delivered at the Wits Institute for Social and Economic Research, 2015; and Ciraj Rassool, 'Re-Storing the Skeletons of Empire: Return, Reburial and Rehumanisation in Southern Africa', *Journal of Southern African Studies* 41, no. 3 (2015): 653–670, https://doi.org/10.1080/03057070.2015.1028002.
434 Erin Osman, 'Should Museums Repatriate Stolen Artefacts? In Conversation with Dr. Njabulo Chipangura', *The Mancunion*, 23 November 2023, https://mancunion.com/2023/11/23/should-museums-repatriate-stolen-artefacts-in-conversation-with-dr-njabulo-chipangura/?swcfpc=1 (accessed 27 November 2023).
435 Adam Maidment, '"Each Thing has Its Own Story" – Manchester Museum Hands Back 174 Aboriginal Artefacts in Landmark Repatriation', *The Manchester Evening News*, 5 September 2023, www.manchestereveningnews.co.uk/whats-on/arts-culture-news/each-thing-story-manchester-museum-27656783 (accessed 27 November 2023).
436 Tony Bennett, 'Introduction: Museums, Power, Knowledge', *Museum Worlds: Advances in Research* 6, no. 1 (2018): 1–6, https://doi.org/10.3167/armw.2018.060102.

437 Walter Mignolo, 'Museums in the Colonial Horizon of Modernity: Fred Wilson's *Mining the Museum* (1992)', *in Globalization and Contemporary Art*, ed. Jane Harris (Hoboken, NJ: Wiley-Blackwell, 2011), 71–85.

438 Rachael Minott, 'The Past is Now: Confronting Museums' Complicity in Imperial Celebration', *Third Text* 33, no. 4–5 (2019): 559–574, https://doi.org/10.1080/09528822.2019.1654206.

439 Lizzie Muller and Caroline Langhill, 'Introduction: How Lively Objects Disrupt Disciplinary Display', in *Curating Lively Objects: Exhibitions Beyond Disciplines*, ed. Lizzie Muller and Caroline Langhill (London: Routledge, 2022), 1–23.

440 Bruno Brulon Soares, *The Anticolonial Museum: Reclaiming our Colonial Heritage* (London: Routledge, 2023), 6.

441 Njabulo Chipangura, 'The Benin Tusk and Zulu Beadwork: Practicing Decolonial Work at Manchester Museum' Through Shared Authority', *Museum Anthropology* 46, no. 2 (2023): 106–116, https://doi.org/10.1111/muan.12279.

442 Minott, 'The Past is Now', 70.

443 Njabulo Chipangura and Jesmael Mataga, *Museums as Agents for Social Change: Decolonisation at Mutare Museum* (London: Routledge, 2021), 1–10.

444 Kassim Sumaya, 'The Museum Will not be Decolonised', *Media Diversified* 11, no. 15 (2017): 1–14, https://mediadiversified.org/2017/11/15/the-museum-will-not-be-decolonised/.

445 Eve Tuck and K. Wayne Yang, 'Decolonisation is not a Metaphor', *Decolonization: Indigeneity, Education and Society* 1, no. 1 (2012): 1–40.

446 Chip Colwell, *Plundered Skulls and Stolen Spirits: Inside the Fight to Reclaim Native America's Culture* (Chicago, IL: University of Chicago Press, 2017), 9.

447 Graham Aplin, *Heritage: Identification, Conservation and Management* (Oxford: Oxford University Press, 2011), 10–28.

448 Tinashe Mawere, 'The Erecting of Nehanda', Centre for Sexualities, Aids and Gender, 18 August 2021, www.csagup.org/2021/08/18/the-erecting-of-nehanda/ (accessed 4 January 2024).

449 Njabulo Chipangura, 'The Politicisation of Liberation-Struggle Exhumations in Eastern Zimbabwe', *Journal of Southern African Studies* 46, no. 5 (2020): 1037–1054, https://doi.org/10.1080/03057070.2020.1807102.

450 Richard Werbner, 'Smoke from the Barrel of a Gun', in *Memory and the Postcolony: African Anthropology and the Critique of Power*, ed. Richard Werbner (London: Zed Press, 1998), 54–58.

451 Jesmael Mataga and Farai M. Chabata, 'Preserving Spiritual Heritage in Zimbabwe: The Case of Gomba/Upper Mazowe Valley', *Zimbabwean Prehistory* 28 (2008): 53.

452 NHM_London, 'Answer to @zimboguide', Twitter, 27 May 2021, https://twitter.com/NHM_London/status/1397896654301323264 (accessed 4 January 2024).

15. *Byéri*:
Ancestor Guardian Figures of the Kwasio People in Southern Cameroon

453   For more on the Kwasio language community, the common origins and the very similarly structured societies of Mbvumbo and Mabi, see Alphonse Kisito Bouh Ma Sitna, *Reconstitution des migrations ancestrales des Kwasio ou Bantu d'Afrique centrale de 1628 à 1906* (Saint-Denis: Edilivre, 2016), 12–17.

454   'An Iconic FANG MABEA figure formerly owned by Félix Fénéon & Jacques Kerchache Achieves €4.4 Million ($5.9 Million) Today at Sotheby's Paris', *Artkhade*, 18 June 2014, www.artkhade.com/en/articles/570/an-iconic-fang-mabea-figure-formerly-owned-by-felix-feneon-jacques-kerchache-achieves-4-4-million-5-9-million-today-at-sotheby-s-paris (accessed 9 November 2023).

455   See Perrick Moritz, 'Paris: une statue Fang Mabea vendue 4,35 millions d'euros chez Sotheby's', *Art Without Skin*, 18 June 2014, https://artwithoutskin.com/2014/06/18/paris-une-statue-fang-mabea-vendue-435-millions-deuros-chez-sothebys/ (accessed 4 July 2023).

456   Eira Rojas, *A Twentieth Century Man: Reevaluating Félix Fénéon, Surrealist Mentor* (London: Courtauld Institute of Art, 2014), 37.

457   '#36 Statue, Fang Mabea, début XIXe siècle', Sotheby's auction catalogue Arts d'Afrique et d'Océanie, 18 June 2014, www.sothebys.com/en/auctions/ecatalogue/2014/arts-afrique-oceanic-pf1408/lot.36.html (accessed 9 November 2023).

458   Sylvester Okwunodu Ogbechie, 'Rethinking the Canon: African Collectors and the Canon of African Art', Canon: A Mini-Symposium, Young Museum, San Francisco, 7 February 2013.

459   Lucie Assi, 'L'art africain chez Sotheby's: l'association gabonaise freine la vente de la collection Leloup', *100% Culture*, 24 June 2023, www.100pour100culture.com/arts-vivants/lart-africain-chez-sothebys-lassociation-gabonaise-freine-la-vente-de-la-collection-leloup/ (accessed 9 November 2023).

460   Database excerpt of the Grassi-Museum für Völkerkunde Leipzig, 10.12.2021. (https://doi.org/10.14279/depositonce-17871) (accessed 21 July 2023).

461   Inventory numbers include III C 6689, III C 7006, III C 7628 and III C 36842 (Berlin), 71.1977.52.1 (Paris), MAf 34108, MAf 27917, MAf 00410, MAf 00411 and MAf 01764 (Leipzig), 035437, 035438 and 48789 (Stuttgart), 96-245 and 29-34-11 (Munich), C677 (Hamburg), 38421, 38658, 38659 and 38660 (Dresden), ET 2355 (Hanover), RAF 806 and RAF 807 (Zürich). Other statuettes that are very similar to Kwasio reliquary figures but attributed to the Fang people can be found in the collections of the Rautenstrauch-Joest Museum in Cologne, the Reiss-Engelhorn Museum in Mannheim, the Museum of Nature and Mankind in Freiburg, the Weltkulturen Museum in Frankfurt, the Völkerkundesammlung in Lübeck and the Museum of Cultures in Basel.

462 Inventory number 4503 at the AMNH was attributed to the skull of a Mabi individual. No information on the context of acquisition of these remains can be retrieved from the archival material that the museum shared with us. This ancestor is part of a collection amassed by the former assistant director of the Berlin Ethnological Museum, Felix von Luschan, which was sold to the North American museum in 1924 after the anthropologist's death. We thank Barry Landua and Kirsten Mable for their cooperative answer to our request.

463 See Dietrich Heißenbüttel, *Ungleiche Voraussetzungen: zur Globalisierung der Künste* (Stuttgart: Merz und Solitude, 2008), 42.

464 See Louis Perrois, *Byeri Fang: sculptures d'ancêtres en Afrique* (Marseille: Musées de Marseille, 1992); also Louis Perrois, *La statuaire Fan, Gabon* (Paris: ORSTOM, 1972).

465 See Pierre Alexandre and Jacques Binet, *Le groupe dit Pahouin: Fang, Boulou, Beti* (Paris: L'Harmattan, 2005).

466 Adolf Rüger, 'Der Aufstand der Polizeisoldaten (Dezember 1893)', in *Kamerun unter deutscher Kolonialherrschaft*, ed. Helmuth Stoecker (Berlin: Rütten & Loening, 1960), vol. 1, 106.

467 Paulin Adjai Oloukpona-Yinnon, *La révolte des esclaves mercenaires: Douala 1893* (Bayreuth: Bayreuth University, 1987), 7. For further reading, see Rüger, 'Der Aufstand der Polizeisoldaten', 103–105; Stefanie Michels, *Schwarze deutsche Kolonialsoldaten: Mehrdeutige Repräsentationsräume und früher Kosmopolitismus in Afrika* (Bielefeld: transcript, 2009), 96–99; and Florian Hoffmann, *Okkupation und Militärverwaltung in Kamerun: Etablierung und Institutionalisierung des kolonialen Gewaltmonopols*, vol. 1 (Göttingen: Cuvilier, 2007), 61–72.

468 Alwin Karl Wehlan, Bericht des Assessors Wehlan über die Bestrafung der aufständigen Mabealeute (Südkamerun), Kamerun (Duala), dated 11 Mai 1893, BArch R1001/4285, 20.

469 See Mabvouer 1989, quoted in Bouh Ma Sitna, *Reconstitution des migrations ancestrales*, 123. See also Jude Sylvain Mboum, *Les Mabi de Kribi. Du génocide à l'ethnocide: histoire et culture meurtries* (Kribi: Self-published, 2022), 94.

470 See Mboum, *Les Mabi de Kribi*, 94; Hoffmann, *Okkupation und Militärverwaltung*, 77–78; and Mabvouer 1989, quoted in Bouh Ma Sitna, *Reconstitution des migrations ancestrales*, 123–126.

471 For all quotes in this paragraph, see Wehlan, Bericht des Assessors, 20.

472 For all quotes in this paragraph, see Wehlan, Bericht des Assessors, 20–24.

473 Wehlan, Bericht des Assessors, 21.

474 See Rüger, 'Der Aufstand der Polizeisoldaten', 106–107; and Oloukpona-Yinnon, *La révolte des esclaves mercenaires*, 29.

475 Wilhelm Vallentin, Abschrift: Untersuchung und Aburteilung der letzten 22 aufständigen Dahomes, Vernehmung des Soldaten Soba, dated 7. March 1894, BArch R1001/4018, 120.

476 Wilhelm Vallentin, Vernehmung des Soldaten Akapo, dated 8 March 1894, BArch R1001/4018, 117.
477 Oertzen 1893, quoted in Wilhelm Vallentin, *Tagebuchblätter eines in Kamerun lebenden Deutschen* (Offprint: Freie Bühne; 5, 1894), 342.
478 Vallentin, *Tagebuchblätter*, 340.
479 Vallentin, *Tagebuchblätter*, 340
480 Oertzen 1893, quoted in Vallentin, *Tagebuchblätter*, 342.
481 Wehlan, Bericht des Assessors, 26.
482 Mabvouer 1989, quoted in Bouh Ma Sitna, *Reconstitution des migrations ancestrales*, 125–126.
483 Eugen Zimmerer, Letter to Reichskanzler Caprivi, Kamerun [Douala], dated 18 Mai 1893, BArch R1001/4285, 17.
484 Zimmerer, Letter to Caprivi, 18. However, this was not to happen. When the appalling news of the terror regime implemented by Leist and Wehlan reached the German public in 1894 via Wilhelm Vallentin, it led to one of the first German colonial scandals. Journalists uncovered 'cruel excesses of violence' which ranged 'from flogging to arbitrary killing, to bestial desecration of corpses' and from which children, women and the elderly were not spared. The outburst of the scandal led to Wehlan and Chancellor Leist being court martialled and convicted for their deeds. For further details, see Frank Bösch, *Öffentliche Geheimnisse: Skandale, Politik und Medien in Deutschland und Großbritannien 1880–1914* (Munich: Oldenbourg, 2009), 267; 264–274.
485 See Rudi Kaeselitz, 'Kolonialeroberung und Widerstandskampf in Südkamerun (1884–1907)', in *Kamerun unter deutscher Kolonialherrschaft*, ed. Helmuth Stoecker (Berlin: Rütten & Loening, 1960), vol. 2, 11–54, 24.
486 See Heißenbüttel, *Ungleiche Voraussetzungen*, 45.
487 Interview with Jules Mana, conducted by Sebastian-Manès Sprute in Kribi, 18 July 2022. Audio file in the possession of the author.
488 Mboum, *Les Mabi de Kribi*, 94.
489 Interview with Jean-Baptiste Nzambi, conducted by Yrine Matchinda in Kribi, 28 February 2021. Audio file in possession of the author.
490 Interview with Joseph Nong, conducted by Yrine Matchinda in Kribi, 1 March 2021. Audio file in possession of the author.
491 Adolphe Mingwuli, 'King Mayesse, Martye et pionnier de la résistance Camerounaise à la Colonisation,' in *Magazine MBALI!, special edition*, September 2014, 3.
492 Interview with Achille Ndtoungou, conducted by Yrine Matchinda in Kribi, 30 August 2021. Audio file in possession of the author.
493 Interview with Achille Ndtoungou, 30 August 2021.
494 Database excerpt, Grassi Museum für Völkerkunde Leipzig, dated 13 September 2021, https://doi.org/10.14279/depositonce-17873 (accessed 21 July 2023).

495	See Alexandre and Binet, *Le groupe dit Pahouin*. On the problem of designations, subdivisions and delimitations of population groups, see Sebastian-Manès Sprute, 'Chaos im Museum: Bestandsaufnahme und Wissensordnung', in *Atlas der Abwesenheit: Kameruns Kulturerbe in Deutschland*, ed. Mikaél Assilkinga et al. (Berlin: Reimer, 2023), 265–296.
496	Interview with Joseph Nong, conducted by Yrine Matchinda in Kribi, 1 March 2021. Audio file in possession of the author.
497	Interview with Jean-Baptiste Nzambi, 28 February 2021.
498	See Yrine Matchinda, 'Gespräche über das Abwesende: Eine Annäherung', in *Atlas der Abwesenheit: Kameruns Kulturerbe in Deutschland*, ed. Mikaél Assilkinga et al. (Berlin: Reimer, 2023), 315.
499	Interview with Achille Ndtoungou, 30 August 2021.
500	Formerly the village of Biang Bwô Mbumbô alias King Mayessè, today on the palm grove of Kienke, owned by the Franco-Belgian industrial group SocFin and run by its subcontractor Socapalm, a plantation where, in the 2000s, employees rose against appalling working conditions (see Fanny Pigeaud, 'Les Camerounais exploités des palmeraies de Bolloré', *Libération*, 11 March 2008. https://web.archive.org/web/20100302113300/http://www.liberation.fr/economie/010176109-les-camerounais-exploites-des-palmeraies-de-bollore [accessed 15 February 2024]).
501	Interview with Achille Ndtoungou, 30 August 2021.

Appendix

MUSEUMS AND COLLECTIONS DISCUSSED

Chapter	Museums and Collections (those holding the cultural assets under scrutiny are listed in bold)	Cultural Asset
Introduction	AfricaMuseum, Tervuren (Belgium) Berlin Ethnological Museum / Humboldt Forum (Germany) British Museum, London (UK) Linden Museum, Stuttgart (Germany) Musée du Quai Branly – Jacques Chirac, Paris (France) Museum der Kulturen, Basel (Switzerland) Smithsonian Institution, Washington, DC (USA) Overseas Museum, Bremen (Germany) Victoria and Albert Museum, London (UK) Weltmuseum, Vienna (Austria) Zeughaus (today, German Historical Museum), Berlin (Germany)	
1	Musée d'Ethnographie du Trocadéro (today, Musée de l'Homme), Paris (France) **Musée de l'Armée, Paris (France)** Musée du Quai Branly – Jacques Chirac, Paris (France) Musée Municipal de Montauban (France) Palais de la Porte Dorée, formerly, Musée National des Arts d'Afrique et d'Océanie, Paris (France)	Samori Touré's headgear

Appendix

Chapter	Museums and Collections (those holding the cultural assets under scrutiny are listed in bold)	Cultural Asset
2	Black Watch Castle and Museum, Perth (UK) Blair Castle, Pitlochry (UK) Brighton Museum & Art Gallery (UK) Bristol Museum and Art Gallery (UK) British Museum, London (UK) Great North Museum, Newcastle upon Tyne (UK) Guards Museum, London (UK) **Highlander's Museum, Fort George (UK)** Kelvingrove Art Gallery and Museum, Glasgow (UK) Museum of Somerset, Taunton (UK) National Army Museum, London (UK) National Museum of African Art, Washington, DC (USA) Osbourne House (Isle of Wight) Rifles Berkshire and Wiltshire Museum, Salisbury (UK) **Royal Engineers' Museum, Gillingham (UK)** Royal Green Jackets (Rifles) Museum, Winchester (UK) Royal Hospital Chelsea, London (UK) Royal Marines Museum, Portsmouth (UK) Royal Regiment of Fusiliers Museum, Warwick (UK) Sir Hector Macdonald Museum, Dingwall (UK) State Hermitage, St Petersburg (Russia) Sudan Archive, University of Durham (USA) Windsor Castle, London (UK)	The Manifesto of the Mahdī

Appendix

Chapter	Museums and Collections (those holding the cultural assets under scrutiny are listed in bold)	Cultural Asset
3	British Museum, London (UK) KwaZulu Cultural Museum, Ulundi (South Africa) Luthuli Museum, KwaDukuza (South Africa) Museum of Archaeology and Anthropology, Cambridge (UK) **Pitt Rivers Museum, Oxford (UK)**	*isiHlangu* (shield) from the Anglo-Zulu war
4	Berlin Ethnological Museum, formerly, Königliche Museum für Völkerkunde (Germany) **Grassi Museum für Völkerkunde, Leipzig (Germany)** Linden Museum, Stuttgart (Germany) Reiss-Engelhorn Museum, Mannheim (Germany)	*Gboguno zipligu*: headgear of a Dagomba war leader
5	Berlin Ethnological Museum (Germany) **Field Museum, Chicago, IL (USA)** Linden Museum, Stuttgart (Germany) Municipal Museum, Braunschweig/Brunswick (Germany)	War coat from Mango
6	British Museum, London (UK) Fowler Museum, Los Angeles, CA (USA) Royal Collections Trust, Windsor Castle, London (UK) Victoria and Albert Museum, London (UK) **Wallace Collection, London (UK)**	Golden trophy head of Kofi Karikari

Appendix

Chapter	Museums and Collections (those holding the cultural assets under scrutiny are listed in bold)	Cultural Asset
7	Berlin Ethnological Museum / Humboldt Forum (Germany) Georg-August University Collections, Göttingen (Germany) Grassi Museum für Völkerkunde, Leipzig (Germany) Landesmuseum Natur und Mensch, Oldenburg (Germany) **Linden Museum, Stuttgart (Germany)**	Carved wooden plaque from an Ngolo *etana*
8	American Museum of Natural History, New York (USA) Berlin Ethnological Museum (Germany) **Grassi Museum für Völkerkunde, Leipzig (Germany)** Linden Museum, Stuttgart (Germany) State Collections Dresden (Germany)	Mangi Meli's cartridge upcycled in a tobacco container
9	**Humboldt Forum / Berlin Ethnological Museum (Germany)** Linden Museum, Stuttgart (Germany)	Ngonnso'
10	Musée d'Ethnographie du Trocadéro (today, Musée de l'Homme), Paris (France) **Musée du Quai Branly – Jacques Chirac, Paris (France) and today at the Fondation Zinsou, Cotonou (Benin)** Museum of the Kings and Amazons of Danxomè (MuRAD), Abomey (Benin)	*Bocio* of three Danxomè kings (Glélé, Ghézo & Béhanzin)

Chapter	Museums and Collections (those holding the cultural assets under scrutiny are listed in bold)	Cultural Asset
11	Berlin State Library (*Staatsbibliothek zu Berlin*, Germany) Bibliothèque Nationale de France, Paris (France) The Bodleian Library, Oxford (UK) **British Library, London (UK)** **British Museum, London (UK)** Cambridge University Library, Cambridge (UK) The John Rylands Library, Manchester (UK) National Museum of Antiquities, Edinburgh (UK) The Royal Library, Windsor Castle, London (UK) Vatican Apostolic Library, Rome (Italy) Wellcome Institute of the History of Medicine, London (UK)	Tabots from the Maqdala library
12	**AfricaMuseum (formerly, Musée Royal d'Afrique Centrale and Musée du Congo Belge), Tervuren (Belgium)** Institut Royal des Sciences Naturelles / Museum voor Natuurwetenschappen, Brussels (Belgium) National Museum of the Democratic Republic of the Congo, Kinshasa (DRC) Porte de Hal (formerly, *Musées royaux* d'Armes, d'Armures, d'*Antiquité* et d'Ethnologie), Brussels (Belgium)	*Nkisi nkonde* of Chief Ne Kuko

Appendix

Chapter	Museums and Collections (those holding the cultural assets under scrutiny are listed in bold)	Cultural Asset
13	AfricaMuseum (formerly, Musée Royal d'Afrique Centrale & Musée du Congo Belge), Tervuren (Belgium) **British Museum, London (UK)** California State University, Fullerton, CA (USA) Hampton University Museum, Hampton, VA (USA) Illinois State Museum, Springfield, IL (USA) Linden Museum, Stuttgart (Germany) Museum für Naturkunde, Berlin (Germany)	*Ngadji* of the Pokomo
14	British Museum, London (UK) Duckworth Laboratory, Cambridge (UK) Manchester Museum (UK) National Archives of Zimbabwe, Harare (Zimbabwe) National Museums and Monuments in Zimbabwe, Harare (Zimbabwe) Natural History Museum, London (UK) Pitt Rivers Museum, Oxford (UK)	Mbuya Nehanda's remains (not found yet)

Appendix

Chapter	Museums and Collections (those holding the cultural assets under scrutiny are listed in bold)	Cultural Asset
15	American Museum of Natural History, New York (USA) Berlin Ethnological Museum (Germany) Grassi Museum für Völkerkunde, Leipzig (Germany) Landesmuseum, Hanover (Germany) Linden Museum, Stuttgart (Germany) MARKK, Hamburg (Germany) Musée du Quai Branly – Jacques Chirac, Paris (France) Museum der Kulturen, Basel (Switzerland) Museum Five Continents, Munich (Germany) Museum für Völkerkunde Dresden (Germany) Museum Natur und Mensch, Freiburg (Germany) Rautenstrauch-Joest Museum, Cologne (Germany) Reiss-Engelhorn Museum, Mannheim (Germany) Rietberg Museum, Zurich (Switzerland) **Sotheby's, Paris (France)** Völkerkundesammlung, Lübeck (Germany) Weltkulturen Museum, Frankfurt am Main (Germany)	Ancestors' guardian figures from *byéri* reliquaries

INDEX

fig refers to a photograph; *ill* to an illustration

Abdülhamid II, Ottoman Emperor 44
Abdulai, Alhaji Ibrahim 62
'Abdullāhi, Khatīfa 37, 38, 41, 43–5
Abeid, Amani 112
Abiodun, Rowland 8
Abomey, Benin 5, 25, 137
Abomey artists 139–40
Abomey treasures 141–4
'absent priesthood' theory 191
Abushiri uprising (1888) 114
Abyssinia (later Ethiopia) 151–3, 157–8
Adibo, Battle of 58*ill*, 61–2, 64–8
Adichie, Chimamanda Ngozi 125
Africa Centre, London 91, 93
AfricaMuseum, Tervuren 164, 169–70, 171, 174
African historiography 16
    see also specific countries
African languages 8, 54, 95
impact of colonialism on 8–9, 130–1
African museums 52
    see also specific museums
Agbidinukun, Daá 141
Aḥmad Faḍīl, Muḥammad 45
    claims to be the Mahdi 38–9, 41
Aksum Kingdom 153–4
al-Nunjūmī, 'Abd-al-Raḥman 43
Albéca, Alexandre d' 142
Alderson, Edwin A.H. 191
Alemayehu, Prince of Ethiopia 157
Algiers 4, 5
Allan, Stuart 3, 4
Almami monarchs 22–3, 24, 28
amaSwati people 50
American Museum of Natural History 111, 202

ancestor veneration 202–3
Andani, Ya Na 62–3, 64–5
Anderssen, Jens 179
Andrews, Kehinde 179
Anglo-Zulu wars 47–56
animal sacrifice 5
animist materialism 152
Anindilyakwa people, Australia 194
Anthonay, Léon d' 27
Antwerp World Fair (1885) 169
Anufo people (Tchokossi) 78–9
war cloak 70*ill*, 72, 74, 76, 80, 82,
apartheid 51, 56
Archinard, Louis 23–4, 25
architecture, looting and destruction of 107–8
Ark of the Covenant 153
Arnim, Albrecht von 100–1
Asante people 87–97
Asante regalia 88, 96–7
Association Internationale Africaine (AIA) 168
Association Internationale du Congo (AIC) 168
Audéoud, Colonel 29
Australia 19
Azoulay, Ariella Aïsha 7

Badji, Cheikh Ousmane 21
Baku, Alphonse, Boma Chief 170, 172
Bakundu, Chief Dibuma 103
Bamena, Cameroon 107
Bamum, King of 15*fig*
Bamum Kingdom 76, 129
Banguiam, Olivier Kodjalbaye 23
Bantu Social Centre, Natal 51
baraza (open-air terrace) 112
Basil, Priya 13

Batanga people 103
Bauche, Manuela 182–3
Beach, David N. 'Charwe: a Woman Unjustly Accused' 191–2
Bebel, August 116
Béhanzin Houedogni, King of Abomey 136*ill*, 139, 141, 143*fig*
    Fondation Zinsou 142
Belgian colonialism 11–12, 163–5, 171–4
Benin, restitution of cultural assets by France (2021) 137, 143–5, 170–1
Benin Bronzes 1, 3, 177–8, 181–2, 184, 185–6
Benin City 5, 6, 25
Benin Expedition (1897) 37
Berlin Conference (1884-85) 4, 5, 61, 114, 115, 137, 152–3, 163, 167
Berlin Postkolonial (organisation) 112
Bertho, Elara 23
Besser, Bernhard von 107
Bevan, Robert 99, 105
Bibliothèque Nationale, Paris 159
Biema Asabiè, Na (chief) of Mango 78–9
Biko, Steve 21
Binns, C.T. *The Last Zulu King* 49
Bismarck, Graf Otto von 114
Black History Month (Chicago, 2023) 76
Black Lives Matter 171
Black Power movement 89
Black Star Film Festival, Philadelphia 95
Black Unity and Freedom Party 88
Blier, Suzanne Preston 139, 141
Blondy, Alpha 21
Boahen, Albert Adu *Histoire Générale d'Afrique* 22
bocio (protective sculpture) 136*ill*, 138–43, 143*fig*
Bodleian Library, Oxford 159
Boma, Congo 165, 167
Bonabéri, Cameroon 99
Botswana 5
Bowdich, Thomas Edward 61
Bratière, Louis 28
Braunschweig Municipal Museum 73
British colonialism 4, 35–8, 44–5, 47–51, 54–6, 61–2, 87, 96, 152–3, 156–8, 189–92
British Expedition to Abyssinia (1867–68) 151–3, 157–8
British Indian Army 157
British Library 152, 158–9
British Museum 5, 51, 54, 88–93, 96, 152, 158–9, 177, 180, 183, 184–5, 186–7, 193–4
    thefts from 1–2, 187
Brussels Museum of International Sciences 172
Brussels World Fair (1958) 142
Bülow, Bernhard von 116
Burton, Richard 139
Burundi 6
Buthelezi, Chief Mangosuthu 55–6
byéri (guardian figures) 200*ill*, 202–3, 206–7, 209*fig*, 210

California State University Museum 180
Call for the Return of the Asante Regalia (1974) 96
Cambridge University. Duckworth Laboratory 193
Cambridge University Library 159
Cameroon 2, 5, 15, 76, 99–108, 126–35, 201–11, 208
    German expeditions in 6*fig*
    Kamerun, German colonial territory 73, 102
Cetshwayo kaMpande, King of the AmaZulu 48–50, 54–5
Chagga people 8, 111, 116
Chardome, Émile 165
Charles III, King xv
Charumbira, Ruramisai 190–1
Chatanda, Cloud 112
Chelmsford, Frederick Thesiger, 2nd Baron Chelmsford 48, 49
Chernoff, John 62
Chevalier, Auguste Jean Baptiste 26
Chilver, Sally 131
Chimurenga (1st 1896-98) 189, 190, 192, 196
Chimurenga (2nd 1964-79) 192, 196
Chinamhora, Nyamasoka 192

Chinodya, Shimmer *Harvest of Thorns* 197
Chipanga, Hosiah 197
Chitepo, Herbert *Soko Risinamusoro* 197
Christian missionaries 78, 116, 191
Christianity 153–4, 156
Church Mission Society 116
Cinema Action Film Collective 91
Cobbing, Julian 191
Collectif Gabon-Occitanie 202
colonialism
    and the Enlightenment 12–13, 194
    recruitment of local people 131–2
    and violence 131–2, 163–4, 204
    see also Belgian Colonialism; British colonialism; French colonialism; German colonialism
Colwell, Chip 196
Congo 163, 164–5, 171–4
Congolese people, displayed in Belgian exhibition 11–12
Cotonou, Benin 141, 144
counter-theft 126–7
Couttenier, Maarten 169–70, 172
Cuban coral 183
Cyprian Bhekuzulu, kaSolomon 56

Dagbon Kingdom 59, 60–8
Dagomba people 62–3, 63–9
    importance of self-defence 66
Dahomey, later Benin 137
Daily Graphic (Ghana) 94
Danxomè Kingdom 137, 145
Debra Tabor, Ethiopia 155–6
decolonisation 179–80, 195, 198–9
Delafosse, Maurice 140, 142
Delcommune, Alexandre 164, 167–9, 173
Deliss, Clémentine 7
Deutsche Staatsbibliothek, Berlin 159
Dhlomo, Herbert Isaac Ernest 52
Diehl, Adolf 64
Digital Benin Project 6

Diop, Mati 97
Djimassé, Gabin 141
Dodds, General Alfred-Amédée 137, 141–2
Dominik, Hans 102
Dorsey, George A. 73
Drummer's Testament, A (website) 62
Du Bois, W.E.B. 27
Dunn, John 55

East India Company 4
Ebune, Joseph B. 100, 102–3
Eckhardt, Wilhelm 129
Edo people 178, 182
Egypt 156, 157
Einstein, Carl 7
Ekplekendo, Akati 145
Ellis, Stephen 163
Entoto Mariyam Church, Addis Ababa 154
Epifano, Angie 23, 30
etana (Ngolo place of assembly) 106, 107–8
État Indépendant du Congo (EIC) 169
Ethiopia 151–6
    Zamana Mesafint era 155–6
Ethiopian Orthodox Church, 149, 154, 160
Ethnological Museum, Berlin 2, 4–5, 64, 65, 66, 73, 79, 101, 111, 127, 129–30, 133, 202
Ethnological Museum, Dresden 202
Eurocentric attitudes 8, 11–13
Ewuare II, Oba 182
Eyo, Ekpo 7, 94
    2000 Years of Nigerian Art 30–1
Ezana, Aksum King 153–4

Fagg, William 89, 96
Fang people 209
Fanon, Frantz 89, 130
Fasilides, Emperor of Ethiopia 155
Fénéon, Félix 201
Field, Marshall 74
Field Museum, Chicago 65, 71–6, 77–6
Finsch, Otto 73
Fischer, Hartwig 1

Flinn Works (arts company) 112
Floyd, George 94, 171
Foliard, Daniel 25
Fongbè language 139
Fowler Museum, Los Angeles 87
France
    relations with Togo 77–8
    restitution of cultural assets to Benin (2021) 137, 143–5, 170–1
French colonialism 4, 23–4, 27, 141
French Dahomey, later Benin 137
Frere, Sir Bartle 48
Friedrich Ebert Foundation 93

Garima Gospels 154–5
Garuba, Harry 152
gboguno zipligu (Dagbon headgear) 7, 60*fig*, 64, 68
gender-based violence 6, 36, 102, 115–6, 130–1
George VI, King, tour of South Africa (1947) 56
German colonialism xv–xvi, 4–6, 63, 68, 77–9, 99–105, 131
Gesellschaft Nordwest-Kamerun 102
Ghana 61, 88
Ghana Broadcasting Co. 93–4
Ghana Focal Team on Reparation and Restitution of Illegally Trafficked and Stolen Cultural Heritage and Artifacts 68–9, 95
Ghézo, King of Dahomey 140–1
    bocio 137, 142
Gibson, Gordon 12
Glauning, Hans 107, 128–30
Glèlè, King of Dahomey 140–2
    bocio 137, 142
Gnassingbé, Eyadéma 78
Godlee, Philip 195
Gondar, Ethiopia 155, 156
Gordon, Major-General Charles 35, 42
Gou (god) sculpture 145
Gouraud, General Henri 24, 28

Au Soudan: Souvenirs d'un Africain 21, 25–6
Grassi Museum für Völkerkunde, Leipzig 59, 61, 64, 67–8, 111, 113, 118, 119, 121, 202, 209
Groote Eylandt, Australia 194
Gruner, Hans 62, 64–5
Guèdégbé, diviner, tablet 145
Gueye, M'Baye 22
Gumboreshumba, Sekuru Kaguvi 189, 192
Guse, Franz 101
Guy, Jeff 51
Gwasira, Goodman 13
Gweagal shield 19
Gwebwaa Palace 64
Gyimah, Michael 61, 67, 68

Habermas, Rebekka 105
Hampton University Museum 180
Hamu, kaMpande 55
Harare, Zimbabwe 198
Harrison, Ian 195
Hassan bin Omari (aka Makunganya) 5
Haylu Kasa *see* Tewodros II, Emperor of Ethiopia
Hermitage Museum, St Petersburg 35
Herskovits, Melville J. 139–40
Hicks, Dan 1–2, 4, 7, 22
Highlanders' Museum, Fort George 39
Ḥitu, ʿAlīwad 45
Hlobane, Battle of 50
Hochschild, Adam 12
Holmes, Richard Rivington 158
Houben, Hans 126, 128–9
Hove, Chenjerai *Bones* 197
human remains 5, 23, 78–9, 119–21, 129–30, 179, 189, 193–4, 202, 205
Humboldt Forum, Berlin 3, 15, 107, 125, 127, 130–1, 170
Hunter, General Archibald 36

Idia, Edo Queen, mask 186
Ife head sculpture 184
Ikenga (Igbo symbol) 125

Index

Ikubor, Divine (Rema) 186
Illinois State University Museum 180
inkhata (Zulu sacred symbol) 54
Institute of National Museum of Congo (IMNC) 171
International Association of Art Critics (3rd Congress, 1973) 171
Isandlwana, Battle of 46*ill*, 48, 50
isiHlangu (Zulu shields) 7, 51, 52–3
Islamic amulets 72
Islamic traditions 30, 72
Itandala, Buluda 4
Itoki people 103
Iyasu I, Emperor of Ethiopia 155

James, Captain C.F. 158
Jazīra Abā, Sudan 39, 40
John Rylands Library, Manchester 159

Kambon-Nakpem Ziblim, Wag-biegu 62, 64, 67
Kamptz, Oltwig von 100–1
Kankanhau, Sosandande Likohim (Sossa Dede) 140, 142
Kasa-Vubu, Joseph 171
Khambula, Battle of 50
Khartoum 42
Khosa, Ntshingwayo kaMahole 49
Kikuku village, Congo 172–3
Kilimanjaro, Tanzania 5, 111, 115–6, 117–8, 121–2
    burial customs in 120
King, Martin Luther 21
King Mayessè Foundation 208
Kitchener, Horatio Herbert, Earl 35–6, 38, 42, 44
Knight, Ian 50
Knutson Waldau & Heilborn Co. 100, 102
Kofi Karikari, Asante King, trophy head of 86*ill*, 96
Kongo people 164, 167–8, 169
Kum'a M'Bape Bele (aka Lock Priso) 99

Kumasi, Ghana 5
Kussmaul, Friedrich 178
Kwamba, Nagyang (King Benga) 203
Kwasio-speaking people 202–3
KwaZulu Cultural Museum, Ulundi 55

Laband, John 50
Lacaille, Agnès 167
Lamche, Schlacke 91
Landesmuseum, Hanover, Germany 202
Langheld, Friedrich Wilhelm 105
language *see* African languages
Lartigue, Raoul 28
Le Corbusier 142
Legbawo-Dzokawo project 9, 81
Leist, Karl Theodor Heinrich 203, 204
Leopold II, King of Belgium 11–12, 163, 167–8, 171
Lessner, Paul Franz Adolf 99, 100, 101–2, 103–4, 105–8
Lidchi, Henrietta 3, 4
Linden, Graf Karl von 107
Linden Museum, Stuttgart 5, 65, 79, 99, 101, 105, 106, 107, 111, 129, 202
Lock, Ron 55–6
London, Caribbean and Black people in 88
Lost Art Foundation, Germany 111
Lumumba, Patrice 21, 171
Luschan, Felix von 64–5, 66, 101, 107
Lusinga, Chief Iwa Ng'ombe 5, 164–5, 172–3
Luthuli, Albert 51, 56
Luthuli Museum, KwaDukuza 51

Mabi people 201, 202–11
Mabvouer, Francois 205
Machel, Samora 196
Macron, Emmanuel xv, 143, 170–1
Magdala *see* Maqdala
Mahdi 37–45
    attitudes to xiv, 42, 78
    claimant to title 38–40
Mahdi banners 7–8, 34*ill*, 38–45

Index

colour coding of 41
Maji Maji war memorial, Tanzania xv, xvi
Mana, Jules 206
Manchester University Museum 193–5, 199
Mandela, Nelson 54
Mandtuo, Etienne Ntunga 209*fig*
Mangi Mareale, Chagga Chief of Marangu 115, 118
Mangi Meli, son of Rindi, Chagga Chief of Moshi 8, 110*ill*, 114–5, 118–23
Mangi Meli Remains (exhibition) 112, 122
Mangi Rindi (aka Mandara, Chagga Chief of Moshi) 115, 116
Mangi Sina, Chagga Chief of Kiboshi 114–5, 121
Manhiya Palace, Kumasi, loans to 96–7
Maphalala, Jabulani S. 48
Maphulomo uprising (1906) 53–4
Maponya, Selbon and Mrs Mama 51
Maqdala, Ethiopia 5, 25, 152–3, 156
    auction of stolen cultural assets 157–9
Maqdala, Battle of (1868) 152–3, 156, 157
Marangu, Tanzania 115
MARKK Museum, Hamburg 202
Marshall Field & Co. 74
Mashayamombe, Chinengundu 190
Massana (artist) 112
Massow, Valentin von 59, 60, 62, 63, 64–5, 66
Matisse, Henri 13
Matundu (god) statue 165
Mavumengwana kaNdlela 49–50
Mawere, Tinashe 196
Mazowe, Zimbabwe 190–1, 198
Mbembe, Achille 8, 152, 193
Mbilini waMswati, Prince 48
Mbombo, kaSimbindumalo 53
Mboum, Jude S. *Les Mabi de Kribi : du Genocide a l'Ethnocide* 206–7
Mbumbô, Bian Bwô (King Mayessè) 203, 205, 208, 211
Mbvumbo people 202
Mehlokazulu, son of Chief Ngobese 49

Mekunda, Doreen 100, 103
Meli, Isaria 113, 117, 118, 120*fig*, 120–1
Menelik I, Emperor of Ethiopia 153
Menelik II, Emperor of Ethiopia 156
Meru people 111–2
Meyer, Birgit 9
Meyo, Yannick Elydjah 202
Mfanawendlela, Chief of the Zungu 55
Michaux, Oscar Isidore Joseph 165
Mijikenda people 180
Mingwuli, Adolphe 208
Mjidho, Baiba Dhidha 184
Mobuto, Sese Seko 171
Moctecuhzoma, Aztec King 3
Mokha, Yemen, blockade of 4
Movement for Black Lives 185
Mpanza, Charles 56
Mudimbé, Vumbi-Yoka 8
Mugabe, Robert 189, 192
Murenga (Shona oracle) 190
Musée d'Ethnographie du Trocadéro, Paris 23–4, 137, 140, 142
    Palais de la Colonisation 27
Musée de l'Armée, Paris 5, 19, 21, 23, 28–30
Musée de l'Homme, Paris 142
Musée de la France d'Outre-Mer 28
Musée des Arts d'Afrique et d'Océanie, Paris (MAAO) 21–2, 28, 31
Musée du Congo Belge, Tervuren 165, 169, 171
Musée du Quai Branly-Jacques Chirac, Paris 5, 24, 28, 142, 202
Musée Municipal de Montauban 28
museum catalogues 11–12
    'dirty data' in 12
museum collections, terminology and naming in 11–14
Museum der Kulturen, Basel 10–11
Museum Five Continents, Munich 202
Museum für Völkerkunde, Dresden 209
Museum of Archaeology and Anthropology, Cambridge 51

Museum of Ethnology, Vienna 178
Museum of Natural Sciences, Brussels 172
Museum of the Kings and Amazons of Danxomè (MuRAD) 145
museums 2, 132–3
    military museums 5, 19
    new museology 9, 10
    photography in 14
    role of 9, 76
    see also specific museums
Mutasa, Garika *The Contract* 197
Mutsvairo, Solomon 192
    Feso 197
Muzenda, Simon 197

Nachtigal, Gustav 204
Nagya, Biwèe (King Massili) 203
Nakeli Nw'embeli 8, 100, 103–4, 108
Napier, General Robert 157
Natal 48
National Army Museum, London 19
National Commission on Repatriation 172, 173, 174
National Museum of Antiquities, Edinburgh 159
National Museums and Monuments of Zimbabwe (NMMZ) 189, 193, 194, 199
Natural History Museum, Berlin 183
Natural History Museum, London 189, 193, 199
Navy and Army Illustrated 38, 43
Ndebele people 191
Ndhlovu, kaThimuni 52
Ndtoungou, Achille 207, 208, 211
Ne Kuko, Chief of Boma 8, 166*fig*, 167–70
Ne Oro, King 168
Nehanda, Mbuya Nyakasikana Charwe 5, 188*ill*, 189–99
Nehanda, Mbuya 5
ngadji (Pokomo drum) 176*ill*, 177–9, 181, 184–5
Ngolo Expedition 99–104

Ngonnso', Queen, and effigy 14, 124*ill*, 125–8, 133, 134*fig*, 135
Ngũgĩ wa Thiong'o *Decolonising the Mind* 8
Nigeria 177, 178, 182
Njobati, Sylvie 125
Njoya, Prince Aboubakar Nijasse 76
Nketia, Kwabena 94
nkisi nkonde sculpture 8, 142, 162*ill*, 164, 167–70
Nkomo, Joshua 192, 198
Nkrumah, Kwame 88
Nondichao, Bachalou ('Ba') 140, 141
Notzing, Albert Schrenck von 118, 119
Nso' people 125–33, 135
Ntshingwayo, Inkosi 50
Ntshingwayo ka Mahole 49
Nxumalo, Otty 54
Nyerere, Julius 196
Nyezane, Battle of 50
Nzambi, Jean Baptiste 207, 209*fig*, 210

Oertzen, Dietrich von 205
Ogbechie, Sylvester Okwunodu 201
Old Moshi, Tanzania 112, 116, 118, 119
Oloukpona-Yinnon, Paulin 203
Olugbohun (Yoruba spirit) 186
Olympio, Sylvanus 77–8
Omdurman, Battle of 35–8, 42, 44
oNdini, Battle of 49, 50, 55
Open Restitution Africa project 3
Opoku, Kwame 8, 96
Oroko people 99–100, 102–3, 106
Ottoman Empire 44, 156, 157
Otumfuo Nana Osei Tutu II 87
Overseas Museum, Bremen 9

Palais de la Marina, Benin, exhibition (2023) 145–6
Pangwe people 209
Paris Short Film Festival 95
Parthenon marbles 1
Pavel, Kurt 128
Perrois, Louis 202, 207

Index

Person, Yves 22, 26
Peters, Carl 115–6
Peterson, Bhekiziwe 50–1
Pfau, Julia 59, 60*fig*
Philadelphia Filmmakers Workshop 94
Philippe, King of Belgium 171, 173
Picasso, Pablo 13
Pioneer Cemetery, Harare 193
Pitt Rivers Museum, Oxford 48, 51, 193–4
Pokomo people 177–81, 184, 185
Pollard, Henry 191
Prah, Margaret Akua 91
Prempeh I, Asante King 96
prize money 4, 19, 37
provenance research 3, 6, 28, 61, 73, 167, 169–70, 173–4, 194–5, 201
Prussian Cultural Heritage Foundation 135
Puttkamer, Jesko von 100

Ranger, Terence 192
rape 6, 102, 131
    see also gender-based violence
Rassool, Ciraj 56, 193
Reiss-Engelhorn Museum, Mannheim 65
religious leaders 192–3
religious symbols 149
Representative Council of Black Associations in France (CRAN) 202
restitution and repatriation 30–2, 95–7, 111, 127, 134–5, 160, 195–6, 210
    opposition to 131, 178, 184
resistance fighters xv–xvi, 8, 21–2, 67, 69, 78, 100–4, 114, 164–5, 189–92, 203–4
Return of Our Cultural Heritage project (*Marejesho*) 111–3, 122
Rhodes, Cecil John 190
Richartz, Father Francis 191, 193
Rietberg Museum, Zurich 202
Rigler, Friedrich 63, 64–5
Robertson, Geoffrey 185
Rorke's Drift 49
Royal Engineers Museum, Gillingham 42

Royal Museum of Antiquity, Armor, Artillery and Ethnology, Brussels 169
Royal Museum of Central Africa, Brussels 179
Rugby World Cup (2023) 47
Rwanda 6

Saanguv, King of Bamum 129
Sagrenti War (1874) 96
Salaga, destruction of 62
Samori Touré (aka The Almami) 20*ill*, 21–3
Samupindi, Charles *Death Throes* 197
Sansanné-Mango, Togo 62, 63, 72
Sarankégny Mori 21, 25–6
    tunic 28–30
Sarr, Felwine 3, 5, 8, 143
    Afrotopia 8
Savoy, Bénédicte 3, 5–6, 143
Schele, Friedrich von 118
Ségou, Mali 5
    treasure of 23, 25–6
Sehm Mbinglo II, Fon of the Nso' 128, 129
    visit to Berlin (2022) 133, 134*fig*
Seitz, Theodor 100–1
Sembène, Ousmane 23, 31
Shaka, King of the amaZulu 52, 55
Shaka iLhembe (tv programme) 56
Shepstone, Sir Theophilus (aka Somtsewu) 48
Shona people 191
Sibanda, Misheck 192
Sigananda, kaSokufa, 55
Sihayo kaXongo 48, 49
Skertchly, Alfred 139, 141
Skiff, Frederick 73
Smithsonian Institution 11, 35
    'Cultural Terms Not In Use' 11
Soares, Bruno Brulon 195
Solomonic dynasty 153, 155
Somé, Malidoma 178
Songea Mbano, Ngoni chief xv
Songea, Tanzania xv
Sotheby's auction house, Paris 201, 202
South Africa 47, 111

apartheid 51, 56
Spiess, Carl 9
Steevens, George 35
Stegall, Carroll R. 116
Steinmeier, Frank-Walter xv–xvi
Stone Press, Sudan 42
Storms, Émile 164–5
Strauch, Maximilian 168
Sudanese wars 35–8
Sufi traditions, Sudan 38, 39, 41–2
Sulemana, Alhaji Alhassan 16, 59–60, 62, 64, 65, 66, 67
Summer Palace (*Yuanmingyuan*), Beijing 26
Sutherland, Efua 94
Sysy House of Fame (organisation) 125

tabots (holy tablets) 152–5, 159
Tabwa people 172
Taiwo, Olufemi *Against Decolonisation* xvi
Tall, El Hadj Omar 23
Talon, Patrice 143
Tamakloe, Emmanuel 62
Tanzania 6, 111–3
Tapiero, Galia 139, 141
Tessmann, Günter (also spelled Günther) 207
Tewodros II, Emperor of Ethiopia 150*ill*, 151, 158, 159
    relations with Britain 156–7
Thierry, Gaston 65, 72–4, 78–9
Thompson, Robert Farris 140
Tibati, Cameroon 5
Tinki of Refem 126
tobacco cartridges 8, 110*ill*, 112–4, 116–9, 121
tobacco production 113–4
Togo 5, 9, 59, 77–80
    German expedition in 6*fig*
Touré, Sekou 22
Traoré, Babemba 21
Trentinian, General Edgard de 26
'tribalism' 182
Trintignant, General 29
Tshisekedi, Félix 171

Tsimba, Chief Madelaine 172
Tsumba, Jean 170, 172
Tūfrīk, Battle of 43
Tullibardine, Lieutenant the Marquis of 36, 37, 43
Tungamirai, Joseph 193
Turner, Hannah 12

Ulundi, Battle of 50, 53, 54
Umber, Lieutenant Heinrich 101
Umlauff, Heinrich 2, 105
Umm Dibeikarāt, Battle of 44
Universal Exhibition, Paris (1900) 27–8
    Exposition des Nègres d'Amériques (US exhibit) 27

Vallentin, Wilhelm 204–5
Vansina, Jan 163
Varèse, Edgard 142
Vatican Apostolic Library, Rome 159
Vera, Yvonne 197
Vergo, Peter 9
Victoria, Queen 37, 54, 156, 157, 197
Victoria and Albert Museum, London 11, 96
vigango (death totem) 180–1
Voncujovi, Célestino Kofi 9, 10*fig*
Voncujovi, Christopher 9

Waetzoldt, Stefan 178
Walda Maryam, Alaqa 155
Wallace Collection, London 96
war regalia 7–8, 19, 66, 70*fig*
    sacredness of 53–4
Wassoulou Empire 21, 22, 29
Waterlot, Georges Emmanuel 140
Watermeyer, John Philip 189, 197
Wehlan, Alwin Karl 203, 204–7
Wellcome Institute, London 159
Weltmuseum, Vienna 3
Wenckstern, Karl von 129
West Africa Magazine 94
Whiteness 179–80

Wilderson, Frank III 185
Wilhelm II, Kaiser 105
Windsor Castle Library 96, 159
Wiredu, Kwasi 13
Wissmann, Hermann von 114−5
Wolfe, Ernie 180
Wolfe, Patrick 180, 189
Wolfrum, Wilhelm 111
Wolseley, Garnet, 1st Viscount 35
 The Soldier's Pocket Book 37
Wynter, Sylvia 158

Xénakis, Iannis 142

Yeefon, Nso' Princess 130
Yendi, Dagbon 61, 62, 63−5, 67, 69
Yendi Heritage and Resource Centre (YHRC) 67
Yohannes IV, Emperor of Ethiopia 156
Yombe people 164, 167−8
Yoruba people 182, 186
You Hide Me (film) 89−95, 90*fig*, 92*fig*

ZANU-PF party 197, 199
Zenker, Georg August 202
Zeughaus, Berlin 5, 19
Zewde, Bahru 153−4
Zibhebhu, kaMaphitha, 55
Zimbabwe 189−93
Zimmerer, Eugen von 205−6
Zintgraff, Eugen 102
Zulfū, 'Ismat Ḥassan 43
Zulu Jazz Club, Durban 47
Zulu kingdom 48
 age regiment system 48−9
Zupitza, Maximilian 101